March of America Facsimile Series

Number 39

A History of New Sweden

Israel Acrelius

A History of New Sweden

by Israel Acrelius

ANN ARBOR

UNIVERSITY MICROFILMS, INC.

A Subsidiary of Xerox Corporation

Foreword

A History of New Sweden by Israel Acrelius, first published in Swedish in 1759, presents a history and description of the Swedish community in the Delaware River Valley from the arrival of the first Swedish settlers there in 1638 to the middle of the 18th century. The history is especially valuable in showing the successive adaptations of the Swedish colonists to Dutch, and later to English, domination. Acrelius wrote the most complete and accurate study of the Swedish settlements in Colonial America yet to appear.

Although Sweden lost out early to rival Dutch and English power in the race to colonize North America, the Swedish government long afterward maintained an active concern in the spiritual well-being of Swedish settlers there. Clergymen from Sweden regularly arrived to occupy pulpits along the Delaware. One such clergyman was Israel Acrelius, who came from Stockholm in 1749 to serve the parish of Christina (now Wilmington, Delaware). Three years after Acrelius' return to Sweden in 1756, he completed the history of New Sweden which he had begun while still in America.

More than half of the history concerns the Swedish church in America. However, the pastor had broad interests. He supplied his readers with political history, with an analysis of colonial administration, and with a careful survey of the regional economy. The customs of the colonists, their manner of living, even a detailed description of what they ate and drank, all fell within the range of his interests.

In describing the imposition of Dutch rule over the colony in 1655 Acrelius reported that "the flower of the Swedish male population were at once torn away and sent over to New Amsterdam." When the English displaced the Dutch in 1664, the Swedes experienced more difficulty, especially from the Pennsylvania Quakers, who, according to Acrelius, coveted Swedish holdings. By the middle of the 18th century Swedish assimilation into the larger English community was still incomplete. Acrelius revealed that the older generation Swedes "hate in their hearts everything that is English. They say that they are Swedish people, although they are in an English country." On the other hand, the pastor continued, many of the younger persons were "so accustomed...to English that they would not afterwards willingly express themselves in Swedish." The confusion of language was symptomatic of a more basic conflict of culture which Acrelius saw particularly in its religious terms.

The present edition was translated from the Swedish in 1874 and includes a historical introduction by the translator, William M. Reynolds. Maps and illustrations accompany the text. More information about New Sweden and about the history written by Acrelius can be found in Gregory B. Keen, "New Sweden, or the Swedes on the Delaware," in *Narrative and Critical History of America*, ed. Justin Winsor (Boston, 1885), IV, 443-502.

Publications

OF THE

Historical Society of Pennsylvania.

THE

HISTORY OF

NEW SWEDEN.

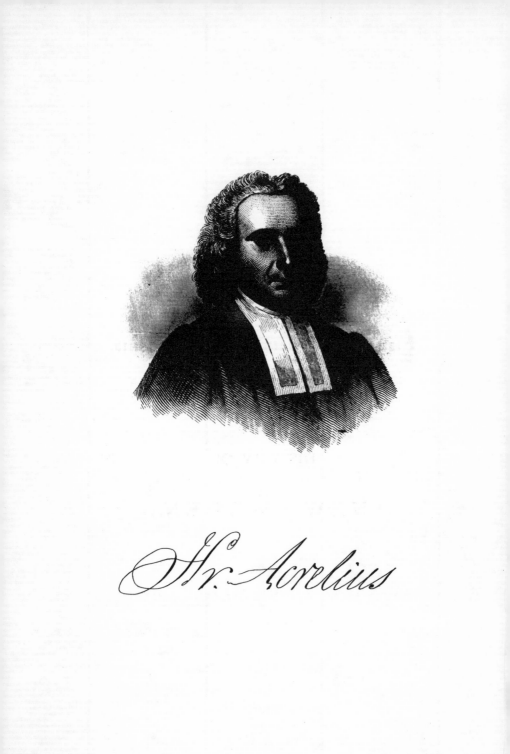

Jr. Acrelius

A

HISTORY OF NEW SWEDEN;

OR,

THE SETTLEMENTS ON THE RIVER DELAWARE.

BY

ISRAEL ACRELIUS,

PROVOST OF THE SWEDISH CHURCHES IN AMERICA, AND RECTOR OF
THE OLD SWEDES' CHURCH. WILMINGTON, DEL.

Translated from the Swedish,

WITH AN INTRODUCTION AND NOTES,

BY

WILLIAM M. REYNOLDS, D.D.,

MEMBER OF THE HISTORICAL SOCIETY OF PENNSYLVANIA, ETC.

PUBLISHED UNDER THE JOINT AUSPICES OF THE
HISTORICAL SOCIETIES OF PENNSYLVANIA AND DELAWARE.

PHILADELPHIA:
PUBLICATION FUND OF
THE HISTORICAL SOCIETY OF PENNSYLVANIA,
No. 820 SPRUCE STREET.
1874.

MEMOIRS

HISTORICAL SOCIETY

OF

PENNSYLVANIA.

....

VOL. XI.

....

PHILADELPHIA:

PUBLICATION FUND OF

THE HISTORICAL SOCIETY OF PENNSYLVANIA,

No. 820 SPRUCE STREET.

1874.

INTRODUCTION.

HE Swedish colony on the Delaware is undoubtedly an important element in those movements of humanity out of which the present position and character of the United States have been developed. Although the number of the colonists thus settled there was small, and the territory of which they took possession but limited, and the political connection with Sweden soon severed, yet the influence of that movement is still felt not only upon the shores of the Delaware, but upon the banks of the Mississippi and the great lakes of the North, and from the Gulf of Mexico to the Californian shores of the Pacific Ocean. The descendants of the original Swedish colonists continue to cultivate the lands of which their ancestors took possession more than two centuries since, and are an essential portion of the population of the three States which now divide among them the territory of the old Swedish colony. New colonists, in still increasing numbers, yearly wend their way from every part of Sweden to the most remote points [1] of the United States. Nor is there any doubt that that first colony of 1638 gives direction and character to these new and increasing masses which now bid fair to make the offspring of the Scandinavian races more numerous in America than in their original homes in Norway, Sweden, and Denmark.

---

[1] Whilst we write (1873), a new Swedish colony is projected in Delaware, near the original starting-point of New Sweden.

The great Gustavus Adolphus first conceived the idea of this colony even as early as the year 1624. "This was one of the few years," says Geijer,[1] "that the King was able to devote to the internal development of the realm." But even then he looked at the subject of colonization in America with the eye of a statesman who understood the wants not only of his own country, but of the world, and was able, with prophetic glance, to penetrate into the distant ages of the future. He proposed there to found a free state, where the laborer should reap the fruit of his toil, where the rights of conscience should be inviolate, and which should be open to the whole Protestant world, then engaged in a struggle for existence with all the Papal powers of Europe. All should be secure in their persons, their property, and their rights of conscience. It should be an asylum for the persecuted of all nations, a place of security for the honor of the wives and daughters of those who were flying from bloody battle-fields, and from homes made desolate by the fire and sword of the persecutor. No slaves should burden that soil, "for," said Gustavus,— and we realize the profound truth of his political economy after an experience of two centuries, at the end of which slavery expired amid the death-throes of our civil war,— "slaves cost a great deal, labor with reluctance, and soon perish from hard usage." But "the Swedish nation is industrious and intelligent, and hereby we shall gain more by a free people with wives and children."[2]

But before his plans for the organization and planting of a colony in America could be matured, Gustavus Adolphus was again hurried away to the battle-field. For the next two years he was engaged in a war with Poland.

---

[1] "Svenska Folkets Historia," Vol. III., p. 128.
[2] "Argonautica Gustaviana," pp. 3 and 22.

terminated by a treaty securing the freedom of worship
alike to Protestants and Papists;[1] and soon after its termination he began to feel the first waves of that terrible
conflict, "the Thirty Years' War," of which he erelong became the great hero, and in which he finally offered up
his life, one of the noblest sacrifices ever made in the
cause of religious liberty. Yet, even amid all these exciting and deeply engrossing events, Gustavus Adolphus
did not forget his meditated colony. "They did but
enlarge his views," says Bancroft;[2] "and at Nuremberg,
but a few days before the battle of Lützen, the enterprise, which still appeared to him as 'the jewel of his
kingdom,' was recommended to the people of Germany,"
as it had already been to those of Sweden. And who
can say what influence this recommendation has had in
preparing the way for the coming of those myriads of
Germans to our shores, by whom such miracles of industry have been performed within the last century and
a half? If it is said that but few of that vast multitude
could ever have heard of the words of Gustavus Adolphus, I answer, that the words of such a man cannot fall
unheeded to the ground, and no one can say where they
will spring up, or what golden harvests of thought and of
action they will produce. It is of such words as these
especially that Milton's profound remark is true, that
"words are not altogether dead things, but do contain a
potency of life within them."

Be that as it may, there was at least one man who
heard and properly pondered, appreciated, and applied
the noble words and wise instructions of Gustavus Adolphus upon this subject of a Swedish colony in America.
That man was Axel Oxenstiern, the friend and prime
minister of Gustavus Adolphus, his successor in the ad-

---

[1] Geijer, *ubi supra*, p. 129.   [2] Bancroft, Hist. U. S., II., p. 285.

ministration of the kingdom; one of the best friends and guardians of his royal master's infant daughter, the wayward Christina; and one of the best and greatest men, not only of his own age and of Sweden, but of any age or any country. The mantle of Gustavus Adolphus could have fallen upon no worthier shoulders than those of Axel Oxenstiern. He carried to a glorious completion, both of war and of peace, the plans so grandly devised by his royal instructor. Baner, Torstensson, and Von Wrangel were the flaming swords which struck down the power of Austria; but the brain that brought to a close the fearful Thirty Years' War, and established Protestantism upon an immovable basis of security, by the peace of Westphalia in 1648, was that of Axel Oxenstiern.

In the meantime, the great Chancellor carried out the wise plans of Gustavus Adolphus in the civil administration of the country, and so also in this of a Swedish colony in America. On the 10th of April, 1633, but a few months after the death of Gustavus Adolphus (which took place on the 6th [1] of November, 1632), Oxenstiern renewed to Germany the offer that the King had previously made relative to the participation of Germany in this American colony, but could only put the plan into execution four years afterwards, in 1637. There can be little doubt that this is the date at which the expedition under Menewe, or Menuet as the Swedes call him, whom the Hollanders called Minuits and Minnewitz, left Sweden; although it may not have reached the shores of the Delaware until the beginning of 1638. Voyages from Europe to America were at that time frequently of six months' duration. But it is evident from Kieft's Protest against the Swedish settlement, which is dated May 6, 1638, that the expedi-

---

[1] Not October 16, as it is, perhaps, by a typographical error in the margin of Bancroft, II., p. 285.

tion must have arrived early in that year. Van der Donck, in his Notes to a Petition sent to the States-General of the United Netherlands in 1649, gives the same date, 1638, but also, incidentally, shows that they had been there a considerable time before Kieft's Protest was made. He there says: "One Minnewits, who had previously been Director at the Manhattans for the West India Company, came to this country eleven years ago, in the year 1638, with the ship *De Kalmers leutel*, and the yacht *De Fogel-gryp*," (he translates the Swedish names of the vessels, "*Kalmars Nyckel*" and "*Vogel Grip*," into Dutch;) "representing, on the contrary, to the Netherlanders who resided at the (South) river, on behalf of the Company, and of Mr. Van der Nederhorst, that he was on a voyage to the West Indies, and that he wished first to transact some business there in passing, and to take in a supply of wood and water, when he should depart. Awhile afterwards some of our people returned thither, and still found them there; but they had already prepared a little garden of salad, potherbs, and such like . . . . The third time it was clearly seen, by the building of a fort, what their designs and intentions were. Director Kieft, on obtaining information of the matter, protested, but in vain." [1] From this it is evident that a considerable time must have elapsed before Kieft issued his Protest against the settlement. The colonists had already made a garden, their seeds had sprung up, and they had erected their fort.

The right of the Swedes to settle upon the Delaware has been discussed with great zeal by Acrelius, on the one side, in favor of the Swedes, and by Van der Donck, on the other, in favor of the Netherlanders. The English also claimed the country by priority of discovery, and, so

---

[1] See the "Documents relating to the Colonial History of New York, Vol. I., pp. 291, 292. Albany, 1856.

far as *discovery* can give a right, there is no doubt that this belonged to the English. Under the patronage of Henry VII. of England, the Cabots had, in 1496, become the first discoverers of the North American continent. In the following year, Sebastian Cabot, the son, explored the same continent, at various points, from the neighborhood of the polar circle to Albemarle Sound in the longitude of Cuba. It was not until 1609 that the Netherlanders began to make voyages of discovery to America. In that year Hudson, as is well known, touched at Cape Cod, entered the bay of New York, and sailed up the river, to which he gave his own name, as far as the village now called after him, and sent a boat even up to the present site of Albany.[1] But it was not until 1623 that Cornelius Mey entered the river, now called the Delaware, and to which he probably gave the name of the South river, as it was called by the Netherlanders as long as they had a foothold on the North American continent. From him also is derived the name of the Cape on the north side of the Delaware; although the original orthography has long been changed to "May." He also ascended the river to the vicinity of the site of Philadelphia, and on Timber creek, at Gloucester Point,[2] in New Jersey, a few miles south-east of Philadelphia, erected a fort, to which he gave the name of Nassau, in honor of the distinguished Prince of that name. But this settlement was by no means permanent. Ten years afterwards, in 1633, when De Vries came up to inquire after the fate of the "few families" whom Mey was said to have left there, he found the Indians in possession of the fort, and

---

[1] It is also claimed that Hudson discovered the Delaware Bay on the 28th of August, 1609, before he entered New York Bay. See Journal of Juet (Hudson's mate) in "New York Hist. Col.," Second Series, Vol. I., p. 320.

[2] Not on Cooper's creek, as stated by some, nor in the neighborhood of Camden, as might be supposed from Bancroft's statement, Vol. II., p. 277.

prepared to destroy him and his men, as they had long since done to those whom Mey had left behind him at that place. Similar to this was the fate of the colony planted by De Vries himself at Hore Kill, a few miles north of Cape Henlopen, in 1631. When he revisited it in the following year, to use his own words, "We found our house destroyed. It was surrounded with palisades instead of parapets or breastwork, but the most of them had been burned. We found the ground strewed with the heads and bones of our murdered men."[1] In regard to this, the author of the "Remonstrance of the New Netherlands," etc., (most probably Adrian van der Donck,) which is contained in Vol. I., pp. 271–318, of the "Documents," etc., says: "In this way was this colony again reduced to nought, howbeit sealed with blood and purchased dearly enough." But they made no further attempts at settling the country upon the Delaware for some years, nor is there any evidence of the occupation of the country by the Netherlanders at any time before the arrival of the Swedes in 1637 or 1638.[2]

Campanius, in his "Description of the Province of New Sweden," (p. 68 of Dr. Du Ponceau's translation,) states that in 1631, or near that time, Charles I. ceded to Sweden all the rights of England to the country upon the Delaware, and that the Swedes purchased of the Hollanders their possessory rights; but both of these statements are highly improbable, nor are they supported by any other historical or documentary evidence. They had, however, that best of all rights to such a territory, that is to say, actual possession, and the cheerful acquiescence of the

---

[1] De Vries' Journal in "Collections of the New York Hist. Soc.," Second Series, Vol. I., p. 251.

[2] The pretence that they had had "peaceable possession" for many years before the arrival of the Swedes (see "Documents," Vol. I., p. 588,) is clearly refuted by De Vries' statements given above.

original occupants of the soil.[1] It was, in fact, the Swedes who inaugurated the peaceful policy of William Penn, for which he has been so deservedly praised, in his purchase of the soil from the Indians, and his uniformly friendly intercourse with them. This was not an accidental circumstance in the Swedish policy, but was deliberately adopted, and always carefully observed. In the Fifth Article of the Instructions given to Governor Printz in 1642, this language is employed: "The Governor . . . . must bear in mind that the boundaries of the country . . . extend, *in virtue of the articles of the contract entered into with the wild inhabitants of the country, as its rightful lords,* from the sea-coast at Cape Hinlopen upwards along the south side of Godin's Bay, and so up the great South river, onward to Minque's Kil," etc. And in the Ninth Article it is said: "The wild nations bordering on all sides the Governor shall treat with all humanity and respect, and so that no violence or wrong be done to them by Her Royal Majesty or Her subjects aforesaid; but he shall rather . . . . exert himself that the same wild people may be gradually instructed in the truths and worship of the Christian religion, and in other ways brought to civilization and good government, and in this manner properly guided. Especially shall he seek to gain their confidence, and impress upon their minds that neither he, the Governor, nor his people and subordinates are come into these parts to do them any wrong or injury, but much more for

---

[1] Gov. Stuyvesant's transaction with the Indians in 1648 (Documents, I., 593.) is of a very doubtful and equivocal character, and entirely inconsistent with the uniformly peaceable intercourse of the Swedes with the Indians. Since writing the preceding part of this note, I have received, through the kindness of Mr. Jos. J. Mickley, a copy of Gov. Rising's treaty with the Indians in 1654, in which two of their chiefs distinctly deny that they had ever made any gift or sale of the lands occupied by the Swedes to Gov. Stuyvesant. The original of this treaty is still preserved (1871) in the Royal Archives in Stockholm.]

the purpose of furnishing them with such things as they may need for the ordinary wants of life." Acrelius, "Beskrifning," etc., p. 24.

This policy was steadily pursued and adhered to by the Swedes during the whole time of their continuance in America, as the governors of the territory of which they had thus acquired the possession; and the consequences were of the most satisfactory character. They lived in peace with the Indians, and received no injuries from them. The Indians respected them, and, long after the Swedish power had disappeared from the shores of the Delaware, they continued to cherish its memory, and speak of it with confidence and affection.

It was not because they were either weak or timid that the Swedish Government pursued this pacific policy with the Indians. Sweden was then still one of the great military powers of Europe, and in her colonial attitude towards Holland showed that she was as ready to wield the sword in America as in Europe.

Holland wrested her Colony from her because Sweden was weak in her naval force, whilst Holland was at that time the leading maritime power of the world. She had just then broken down the colossal naval power of Spain, and was in the midst of that contest for the control of the ocean with Great Britain, in which it was so long doubtful which should place itself at the head of the empire of the waves. It is self-evident that no nation, however strong and warlike, can establish and maintain colonies separated from her by a wide and boisterous ocean, unless she has not only an abundance of ships in which to transport her colonists, and the supplies which they require from home, but also a sufficient naval force with which to protect them from hostile attacks upon the sea, which, unless properly resisted, may readily cut off their connection and communication with their mother country. In addition to this, the Hollanders at Manhattan, as New York was then called, had, at only the distance of a couple of hundred miles, a force ten times as great as that of the Swedish colony, which they could readily precipitate upon it, and with which, in fact, they did surprise and crush it in the course of a few weeks. Governor Stuyvesant, leaving New Amsterdam at the close of August, 1655, before the end of September following had captured both the Swedish forts, and had undisputed possession of the whole Swedish Colony. Stuyvesant's force was from six hundred to seven hundred men strong. The Swedes had in Trinity Fort (now New Castle) less than fifty men,[1] and scarcely one hundred in Fort Christina.

This weakness of the Colony was a natural result of the decline of the mother country. Sweden had exhausted herself by the superhuman efforts which she had made under the great Gustavus, and the great Chancellor whom he left at the head of affairs. Christina was too weak in character to restore, by wise government in peace, the strength of the kingdom, exhausted by wars of so many years' continuance. Oxenstiern had scarcely brought to a successful termination the Thirty Years' War, by the peace of 1648, when he fell into disgrace with the young Queen. But Christina was unable to govern the country without Oxenstiern, and on the 6th of June, 1654, she abdicated her throne. On the 28th of August following, Oxenstiern breathed his last earthly sigh, with proud remembrance of the father, and pity for the daughter, in the words : " She is still the daughter of the great Gustavus,"[2] and so descended to his honored grave. Charles Gus-

---

[1] Hudde, in his "Report," (found in "New York Hist. Col.," p. 428, New Series,) says that, in 1645, it was "usually garrisoned by twelve men."

[2] Geijer, "Svenska Folkets Historia," III., p. 481.

tavus, who succeeded to the throne of Sweden, the son of the Elector Palatine and Catharine, the favorite sister of Gustavus Adolphus, is said to have had some idea of the importance of this Colony to Sweden; but he was too much taken up with the wars in which he was almost immediately involved to be able to devote any attention to this distant point of his government. Vessels that he sent with reinforcements to the Colony are said to have been captured by the Spaniards; besides which he was engaged in incessant wars with Poland and Denmark until the close of his brief reign in 1660. Then followed the long minority of his son, Charles XI., who was only five years of age at the time of his father's death. During this interval the claims of the lost Colony upon the Delaware appear to have been wellnigh forgotten.

But it is to the enduring honor of the Crown of Sweden, the Swedish people, and the Swedish Church, that they never forgot nor deserted those whom they had sent forth into the western wilderness as their pioneers, and as heralds of the Gospel to the poor heathen who were wandering there. The Gospel finally proved itself to be a firmer bond between Sweden and her colonists in America than either Political Economy, Statesmanship, or Military Power. In less than forty years (from 1655 to 1693), the handful of Swedes whom their last Governor, Rising, had left behind him on the Delaware had increased to about one thousand. We have, in Acrelius, a list of nearly two hundred families, embracing over nine hundred individuals; and there is no doubt that there were at that time many more Swedes and their children in the adjacent country not thus enrolled. These people still cherished the simple faith of their ancestors, and were very anxious to have the services of the Church and a regular Minister. Upon the overthrow of the Swedish administration in

2

1655, one Minister, Lars Lock, who had come to the country with Governor Printz in 1642, remained with them, and continued to officiàte until 1688, when he was removed by death. In the meantime, in 1677, they had called another Minister, the Rev. Jacob or James Fabritius, two Ministers being required for the increasing population, which was also scattered from the present site of Philadelphia to New Castle, in Delaware, and Salem, in New Jersey. Fabritius, who had come from Holland, officiated in that language, which the Swedes seem generally to have acquired under the Dutch administration; which, however, lasted only ten years, the English Government, under the Duke of York, taking possession of the whole Netherlands territory, from the North to the South rivers, in 1664.

Their only surviving Minister, Fabritius, becoming incapacitated by age for longer service, in 1691, the Swedish colonists made repeated efforts to obtain another as his successor. It was not, however, until 1696 that these efforts were successful. In 1693, one of their letters was laid before Charles XI., king of Sweden, and, being earnestly supported by Dr. Svedberg, afterwards Bishop of Skara, resulted in the establishment of the "Swedish Mission in America," by which, for nearly a century, the Swedish churches upon the Delaware continued to be supplied, not only with a succession of pious and learned Ministers, but also with religious books, assistance in building their churches, and other appliances for the development of their religious life. It was only after the Swedish language had almost entirely disappeared from among the descendants of the colonists sent from Sweden, and the great body of the members of their churches upon the Delaware spoke the English language exclusively, that the Swedish nation ceased to supply them with their

Ministers. There is not upon record a more remarkable
instance of disinterested care for its expatriated citizens,
than that of the Swedish Government for these obscure
members of its race, no longer bound to it by any political
ties, and separated from it by the wide expanse of the
stormy Atlantic. From 1696 to 1786 the Swedish Government sent to the churches on the Delaware no less than
twenty-four (24) Clergymen, generally giving them an
outfit, and paying the expenses of their voyage from
Sweden to America, as also of their return voyage when,
after many years of faithful labor, they returned to their
native land, where they were again received with open
arms, and often invested with pastorates of the most
desirable character. How much money the Swedish Government thus expended, it is now impossible to determine.
As much as $600[1] silver mint was for some time given
to each Missionary for his voyage to America, and
$400 for his return voyage. The Provost received
from $250 to $400 annual salary from Sweden, which
was altogether independent of what he received from
his congregation in America. Special grants were also
frequently made to Clergymen of distinguished merit,
or to those whose necessities were urgent. The amount
thus expended by the Swedish Government cannot have
been less than $100,000, and may have reached double
that sum.[2] It must also be borne in mind that money was
scarce during that period, and that Sweden was then in a
declining condition, and frequently suffering from financial
embarrassment. The country, exhausted by the expenditure of blood and treasure in the "Thirty Years' War,"
was brought to the verge of bankruptcy by the disastrous

---

[1] See notes on pp. 224, 368.

[2] See "Historical Sermon" of the Rev. O. Perinchief, of the Swedes'
Church, Upper Merion, 1873, p. 11.

conclusion of the reign of Charles XII. We cannot, therefore, but admire the liberality of Sweden towards the descendants of the handful of colonists whom, in the days of her power and prosperity, she sent forth to America, but whose spiritual necessities she was anxious to provide for even in times of her own deepest depression.

There is no doubt, also, that this Mission to the Swedes in America was originally designed for the Christianization of the heathen aborigines by whom they were at that time (1693) surrounded. This work had been begun by the elder Campanius, when the country was still in the hands of the Swedes, under Governor Printz's administration (in 1642). This was four years before Eliot (who has been called "the morning star of missionary enterprise"[1] and "the Apostle of the Indians") commenced his labors in New England (1646). His Dialogues and Vocabularies of the language of the Delawares (which may be seen in his grandson's book[2]), and his translation of Luther's Shorter Catechism, were probably the first attempts at reducing the language of our North American Indians to writing. The Catechism, printed in Sweden at the King's expense, was sent over to America with the Missionaries of 1696. Bishop Svedberg, the father of the well-known Emanuel Swedenborg, was the zealous counsellor of King Charles XI. as well in these benevolent plans for the benefit of the Indians as for the Mission generally; and so continued throughout his life. He was a man of no less marked character than his eccentric and mystical son. During forty years (from 1695 to 1735, which last is the date of his death,) he continued to devote himself to this work, of which he was,

---

[1] Bancroft, "Hist. of U. States," Vol. II., p. 94.
[2] Th. Campanius Holm. "Description of New Sweden," etc., Du Ponceau's Translation, pp. 144-159.

in fact, during all that time, the superintendent. He presented the churches on the Delaware with some hundred copies of his excellent hymn-book (three hundred by the first Missionaries, and more afterwards), and never grew weary in his services to them. He sent his own son over to them as a schoolmaster, and several of his relatives as Clergymen. He maintained a constant correspondence with them, and wrote an extensive work (entitled "America Illuminata") on the subject of Missions in America, of which, however, only an abridgment has been published. In 1712, the English "Society for the Propagation of the Gospel" thanked the King for his care of the Swedes in America, and elected Bishop Svedberg as one of its honorary members. It was in accordance with his instructions that the Swedish Missionaries in America maintained such intimate relations with this Society and the Episcopal Clergymen and churches in the same field of labor.

Various other distinguished Swedes either took part in this Mission or manifested a lively interest in it. It is a very curious circumstance that Charles XII., even during his most arduous campaigns in Poland, in Russia, and even during his unfortunate sojourn in Turkey, found time to devote his attention to this apparently insignificant Mission — several of his orders in regard to it being dated from his camps in those countries, e. g., from his headquarters at Smorgonia, in the Polish province of Lithuania, and from his camp at Tamerlash, near Adrianople, in Turkey. We infer from this that, notwithstanding the impetuosity of his character, Charles XII., like every great military genius, was as careful in attention to details as he was comprehensive in his grasp of the vital points of his circumstances.

The celebrated naturalist, Peter Kalm, Professor of

Œconomics in the University of Åbo, in Finland, (then still an integral part of Sweden,) also took an active interest in that part of the Swedish Mission which was in New Jersey. He made this locality his head-quarters during a considerable part of his sojourn in North America. The two volumes of his travels in this country are well known to the scientific world, and also contain much that is interesting to the student of American history, as, like Acrelius, he was in this country only a few years before our great revolutionary struggle (from 1748 to 1750), when the causes that led to that great event were just making themselves felt, and men of sagacity already foreboded the great political storm that was gathering. But in these two volumes, so full of details in regard to plants, trees, birds and beasts, agriculture, manufactures, commerce, and politics, Kalm nowhere refers to the somewhat romantic episode in his travels, by which his frequent visits to the sands of Southern Jersey, and his rather protracted sojourn there, are explained. Acrelius supplies us with this. He tells us that Professor Kalm there found the widow of the Missionary, the Rev. John Sandin, who had remained there, a stranger in a strange land, with her two children, both in their infancy, ever since the death of the husband and father. The worthy Professor became very much interested in this unfortunate family, visited them more and more frequently, often officiated in the now vacant Parish of the deceased Clergyman, and before he left the country, in 1750, became the husband of the widow, who, with her two children, accompanied him on his return to Sweden and Finland.

One of the most interesting and efficient men who took part in the Swedish Mission in America was Charles Magnus von Wrangel, who, in 1759, received the appointment of Provost of the Swedish churches on the Delaware, in which capacity he labored there for about nine years, returning to Sweden in 1768. He belonged to one of the most distinguished families in Sweden — that of the great General von Wrangel, who had distinguished himself in the army of Gustavus Adolphus, and afterwards, in conjunction with Baner and Torstensson, showed that he was no unworthy scholar of the great soldier. Charles Magnus von Wrangel had studied in his native country at Westerås and Upsala, and then going to the University of Göttingen in Germany, received there the degree of Doctor of Divinity. Soon after this he was nominated as a Court Preacher in the Royal chapel in Stockholm; but, at the request of the Archbishop, Samuel Troilius, relinquished this for the Provostship of the American Mission. In this position Von Wrangel's labors were of the most active and influential character. He reorganized the decaying Swedish churches, procured new and improved charters for them from the government of Pennsylvania, and united them into a compact body. He also added several new congregations[1] to their number. He published (in Dr. Franklin's printing-office) a translation of Luther's Shorter Catechism into English[2]—probably the first appearance in English of that well-known manual of the elements of Christian doctrine. We are told by Dr. Clay[3] that "he possessed a most winning and captivating eloquence," so that "he was usually obliged to preach in the open air on account of the great crowds who attended upon his ministry." But Dr. Clay is mistaken when he says "that he was, upon his return to Sweden, made a Bishop." On the contrary, although upon his return he

---

[1] Clay's "Annals," p. 125.
[2] "Nachrichten aus Pennsylv.," pp. 384 and 867.
[3] *Ubi supra.*

received the position of "First Court Preacher," he died
(in 1786) as the Rector of Sala. He occupied, however,
a distinguished position among the Swedish Clergy, and
was one of the founders of the Swedish Society "*Pro fide
et Christianismo*," which was established in 1771.[1]

Quite a number of the Swedish American Pastors
manifested considerable literary ability, and several of
them published books or tracts on the state of the Swedish
Church in America — more particularly And. Hesselius,
Tobias E. Björck, and our author. Björck wrote in Latin
a small quarto of thirty-four pages, under the title "Dissertatio gradualis de Plantatione Ecclesiæ Svecanæ 'in
America" (Upsala, 1731). The Dedication, in English
verse, "To the Most Honorable Lord, Count Charles
Gyllenborg, Senator in the Kingdom of Sweden and
Chancellor of the University of Lund," is a poor specimen
of English; but his Latinity is respectable.

Of all these, however, the work of Acrelius is the most
complete and respectable. As a history, it is more authen-
tic as well as more extensive than that of the younger
Campanius, who was never in America, and so not personally cognizant of the matters in regard to which he
wrote. Acrelius, of course, availed himself of the labors
of Campanius as well as of his other predecessors; and,
in fact, the greatest mistake that he makes — that of
regarding Jac. Chartiers as an English discoverer of
America — is occasioned by his reliance upon the au
thority of Campanius. But in regard to the importance
and superior value of Acrelius' work, we have the testimony of Dr. Du Ponceau, the translator of Campanius.
In his Preface to that work (pp. ix. and x.), he says,
"There is a later Swedish work on the same subject,
which we have already alluded to, and which deserves to

---

[1] Cornelius' "Handbok," etc., p. 248.

INTRODUCTION. XXV

be made known. It is entitled "A Description, etc. By
the Rev. Isaac[1] Acrelius," etc. . . . . . "and that history is,
in our opinion, much more complete, and in every respect
superior to that now presented to the public; to which,
however, as being the oldest, the preference has, for the
present, been given." It was inferred from this that it
was the intention of Dr. Du Ponceau to translate the work
of Acrelius also; and it was also reported, after his death,
that he had left the work behind him in manuscript,
which is one reason why its translation was not undertaken by others. Dr. Du Ponceau may also have been
prevented from accomplishing this work by the impres-
sion that it had been already performed by the Rev. Dr.
Collin, the last Swedish Rector of the churches on the
Delaware, who, as early as 1799, translated a considerable
portion of Acrelius for the benefit of the Rev. Dr. S.
Miller, of Princeton, N. J., who was then engaged in preparing his "Church History." Dr. Miller appears to
have transferred this translation to the American Philosophical Society of Philadelphia, by whom it was again
transferred to the New York Historical Society for publication in their "Collections," Vol. I., New Series, 1841,
of which it forms a portion from page 401 to page 448.
The Editor of that volume, in his "Introductory Note"
on page 405, also says, "A complete version of Acrelius
would be a valuable contribution to the stock of American
history."

A still stronger desire for the publication of a translation of Acrelius was expressed by Benjamin Ferris, the
author of "A History of the Original Settlements on the
Delaware," (Wilmington, 1846.) In his Preface, p. iv.,

---

[1] "Isaac" is, of course, a slip of the pen for "Israel," which has also been
copied by the editor of the "Documents relating to the Hist. of N. York," in
his note to p. 168 of Vol. VII.

he says: "A good translation of Acrelius' 'History of New Sweden' would undoubtedly add much to our stock of knowledge. The small part of it already published is composed of extracts selected by Nicholas Collin, and relates chiefly to the controversies between the Dutch and the Swedes. Such detached portions of the work impair the connection of the history, and present its author in a less favorable point of view than he may justly merit."

An interesting personal notice is given of Acrelius by one of the most distinguished of his cotemporaries in America, Dr. William Smith, at that time Provost of the Philadelphia Academy, and who subsequently took so active a part in the American Revolution. In a letter to Dr. Secker, at that time (November 1, 1756,) Bishop of Oxford, but subsequently Archbishop of Canterbury, he says: "The bearer of this is the Rev. Mr. Israel Acrelius, a learned Swede, who has been several years Commissary to the Swedish Congregations on the Delaware, and now returns to considerable preferment in his own country as a reward of his faithful labors. He is well entitled to the honor of Your Lordship's notice, and knows the state of all the Missions in this Province perfectly well. There is a good deal of confusion in some of them; and as he is an impartial person, his account will, no doubt, be of weight should he be called upon. He has often preached in English, and made use of our service. His chief abode was near Newcastle. . . . . I leave all to Mr. Acrelius, who will be on the spot, and can have no interest in being partial, as he is never to return to this place." [1]

It is somewhat remarkable that Acrelius' labors as a

---

[1] "Documents relative to the Colonial History of the State of New York," Vol. VII., p. 168, where there is also a note by the editor giving an account of Acrelius' History of N. S.

historian, and especially as a church-historian, has been
so little recognized either in his own country or abroad.
The only notice we find of him among church-historians
is in Skarstedt's "Manual of Swedish Church History," [1]
p. 196, where we have an account of his controversy with
Alnander, in 1761, in regard to the doctrinal relations of
the churches of England and of Sweden to each other;
but no reference either to his residence in America or his
work on New Sweden. Even Dr. Rudelbach, who devotes
the fifth number of his "Christian Biography" [2] to an
extensive sketch of Bishop Svedberg, in which his connection with the American Mission is particularly noticed,
makes no mention of this work, in which Svedberg's missionary zeal is so amply illustrated. We infer from this
that but a small edition of the work was printed, and that
it had a very limited circulation, which is further confirmed
by the fact that so few copies of it are now to be found
either in this country or in Sweden. Acrelius lived over
thirty years after his return to his native land, dying, in
the year 1800, at the patriarchal age of eighty-six.

We have endeavored to translate our author into English as simple and unpretentious as its Swedish original.
Swedish orthography has, however, undergone a considerable change within the century that has elapsed since
Acrelius wrote, and Swedish literature and style have
kept pace with the progress of thought and of society in
all parts of the world. But we believe that it will be found
that the simple narrative of Acrelius will still meet the
objects for which it was originally composed, and for
which it is now presented to the American public. Near

---

[1] "Handbok i Sweriges Kyrkohistoria för skolan och hemmet, of C. W.
Skarstedt:" Stockholm, 1867, pp. 244.

[2] "Christliche Biographie, von Dr. A. G. Rudelbach:" Leipzig, 1849. pp.
293–370, 4te u. 5te Lieferungen.

the close of the first century of our national existence as a republic, and far advanced in the third century since our "Pilgrim Fathers" from various lands first moored their barks in the James, the Hudson, Plymouth Bay, and the Delaware, we begin to revert with more and more interest to the obscure twilight in which our ancestors first landed upon these shores, where so bright and glorious a dawn has finally burst forth upon their descendants. Acrelius not only throws light upon the first colonization of the shores of the Delaware, but he also places us in the midst of those stirring events which immediately preceded the great Revolution of 1776 — Braddock's war of 1755, and the popular agitation of the Colonies, Pennsylvania and Delaware especially, by which it was attended.

The translator has endeavored, as far as possible, to elucidate all the points of topography and local history involved in the author's narrative, and by the insertion of several cotemporaneous (Lindström's) maps to give clear views not only of the Swedish Colony, but also of the country as known to the author during his five years' residence upon the banks of the Delaware and the Christina.

As the printing of this volume approached its completion, there appeared the admirably written volume entitled " Memorial of Thomas Potts, Junior, who settled in Pennsylvania; with an Historic-Genealogical Account of his Descendants to the Eighth Generation," from the pen of Mrs. Thomas Potts James. It gives a very full account of the early iron-works in the valley of the Schuylkill; and the reader of this volume who may chance to be interested in the subject of its chapter xi., pp. 164 to 170, is referred to the work of Mrs. James, pp. 26, 28, 30, 40, 42, 49, 53, 70, and 71. The two latter contain a list of furnaces in Pennsylvania in or about the year 1788.

The translator should not close these introductory remarks without the expression of his thanks for the aid rendered by Mr. Joseph J. Mickley. This gentleman's knowledge of Swedish Colonial history, and of the Swedish language, perfected during a sojourn in that country, was freely given to elucidate any obscurity or idiom ; and it is believed has secured the translation from any very serious error. To Messrs. John Jordan, Jr., and Townsend Ward, of the Historical Society of Pennsylvania, his thanks are due for the most valuable aid in the revision of his translation, and in everything connected with its passage through the press and publication. To the Rev. William C. Reichel, of Bethlehem, who is also a valuable member of the Society, he would express his obligations for most of the notes attached to the author's appendix, giving an account of his visit to Bethlehem.

On the return of Acrelius to Sweden in 1756, he sent his portrait to the widow of Petrus Tranberg, his predecessor. At her death, it, and also a portrait of Tranberg, went to her daughter Elizabeth, who married Oloff Parlin, Pastor of the Wicaco Church. In 1802, the yellow fever carried off every member of Mrs. Parlin's family who resided in Wilmington, Del., except her granddaughter, who afterwards married John Gordon of that city, and inherited the portraits, and sent them to the parsonage of the Swedes' Episcopal Church, Spring Alley and Walnut St. Having never been reclaimed, they are now recognized as the property of the church, and are fully identified by the family of the late Mrs. Gordon, of Wilmington. The portrait of Acrelius has been engraved for this volume.

The valuable map which accompanies the volume has been engraved from a fac-simile copy, made for Mr. Mickley, from the original of Peter Lindström, the Royal Swedish Engineer.

THE SWEDES' CHURCH WICACO.

DESCRIPTION

OF THE FORMER AND PRESENT CONDITION

OF THE

SWEDISH CHURCHES,

IN

WHAT WAS CALLED NEW SWEDEN,

AFTERWARDS

NEW NETHERLAND,

BUT AT THE PRESENT TIME

PENNSYLVANIA, TOGETHER WITH THE ADJACENT PLACES ON THE RIVER DE LA WARE, WEST JERSEY, AND NEW CASTLE COUNTY, IN NORTH AMERICA.

PUBLISHED BY

ISRAEL ACRELIUS,

FORMERLY PROVOST OF THE SWEDISH CHURCHES IN AMERICA AND PASTOR
AT CHRISTINA, BUT NOW PROVOST AND PASTOR IN FELLINGSBRO.

STOCKHOLM:
PRINTED BY HARBERG & HASSELBERG.
1759.

Imprimatur

N. von OELREICH.

TO THE

Most Mighty and Most Gracious Queen,

QUEEN LOUISA ULRICA,

Queen of the Swedes, the Goths, and the Vends.

MOST MIGHTY AND MOST GRACIOUS QUEEN!

BEFORE the throne of Your Royal Majesty, a Swedish American offers this description of the former and of the present condition of the Churches among which, in a service of eight years, he offered up the powers of his life amid laborious official duties, toilsome journeys, and the endurance of severe sicknesses.

Most Gracious Queen! That land upon the river De la Ware which Queen CHRISTINA purchased of the wild heathen according to the laws and rights of nations; that land whereon her soldiers built forts and erected the arms of the Swedish Crown; that land which its first Colonists brought forth from its solitude — that land was ours. Peace, the beneficent mother of all useful arts, gave occasion to our great King GUSTAF ADOLPH to undertake an enterprise so profitable; but war, the destruction of all people, hindered its execution. Peace, renewed under Queen CHRISTINA, carried the plan to an admirable success; but the war under CHARLES X. threw everything into confusion, and placed Sweden in a condition in which she could no longer avail herself of those advantages.

Those who have represented that land as poor and unprofitable to Sweden, have either concealed the truth, or betrayed their ignorance. The land when cultivated þrings forth an abundance of grain, every kind of the necessaries of life, copper, iron, and beautiful species of trees; it is adapted to tobacco, to the culture of silk, and to vineyards, whilst its commerce would also bring to us sugar, coffee, chocolate, indigo, rice, cotton, yea, even gold and silver at reasonable prices.

This is little more than dreaming what, under certain circumstances, might have been possible. Yet, as Queen CHRISTINA's name upon the De la Ware shall adorn Church, Parish, Fort, Hundred, stream, and the like, even unto the world's end, so it is Your Gracious Majesty's permission that this book, which treats of that country, should derive its highest worth from the dear name of Your Royal Majesty as long as a leaf remains in it; and as Queen ULRICA ELEANORA, of most glorious memory, always cherished her Swedish Americans with especial Royal grace, and also assured them of this in her letter of April 15th, 1719, so I, a Provost of those Churches, recalled home, beg to include my brethren in office still remaining there, and their hearers, in the same Royal grace which has been accorded to me in the richest measure since my return home, and which I trust that I may retain for all time to come.

Live, Queen LOUISA ULRICA! May you long live to adorn the Royal House of Sweden! May you live happy and prosperous, to the common joy of your faithful subjects! May the God of heaven crown Your Royal Majesty with peace and gladness in time, and with the unfading crown of glory in eternity, wishes and prays from his heart,

MOST MIGHTY AND MOST GRACIOUS QUEEN,

YOUR ROYAL MAJESTY'S

Most humble and most faithful subject,

ISRAEL ACRELIUS.

PREFACE.

ITH what propriety can a Pastor write histories and secular books, when no time seems left him which ought not to be applied to spiritual duties and the edification of the soul? This is a question of conscience, which might arise now, as well as upon many other occasions. We usually excuse ourselves by the idea that only leisure hours of mental relaxation are thus employed; but what leisure is there for a faithful laborer in the Lord's vineyard, where the labor is itself rest? Those who know what laborious official duties and toilsome journeys are demanded by the care of churches in America, might think that I there had less excuse for such employments than any one else. Often has this subject so weighed upon my mind, that I have for some time laid it entirely aside, and have now first since my return home taken it up again, and employed for its completion the leisure which Providence has here bestowed upon me.

The love of my foster-land; a loving remembrance of my former dearly beloved Parishioners; together with a special opportunity of making use of some of the principal documents in the New York Archives, which contain accounts of the first settlement of the Swedes upon the De La Ware, their trade and government there, which never before presented itself, and which no Swede might ever again have the opportunity of inspecting — these considerations have induced me to believe that I had not discharged my duty, if I did not therefrom collect that which might somewhat contribute to throw light upon so dark a point in Swedish history, detailing circumstantially that upon which others had only partially touched, and correcting the mistakes which they had made from want of correct information.

The Swedish authors of whom I have made use, although I have not everywhere depended upon them, are the following: "*Superintendent And. Rudman's Manuscript*" in the Wicacoa Church-Book. This is

a collection of information derived from the oldest Swedes upon
Rudman's arrival in America in the year 1697. "A short description
of the Province of New Sweden in America," by Thom. Campanius,
Holm., 1702. "*Dissertatio gradualis de Svionum in America Colonia,
Præs. M. Pet. Elvio, Resp. John D. Swedberg, Ups.*, 1709." "*A
Short Account of the present Condition of the Swedish Church in
America,*" by And. Hesselius, 1725. "*Dissertat. Grad. de Planta-
tione, Ecclesiæ Svecanæ in America, Præs. M. And. Grænwall, Resp.
Tobias B. Bjoerk, Ups.*, 1731." "*America Illuminata,*" an exten-
sive work in manuscript, but afterwards published in an abbreviated
form, by Dr. Jesper Svedberg, Bishop of Skara, in 1732.

The Church-Books of the several congregations were in former times
kept with much care, and contain many useful observations. The
above-named authors have, for the most part, followed Th. Campanius,
whom I have found myself under the necessity of correcting in regard
to the Swedes' first departure to America, as well as in relation to other
circumstances relative to their government. In addition to this, after
my return home, the well-born Lord And. Anton von Stiernman, Counsellor of the Chancery, and Knight of the Royal Order of the North
Star, with his accustomed zeal for Swedish history, and regardless of all
trouble, brought forth from the Archives of the Kingdom most important documents, not hitherto made use of, which he most graciously
communicated to me.

Although my recreation consisted, in a great measure, in the collection of insects, birds, fish, quadrupeds, plants, ores, gravels, clay, etc.,
which I gathered at the expense of his Excellency, the Chamberlain,
Mr. Charles de Geer, for his valuable cabinet, and whereof, after my
return home, I very humbly presented a part for the gratification of my
most gracious Queen ; yet I carefully abstained from the department of
Natural History, inasmuch as the celebrated Professor Kalm, somewhat before, and during my time, was visiting the same regions for this
special object, being sent out by the Royal Academy of Science. And
as I neither had occasion to attempt rivalling that learned man, nor to
doubt that the publication of his Journals would meet the universal expectation, so I had no reason to employ myself in that way.

As the Most Gracious Rulers of Sweden still, at considerable expense,
watch over the spiritual welfare of the descendants of their Swedish
subjects in America, who also cease not to honor and recognize this
care with the most humble gratitude, so, in the preparation and publication. of this work, it has been my principal aim to point out
the faithful upholding of the Church, or its dangerous decline,

which, indeed, depends chiefly upon the unwearied, faithful, and conscientious supervision and exhortations of the Clergy during the time prescribed to them to reside among their countrymen in that remote part of the world; and the reward that they have to expect is in eternity from the Great Chief Shepherd, whilst assured of respectable promotion upon their return to their native land. In the case of this latter matter, the Right Reverend Doctor Henry Benzelius, during his lifetime, the zealous and deservedly renowned Archbishop of Sweden, who has lately fallen asleep in the Lord, vied with all his worthily renowned predecessors, and especially with the late Bishop of Skara, Dr. Jesper Svedberg, who will be held in everlasting remembrance among the Swedish churches in Pennsylvania.

For the very considerable expenditures devoted to that Missionary work, our realm does not, indeed, receive any temporal advantage or return. But as Pennsylvania every year receives important contributions from liberal hands in England for the use of the English churches, from Holland for the German Reformed, from various parts of Germany for the German Evangelical Churches, and from Scotland for the lately established Free Schools, so let none grudge that our own Sweden supports the descendants of her countrymen in the way of salvation, who might otherwise be scattered amid every form of error. When the Lord shall bring to light that which is now involved in darkness; when the inhabitants of God's kingdom shall be gathered from the East and from the West; then shall be manifested the fruits of all the expenditures, all the toil and labor, the dangers of life and the snares of death which have been encountered; and then shall each and all have their reward from God. To God alone be the glory. Amen.

ISRAEL ACRELIUS.

STOCKHOLM, August 18, 1758.

CONTENTS.

PART FIRST.

OF THE SWEDISH ADMINISTRATION.

CHAPTER I.

OF THE FIRST ARRIVAL OF THE SWEDES, UNDER COMMANDANT MENEWE.

CHAPTER II.

THE ADMINISTRATION UNDER GOVERNOR PRINTZ.

CHAPTER III.

The Administration of Director-General Rising.

PART SECOND.

Of the Holland Administration.

CHAPTER I.

The Administration under Governor Paul Jaquet.

CHAPTER II.

The Administration under Governors Alrich and Beckman.

CHAPTER III.

The Administration under Governor Alexander Hinoyosa and Vice-Governor W. Beckman.

PART THIRD.

THE ENGLISH ADMINISTRATION.

CHAPTER I.

THE GOVERNMENT UNDER THE DUKE OF YORK.

CHAPTER II.

THE ESTABLISHMENT OF THE GOVERNMENT UNDER THE PROPRIETOR WILLIAM PENN.

CHAPTER III.

OF CHANGES IN THE GOVERNMENT, AND ITS PRESENT CONDITION.

CHAPTER IV.

MISUNDERSTANDING BETWEEN PROPRIETOR PENN AND THE SWEDES IN REGARD TO RIGHTS TO THEIR LANDS.

CHAPTER V.

MISUNDERSTANDING BETWEEN THE PROPRIETORS AND THE PROVINCE IN LATER TIMES.

CHAPTER VI.

OF THE TOWNS AND THEIR TRADE.

CHAPTER VII.

OF AGRICULTURE.

CHAPTER VIII.

OF STOCK RAISING.

CHAPTER IX.

THE MANNERS AND CUSTOMS OF THE PEOPLE GENERALLY.

CHAPTER X.

CHAPTER XI.

CHAPTER XII.

PART FOURTH.

THE STATE OF THE CHURCH FROM 1655–1696.

CHAPTER I.

THE CHURCHES FALL INTO A DECLINE.

CHAPTER II.

REVIVAL OF THE MISSION.

PART FIFTH.

OF WICACOA CHURCH.

CHAPTER I.

OF MR. RUDMAN'S TIME.

CHAPTER II.

OF MR. SANDEL'S TIME.

CHAPTER III.

OF MR. LIDMAN'S TIME.

CHAPTER IV.

OF MR. FALK'S TIME

CHAPTER V.

OF MR. DYLANDER'S TIME.

CHAPTER VI.

OF MR. NAESMAN'S TIME.

CHAPTER VII.

OF MR. PARLIN'S TIME.

PART SIXTH.

OF CHRISTINA CONGREGATION.

CHAPTER I.

OF MR. BJÖRK'S TIME.

PART SEVENTH.

THE CHURCHES AT RACOON AND PENNSNECK.

CHAPTER I.

OF THE TIME BEFORE RACOON AND PENNSNECK BECAME PARISHES.

CHAPTER II.

OF MR. LIDENIUS' TIME.

CHAPTER III.

OF TRANBERG AND WINDRUFVA'S TIME.

CHAPTER IV.

OF AN UNFORTUNATE VACANCY.

CHAPTER V.

OF MR. SANDIN'S TIME.

4

CHAPTER VI.

OF MR. UNANDER'S TIME.

CHAPTER VII.

OF THE TIME OF THE YOUNGER LIDENIUS.

THE CHURCHES OF KINGSESSING AND UPPER MERION.

PART EIGHTH.

OF THE CHURCHES IN GENERAL.

CHAPTER I.

OF VARIOUS ORDERS AND DISORDERS.

CHAPTER II.

CHAPTER III.

OF THE PRIVILEGES AND MEANS OF THE MISSION.

A
HISTORY OF NEW SWEDEN.

PART FIRST.

OF THE SWEDISH ADMINISTRATION.

CHAPTER I.

OF THE FIRST ARRIVAL OF THE SWEDES, UNDER COMMANDANT MENEWE.

1. THE DISCOVERY OF AMERICA.

FTER that the magnanimous Genoese, Christopher Columbus, had, at the expense of Ferdinand, king of Spain, in the year 1492, discovered the Western hemisphere, and the illustrious Florentine, Americus Vespucius, sent out by King Emanuel of Portugal, in the year 1502, to make a further exploration of its coasts, had had the good fortune to give the country his name, the European powers have, from time to time, sought to promote their several interests there. Our Swedes and Goths were the less backward in such expeditions, as they had always been the first therein. They had already, in the year 996 after the birth of Christ, visited America, had named it Vinland the Good, and also Skrællinga Land, and had called its inhabitants " the Skrællings of Vinland."[1] It is therefore evident that the Northmen had visited some part of North America before the Spaniards and Portuguese went to South

---

[1] *Olof Tryggvason's Saga*, pp. 320, 321; also from p. 329 to 348.

America. But the question is, what would have been thought about Vinland, if no later discoveries had been made, and what they thought about it before the time of Columbus?

2. THE DISCOVERY OF VIRGINIA.

Every region in America was discovered in its own separate time. Virginia was discovered in the year 1497, by Sebastian Cabot, a Portuguese, who was then the captain of an English ship. Its coasts were afterwards visited by those brave knights, Sir Francis Drake and Sir Walter Raleigh, the latter of whom called the land VIRGINIA, after Queen Elizabeth of England, who lived unmarried. Under this name was included all the country stretching from Cape Florida to the St. Lawrence river, which was formerly called Florida, when separate names were not yet given to its coasts. That was done about the year 1584. Captain De la Ware, under the command of the English Admiral James Chartiers,[1] was the first who discovered the bay in which the Indian river Poutaxat debouched, and gave his name, Delaware, to both the river and the bay, in the year 1600 These countries were repeatedly visited by the English; first by those sent out by Sir Walter Raleigh from Bristol, in the year 1603, and afterwards by Sir G. Popham and Captain James Davis, but little more was accomplished than that they learned to know the people, erected some small places and forts, which, however, were soon destroyed by the savages. In the year 1606 a body of emigrants was sent to the northern regions, by two companies, called the London and the Bristol Companies. The former settled southward on the Chesapeake Bay, the latter on the Kennebeck, or Sagadahoc river. Each had its territorial rights secured by a patent. In the year 1620 a dispute arose between them about the fisheries at Cape Cod, when a new patent was given. The Bristol Company, which received an accession of some persons of rank and distinction, changed its name to that

---

[1] [Acrelius has been led into this singular mistake by Campanius, whom he here follows — James Cartier (not Chartiers) was a French subject, and discovered the St. Lawrence in 1534. Lord (not "captain") De la Ware was appointed Governor of Virginia in 1610, and arrived at Jamestown on the 10th of June of the same year. He probably entered the Delaware on his way to Virginia.]

of the Plymouth Council, and obtained a right to all the lands lying above the 40th degree up to the 48th degree of North latitude, which was three degrees farther north than the former grant, and included the greater part of Acadia, or New Scotland; and also extended westward from the Atlantic to the Pacific Ocean; all this was included in New England.[1] The rest remained under Virginia.

3. The Entrance of the Hollanders into the New World.

About the same time the Hollanders undertook to steal into these American harbors. They took a fancy to the shores of the bay called by the Indians Menahados, and the river Mohaan.[2] Henry Hudson, an Englishman in the service of the Holland East India Company, had first discovered those places,[3] and called the bay after his own name, Hudson's Bay. This East India Company, in the year 1608, sold its right to the country, which it based upon its priority of discovery, to some Hollanders. These obtained from the States-General of Holland an exclusive privilege (*privilegium exclusivum*) to the country, and took the name of " The West India Company of Amsterdam." In the year 1610 they began to traffic with the Indians, and in the year 1613 built a trading post (*magazin*) at the place now called Albany, and in the following year placed some cannon there. Samuel Argall, the Governor of Virginia, drove them out in 1618,[4] but King James I. gave them permission to remain, that their ships might obtain water there in their voyages to Brazil.[5] From that time until 1623,[6] when the West India Company

---

[1] Comp. "*The History of the New World, called America*," pp. 106, 107. Also, John Smith's, Rich. Grenville's, and Rich. Waitborn's Descriptions of America. Also, "*The Present State of North America*," London, 1755.

[2] [Evidently the Mohawk, although we do not anywhere else find that river so called. The connection would indicate the Hudson river, but that is never so designated, but was called by the natives the Cohatatea, or Ofogue. See O'Callaghan, "History of New Netherland," I. 44, and II. 300.]

[3] [In the year 1609.]

[4] [O'Callaghan, I., p. 69, places this visit of Argall in 1613, but he was not Governor of Virginia until 1617.]

[5] "The History of the New World," etc., p. 106.

[6] [The West India Company obtained its charter June 3, 1621.]

obtained its charter, their trade with the Indians was conducted almost entirely on shipboard, and they made no attempts to build any house or fortress until 1629. Now, whether that was done with or without the permission of England, the town of New Amsterdam was built and fortified, as also the place Aurania, Orange, now called Albany, having since had three general-governors, one after the other. But that was not yet enough. They wished to extend their power to the river Delaware also, and erected on its shores two or three small forts, which were, however, soon after destroyed by the natives of the country.

4. ARRANGEMENTS IN SWEDEN FOR A COLONY.

It now came in order for Sweden also to take part in this enterprise. William Usselinx,[1] a Hollander, born at Antwerp in Brabant, presented himself to King Gustaf Adolph, and laid before him a proposition for a Trading Company, to be established in Sweden, and to extend its operations to Asia, Africa, and Magellan's Land (Terra Magellanica), with the assurance that this would be a great source of revenue to the kingdom. Full power[2] was given him to carry out this important project; and, thereupon a contract[3] of trade was drawn up, to which the Company was to agree, and subscribe it. Usselinx published explanations of this contract, wherein he also particularly directed attention to the country on the Delaware, its fertility, convenience, and all its imaginable resources.[4] To strengthen the matter, a charter (octroy[5]) was secured to the Company, and especially to Usse-

---

[1] [As early as 1604 Usselinx, who was a merchant, proposed the formation of such a company in Holland. See O'Callaghan's History of New Netherland, I., 30.]

[2] "Fullmagt för Willam Usselinx at inrätta et Gen. Handel's Comp. til Asiam, Afr., Amer., och Terra Magell., Dat. Stock., d. 21 Dec., 1624."

[3] "Sw. Rikes Gen. Handel's Compagnies Contract, dirigerat til Asiam, Africam, och Magellaniam samt, desz conditiones, etc. Stock., år 1625."

[4] "Usselinx Förklaringar öfver Handel's Contractet." See the "*Argonautica Gustaviana*," printed at Frankfurt on Main, in the year 1633. The original was in the Holland language, but was translated by Eric Shroderus, the king's translator, in the year 1626.

[5] "Octroy eller Privilegier som then Stormägtigste Högborne Furste och Herre, Herr Gustaf Adolph, Sweriges, Göthes och Wendes Konung u. Det Swenska nyss uprättade Södra Compagniet nädigst hafver bebrefwat, Dat. Stockholm, d. 14 Junii, 1626."

linx, who was to receive a royalty of one thousandth upon all articles bought or sold by the company.

5. THE EXECUTION OF THE PROJECT.[1]

The powerful king, whose zeal for the honor of God was not less ardent than for the welfare of his subjects, availed himself of this opportunity to extend the doctrines of Christ among the heathen, as well as to establish his own power in other parts of the world. To this end he sent forth Letters Patent,[2] dated at Stockholm, on the 2d of July, 1626, wherein all, both high and low, were invited to contribute something to the Company, according to their means. The work was completed in the Diet of the following year, 1627, when the estates of the realm gave their assent, and confirmed the measure. Those who took part in this Company were: His Majesty's mother, the Queen Dowager Christina, the Prince John Casimir, the Royal Council, the most distinguished of the nobility, the highest officers of the army, the bishops and other clergymen, together with the burgomasters and aldermen of the cities, as well as a large number of the people generally.[3] The time fixed for paying in the subscriptions was the 1st of May of the following year (1628).[4] For the management and working of the plan there were appointed an admiral, vice-admiral, chapman, under-chapman, assistants, and commissaries, also a body of soldiers duly officered.

6. RENEWAL OF THESE PLANS.

But when these arrangements were now in full progress and duly provided for, the German war and the king's death occur-

---

[1] Art. xxiii. of the octroy.

[2] [Bancroft (in his History of the United States, II. 284, 285) correctly quotes this letter as given in the Argonautica Gust.]

[3] Joh. Loccenii, Hist. Svec., p. m. 556.

[4] "Mandat at alle som uti Söderländska Compagniet sig upteknadt hafva," etc. "Order that all who have made subscriptions to the Southern Company, shall pay in the same without delay by the 1st of May, or be liable to the Company for all hindrance and damage." Dated at Stockholm, January 11, 1628. See "Samling af Kongl Bref, Stadgar, ock Förordningar angående Swerige's Rikes Commerce, Politie ock Oeconomie," etc., made by the Royal Councillor Anders Anton von Stiernman, in the year 1750.

red, which caused this important work to be laid aside. The Trading Company was dissolved, its subscriptions nullified, and the whole project seemed about to die with the king. But just as it appeared to be at its end, it received new life. Another Hollander, by the name of PETER MENEWE, sometimes called MENUET,[1] made his appearance in Sweden. He had been in the service of Holland in America, where he became involved in difficulties with the officers of their West India Company, in consequence of which he was recalled home and dismissed from their service. But he was not discouraged by this, and went over to Sweden, where he renewed the representations which Usselinx had formerly made in regard to the excellence of the country, and the advantages that Sweden might derive from it.

7. UNDER QUEEN CHRISTINA.

Queen Christina, who succeeded[2] her royal father in the government, was glad to have the project thus renewed. The royal chancellor, Count Axel Oxenstierna, understood well how to put it in operation. He took the West India Trading Company into his own hands, as its president, and encouraged other noblemen to take shares in it. King Charles I. of England had already, in the year 1634, upon representations made to him by John Oxenstierna,[3] at that time Swedish ambassador in London, renounced, in favor of the Swedes, all claims and pretensions of the English[4] to that country, growing out of their rights as its

---

[1] [An autograph letter found in the royal archives in Stockholm gives the name as commonly written in English, MINUIT.]

[2] [Christina succeeded her father, the great Gustaf Adolph, in 1632, when only six years of age, and the kingdom remained under a regency until she was eighteen, in 1644; consequently, she was only eleven years of age in 1637, when the American colony was established.]

[3] [The brother of the great Chancellor.]

[4] Th. Campanius, p. 62, confirmed by Von Stiernman out of the official documents, although the date of the year is given incorrectly. The articles of cession were found in the royal archives before the burning of the castle, where they were preserved. [Campanius (p. 68 of Duponceau's translation) says, "in or about the year 1631." It is significant that Acrelius says nothing about "the purchase of their claim from the Hollanders," to which Campanius refers in the place just cited, and of which he says, "the treaty which confirmed that purchase was shown to me by the Hon. Mr. Secretary Elias Palmskiold."]

first discoverers. Hence everything seemed to be settled upon a firm foundation, and all earnestness was employed in the prosecution of the plans for a colony.

8. MENEWE'S DEPARTURE.

As a good beginning the first colony was sent off,[1] and Peter Menewe was placed over it, as being best acquainted in those regions. They set sail from Götheborg in a ship-of-war, called the *Key of Calmar*, followed by a smaller vessel, bearing the name of the *Bird Griffin*, both laden with people, provisions, ammunition, and merchandise suitable for traffic and gifts to the Indians. The ships successfully reached their place of destination. The high expectations which our emigrants had of that new land were well met by the first views which they had of it. They made their first landing on the bay or entrance to the river Poutaxat, which they called the river of New Sweden, and the place where they landed they called *Paradise Point*.[2]

9. PURCHASE OF LAND.

A purchase of land was immediately made from the Indians, and it was determined that all the land on the western side of the river, from the point called Cape Inlopen, or Hinlopen,[3] up to the fall called Santickan,[4] and all the country inland, as much as was ceded, should belong to the Swedish crown forever. Posts were driven into the ground as landmarks, which were still seen in their places sixty years afterwards.[5] A deed was

---

[1] [In August, 1637, although it did not reach the Delaware until 1638. See Odhner "Sveriges Inre Historia," p. 302. He reached the Delaware in the middle of April.]

[2] [In the neighborhood of what is now Lewes, in the State of Delaware.]

[3] [Now Henlopen, according to O'Callaghan (Hist. of New Neth., I. 73), originally called "*Hindlopen*" by Captain Cornelis Mey, after a town of the same name in Friesland. Mey also gave his own name to the southern cape of New Jersey, which we now call Cape May. He visited the country about the year 1614.]

[4] [Trenton Falls, which Campanius (p. 49 of Transl.) calls "the falls of Assinpink." On Visscher's Map of Pennsylvania, given in Duponceau's translation of Campanius, to face p. 78, we find "*Sanhiccans*" given as the most northern point.]

[5] The Provost, Magister Andr. Rudman, upon his arrival in the country in 1697, made a careful investigation among the oldest Swedes in regard to the first settlement of the country. His manuscript remarks on the point are found in the Wicacoa Church book, and will be cited hereafter.

drawn up for the land thus purchased. This was written in Dutch, because no Swede was yet able to interpret the language of the heathen. The Indians subscribed their hands and marks. The writing was sent home to Sweden, to be preserved in the royal archives. Måns Kling was the surveyor. He laid out the land and made a map of the whole river, with its tributaries, islands, and points, which is still to be found in the royal archives in Sweden. Their clergyman was Reorus Torkillus of East Gothland.

10. Christina the First Place Built.

The first abode of the newly arrived emigrants was at a place called by the Indians Hopokahacking. There, in the year 1638, Peter Menuet built a fortress, which he named Fort Christina, after the reigning queen of Sweden. The place, situated upon the west side of the river, was probably chosen so as to be out of the way of the Hollanders, who claimed the eastern side—a measure of prudence, until the arrival of a greater force from Sweden. The fort was built upon an eligible site, not far from the mouth of the creek, so as to secure them in the navigable water of the Maniquas, which was afterwards called Christina Kihl, or Creek.

11. The Country Wild and Uninhabited.

The country was wild and uninhabited by the Hollanders They had had two or three forts on the river — Fort Nassau, where Gloucester now stands, and another at Horekihl, down on the bay. But both of these were entirely destroyed by the Americans, and their occupants driven away. The following extract from the History [1] of the New Netherlands, which Adrian van der Donck published in the year 1655, with the

---

[1] [This work is evidently different from the one translated in the "Collections of the New York Historical Society," Vol. I. (New Series), from p. 129 to 242; but was, no doubt, based upon "*The Remonstrance of New Netherland, and the Occurrences there*," presented "to the High and Mighty Lords, the States-General," etc., by Van der Donck and others, in the name of "the people of New Netherland," in the year 1649, which may be seen in the first volume of the New York "Documents," pp. 270–318.]

license and privilege as well of the States-General as of the West India Company, will serve as proof of what we have said:[1]

"The place is called Hore-kihl,[2] but why so called we know not. But this is certain, that some years back, before the English and the Swedes came hither, it was taken up and settled as a colony by Hollanders, the arms of the States being at the same time set up in brass. These arms having been pulled down by the villany of the Indians, the Commissary there resident demanded that the head of the traitor should be delivered to him. The Indians, unable to escape in any other way, brought him the head, which was accepted as a sufficient atonement of their offence. But some time afterwards, when we were at work in the fields, and unsuspicious of danger, the Indians came as friends, surrounded the Hollanders with overwhelming numbers, fell upon them and completely exterminated them. Thus was the colony destroyed, though sealed with blood, and dearly enough purchased."

12. THE HOLLANDERS PROTEST.

Notwithstanding all this the Hollanders believed that they had the best right to the Delaware river, yea, a better right than the

---

[1] The extract may be seen on pages 37, 38, and 39 of said work. The author was more devoted to the honor and interests of his countrymen than to truth and justice. In the passage quoted he gives strong evidence directly the reverse of his intention. He calls Fort Nassau the first of the four fortresses of the Hollanders in America, which no one can understand. He speaks of the colony at Hore-kihl as quite considerable, although it consisted of very few persons who undertook to settle there, and although twenty-eight years afterwards, when the whole river was under the government of the Hollanders, they dared not erect there even a small fort, without having first, with great care, made the show of a purchase from the Indians. He makes Hore-kihl like the Delaware in depth and size, which no one can notice without a smile.

[2] [Horekill (variously written Horeskill, Hoarkill, and Whorekill) is, no doubt, a corruption of Hoornkill, so called from Hoorn, a city in Holland, from which Captain Mey sailed upon his expedition to America, when he discovered, or made his first visit to the Delaware. The derivation of the name suggested by Van Sweringen, in his " Account of the Settling of the Swedes and Dutch at the Delaware," (contained in Vol. III., pp. 342–347 of " Documents Relating to the Colonial History of New York," etc.,) is of a piece with the rest of his narrative, and entitled to no consideration. Horekill was about two leagues from Cape Henlopen, and is probably the stream now called Lewis' Creek, in the State of Delaware. See also the note to p. 21 of Ferris's " Original Settlements on the Delaware."]

Indians themselves. It was their object to secure at least all
the land lying between said river and their city of New Amsterdam, where wás their stronghold, and which country they once
called "The New Netherlands." But as their forces were still
too weak, they always kept one or another of their people upon
the east side of the river to watch those who might visit the
country. As soon, therefore, as Menuet landed with his Swedish
company, notice of the fact was given to the Director-General
of the Hollanders in New Amsterdam. He waited for some
time, until he could ascertain Menuet's purpose; but when it
appeared that he was erecting a fortress for the Swedes, he sent
him the following protest:[1]

"THURSDAY, May 6, 1638.

"I, William Kieft, Director-General of the New Netherlands,
residing upon the island of Manhattan, in the Fort Amsterdam,
under the government belonging to the High and Mighty States-
General of the United Netherlands, and the West India Company, chartered by the Council Chamber in Amsterdam, make
known to you, Peter Menuet,[2] who style yourself Commander[3]
in the service of Her Royal Majesty, the Queen of Sweden;
that the whole South river of the New Netherlands, both above
and below, hath already, for many years, been our property,
occupied by our forts, and sealed with our blood; which was
also done when you were in service in the New Netherlands,

---

[1] *New York Office in the General Index to the Dutch Records, Lib. A.* — The
Swedish annalists, who have given any account of this Swedish colony in America,
have represented the first emigration as taking place in the time of King Gustaf
Adolph, about the year 1627. This was the opinion of Th. Camp. of Holm. See
his *"Nya Swerige"* (New Sweden), pages 57, 58, 72, 73, which others have followed. See the *" Dissert. de plant, Ecclesiæ Swec, in America,"* p. 5. But this was
only a conjecture suggested by the great preparations which were made at that time,
but which were suddenly broken off. It would undoubtedly have been all the better
if the work had been taken hold of at that time with all earnestness. But this protest is proof to the contrary, and shows that the first arrival must have taken place
some time in the year preceding the building of the fortress [that is to say, in 1638].

[2] [According to O'Callaghan, Minuit arrived in the New Netherlands in 1624,
and left the country in 1632. See Hist. of New Neth., I., pp. 100 to 128, for his
administration. It was, therefore, under his government that De Vries made his
attempt to establish a colony on the Delaware.]

[3] ["Commandant," in the original, is equivalent to chief officer.]

and you are, therefore, well aware of this. But whereas you have now come among our forts to build a fortress to our injury and damage, which we shall never permit; as we are also assured that Her Royal Majesty of Sweden has never given you authority to build forts upon our rivers and coasts, nor to settle people on the land, nor to traffic in peltries, nor to undertake anything to our injury: We do, therefore, protest against all the disorder and injury, and all the evil consequences of bloodshed, uproar, and wrong which our Trading Company may thus suffer: And that we shall protect our rights in such manner as we may find most advisable." [1] Then follows the usual conclusion.

13. ANOTHER PROOF OF THIS.

In his history of the New Netherlands already cited, Adrian van der Donck likewise relates how protest was made against the building of Fort Christina, but there also he gives evidence of the weakness of the Hollanders in the river on the first arrival of the Swedes, and that their strength consisted almost entirely in great words.

"On the river," he says, "lies, first, Maniqua's Kihl, where the Swedes have built Fort Christina, where the largest ships can load and unload at the shore. There is another place on the river called Schulkihl, which is also navigable. That, also, was formerly under the control of the Hollanders, but is now mostly under the government of the Swedes. In that river (Delaware) there are various islands and other places formerly belonging to the Hollanders, whose name they still bear, which sufficiently shows that the river belongs to the Hollanders, and not to the Swedes. Their very commencement will convict them. Before the year 1638 one Minnewits, who had formerly acted as Director for the Trading Company at Manhatans, came into the river in the ship *Key of Colmar*, and the yacht called the *Bird Griffin*. He gave out to the Hollander, Mr. van der Nederhorst, the agent of the West India Company in the South river, that he was on a

---

[1] [The translation of this protest given by Dr. O'Callaghan, in his Hist. of New Netherland, Vol. I., p. 191, being made from the Dutch, is naturally somewhat different in its language from the above, which is made from the Swedish. But we presume that the omission of the reference to the traffic in peltries is a slip of the pen.]

voyage to the West India islands, and that he was staying there
to take in wood and water.   Whereupon said Hollander allowed
him to go free.   But, some time after, some of our people going
thither found him still there, and he had planted a garden, and
the plants were growing in it.   In astonishment we asked the
reasons for such procedure, and if he intended to stay there ?
To which he answered evasively, alleging various excuses for
his conduct.   The third time they found them settled and building a fort.   Then we saw their purpose.   As soon as he was
informed of it, Director Kieft protested against it, but in vain." [1]

14. PETER HOLLENDARE MENEWE'S SUCCESSOR.

Thus Peter Menuet made a good beginning for the settlement
of the Swedish colony in America.   He guarded his little fort
for over three years, and the Hollanders neither attempted, nor
were able to overthrow it.   After some years of faithful service
he died at Christina. [2]   In his place followed Peter Hollendare,
a native Swede, who did not remain at the head of its affairs
more than a year and a half.   He returned home to Sweden, and
was a major at Skepsholm, in Stockholm, in the year 1655. [3]

---

[1] [See " Documents relating to the Colonial History of New York," etc., Vol. I.,
p. 291, where this passage, as well as the one already quoted from Van der Donck
in § 11 above, is found.   Van der Donck here says explicitly that Menuet came
"before the year 1638," which also serves to fix the arrival of the Swedes in 1637.]

[2] [C. T. Odhner (in his " Sveriges Inre Historia "), for a knowledge of which I
am indebted to Mr. Joseph J. Mickley, of Philadelphia, informs us that Minuit
returned to Sweden in 1639, and does not again make his appearance in the Swedish
service, either in America or in Europe, and that in July, 1639, Lieutenant Peter
Hollendare (a knight) was nominated as commandant at Fort Christina.   See
Odhner, p. 302 — printed at Stockholm, 1865.]

[3] Rudman's MSS.

CHAPTER II.

THE ADMINISTRATION UNDER GOVERNOR PRINTZ.

I. THE SECOND SWEDISH COLONY.

THE second emigration took place under Lieutenant-Colonel JOHN PRINTZ, who went out with the appointment of Governor of New Sweden.   He had a grant of four hundred rix dollars for his travelling expenses, and one thousand two hundred dollars silver as his annual salary.   The Company was invested with the exclusive privilege of importing tobacco into Sweden, although that article was even then regarded as unnecessary and injurious, although indispensable since the establishment of the bad habit of its use.[1]   Upon the same occasion was also sent out Magister John Campanius Holm,[2] who was called by their excellencies, the Royal Council and Admiral Claes Flemming, to become the Government chaplain, and watch over the Swedish congregation.

The ship on which they sailed was called the *Fama*.   It went from Stockholm to Götheborg, and there took in its freight. Along with this went two other ships of the line, the *Swan* and the *Charitas*, laden with people and other necessaries. Under Governor Printz ships came to the colony in three distinct voyages.   The first ship was the *Black Cat*, with ammunition, and merchandise for the Indians.   Next the ship *Swan*, on a second voyage, with emigrants, in the year 1647.   Afterwards two other ships, called the *Key* and *The Lamp*.   During these times the clergymen, Mr. Lawrence Charles Lockenius and Mr. Israel Holgh, were sent out to the colony.

The instructions for the Governor were as follows:

---

[1] Placat on tobacco for the year 1641.

[2] [It was long a favorite usage in Sweden to designate clergymen by the name of the place or province in which they were born, so that Holm may here be equivalent to "a native of Stockholm."]

"Instructions, according to which Her Royal Majesty, our Most Gracious Queen, will have the Lieutenant-Colonel, now also the appointed Governor over New Sweden, the noble and well-born JOHN PRINTZ, *to regulate himself, as well during his voyage as upon his arrival in that country.   Given at Stockholm, the* 15*th of August,* 1642.

"Inasmuch as some of the subjects of Her Royal Majesty and of the Crown of Sweden have, for some time past, undertaken to sail to the coasts of the West Indies, and have already succeeded in conquering and purchasing a considerable tract of land, and in promoting commerce, with the especial object of extending the jurisdiction and greatness of Her Royal Majesty and of the Swedish crown, and have called the country NEW SWEDEN; wherefore, and inasmuch as Her Royal Majesty approves and finds this their undertaking and voyaging not only laudable in itself, but reasonable, and likely, in the course of time, to benefit and strengthen Her Royal Majesty and the Swedish throne : So has Her Royal Majesty, for the promotion of that work, and for the assistance of those who participate therein, furnished them for the making of that important voyage, and also for the confirming and strengthening of that important work thus begun in New Sweden, for said voyage, two ships, named the *Fama* and the *Swan*, as well as some other means necessary thereto, under a certain Governor, whom Her Majesty has provided with sufficient and necessary powers, having thereunto appointed and legitimated Lieutenant-Colonel John Printz, whom she has, accordingly, seen good to instruct upon the points following.

" 2. The ships above named having proceeded to Götheborg, John Printz, the Governor of New Sweden, shall now, without any delay, take his departure to said place, so arranging his journey by land that he may reach there by the first opportunity. Going down to Götheborg, he shall assist in ordering and arranging everything in the best manner possible, and especially in accordance with the best regulations that the members of the Company can have made; and as concerns his own person, and that of his attendants, he shall so arrange his affairs that he may immediately, in the month of September next following, set sail from this country and proceed to sea.

" 3. But either before, or at the time when the ships are about to set sail from Götheborg, the Governor shall consult with the skippers and officers of the ships, considering and deciding, according to the state of the wind and other circumstances, whether he shall direct his course to the north of Scotland, or through the channel between France and England.

" 4. Under way and on the journey, he must see to it that the officers and people of the ships perform their duties at sea truly and faithfully; and in all important and serious matters he can always avail himself of the aid and counsel of the persons afore-said who usually form the council of a ship; he shall also have every important occurrence carefully noted, causing a correct log, or journal, thereof to be kept, of which also he shall, by every opportunity, send hither a correct copy.

" 5. The Governor, God willing, having arrived in New Sweden, he must, for his better information, bear in mind that the boundaries of the country of which our subjects have taken pos-session extend, in virtue of the articles of the contract entered into with the wild inhabitants of the country, as its rightful lords, from the sea-coast at Cape Hinlopen,[1] upwards along the west side of Godin's Bay,[2] and so up the Great South river,[3] on-wards to Minque's Kil,[4] where Fort Christina is built, and thence still farther along the South river, and up to a place which the wild inhabitants call Sankikans,[5] where the farthest boundaries of New Sweden are to be found. This tract, or district, of country extends in length about thirty (30) German miles, but in breadth, and into the interior, it is, in and by the contract, con-ditioned that Her Royal Majesty's subjects, and the participants in this Company of navigators, may hereafter occupy as much land as they may desire.

" 6. Recently, and in the year last past — viz., 1641 — several English families, probably amounting to sixty persons in all, have

---

[1] [Cape Henlopen — we follow the orthography of the text.]

[2] [Usually written " Godyn's," Delaware Bay being so called by the Hollanders, after Samuel Godyn, who, in 1629, received a patent for a large tract of land there as its patroon.]

[3] [The river Delaware.]   [4] [Now Christiana Creek.]

[5] [Trenton Falls, ninety (90) miles from the mouth of Delaware Bay.]

settled, and begun to build and cultivate the land elsewhere,
namely, upon the east side of the above mentioned South river, on
a little stream named Ferken's Kil;[1] so have also the above named
subjects of Her Majesty, and participants in the Company, purchased for themselves of the wild inhabitants of the country the
whole of this eastern side of the river, from the mouth of the
aforesaid great river at Cape May up to a stream named Narra-
ticen's Kil,[2] which tract extends about twelve (12) German miles,
including also the said Ferken's Kil, with the intention of thus
drawing to themselves the English aforesaid. This purchase
the Governor shall always, with all his power, keep intact, and
thus bring these families under the jurisdiction and government
of Her Royal Majesty and the Swedish Crown; especially as we
are informed that they themselves are not indisposed thereto;
and should they be induced, as a free people, voluntarily to
submit themselves to a government which can maintain and
protect them, it is believed that they might shortly amount to
some hundred strong. But however that may be, the Governor
is to seek to bring these English under the government of the
Swedish Crown, inasmuch as Her Royal Majesty finds it to be
thus better for herself and the Crown as partners in this undertaking; and they might also, with good reason, be driven out
and away from said place; therefore, Her Most Royal Majesty
aforesaid will most graciously leave it to the discretion of Governor Printz so to consider and act in the premises as can be
done with propriety and success.[3]

"7. There is no doubt that the Holland West India Company
will seek to appropriate to themselves the place aforesaid, and

---

[1] [Written also "Varken's Kil," i. e. "Hog's Creek," which is now called Salem
Creek. The Indians called it Oitsessingh, or Wootsessungsing.]

[2] [Raccoon Creek. The "Naraticongs" are mentioned as an Indian tribe north
of the Raritan. See O'Callaghan, I., 49.]

[3] [It is not known whence these English settlers came, or the precise time of their
coming. According to the text above, it was in 1641. Ferris, in his "History of
the Original Settlements on the Delaware" (Wilmington, 1846), p. 55, on what
authority he does not tell us, says that it was in 1640, and adds, "Some have supposed they were squatters from New Haven; some, adventurers from Maryland;
and others, the pioneers of Sir Edmund Ployden." In all probability, they were
the same party of people from New Haven who in the spring of 1642 settled on the
Schuylkill.]

the large tract of land upon which the English have settled, and
the whole of the above named east side of the Great South
river, and that so much the rather as their fort or fortification
of Nassau, which they have manned with about twenty (20) men,
is not very far therefrom, upon the same eastern side of the river,
just as they also make pretensions to the whole western side of
the aforesaid South river, and consequently to all that of which
our subjects aforesaid have taken possession, which they have
seized, relying upon their Fort Nassau, whereby they would
take possession of the whole South river, and of the whole
country situated upon both sides of the same river. It is for
this that they have protested against the beginning which her
before mentioned Majesty's subjects have made in settling and
building, and, so far as they could, have always opposed and
sought to prevent our people from going up the South river
and past their Fort Nassau. Therefore shall the Governor take
measures for meeting the agents and participants of said Holland
West India Company in a proper manner, and with mildness,
but firmly, remonstrate, and make known to them the upright
intentions of Her Royal Majesty and her subjects in the premises, that nothing has herein been sought, or is now sought,
other than a free opening for commerce; that Her Royal
Majesty's subjects have, in a just and regular manner, purchased
of the proper owners and possessors of the country that district
of which they have taken possession, and which they have begun
to cultivate, and that they cannot, therefore, without injustice,
oppose Her Royal Majesty or her subjects, or seek to disturb
them in their possessions without doing them great injury. But
should the same Holland Company, contrary to all better hopes.
allow themselves to undertake any hostility, or make any attack,
then, in such case, it will only be proper to be prepared with the
best means that circumstances will allow, and so seek to repel
force by force; therefore as this, like everything else, is best
judged of and decided on the ground, so also does Her Royal
Majesty place it in the Governor's discretion to meet such vex-
ations in the first instance with kind admonitions, but if these
are not effective, then with severity, according to the best of his
understanding, so as to arrange everything to the best advantage

and honor alike of Her Royal Majesty and the members of the Company. But if no such troubles arise, which it is hoped will be the case, and Her Royal Majesty and her subjects remain undisturbed in that which they have rightfully brought into their possession, then shall the Governor hold good friendship and neighborhood with the aforesaid Hollanders at Fort Nassau, and with those who dwell upon the North river at Mankatan's,[1] or New Amsterdam, as also with the English who dwell in the country of Virginia, and make no inroads upon any of them, nor interfere with that of which they are in the actual possession. Especially, since the adjacent English in Virginia have already commenced to offer Her Royal Majesty's subjects in New Sweden all kinds of useful assistance, and to let them procure, upon reasonable payment, such cattle and seed-corn as they may desire; therefore shall the Governor continually seek to give free and undisturbed course to the correspondence and commerce thus begun with the English, to the use and benefit of Her Royal Majesty's subjects aforesaid.

" 8. Those Hollanders who have emigrated to New Sweden, and settled there under the protection of Her Royal Majesty and the Swedish Crown, over whom Jost von dem Boyandh[2] has command, the Governor shall treat according to the contents of the charter and privileges[3] conferred by Her Royal Majesty, of the principles whereof the Governor has been advised; but in other respects he shall show them all good-will and kindness, yet so that he shall hold them also to the same, that they also upon their side comply with the requisitions of their charter, which they have received. And inasmuch as notice has already been given them that they have settled too near to Fort Christina, and as houses are said to be built at the distance of almost three miles from that place, they should therefore leave that

---

[1] [Usually called " Manhattan's," also " Manhattoe," from an Indian tribe of that name. See O'Callaghan's " History of New Amsterdam," I., p. 47.]

[2] [O'Callaghan, in his " Hist. of New Netherland," I., p. 366–7, calls this person *Joost de Bogaert*, and (in his note on p. 367) says that, " In the translation in the New Series of N. Y. Hist. Soc. Trans., p. 411, the name is misspelled." The spelling, however, is that of Acrelius, which we give above.]

[3] [" Octroy och privilegio."]

place and betake themselves to a somewhat greater distance from the said fort. So also does Her Royal Majesty leave it to the good pleasure and prudence of the Governor, when on the ground, duly to consider the deportment of said Hollanders and the situation of the place of which they have taken possession, and, according to his judgment, either let them remain there quietly, or make such a disposition and settlement of the matter as he shall find most suitable and advantageous to Her Royal Majesty and the participants in said Company of navigation.

"9. The wild nations,[1] bordering upon all other sides, the Governor shall understand how to treat with all humanity and respect, that no violence or wrong be done to them by Her Royal Majesty or her subjects aforesaid; but he shall rather, at every opportunity, exert himself, that the same wild people may gradually be instructed in the truths and worship of the Christian religion, and in other ways brought to civilization and good government, and in this manner properly guided. Especially shall he seek to gain their confidence, and impress upon their minds that neither he, the Governor, nor his people and subordinates are come into those parts to do them any wrong or injury, but much more for the purpose of furnishing them with such things as they may need for the ordinary wants of life, and so also for such things as are found among them which they themselves cannot make for their own use, or buy or exchange. Therefore shall the Governor also see thereto that the people of Her Royal Majesty, or of the Company who are engaged in trading in those parts, allow the wild people to obtain such things as they need at a price somewhat more moderate than they are getting them of the Hollanders at Fort Nassau, or the adjacent English, so that said wild people may be withdrawn from them, and be so much the more won to our people.

"10. In regard to the Governor's place of residence, Her Royal Majesty leaves it to him to provide and choose the same according

---

[1] [The Lenni Lennape, called by the elder Campanius "Renni Rennappe;" by the English, Delawares. The Delawares were subdivided into the tribes of the Assinpinks, in the north; the Andastakas, on Christina Creek, Del.; the Rankokas, or Chichequaas, and the Mingoes, the Neshaminies, in Bucks Co., Pa.; the Shackamaxons, the Mantas, and the Minnesinks, above the forks of the Delaware.]

as he finds the case to be in the place, or it can be continued
where it now is, and the residence arranged and ordered in the
most convenient manner possible; in like manner shall the
Governor also provide a suitable place for a fortress, either at
Cape Hinlopen, or the island called "James' Island,"[1] or wherever else a good site for the same may be found: wherein he
has especially to keep in view these considerations above all
others, namely, that by such a fortification it should be possible
to close up the South river, having it commanded by the same
fortress, and that there should also be found there, without great
difficulty, a suitable harbor wherein the ships of Her Royal
Majesty and her subjects could be in security, and, if need so
were, continue to lie there over winter.

"11. And if the Governor does not find it necessary at once
and hastily to fortify another new place, but can for the present
properly defend himself by Fort Christina, then shall he so much
the more zealously at once arrange and urge forward agriculture
and the improvement of the land, setting and urging the people
thereto with zeal and energy, exerting himself above all other
things that so much seed-corn may be committed to the ground
that the people may derive from it their necessary food.

"12. Next to this, he shall pay the necessary attention to the
culture of tobacco,[2] and appoint thereto a certain number of
laborers, so arranging that the produce may be large, more and
more being set out and cultivated from time to time, so that he
can send over a good quantity of tobacco on all ships coming
hither.

"13. That better arrangements may be made for the production
of cattle, both great and small, the Governor shall at once exert
himself to obtain a good breed of cattle of all kinds, and especially of that which is sent out from this country, and also seek to
obtain a supply from the neighboring English, dividing everything with those who will use and employ it in agriculture in
exchange for seed, and with such prudence as he shall find most
serviceable to the members of the Company.

---

[1] ["Jaques Eyland" was in the neighborhood of Fort Nassau, probably between
that and where Philadelphia now is.]

[2] ["*Toback*" is the spelling here; in modern Swedish it is "*tobak*."]

" 14. Among and above other things, he shall direct his attention to sheep, to obtain them of good kinds, and as soon as may be seek to arrange as many sheep-folds as he conveniently can, so that presently a considerable supply of wool of good quality may be sent over to this country.

" 15. The peltry-trade with the natives he shall also, so far as possible, seek to sustain in a good state,[1] exercise a careful inspection of all engaged in it, prevent all frauds in established commissions, and take care that Her Royal Majesty and her subjects, and the members of the Company, may have reason to expect good returns for their cargoes.   In like manner, he shall provide that no other persons whatever be permitted to traffic with the natives in peltries; but this trade shall be carried on only by persons thereto appointed in the name of the whole Company, and in its ways.

" 16. Whatever else it may at present be necessary to do in that country will be best committed to the hands of the Governor in the country, according to the circumstances of the time and place; more especially as the same land of New Sweden is situated in the same climate with Portugal;[2] so, apparently, it is to be expected that salt-works might be arranged on the sea-coasts.   But if the salt could not be perfectly evaporated by the heat of the sun, yet, at the least, the salt water might be brought to such a grade that it might afterwards be perfectly condensed by means of fire, without great labor or expense: which the Governor must consider, and make such experiment, and, if possible, put it into operation and make it effective.

" 17. And as almost everywhere in the forests wild grapevines and grapes are found, and the climate seems to be favorable to the production of wine, so shall the Governor also direct his thoughts to the timely introduction of this culture, and what might herein be devised and effected.

" 18. He can also have careful search made everywhere as to whether any metals or minerals are to be found in the country, and, if any are discovered, send hither correct information, and then await further orders from this place,

---

[1] [In the original, " i godt *esse.*"]

[2] [Portugal is situated between 37° and 42° N. latitude, and New Sweden was between 38° and 41° of the same latitude.]

" 19. Out of the abundant forests, the Governor shall examine and consider how and in what manner profit may be derived from the country; especially what kind of advantages may be expected from oak-trees and walnut-trees, and whether a good quality of them might be sent over here as ballast. So also it might be examined whether oil might not be advantageously pressed out of the walnuts.

" 20. The Governor shall likewise take into consideration and correctly inform himself how and where fisheries might be most profitably established; especially as it is said that at a certain season of the year the whale fishery can be advantageously prosecuted in the aforesaid Godin's Bay,[1] and adjacently; he shall therefore have an eye upon this and send over hither all needed information as to what can be done in this and other matters connected with the country, and what further hopes may be entertained in reference thereto.

" 21. The Governor shall also carefully inquire, and inform himself in regard to the food and convenience for keeping a great number of silkworms, wherewith a manufacture might be established; and if he discovers that something useful might thus be accomplished, he shall take measures for the same.

" 22. Whatever else could be done in connection with the successful cultivation of the land, but cannot be introduced just for the present, this Her Royal Majesty will graciously have entrusted to the fidelity, foresight, and zeal of the Governor, with the earnest command and admonition that he seek in all matters to uphold the service and dignity of Her Royal Majesty and the crown of Sweden, as also to promote the advantage and interest of the members of the Company, in the conservation of the same land of New Sweden, its culture in every way possible, and the increase of its profitable commerce.

" 23. But far above all this, as to what belongs to the political government and administration of justice, everything of this kind must be conducted under the name of Her Royal Majesty and the Crown of Sweden, for no less reason than that the coun-

---

[1] [The Dutch, under De Vries, in 1630, tried to prosecute the whale fishery in the Delaware, but found it unprofitable. See New York Hist. Collect., New Series, Vol. I., p. 250.]

try enjoys the protection of Her Royal Majesty and of the Crown, and that the interest of the Crown is in the highest degree involved in the protection of that country, its cultivation, and active trade and commerce. To give the Governor specific information herein cannot so well and effectually be done at so great a distance; it must therefore be left to his own discretion and good sense that he upon the ground provide, arrange, and execute whatever conduces to bring matters into good order and a proper constitution, according as he finds the necessities of the time and place to require. At first, and until matters can be brought into a better form, the Governor may use his own seal, but in a somewhat larger form, in briefs, contracts, correspondence, and other written documents of a public character.

" 24. He shall decide all matters of controversy which may arise according to Swedish law and right, custom and usage ; but in all other matters also, so far as possible, he shall adopt and employ the laudable customs, habits, and usages of this most praiseworthy realm.

" 25. He shall also have power, through the necessary and proper means of compulsion, to bring to obedience and a quiet life the turbulent and disorderly who will not live quietly and peacefully, and especially gross offenders, who may possibly be found; he may punish not only with imprisonment and the like duly proportioned means of correction, but also, according to their misdeeds or crimes, with the loss of life itself; yet not in any other than the usual manner, and after the proper hearing and consideration of the case, with the most respectable people and the most prudent associate judges who can be found in the country as his counsellors.

" 26. Above all things, shall the Governor consider and see to it that a true and due worship, becoming honor, laud, and praise be paid to the Most High God in all things, and to that end all proper care shall be taken that divine service be zealously performed according to the unaltered Augsburg Confession, the Council of Upsala, and the ceremonies of the Swedish Church; and all persons, but especially the young, shall be duly instructed in the articles of their Christian faith ; and all good church discipline shall in like manner be duly exercised and received. But

so far as relates to the Holland colonists that live and settle
under the government of Her Royal Majesty and the Swedish
Crown, the Governor shall not disturb them in the indulgence
granted them as to the exercise of the Reformed religion
according to the aforesaid Royal Charter.[1]

" 27. In all else which cannot here be set down in writing, the
Governor shall conduct himself as is suitable and becoming to a
faithful patriot, and take into due consideration whatever is cor-
respondent to his office, according to the best of his understanding, and with the greatest zeal and care, also regulating
himself in accordance with that which may be here communicated to him by word of mouth; and there is herewith given
him a special list of the people who accompany him, and of the
means and equipment of his office.

" 28. Finally, Her Royal Majesty is also well satisfied that the
said office of his government shall continue and exist for three
years, after the lapse of which he, the said John Printz, shall be
free to return hither again, after the necessary arrangements have
been made in regard to his successor, or some substitute in the
said service.   Should he, the said John Printz, have a desire to
continue longer in this charge, he shall have the preference over
others therefor, provided that the advantage and service of Her
Majesty and the Crown, and of the Company, so demand.   Given
as above.

" PAEHR BRAHE,   HERMAN WRANGEL,
CLAES FLEMMING,   AXEL OXENSTIERNA,
GABRIEL BENGTSSON OXENSTIERNA.[2]

AND. GYLLENKLOU."[3]

---

[1] [" Octroy," given to Henry Hochhammer in 1641. See O'Callaghan's " New
Netherlands," I., p. 366.]

[2] [These five names are historical. They formed at that time the Swedish Council
of State who carried on the government immediately after the death of Gustaf Adolph
the Great, and during the minority of his daughter Christina, who was not quite six
years old at the time of her father's death (November 6, 1632), and, consequently,
in her seventeenth year at the date of this document. She ascended the throne as
actual sovereign on her eighteenth birthday, viz., December 6, 1644. The Swedish
colony in America was, undoubtedly, the work of the great Chancellor Axel Oxenstiern, though first suggested by Gustaf Adolph.]

[3] [Gyllenklou was secretary of the Council.]

2. THE FORMER ROUTE TO NORTH AMERICA.

The voyage to New Sweden was at that time quite long. The watery way to the West was not yet well discovered, and therefore, for fear of the sand banks off Newfoundland, they kept their course to the east and south as far as to what were then called the Brazates.[1] The ships which went under the command of Governor Printz sailed along the coast of Portugal, and down the coast of Africa until they found the eastern passage,[2] then directly over to America, leaving the Canaries[3] high up to the north. They landed at Antigua, then continued their voyage northward, past Virginia and Maryland, to Cape Hinlopen. Yet, in view of the astonishingly long route which they took, the voyage was quick enough in six months' time — from Stockholm on August 16, 1642, to the new fort of Christina, in New Sweden, on February 15, 1643.[4]

3. THE EMIGRANTS OF VARIOUS CLASSES.

The Swedes who emigrated to America belonged partly to a trading company provided with a charter, who for their services, according to their condition or agreement, were to receive pay and monthly wages;[5] a part of them also went at their own

---

[1] [The Azores.?]   [2] ["Passaden" in the original.]

[3] [If they sailed due west to Antigua, they must have gone down south to the latitude of the Cape de Verde Islands.]

[4] Th. Camp. Holm, p. 63. Compare "Sam. Pufendorfii Commentar. de Reb. Swec.," Lib. XIV., p. 506, § 75, where, about the year 1642, he says: "In this year John Printz is sent as Governor to New Sweden in North America, to arrange the affairs of the new province, where, some years before, certain Batavian merchants had begun to form a colony under the auspices of Queen Christina. Here an agreement had been made with the barbarians, the natives and lords of that country, that the boundaries of that New Sweden should extend from the promontory of Hinlopen up the western side of Godwin's Bay (Godyn's Bay) to the bank of the Great South river up to Minque's Kil, where Fort Christina is situated; thence farther along the banks of said river as far as to a place called by the natives Sankikas, where the last Swedish fort is. This tract extends thirty German miles in length; but as to its breadth into the interior, it was agreed that the Swedes might occupy as much land as they wished. But the Hollanders who had erected the fort which they called Nassau, upon the eastern bank of the South river, laid claim to all the country on the western bank of the same which was occupied by the Swedes, which they also, some years after, got possession of for themselves by excluding the Swedes."

[5] Octroy och Priv. foer participanterne af det til Afr. As. och Amer. anstaeldte

impulse, to try their fortune. For these it was free to settle and live in the country as long as they pleased, or to leave it, and they were therefore, by way of distinction from the others, called freemen. At first, also, malefactors and vicious people were sent over, who were used as slaves to labor upon the fortifications. They were kept in chains, and not allowed to have intercourse with the other settlers; moreover, a separate place of abode was assigned to them. The neighboring people and country were dissatisfied that such wretches should come into the colony. It was also, in fact, very objectionable in regard to the heathen, who might be greatly offended by it. Whence it happened that when such persons came over in Governor Printz's time, it was not permitted that one of them should set foot upon the shore, but they had all to be carried back again, whereupon a great part of them died during the voyage, or perished in some other way. Afterwards it was forbidden at home in Sweden, under a penalty, to take for the American voyage any persons of bad fame, nor was there ever any lack of good people for the colony.[1]

4. TENAKONGH, THE GOVERNOR'S RESIDENCE.

Governor Printz was now in a position to put the government upon a safe footing to maintain the rights of the Swedes, and to put down the attempts of the Hollanders. They had lately, before his arrival, patched their little Fort Nassau. On this account he selected the island of Tenackong as his residence, which is sometimes also called Tutaeaenung and Tenicko,[2] about three Swedish miles from Fort Christina. The convenient situation of the place suggested its selection, as also the location of Fort Nassau,[3] which lay some miles over against it, to which he

---

Handels Comp. och Skepsfart at njuta uti foeljande Tjugu fyra års tid. — Dat. Stock. d. 15 Dec., 1649, § 2.

[1] Th. Campanius, pp. 66, 67.

[2] [Now Tinicum, in Delaware co., Pa., about nine miles S.W. of Philadelphia.]

[3] [Fort Nassau was built near the mouth of Timber Creek, below Gloucester Point, in New Jersey. It is said to have been built by Cornelius Mey in 1623; but when visited by De Vries, ten years afterward (January 5, 1633), it was in the possession of the Indians, among whom he was afraid to land. We have no evidence that the fort was reoccupied by the Dutch before the establishment of the Swedish colony in 1638. See Voyages of De Vries in N. York Hist. Col., New Series, Vol. I., p. 253.]

could thus command the passage by water. The new fort, which was erected and provided with -considerable armament, was called New Götheborg. His place of residence, which he adorned with orchards, gardens, a pleasure-house, etc., he named Printz Hall. A handsome wooden church was also built at the same place, which Magister Campanius consecrated, on the last great prayer-day which was celebrated in New Sweden, on the 4th of September, 1646. Upon that place also all the most prominent freemen had their residences and plantations.

5. Intrusion of the Hollanders.

The Hollanders intruded upon the Swedes in their traffic with the Indians, and Printz, therefore, sought to keep them under. In the name of the High and Mighty States-General and of the West India Company,[1] under which all their transactions were carried on, they had never bought as much as a foot's breadth of land; but from time to time sent in some particular persons, who treated with the heathen on their own account, and thus tried to find out what course the Swedes would pursue in consequence. In the year 1646 came one Thomas Broen with a permit from Peter Stuyvesant,[2] the Holland Director at New Amsterdam, to settle himself at Mantas[3] Huck, on the other side of the bay, directly opposite Tenakongh. This permit he showed to Governor Printz, and desired his aid in the building of his abode. The Governor promised this upon condition that he would place himself under the Swedish government. But when he saw beneath this the trick of the Hollanders, he himself bought of the Indians the land from Mantas Huck to Narraticon's, or Raccoon's Kihl, and raised upon it a post to which the Swedish coat-of-arms was affixed, whereby the plan of the Hollanders was frustrated for the time.

---

[1] [The Dutch West India Company received its charter from the States-General of the United Netherlands on the 3d of June, 1621. See the Charter in Appendix to O'Callaghan's Hist. of New Neth., pp. 399-407.]

[2] [Peter Stuyvesant was appointed Director of New Netherland on the 28th of July, 1646, but did not arrive there until May 11, 1647. It is, therefore, probable that "1646" is a typographical error for 1649.]

[3] [O'Callaghan, ubi supra, p. 165, calls this place "Mantuas Hoeck," and represents it as being "above Fort Nassau;" whereas Acrelius places it "opposite Tenakongh," some miles below.]

6. FURTHER IN THIS MATTER.

Andries Hudde, appointed commandant *ad interim* at Fort Nassau on the 12th of October, 1645, protested in writing against Printz's land-purchase of the 8th of September, 1646, and gave information of the same to the Director, Peter Stuyvesant, namely, that Governor Printz sought to procure for himself all the land east of the river; that if he could make himself master of both sides, it was probable that he would export annually thirty or forty thousand beaver skins.   Now, as the Holland Company's treasury was entirely empty, and the Hollanders saw that they had no time to lose, they resorted to another plan. Some freemen — Simon Ruth, Cornelius Marizen, Peter Hermansson, Andries Hudde, Alexander Boyer, and David Davids — united together and purchased of the Indians a piece of land extending from Ancocus Kihl[1] to Tenakongh Island,[2] another place higher up on the river than where the Governor had his residence, and also took a title therefor; but with the reservation that if the Company wished to purchase it for themselves, they might do so by refunding their purchase money to them. Governor Printz protested against this as an unbecoming proceeding, which protest also Hudde sent over to New Amsterdam.   Peter Stuyvesant, in his answer, complains of their inability to maintain their rights, and promises money to buy all the land from Narraticon's Kihl to the bay, which, however, was never done.[3]

7. THE HOLLANDERS' PURCHASE OF LAND, AND BUILDING OF FORT CASIMIR.

Governor Printz had blocked up the passage of the Hollanders to Fort Nassau by water, but they devised another method of evading his superior power.   They entered into a treaty with the

---

[1] [On the map "Kancoques," now Rancocas Creek.]

[2] [Near Burlington, N. J.]

[3] [O'Callaghan (Hist. of New Neth., I., p. 371) is evidently mistaken in placing the appointment of Hudde in the year 1646.   Hudde's Report (contained in the N. Y. Hist. Col., New Series, I., pp. 428 to 442) fixes it on November 1, 1645.   That document covers the whole period from 1645 to 1647, and was directed to Governor Stuyvesant after his arrival in America.]

Indians for the land which lies between Maniqua's or Minqua's Kihl and the river, as far down as Bombe's Huck or Bambo Hook[1] (Canarosse), and concluded the purchase on the 19th of July, 1651.[2] That agreement was the only one which had yet been made in the name of the States-General and the West India Company. But by that they bought the land which the Minquesses[3] had already, in Menewe's time, sold to the Swedes, and it is therefore unreasonable to believe that the true owners of the land subscribed that bill of sale. Shortly after this Fort Casimir[4] was built at Sandhuk. Governor Printz at once protested against it; but either he had not the means of hindering it, or had not time for it, and so the matter rested.

8. THE INJURY REMEDIED BY THE BUILDING OF ELFSBORG.

To remedy the injury which the Hollanders inflicted by Fort Casimir, Governor Printz erected upon the place called Wootsessung Sing[5] another Swedish fort, which he called Elfsborg, one Swedish mile[6] below Sandhuk, and two miles below Christina, but on the eastern shore, from which that district of country was in former times, and even now is called Elsingborg.[7] From this was fired a Swedish salute upon the arrival of Swedish ships. But its principal object was to search the Holland ships which came before it, and (which stuck very hard in their maw) to make them lower their flag. The fort was afterwards abandoned by the Swedes and destroyed, as it was almost impossible to live there on account of the gnats (*myggor*);[8] whence it was for some time called Myggenborg.

---

[1] [Acrelius elsewhere (p. 48, inf.) calls this point " *Spinnel Udden* " or " Spider's Point," which, however, is distinct on Lindström's Map.]

[2] The General Index, &c., ubi supra.

[3] [Campanius calls these tribes Minques or Minckus, whom the English called Mingos and Iroquois. They had subdued the Lenni Lennapi, or Delawares, and this may account for the conflicting sales of land.]

[4] [Now New Castle, in the State of Delaware.]

[5] [Lindström calls this place on his map " Elfzborg, or Asamehaking"; Campanius, " Oitsessing, Elfsborg, or Asamohackingz," which is the Dutch Varcken's Kil (Hog Creek), now Salem Creek, as already explained above.]

[6] [A Swedish mile is 6.648 English miles, or 11.700 yards.]

[7] [Elsinborough twp. is three miles N. E. of Salem.]

[8] [No doubt mosquitoes, which are sometimes very troublesome in that part of New Jersey. Compare the English " *midge*."]

9. OTHER FORTS.

Besides these there were Fort Korsholm, at Passäyunk,[1] where the commander, Sven Schute, had his residence. Manäyungh, on the Skörkihl, or Skulkihl,[2] was a fine little fort of logs, having sand and stones filled in between the woodwork, and surrounded by palisades, four Swedish (twenty-seven English) miles[3] from Christina, eastwardly. Mecoponacka, Upland,[4] was two Swedish miles from Christina, and one mile from Götheborg, upon the river shore, on the same plan, with some houses and a fort.

10. OTHER PLACES.

Other places were equally well known, though not fortified. Chinsessing,[5] a place upon the Schuylkill, where five families of freemen dwelt together in houses two stories high, built of white-nut tree (hickory), which was at that time regarded as the best material for building houses, but in later times was altogether disapproved of for such purposes. *Karakung*[6] had a watermill, which the Governor had built for the people, which was the first in the country. *Chamassung*[7] was also called Finland, a district where the Fins dwelt by the waterside, and *Neaman's Kihl*,[8] one and a quarter miles from Christina. Manathaan,[9] or Cooper's Island, was an island opposite Fort Christina, so called from a cooper, who dwelt there with two Hollanders, and made casks, or wooden vessels and small boats. Techoherassi was Olof Stillé's[10] place.

---

[1] [In the southern part of Philadelphia. In this and the following word (Manayunk), I have changed the Swedish *j* into its English equivalent, *y* — Passayunk = Passajungh. — TR.]

[2] [Now Schuylkill, according to the Dutch orthography.]

[3] [Campanius (p. 8, Du Ponceau's translation) has evidently made a mistake in saying "four *German* miles" instead of Swedish.]

[4] [Now Chester, Pa.]

[5] [Kingsessing, three miles S.W. of Philadelphia, on the Schuylkill.]

[6] [Karakung is the Indian name of Cobb's Creek. The mill stood above the bridge near the Blue Bell Inn. The iron bolts by which the framework was fastened to the rock in the bed of the stream are still to be seen. Record of Upland, p. 88.]

[7] [We have no satisfactory details in regard to this Finnish settlement.]

[8] [Called also Naaman's Creek, a small stream in the N. E. of Delaware.]

[9] [This is no longer an island, though it is still called "Cherry Island Marsh."]

[10] [Or, Stillé's Land. "He was the ancestor of the Swedish Stillés in America. His native place was Roslagen, in the parish of Länna, and Penningsby Court, as his passport still shows," says Acrelius in his note in loco.]

Gripsholm,[1] Nya Wasa, etc., which are marked upon the oldest maps, were places laid out and occupied, but did not get established under the Swedish administration.

11. To what Land the Swedes had a Right, partly by Purchase and partly by Agreement.

The land on the west side of the river, which the Swedes had purchased of the heathen, first in Menewe's time, and afterwards under Governor Printz, or had acquired a right to by agreement, stretched from Cape Hinlopen to the Falls of the Delaware, and thence westward to the Great Fall in the river Susquehanna, near the mouth of the Conewâga[2] Creek. These Indians were called, by Europeans in general, Delawares; but within a circle of eighteen miles around the Swedes, there were ten or eleven separate tribes, each having its own sackkewan,[3] or king. Among these were especially the Minesinkos, the Mynkusses, or Minequesses, upon the so-called Maniquas, or Minqua's Kihl (Christina), with whom the Swedes formed a special friendship.[4]

---

[1] [These places were probably on the Schuylkill, S.W. of Philadelphia.]

[2] [The accompanying sketch and remarks, by Samuel W. Mifflin, of Columbia, Pa., one of the most accomplished civil engineers of our country, fully elucidate the locality of the point fixed by the Swedes as their western boundary on the Susquehanna:

"I inclose a tracing (see p. 48) from a county map, on a scale of one (1) mile to an inch, of the falls of Conewago. You will perceive that there are two Conewago creeks, one on each side of the river; that on the east side is much the smaller stream, and forms the boundary between Lancaster and Dauphin counties. The falls begin on a line directly opposite the mouth of this stream. They lie on both sides of the barren island which divides the river, and extend about three-quarters of a mile down the river,—not quite so far down as the mouth of the western stream. The height of the falls is fifteen feet, and the channel, though very rough, is not considered dangerous for rafts when skilfully handled. York Haven, the nearest point to the falls, is about eleven miles from York, and fourteen from Columbia, being about half way between Columbia and Harrisburg."]

[3] [Commonly written "sachem" by English writers.]

[4] [The Delawares, properly called Lenni Lennape, belonged to the great Algonkin family, which stretched from the mouth of the St. Lawrence north to Hudson's Bay, and west to the Rocky Mountains, and south down the Atlantic coast to the neighborhood of Florida, where they were met by the Choctah-Muskogees, Catawbas, Tuscaroras, and the Cherokees, north of which tribes they stretched to the Mississippi. The Iroquois, whom the Swedes called "Minques" and "Minekas," were an intrusive race, extending from Lake Champlain on the east, and thence on the south of the St. Lawrence, and on both sides of Lakes Ontario and Erie, and south to the Susquehanna and Ohio. The Tuscaroras in southern Virginia were also Iroquois.]

6

These extended twelve Swedish miles[1] into the interior of the country, on to the Conestoga and the Susquehanna, where they had a fort which was a square surrounded by palisades, with some iron pieces on a hill, and some houses within it.[2]

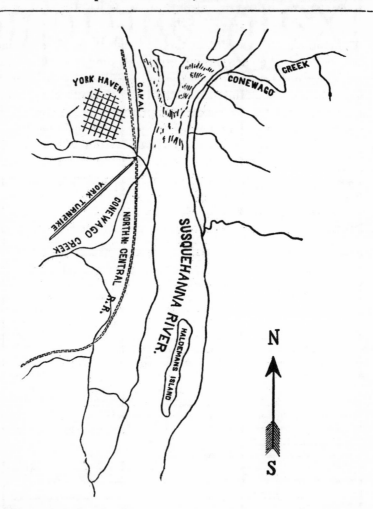

---

[1] [Ninety-three (93) English miles.]

[2] [Campanius (p. 124 of Du Ponceau's translation) gives a plate of an Indian fort, which may correspond to the statement of Acrelius. But we have no notices of Indian fortifications provided with artillery.]

But some of them were with the Swedes every day, who, also, once or twice in a year, made a journey up into the country among the Minequesses, with their wares for sale. The road was very difficult, over sharp gray stones, morasses, brooks, and streams, which can still be very well seen by those who travel between Christina and Lancaster.

12. PROOF OF THIS.

The old Indians still tell of the treaties which their forefathers made with the Swedes, as also how far they were disposed to admit them into their country. Of this it may serve as evidence to introduce the following extract from the minutes of the treaty made in Lancaster :[1]

"THE COURT-HOUSE IN LANCASTER,
June 26, 1744, P. M.

"*Present.* — Hon. George Thomas, Kt., Lieutenant-Governor of Pennsylvania, etc.; the Hon. Commissioners of Virginia; the Hon. Commissioners of Maryland; the Deputies of the Six Nations of Indians. Conrad Weiser, Interpreter.

"Canasatego, the Indians' spokesman, spoke as follows:

"Brother, the Governor of Maryland: When you spoke of the affair of the land yesterday, you went back to old times, and told us you had been in possession of the province of Maryland above one hundred years. But what is one hundred years in comparison to the length of time since our claim began?—since we came up out of this ground? For we must tell you that, long before one hundred years, our ancestors came out of this very ground, and their children have remained here ever since. You came out of the ground in a country that lies beyond seas; there you may have a just claim, but here you must allow us to be your elder brethren, and the lands to belong to us long before you knew anything of them. It is true that, about one

---

[1] [Acrelius seems to translate from the original minutes of the treaty, and his translation differs in various particulars from that given in Vol. IV. of the "Colonial Records" of Pennsylvania, as published by that State. I subjoin a copy of the minutes, as there given, for purposes of comparison, and so as to present entire this remarkable and genuine specimen of Indian eloquence.]

hundred years ago, a German ship came hither and brought
with them various articles, such as awls, knives, hatchets, guns,
and many other things, which they gave us. And when they
had taught us to use these things, and we saw what kind of a
people they were, we were so well pleased with them that we
tied their ships to the bushes on the shore. And afterwards,
liking them still better, and the more the longer they stayed with
us, thinking that the bushes were too weak, we changed the
place of the rope, and fastened it to the trees. ' And as the trees
might be overthrown by a storm, or fall down of themselves (so
strong was our friendship for them), we again changed the place
of the rope, and bound it to a very strong rock. [Here the
Interpreter said, They mean the land of *Onondago*.[1]] There we
fastened it very securely, and rolled wampum[2] around it. For
still greater security, we stood upon the wampum, and sat upon
it to fasten it, and to prevent all injury, and we took the greatest

---

[1] [Probably Hotinnonchiendi, "the Complete Cabin," the name by which the Five
Iroquois nations called themselves. See O'Callaghan's Hist. of the New Neth.,
II., p. 303, note 1.]

[2] Wampum is a kind of oblong pearls or beads made of oyster-shells, or of mussels
called clams, white, brown, or bluish-red. These are a kind of holy relics for the
Indians, who formerly made them for themselves, but now generally buy them in the
stores. They are used — 1. For ornament. Strung upon strings, and fastened upon
leather, they serve them as belts, bracelets, necklaces, and bands around their heads.
Sometimes, also, they hang down, being fastened in their ears, or nose. 2. As tokens
of friendship. When their meetings (councils) were held, for each *article* which was
set forth or adopted, a string or belt of wampum was given, according to the importance of the point. This custom is still maintained very carefully in their intercourse
with Europeans, who also pay them back again, in like manner, with suitable gifts;
sometimes also with wampum. 3. Formerly, also, *for money*. The brown, or blue
and red, were of double the value of the white. *Six* white ones were worth *one*
stiver (two cents); *three* brown, or blue and red, *one* stiver; twenty stivers were one
guilder of the country (forty cents); five country guilders, *one* guilder of Holland.
Wampum was strung upon thread or strings, usually a fathom long, which was worth
five guilders. The way of counting the wampum, for its value in stivers, was on the
thumbs, in this wise: from the end of the nails to the first joint, for the string within
that distance contained either six white ones, and so one stiver, or six brown ones,
and so two stivers. The manner of proving the goodness of the wampum was to
draw the wampum over the nose. If the string ran over it as smooth as glass, the
wampum was good; otherwise, not. For as the corners were worn off by use, so
that they were no longer close upon the threads, they were no longer good. See
hereon P. Lindström's account in Th. Campanius, l. c., pp. 138, 139. [Translation,
pp. 131, 132.]

care to keep it uninjured for all time. As long as that stood, the newly-arrived Germans recognized our right to the country, and from time to time urged us to give them portions of our land, and that they might enter into a union and treaty with us, and become one people with us." [1]

That this is more correctly said of the Swedes than of the Hollanders can be inferred from this, that the Hollanders never made such a purchase from them as to include their whole country, which the Swedes did; yet the English are rather disposed to explain this in favor of the Hollanders. The savages regarded both the Swedes and Hollanders, being Europeans, as one people, and looked upon their quarrels as disagreements between different families. [2]

---

[1] The History of the Five Indian Nations of Canada, pp. 103, 104.

[2] We are indebted to John F. Huston, Esq., of Harrisburg, Pa., for the following extract from the "Colonial Records," Vol. IV.:

"At a council held in the Court-house at Lancaster, June 26th, 1744, there being present Hon. George Thomas, Lieutenant-Governor of Pennsylvania, the Honorable Commissioners of Virginia, the Honorable Commissioners of Maryland, the Deputies of the Six Nations, and Conrad Weiser, Interpreter, Canassatego spoke as follows:

"Brother, the Governor of Maryland: When you mentioned the affair of the land yesterday, you went back to old times, and told us you had been in possession of the province of Maryland above one hundred years; but what is one hundred years in comparison to the length of time since our claim began? — since we came out of this ground? For we must tell you that, long before one hundred years, our ancestors came out of this very ground, and their children have remained here ever since. You came out of the ground in a country that lies beyond seas; there you may have a just claim, but here you must allow us to be your elder brethren, and the lands to belong to us long before you knew anything of them. It is true that, about one hundred years ago, the Dutch came here in a ship, and brought with them several goods, such as awls, knives, hatchets, guns, and many other particulars, which they gave us. And when they had taught us how to use their things, and we saw what sort of people they were, we were so well pleased with them that we tied their ship to the bushes on the shore, and afterward, liking them still better the longer they stayed with us, and thinking the bushes too slender, we removed the rope and tied it to the trees; and as the trees were liable to be blown down by high winds, or to decay of themselves, we, from the affection we bore them, again removed the rope, and tied it to a strong and big rock [here the interpreter explained that they meant the Oneida country]. And not content with this, for their further security, we removed the rope to the big mountains [here the interpreter explained that they meant the Onondago country], and there we tied it very fast, rolled wampum about it, and, to make it still more secure, we stood upon it, and sat down upon it to defend it, and did our best endeavors that it might remain uninjured forever. During all this time the new-

13. How Purchases of Land were made from the Heathen.

Purchases of land from the wild tribes were made in this way:
Both parties set their names and marks under the purchase-con-

comers, the Dutch, acknowledged our right to the lands, and solicited us from time
to time to grant them parts of our country, and to enter into league and covenant with
us, and to become one people with us. After this the English came into the country,
and, as we were told, became one people with the Dutch. About two years after the
arrival of the English, an English Governor came to Albany, and finding what great
friendship subsisted between us and the Dutch, he approved it mightily, and desired
to make as strong a league, and to be on as good terms with us as the Dutch were,
with whom he was united, and become one people with us. And by his farther care
in looking at what had passed between us, he found that the rope which tied the ship
to the great mountain was only fastened with wampum, which was liable to break,
and rot, and to perish in the course of years. He, therefore, told us that he would
give us a silver chain, which would be much stronger, and last forever. This we
accepted, and fastened the ship with it, and it has lasted ever since. We have, indeed, had some small differences with the English, and during these misunderstandings some of their young men would, by way of reproach, be every now and then
telling us that we should have perished if they had not come into the country and
furnished us with swords, and hatchets, and guns, and other things necessary to the
support of life. But we always gave them to understand that they were mistaken;
that we lived before they came among us, and as well or better, if we may believe
what our forefathers have told us. We had then room enough, and plenty of deer,
which was easily caught; and though we had not knives, hatchets, or guns, such as
we have now, yet we had knives of stone, and hatchets of stone, and bows and arrows,
and these served our uses as well then as the English ones do now. We are now
straitened and sometimes in want of deer, and liable to many other inconveniences
since the English came among us, and particularly from that pen-and-ink work that
is going on at the table [pointing to the secretaries]. And we will give you an instance of this: our Brother Onas,* a great while ago, came to Albany to buy the Susquehanna lands, but our brother, the Governor of New York, who, as we suppose,
had not a good understanding with our Brother Onas, advised us not to sell him any
land, for that he would make an ill use of it; and pretending to be our good friend,
he advised us, in order to prevent Onas or any other persons imposing on us, and that
we might always have our land when we should want it, to put it into his hands, and
told us he would keep it for our use, and never open his hands, but keep them close
shut, and not part with any of it, but at our request. Accordingly, we trusted him,
and put our land into his hands, and charged him to keep it safe for our use. But
some time after he went away to England, and carried our land with him, and then
sold it to our Brother Onas for a large sum of money! And when, at the instance
of our Brother Onas, we were minded to sell him some land, he told us that we had
sold the Susquehanna lands already to the Governor of New York, and that he had
bought them from him in England; though when he came to understand how the
Governor of New York had deceived us, he very generously paid us for our lands
over again.

* [So the Indians called the Governor of Pennsylvania.]

tract. Two witnesses were also taken by the Christians. When these made their oath that they were informed as to the transaction, and had seen the payment made, then the purchase was valid. If the kings or chiefs of the Indians signed such an agreement in the presence of a number of their people, then it was legitimate on their side. In former times they were quite truthful, although oaths were not customary among them. But it was not so in later times, after they had had more intercourse with Christians. Payments were made in awls, needles, scissors, knives, axes, guns, powder and balls, together with blankets of frieze or felt, which they wrap around them. One blanket suffices for their dress. These wares they procured for themselves, for their skins of beavers, raccoons, sables, gray foxes, wildcats, lynxes, bears, and deer.

14. THE INDIANS A DISSATISFIED PEOPLE.

It is true the savages sold their lands at a low rate, but they were a discontented people, who, at no great intervals, must have new gifts as new reminders, if their friendship was to

---

"Though we mention this instance of an imposition put upon us by the Governor of New York, yet we must do the English the justice to say, we have had their hearty assistance in our wars with the French, who no sooner arrived among us than they began to render us uneasy, and to provoke us to war; and we have had several wars with them, during all which we constantly received assistance from the English, and by their means we have always been able to keep up our heads against their attacks.

"We now come nearer home. We have had your deeds interpreted to us, and we acknowledge them to be good and valid, and that the Conestoga or Susquehanna Indians had a right to sell those lands to you, for they were then theirs; but since that time we have conquered them, and their country now belongs to us, and the land we demand satisfaction for, and part of the lands comprised in those deeds. They are the Cohongorontas' lands; those we are sure you have not possessed one hundred years — no! nor above ten years. And we made our demands so soon as we knew your people were settled in those parts. These have never been sold, but remain still to be disposed of, and we are well pleased to hear you are provided with goods, and do assure you of our willingness to treat with you for those unpurchased lands, in confirmation whereof we present you with this belt of wampum." Which being received with the usual ceremony, Cannasatego added: "That as the three Governors of Virginia, Maryland, and Pennsylvania had divided the lands among them, they could not, for this reason, tell how much each had got, nor were they concerned about it, so that they were paid by the several Governors for the several parts each possessed, and this they left to their honor and justice."]

remain firm. Such they always have been, and still are As
they regarded the Swedes and the Hollanders as one people,
it was all the same to them which of them had their land, so
that they only frequently got gifts. Three years after Governor
Printz's arrival, as gifts were withheld, and Swedish ships came
but seldom, the Indians murmured that they did not receive
more, and that the Swedes had no more goods for their traffic.
Then there came out a rumor that the savages had a mind to
fall upon and exterminate them. This went so far that in the
year 1654 their Sackkewàn sent out his son, called his elders
together, and had a consultation as to what was to be done.
But as they regarded the Swedes as a warlike people, who were
not to be trifled with, as also that they had dealt justly with
them, and were shortly expecting other ships with costly wares,
they prudently laid aside all hostile thoughts, and confirmed
anew their former friendship.[1]

15. THEY FREQUENTLY VISITED THE SWEDES.

After the Christians came in, and the savages gave over their
country to them, the latter removed farther into the forests in
the interior of the country. But it was their custom, at certain
times of the year, to come forth in great numbers to visit the
Swedes, and trade with them. That was done for the most part
after they had planted their maize, namely, in the month of June,
and so they remained for some time after the close of summer,
when they gathered wild pease, which grew along the river, and
dried them. These pease, in their language, were called *Tachy*.
The Indians were not troublesome, as in the mean time they supported themselves by fishing and hunting, which custom they kept
until within fifty years since. These tribes were the Delawares,
the Mynquesses, or Minnesinks, who called the Swedes their

---

[1] On this can be read Mag. Joh. Campanius' Dialogue, which he has composed
upon this subject in the dialect of the barbarians He was himself at that time present
in the country, and so is the best witness; in Thom. Camp., l. c., pp. 68, 173. [See
pp. 74 and 153–156 of Du Ponceau's Trans. Acrelius has here confounded two different councils of the Indians. The elder Campanius could not have been present at
an Indian conference in 1654, or have had any personal knowledge of it, as he left
the country in 1648. The younger Campanius tells us that the conference of 1654
was held with Governor Risingh.]

brothers. Sometimes there came with them some of that race which the Swedes called Flatheads,[1] for their heads were flat on the crown. These were dangerous, and murdered people, when they found them alone in the woods. They first struck the person on the head, so that he either died or swooned, after which they took off the skin of the head, notwithstanding which, some persons revived again. That is called scalping, and is still in use among all the American Indians, and the skin of the head is called a scalp, which is their usual token of victory. An old Swedish woman, called the mother of Lars Buré, living at Chinsessing, had the misfortune to be scalped in this manner, yet lived many years thereafter, and became the mother of a number of children. No hair grew on her head again, except what was short and fine.[2] On their account the people were compelled to live close together, as also to have stories on their houses provided with loopholes. By their intercourse with the savages the Swedes became well acquainted with the Indian language, and there are still some of the older ones who express themselves quite well in it. The savages were very much attached to Olof Stille, of Techoherassi, in his old age ; but they wondered much at his thick black beard, from which also they gave him a special name.[3]

---

[1] [Probably Iroquois.]

[2] It is told of an English soldier, who was on picket-duty at Oswego in 1755, that, in a drunken fit, he laid himself down upon his arms and went to sleep. A hostile Indian saw and scalped him, taking him to be dead, and so left him. When the relief came, he waked up, shook himself, and said he had been somewhat drunk, and that his head was not yet quite right; but, upon further examination, it was found that his scalp was gone.

[3] It is remarkable that the Indians hate a beard, and that neither men nor women among them have hair upon their body, except the head. Comp. Joh. Bertram's " Travels through a part of Pennsylvania," p. 7. Conrad Weiser, a man of German descent, but born in the country,* was greatly beloved by the Indians, and very well acquainted with their language. He stayed at one time in the Ephrata cloister, among the monks, called Beiselians, Dunkards, or Dumplars, a kind of Anabaptists. During that time he also let his beard grow, according to the law of the order. He was for many years an Interpreter between the Indians and the English in their councils. The former had the same confidence in him as in one of their own race. They have given him the name of *Tarachawagon.* When a sale of land is made, the Indians

---

* [Conrad Weiser, according to his own statement, was born in Germany in the year 1696, and came to this country in his fourteenth year. See Hall, Pennsylv. Nach., p. 973.]

16. Gov. Printz chastises the Hollanders, and searches their Ships.

Governor Printz, for some time, played the master in the river of New Sweden, and held the Hollanders under him, although he did not exterminate them. Adrian van der Donck, in the passage before cited, testifies how he chastised them at Fort Elfsborg:

"The Swedish governor, thinking that now is the right time, has built a fort called Elsingborg. There he holds a high hand over each and all, even over the vessels of our Trading Company, and all those who sail up into the South river, compelling them to strike their flags, without exception. He sends two men on board to inquire where they come from. Which is scarcely better than searching us, to which it will come at last. We cannot understand what-right those people, the Swedes, have to act so; or how the officers of another power, as these give themselves out to be with full powers, can take upon themselves such high authority over another people's lands and wares, which they have so long had in possession, and sealed with their own blood: especially as we hold it by a charter."[1]

17. Has the Arms of the States-General torn down.

The Holland Commander[2] had erected the arms of the States-General upon the shore of the river, but the Swedish Governor

---

subscribe on the one side, and the English Commissioners upon the other. Then the Interpreter must write his name, *Tarachawagon*, first, under those of the Indians, and then "*Conrad Weiser*" under the English, as a sign that each has an equal share in him. So it also went with his beard. At the meeting in Lancaster in 1744 (June), when they came together, and before they began to consult, they first took half of his beard off of him, as their own right. Next, it was among their principal representations to the meeting, and especially to the Governor of Pennsylvania, that he should take off the other part of Tarachawagon's beard, since he would otherwise scare their children when he came among them. To give their speech the greater weight, they here delivered a string of wampum, as is the custom. The Governor, before his departure, assured them that he would take off the other part of the beard, and that he had already given an order for this. In confirmation of this, he also gave them a string of wampum, which was received with their usual exclamation of joy, "Yo-hah, yo-hah." "The History of the Five Indian Nations," etc. The Treaty of Lancaster, p. 151.

[1] [See "Documents relative to the Colonial Hist. of the State of New York," etc., Vol. I., p. 291. (The differences of phraseology are to be referred to the retranslation from Swedish into English.)]

[2] [Sw., "Commendanten."]

ordered them to be torn down. A Swedish Lieutenant was bold enough to perform this errand at Santhickan, now the town of Trenton, where the falls of the river are. When the Hollanders asked him, "How dare you do such a thing?" he answered, "If the very standard of the States-General stood there, I would treat it in the same manner." This was done on the 8th of September, 1646.

Adrian van der Donck refers to this in the passage before cited, where he says:

"A further proof: Above Maghchachansie or Mechakanzjiåå,[1] at Santhickan,[2] the arms of their High Mightinesses were erected, in consequence of Director Kieft's orders, as a token that the river and all its parts belonged to th dominion, and were the property of the States. But what advantage had we from this? Nothing else than shame, and a diminution of our honor. For the Swedes, in their intolerable haughtiness, threw them down, and now, whilst we keep quiet, they think that they have performed a heroic exploit. Although we have protested against that and various other trespasses, they regard it no more than as if a crow should fly over their heads. If the Swedish Governor gets reinforcements in time, we should have more to fear from him than from the English, or any of their Governors. That is in brief what relates to the Swedes, whereof the Company's servants could give fuller information, to whose Journals and Documents we appeal."[3]

18. THE SWEDES AND HOLLANDERS UNITE IN DRIVING OUT THE ENGLISH.

However jealous the Hollanders were of the Swedes for the advantages which they thus gained, and however they contended

---

[1] [In the N. York Hist. Doc., *ubi supra*, this name is written "Machihachansio," where a note also tells us that this is "*Magechqueshou*" of the Dutch maps, and supposed to be the creek at Bordentown, N. J.]

[2] In Van der Donck, "Sankikans."

[3] [Acrelius appears to have condensed Van der Donck's rather diffuse style. The English translation in the "Documents relating to the Colonial History," etc., p. 292, is, apparently, closer to the original. Andreas Hudde, in his "Report" of 1645, seems to have given the "fuller information" of the operations of the Swedes on the Delaware for which Van der Donck here calls. See the Report translated by —— in the "New York Hist. Col.," New Series, Vol. I., pp. 428 to 442.]

with each other for these things, yet they were always equally united when it came to shutting the English out of the river. Already in those times the Englishman sought to settle himself on those coasts, and had so far a claim to it as the western shore was regarded as the rear of Virginia, especially as the times then gave him the best right who had the most strength. The year before Governor Printz landed, the English had fortified a place upon the Schulkihl, to drive out whom the Commissary at Fort Nassau received the following orders :

" May 22, 1642.

" *Instructions for* JAN JANSSON ILPENDAM, *Commissary of the West India Company, how to conduct himself upon the South river of the Netherlands :*

" So soon as the sloops Real and S. Martin reach land, he, the said Jan Jansson Ilpendam, shall repair to both or either of the said sloops (and, if he finds it necessary, he shall collect as great a force as he is able), and go into the Schulkihl, to the place which the English have lately taken possession of, and immediately land there, and demand their orders, and by what authority they undertake to rob us of our land and trade. If they have no royal authority, which expressly commands them to set themselves down upon our boundaries, or a copy of the same, he shall compel them, in a polite manner, to remove, so that no blood may be shed. If they refuse this, he shall take them in custody, and convey them on board the sloops, and in other respects see to it that he may maintain the supremacy, and protect the honor of their High Mightinesses, as also of the Most Honorable the West India Company. But if the English are either taken or driven away, he shall completely demolish the place. The said Jan Jansson shall also see to it that the English are not injured in their property, of which a full inventory shall be made out in their presence. Done in our Council in the Fort of Amsterdam, and given as aforesaid." [1]

19. PROOF THEREOF.

That the Swedes very willingly assisted in this, and did the most for its accomplishment, is also testified by Adrian van der

---

[1] [This was during Gov. Kieft's administration, and the " Instructions," of course, proceeded from him.]

Donck in the place already referred to, although he is greatly mistaken as to the situation of the place.

"There lies another creek (Kihl) on the eastern shore, three miles down towards the mouth of the river, called Varckens Kihl (Hog creek, or Salem creek), where some English settled, but Director Kieft drove them away, and protested against them, being in part supported by the Swedes; for they had both agreed to drive the English away," page 39. "The English have, at various times, and in various places, striven to get possession of that river, to which they insist that they have the best right. This has thus far been prevented by protests and forcible expulsion, as we well know that if we allow them to establish themselves, the river will be lost, or we shall be put to great inconvenience, as they will swarm into it in great crowds. It is given out as certain, that many English families are now on their way thither. But if they once get a firm footing, it will soon be all over with both Hollanders and Swedes; at all events, we shall lose a great deal, if reinforcements are not speedily sent." [1]

20. The Weakness of the Hollanders.

It now seems that it may be reasonably concluded that the strength of the Hollanders in the river was considerable, seeing that they could effect so much; but these movements did not amount to much. A few unarmed English families might be driven out of the country by a small force. On the contrary, they neither drove any trade at that time, nor had they any military force, which reflected the least honor on the Commandant.

21. Proof of This.

The Commandant and Commissary, Jan Jansson Ilpendam, who commanded at Fort Nassau, was, on the 12th of October, 1646, called to New Amsterdam, to render an account of goods which he had on hand, for both the West India Company and some private persons. Andries Hudde was sent to Fort Nassau to examine his books, and return such goods as were unnecessary, but was himself to remain as Commandant until further

---

[See "Documents . . . Colonial Hist. of N. York," Vol. I., p. 292.]

orders, and repair the fort that same year. The magazine there was in no better condition than that Ilpendam in his account specifies the receipt of two bales of Harlem cloth, and two packs of beaver-skins, which he had on hand during his time, and that was all that he was now to account for.[1]

22. FURTHER PROOF.

Neither could that command have been of much honor or revenue. Andries Hudde, who had been appointed as Commander, *ad interim*, at Fort Nassau, on the 31st of December, 1654, petitioned the Governor and his Council in New Amsterdam, that he might be employed as schoolmaster for New Amsterdam, but the matter was referred to the preachers and their consistory. A singular descent from Commander to schoolmaster![2] But neither would that take shape, for in the year 1660 he was Secretary to the Governor at Altona (Christina), and at the same time Sexton of the Church.

23. THE EXPENSES OF THE COLONY.

The support of the Governor and of the garrison amounted annually to twenty-six hundred and nineteen rix-dollars,[3] to be drawn from the excise on tobacco in Sweden, and as the income from this did not amount to so much, the Crown's third of all confiscated tobacco was added to it, as also the fines for the offence. If any loss occurred in the management, it was to be made up out of the department of the excise. All the merchandise which was brought from Holland to Götheborg, to be shipped to New Sweden, together with all the tobacco and peltries from New Sweden, were to go free of duty. But the tobacco which the Company imported from Holland was to be subject to a duty.[4]

---

[1] New York Archives in the General Register of Holland Transactions, Lib. A.

[2] New York Archives, Lib. C., p. 342.

[3] [It is, no doubt, a misprint in O'Callaghan's "Hist. of N. Netherlands," I., p. 367, when he says, "Her Majesty appropriated two *millions* six hundred and nineteen dollars" for the support of the province of New Sweden — the "millions" should be "thousands," as is apparent not only from Acrelius, but from the note of O'Callaghan on the same page.]

[4] "Open Letter relative to the State of New Sweden," Jan. 20, 1648.

24. GOVERNOR PRINTZ RETURNS HOME, AND LEAVES THE AD-MINISTRATION IN THE HANDS OF JOHN PAPEGOIJA.

Governor Printz clearly saw the weakness of the Hollanders, but prudence suggested to him doubts as to how long that might continue, and what might follow thereafter. He looked upon New Amsterdam as a place from which a sudden thundering and lightning might burst forth. Now he was strong enough to drive the Hollanders out of the river, but how he was afterwards to preserve his advantages he did not know. He had not for a long time had a message from home. The reinforcements which he expected were delayed until his hope turned into despair. Neither were the Indians to be relied upon. As long as the Swedes had anything that they wanted, everything was well; but without that, murmurs and misunderstandings speedily arose. He sent some persons home to Sweden with representations in regard to the existing state of affairs, together with complaints concerning the intrusions by his neighbors, among whom the old Schut[1] was one. But Governor Printz was afraid that he should have to wait too long; he had not patience to wait for either answer or reinforcement, and therefore, in the year 1652, returned home to Sweden, after he had been in the country ten years. In his place he appointed his son-in-law, Mr. John Papegoija, as Vice-Governor.[2]

---

[1] [Holland officer — probably Hudde.]

[2] See Anton von Stiernman's "Matrikel öfver Sveriges Rikes Ridderskap och Adel" for the year 1754, p. 350, where we have the following: "Printz, John. Ennobled on July 20, 1642. Introduced in 1643. After well-spent studies in home and foreign universities, he turned his attention to military life, and rose therein, during the Prussian and German war, until, in the year 1638 (May 28), he became Lieutenant-Colonel of the West Götha cavalry. In 1640 he most shamefully and disgracefully surrendered the fortress of Chemnitz, and thereupon went off without the authority of the Field-Marshal John Baner, his leave or permission, and returned to Stockholm. Here he was put under arrest; but after six weeks was dismissed, having given bail, yet with the proviso that he was to appear before a court-martial, which decided that he should be deprived of his commission, which sentence was confirmed by the Council of State on the 17th of February, 1641. But his wife, children, and furniture, that had been placed under arrest in Halberstadt, were, upon his humble petition, released in the first-named year, 1640, on the 29th of August. He was afterwards, on the 16th of August, 1642, appointed Governor of New Sweden. After his return thence he was made a General, and, in the year

CHAPTER III.

THE ADMINISTRATION OF DIRECTOR-GENERAL RISING.

1. JOHN CLAUDIUS RISING.

IN the year 1654 the ship *Eagle* arrived from Sweden. Upon it came John Claudius Rising, formerly Secretary in the Royal College of Commerce, but now appointed Commissary and Governor's Assistant-Councillor in New Sweden. In his company was the engineer, Peter Lindström,[1] together with various officers, officials, and military. Their clergyman was one named Peter. The inhabitants of the country, submitting to the Swedish government, should enjoy free allodial grants for themselves and their heirs, have the liberty of trading with the natives at their pleasure, introduce their goods into New Sweden, export them at two per cent., and then be free from all duties in Sweden and its subject provinces.[2]   The special privileges, given to certain participants in the tobacco trade in the year 1653, were also revoked, as they had fallen into disorder, whilst, on the other hand, the exclusive privilege of the American Company to the enjoyment of that trade was renewed.[3]   The inclination to emigrate from Sweden to America was so strong that when the ship set sail, over one hundred families of good and respectable people, provided with good passports and recommendations, were compelled to remain in Götheborg. They had sold house and home and all their goods in the expectation of becoming Americans along with their wives and children, but could not get away for want of room on the ships.

1658, Governor of the district of Jönköping.   He was born in the parsonage of Bottneryd.   He died in 1663, without male issue, and the family ended with him on the Swedish side."

[1] [The MS. of Lindström's Memoir of this expedition to New Sweden is still preserved in the Royal Library in Stockholm, of which, also, Mr. J. J. Mickley, of Philadelphia, is having a copy made to bring to this country.]

[2] Placat angående Handelen och Seglation på Nya Sverige år 1654 d. 15 Mart.

[3] Privilegium för det Americanska Compagniet d. 23 Dec., 1654.

2. First Salute. The taking of Fort Casimir.

They arrived safely, and immediately came to at Fort Casimir, the fort upon Sandhuk,[1] which they first saluted with two guns. Then they sent up to the Commandant to ask whether he would surrender the fort which had been so improperly erected upon the Swedes' ground and against their protests. But when the Commandant required rather a long time for deliberation, Commissary Rising landed about thirty soldiers, against whom the fort was not strong enough to defend itself; yet the Hollanders did not at that time purchase any right to the land with their blood.[2] A correct inventory was made of everything in the fort, and every one was allowed to carry off his property, whether belonging to the Company or to private individuals. The people were left at liberty either to go away, or, after taking the oath of allegiance to the Swedish Crown, to remain and be protected in all their rights.[3] This was done upon Trinity Sunday, on which account the fort was called by the Swedes the Fort of the Holy Trinity. It was afterwards, according to the plans and measurements of the engineer, Peter Lindström, as good as built anew, and was at the same time improved with outworks.

3. Council with the Indians at Printz Hof.

The Vice-Governor, John Papegoija, had determined to take his departure from the country, and the government was, therefore, handed over to the said Commissary, John Rising, after which he assumed the title of " General Director of New Sweden." He at once devoted himself to the strengthening of the old treaty with the Indians, of which the engineer, Peter Lindström, gives the following account in Chap. II. of his manuscript treatise :

---

[1] [Now New Castle, in Delaware, about four miles below Christina.]

[2] [A quiet hit at Adrian van der Donck's expression on the title of the Hollanders to the countries on the South river, above quoted.]

[3] [O'Callaghan in his " Hist. of New Neth.," II., p. 167, says that Gov. Stuyvesant had acted without orders in the erection of Fort Casimir, and that the West India Directors were not altogether disposed to sustain him in that procedure.]

"On the 17th of June, 1654, there were assembled at Printz Hall ten sachems, or chiefs of the barbarians. There a talk was made to them on behalf of the great Queen of Sweden, and it was sought to renew the ancient league and friendship that subsisted between them and the Swedes, who had purchased of them the lands which they occupied. The Indians complained that our ships had brought much evil upon them, as so many of them had since died. Yet they took the gifts and divided them among themselves. They then went out and conferred among themselves. Then they came in again, and one of them, named Naaman, reproached the others for having spoken ill of us and done us injury, for we were good people. 'See there,' said he, 'what they bring us, and offer us their friendship.' So saying, he stroked himself three times down his arm, which among them is a sign of especial friendship. He then returned thanks on behalf of all of them for the present, and said that hereafter we should keep a much firmer friendship; that as they had heretofore, in the time of Governor Printz, been as one body and one heart (striking his breast as he spoke), so they should hereafter be as one head with us. Whereupon he took hold of his head, waving his hands around as if he were tying a tight knot, and then he gave an amusing comparison, namely, that as the callibash is a round growth, without a rent or a seam, so should we hereafter be as one head without a crack. So if any one should propose to make an attack upon them, we should make it known to them ; and if they heard of any such thing against us, they would warn us even if it were at the darkest hour of midnight. To this it was answered that this was very good if they would so affirm and observe this, whereupon they all uttered a loud shout, and assented. Thereupon the great guns were fired, which greatly pleased them, so that they cried, '*Pu hu hu, mokirich pickon*,' that is to say, 'Hear now! can believe! the great guns are firing.' Then wine and brandy were given them. Then another stood up and said that all who were present should hold that alliance fast, and never do us any injury. They should not kill our swine or our cattle; and if it should be proved upon any one that he had done this, he should be punished for it to the warning of others. They then advised us to settle some colonies in Passayung, where most of them lived, to see if any one acted to the contrary, and then he should be punished. They also declared that all the land which we had purchased should belong to us.   Thereupon the deeds of purchase were taken up, — although only a part of them were there present, the rest being in Stockholm, — and the names that were in them were read over.   When they heard their names they were greatly pleased by it; but when any one was named who was dead, they hung down their heads.[1]   In the meantime two large kettles and other vessels filled with suppan[2] were set upon the ground.   That is a mush of maize, or Indian corn, which grows there.   The chiefs kept their seats, and the common people eat their full."[3]

4. DESCRIPTIONS OF THE COUNTRY MADE OUT.

Director Rising and the Engineer Lindström employed the time which they spent in New Sweden very creditably in making an accurate investigation of the situation of the country, and its fertility. These observations were subsequently set forth in regular descriptions, of which the Director prepared one, and Lindström two, all of which still remain in manuscript.[4]   The suitableness of the climate for human health; the power of the soil to send forth its products; the ability of animals to reproduce their kind; also, the rich supplies of the precious metals, gold and silver, as also the minerals valuable to science and the arts — all these were extravagantly[5] set forth.   But in this the authors

---

[1] [O'Callaghan (Hist. N. Neth., II., p. 81) informs us that in 1648 the Indians of the Schuylkill confirmed to the Dutch a grant of land there made to them some time previously.   They were evidently a different party; but which were the rightful owners it is now impossible to tell.]

[2] [Du Ponceau (p. 78 of his translation of Campanius) spells the word "sappaun." The last syllable, "paun," is, no doubt, the same word which Campanius in his Indian Dialogues writes "*poon*" = "bread," whence our word "pone."]

[3] Th. Camp., p. 70, etc.

[4] ["A French translation of Lindström's relation is in the library of the American Philosophical Society, which was procured for them from the archives of the government at Stockholm."   Du Ponceau, in the preface to his translation of Campanius, p. 8.]

[5] ["Hyperpoliskt" in the original; apparently a misprint for "hyperboliskt" — "hyperbolically."]

were justifiable, for, on the one hand, they described their own country, whilst, on the other hand, other writers have employed the same method to bring to the light unknown regions, for the purpose of enticing people over the great sea, and to procure settlers.[1]

---

[1] The engineer, Peter Lindström in his Treatise (Tractat), which is preserved in the Royal Archives (Cancelliet), in Chap. 5, relates thus: "There was once an American with Governor Printz, who, when he saw that his wife had a gold ring upon her finger, inquired of her why she wore such a trifle upon her finger? The Governor hearing this, asked the American whether he could procure such stuff for him? If he could, he would give him a great deal that was good in return. Whereupon the American answered, 'I know where there is a whole mountain full of this.' On this the Governor took an armful of red and blue cloth, also lead, powder, looking-glasses, needles, etc., and showing them to him, said, 'See here what I will give you if you will bring me a piece of that in proof of what you have said; but I will send two of my people along with you.' To this he would not agree, but said, 'I will first go and bring you the proof; if that satisfies you, then there is time enough for you to send some one with me.' Promising the proof, he thereupon received some pay. A few days thereafter he returned with a piece as large as two fists, which the aforesaid Governor tested, and found that it abounded in good gold, and obtained a considerable quantity from it, from which he afterwards had gold rings and bracelets made. He therefore promised the American a much greater reward if he would show our people, whom he would send with him, where that mountain was situated; which he also promised to do, but said that he had not leisure for it at that time, but would come back again after some days; and then he again received some presents. After this American came to his countrymen and began to boast before them, they compelled him to tell for what he had received his gifts; and when they came to know it, they put him to death, so that that place might not become known to us, supposing that it might bring some mischief upon them," etc. It is difficult to establish the trustworthiness of that report, for no gold-mountain has as yet been discovered, although the English have well understood how to search for it. See Th. Camp., 35. (Transl., pp. 44, 45.)

In the same manner is to be understood p. 39, l. c., where it is told of grains of silver found in flint-stones not far from Racoon's Kihl, as an indication that the adjacent hills contain good silver ore. So also, p. 41, of black clay in Varge Kihl, serviceable for making ink, also for painting with as lampblack; also, in the same place, blue earth that can be used for blue paint; p. 42, of a white clay in Swapecksisko, or Hwhitler's Kihl, which, when it becomes dry and tempered, is good for white paint; ibid., of red clay, in Hwiskakimensi, or Red-clay creek, which, when dried, pounded, and well prepared, is used instead of cinnabar. Of both the last named it can be said with certainty that neither has been proved to the present time.

Captain John Smith, in the account of his Travels in Virginia, expresses himself as follows: "And that I may in few words describe that country, it is so fashioned that all that Muscovia and Polonia have of various kinds of resins and pitch, fish, and many other things; what France has in wine and salt, Spain in iron, steel, figs, wine,

5. Map of the Principal Places.

Said Engineer Lindström's description of New Sweden, which was placed in the Royal Archives, was accompanied by a map of all the places known upon the Swede's river. The map begins at the mouth and extends up to the falls, upon both sides of the river.

On the east side of the river were:

Cape May, which is still so called; Astvehoens [1] river in Indian, called in Swedish Riddare Kihl, now commonly [2] (English) Prince Maurice river; Fogelsand, Sw., now Egg Island; Sepahacking, or Cohanzy creek, the Indian name being retained in English; Roiter river, now Atlevas, [3] (Alloway's?) or Oliver's creek; Asamohacking, Oijtsessing, Wootsessungsing, Ind., Elfsborg, Sw., now Elsingburg; Warkens Kihl in Dutch, Hog creek in Eng., now Salem creek; Obisquahosit, Ind., now Pennsneck; Kagkikanizackins Kihl, Ind., Aldmans Kihl, Sw., now Olmutz [4] creek; Memiraco, Narraticon, Ind., now Raccoon creek. N. B. This name has undergone various changes: Memiraco, Racoon, Racuun, Narraticon, Araratcung, Ratcung; Mackles Kihl, now Manto's creek; Piscozackasings Kihl, Ind., now Woodbury creek; Tetamekanckz [5] Kihl, Ind., now Timber creek; Arwames, Tekoke, Tekååcho, Hermaomissing, Ind., Fort Nassau [6] in Hol-

---

and much more, this (according to the reports of Englishmen) we may have there within the space of half a hundred miles in great abundance for the whole realm." Yet the matter is found quite otherwise. [This seems to be an epitome of Smith's statement as given in his " Virginia," p. 33 of Pinkerton's Vol. XII. — R.]

Mr. William Penn has given out that when he made his first voyage to Pennsylvania, which was in November, 1682, when they came near the land they noticed so pleasant and delightful an odor in the air, as though it came from the sweetest smelling orchard when first coming into bloom. Obs. — At that time everything lies waste, and it is most unhealthy!

[1] [On the copy of the map published in Du Ponceau's translation of Campanius, the name appears to be " Astvetioens river; " but neither form has a distinct Indian type.]

[2] Acrelius uses the Latin " *vulgo* " to denote the current name, which is usually English. In our translation Sw. stands for Swedish; Eng., English; Ind., Indian, etc.

[3] I suspect that " Atlevas " is a typographical error for " Alloway's," as the creek is now called — not " Oliver's."

[4] Now Oldman's, not " Olmutz " creek.

[5] [Tetamekonchz on the map.]

[6] [This variety of names may have arisen from the fact that the first fort of 1623 or

land, now Gloucester Point; Rancoques or Ancocus, Ind.;
Aquikonasra, Werentapecka, Traconick, Poaetquessing, Menei-
eck, etc., etc., are forgotten places.[1]

On the west of the river:

Cape Hinlopen (Holland), now Cape Henlopen; Horekihl,
Sw.; Paradiset,[2] Sw., now Lewistown; Paradise Point, Sw., in
English, Prime Hook;[3] Mördare Kihl, Sw., now Mother creek;[4]
Warge Kihl, Sw., now Dover creek; Spinnel Udden,[5] Sw., Bom-
tie's Hook, Hol., now Bambo[6] Hook; Amke Kihl, Ind., now
Duck creek; Aekan, Ind., now Blackbirds' creek; Minquess
Kihl, Menejackse, or Apoquemeny, Ind., and still so called;
Niew Claus Land, Hol., now St. George's and Red Lion Hun-
dred; Drufve-udden, Sandhuken, Sw., Fort Casimir, Hol., now
New Castle; Maniquas, Minquas, Ind., Christina Kihl, Sw., now
Christiana, Christine, and Christeen; Hopokohacking, Ind.,
Fort Christina, Sw., now Rocksen; Swapecksisko, Ind., Hwit-
ler's Kihl, Sw., now White Clay creek; Hwiskakimensi, Ind.,
Rödlers Kihl, Sw., now Red Clay creek; Nöteboms Oen,[7] Sw.,
Knes ad Bradz oen, Hol., now Bread and Cheese Island;[8] Tas-
woyen, Sickpeckon, Ind., now Elk river, which falls into Chesapeake
Bay in Maryland; Fiske Kihl, Bränwins creek, now Brandywine
creek; Strömkihlen, Skyllpott or Skylpadde Kihl, Sw., now
Skyllpott; Manathaan, Ind., Kyperölandet, Sw., now Cherry
Island; Nyman's Kihl,[9] Sw., and now in use; Chamassung,
Ind., Finland,[10] Sw., now Marcus Hook; Mecoponacka, Ind.,
Upland, Sw., now Chester; Techoherassi, Ind., Olof Stillé's Land,

---

1624 (according to Report in Documents, Hist. of N. York, I., p. 149) was destroyed,
and the position of the second one somewhat changed.]

[1] [The survey extended up to Trenton Falls. The name of Asinpink is still preserved in a stream of that name.]

[2] [The termination *et* is the Swedish definite article — "*The* Paradise."]

[3] [Near Mespillon creek, in Delaware.]

[4] [Probably a misunderstanding of "Mutherer's creek," now called "Murderer's,"
which the Swedish meant.]

[5] ["Spiders' Point."]

[6] [Du Ponceau (in Campanius, p. 46) calls it Bombay Hook.]

[7] [Nut "Island."]

[8] [A translation of the Dutch name.]

[9] [Probably an error for Naaman's Kihl — Naaman was an Indian chief.]

[10] [This and the following places are in Pennsylvania.]

Sw.; Tenakon, Tutaeaenung, Teniko, Ind., Nya Götheborg, Sw., now Tenakon;[1] Sipæssing, Ind., Bond's Island, Sw. and Eng.; Nyeck's Kihl, Ind., now Darby creek; Chinsessing, Ind., now Kingsessing; Manajung, Ind., Skörkihl,[2] Sw., Schuylkill; Passayungh, Moyamensing, Wicacoa,[3] Pennipack,[4] Nitshamene,[5] still retain their Indian names; Sanchichan, Santickan, Asinpinck,[6] and Alumingh are all Indian names denoting the river's fall; Nittabaconck, Merekaz, Plom Point, Wickon, or Gädde Kihl, etc., are now unknown.

The aforesaid map was of the length of four ells, and two ells in breadth, and until the year 1696, when His Royal Majesty King Charles XI. renewed the Swedish mission in America, was hung up in the Royal Council Chamber in the castle at Stockholm. Then the king directed that this map should be copied off in smaller form and engraved on copper, whereby it was preserved from the destruction which overtook the castle in Stockholm by the lamentable fire of the year 1697 (May 7). A copy of this is found in Th. Camp. Holm's Description of New Sweden.

6. A Plan of Fort Christina.

The Engineer Lindström also prepared another chart, namely, of Fort Christina and its siege by the Hollanders. Together with the fort, which was favorably situated, four batteries were sketched: Slangenborg, across Christina Kihl by the ferry; Myggenborg, on the heights west of the fort; Rotteborg, on the approach to the fort on the land side; and Fligenborg, on the hill east of the fort on the other side of Fish Kihl, or what is now called Brandywine creek. But that he marks out Christina Haven as a besieged place, although there was as yet no town there, and the place still in part consists of timber-land,

---

[1] [Tinicum.]

[2] On the map " Skiär eller linde Kil; " that is " Linden creek."

[3] [Also called " Wickquakonich," on the map Wichacoing, of which " Wicaco" is a contraction, one of the six Indian towns mentioned by Campanius, p. 46.]

[4] [Called by Campanius " Pennickpacka," also an Indian village.]

[5] [Nishamany.]

[6] [As Asinpinck is the name of a stream, it is doubtful whether it has the signification here indicated.]

which was never cleared; also that Tenakong is laid down as
directly over Christina Kihl, although it lies more than three
Swedish miles up the river — that is to be set down to his own
account.

7. Unreasonableness of the Hollanders.

The Hollanders could not digest the affront put upon them
when Director Rising captured Fort Casimir, and at the same
time drove them out of New Sweden. From that day they
began to collect their forces, but could not immediately show
what they had in their mind. Meanwhile, to their great joy, it
happened that Mr. Deswijk,[1] captain and supercargo of a Swedish
ship called the *Golden Shark*, which was sent to reinforce the
Swedes, as well as to carry goods back again, had the misfortune
to cast anchor alongside of their coast, whilst he regarded the
Hollanders as old friends and neighbors, but was immediately
seized by them and considered a good prize. The following
extracts from the New York Records will give the facts of this
seizure :

"*October* 17–24, 1654. Captain Deswijk declares that his
ship was compelled by an oversight of the pilot to go up into
the Raretan river, where the Hollanders forcibly seized them,
and keep him a prisoner in New Amsterdam, whither he came
to obtain a pilot who should conduct him to the South river, or
the river of New Sweden. You now pretend, says he, that Mr.
John Rising, the Governor of New Sweden, had taken Fort
Casimir from you, to which you pretend to have a right; which
pretension has no ground nor certainty. That fortress was built
by your General-Director in the year 1651, rather by force and
violence than by right and justice, on the South river, a soil and
country belonging to Her Royal Majesty of Sweden, my Most
Gracious Queen — against which Governor John Printz protested.
Therefore, said John Rising has not taken it from you, but has
only taken back property which belongs to her Majesty of
Sweden. It cannot be proved that he has taken a single penny

---

[1] [O'Callaghan, Vol. II., p. 276, of his Hist. of N. Netherlands, calls him "Captain Van Elswyck." — "Daswick," in Dr. Collin's translation, in Vol. I., p. 414, of
N. York Hist. Col. N. S., is probably a typographical error.]

of any of your subjects. But when the free people, who lived there and wished to remain permanently, had given their oath of allegiance, they were all protected in their rights. Further, no man who lives or lands there has ever been detained, but has always been left at liberty to go where he pleased, and also to take his goods and chattels with him. But as concerns myself, you treat me in a very different way," etc.

To this Governor Stuyvesant[1] and his Council answered as follows :

" To the unfounded protest presented by Mr. Deswijk, Factor of the Swedish Company, it is answered: that although he pretends to have sailed into this river by the oversight of his pilot, and had sent his people to us as to good friends and neighbors, the facts do not so appear to us. Director Rising's hostile conduct is well known, when, under an appearance of friendship, he came before our fortress Casimir on the South river in the New Netherlands, gave two salutes, and sent thirty men on shore, who were welcomed by our commandant and official as friends and neighbors. But when they saw the weakness of our garrison, they did not treat our few soldiers as friends and neighbors of the Crown of Sweden, but as declared enemies, though they belonged to the States-General and the West India Company : with force and arms they made themselves masters of Fort Casimir, with all its ammunition, houses, and other things belonging to the far-famed West India Company, in direct opposition to all rights and usages of war — and they still hold the same. They have also compelled some of our officers, together with other free people who represented the States-General and the West India Company, to renounce their oath of allegiance, and submit to the Crown of Sweden," etc. Other supposed injuries and insults were also recounted,[2] etc.

What lame pretexts are here urged for that outrage all the

---

[1] [Peter Stuyvesant was appointed Governor of the New Netherlands July 28, 1646, and arrived at the Manhattans (now New York) on the 11th of May, 1647. His administration lasted until September 8, 1664, when he surrendered to the English under Col. Nichols, and the name of New York was substituted for that of New Amsterdam, and the New Netherlands disappeared from the New World.]

[2] Arch. in New York; the Gen. Index, Lit. C., p. 280.

world can see.   What the Hollanders had, on various occasions
before this, done to the English, compelling them to relinquish
places which they had occupied, and allowing the people to
depart with their property, or to remain in the country as their
subjects, that they now determined to do to the Swedes, in conflict with all the laws and usages of nations, because this best
pleased themselves. Although it was an entirely different matter
to take possession of one's own land from a foreign power and
its garrison, which sought the injury of the country and its
government, where all had liberty to go their way, and take
along with them that which belonged to them — and to keep a
ship with its goods and people, which had come into their
harbor of necessity, but was willing to leave it immediately, and
without creating the least disturbance.

8. FORT TRINITY TAKEN.

Finally their hostility burst forth in a full flame.   On the 30th
of August, 1655, came the Holland Gov. Peter Stuyvesant, with
seven vessels, great and small, and from 600 to 700 men strong,
from the North river and New Amsterdam up into the river of
New Sweden, and fell violently upon the Swedes. He made his
first night-camp in the abandoned and decayed Fort Elfsborg,
where he arrayed his soldiers, and took some freemen prisoners.
The following day he sailed past Fort Trinity, and landed upon
a point which is now called Swanevik.   There they began to
throw up some entrenchments, and with threats and arguments
to demand the surrender of the fort.

Sven Schute,[1] the commander there, endeavored partly to
dissuade and partly to hold out against their attack until he
could receive reinforcements from Christina; but all in vain.
The road to Christina had already been beset by the Hollanders,
so that no one could either go or come from that place.   Commander Schute's proceedings were entirely disapproved by
Director Rising, especially that he gave up the fort without the

---

[1] [Mr. Marsh, in his translation of Gov. Rising's Report, in the New York Hist.
Col., New Series, Vol. I., p. 443, writes this name " *Schüte*," and in a note says that
" the modern orthography is *Skytte*."

least resistance. But the excuse was, that necessity knows no law. The Commander was allowed to march out of the fort with some few men; but the other officers were taken prisoners and kept within the fort, and the common soldiers were put on shipboard and sent over to New Amsterdam. That was, indeed, said to be done of their own good will, thus to submit to the power of the Hollanders; but the people's own words witnessed to the contrary. As to the rest, all posts were filled with Holland soldiers. The Swedish flag was hauled down, and that of Holland put in its place. The following document informs us more fully of these transactions:

Extract from Governor Stuyvesant's Journal, dated September 10–17, 1655.

"This day, eight days since, we came into the bay of the South river, and were delayed during Sunday by the ebb and flood tide.

"On Thursday following we came before the deserted Fort Elsingburg, and there held a review, and divided our troops into five companies.

"On Friday morning, the wind and tide being favorable, we passed Fort Casimir without any hostile demonstration on either side, and cast anchor a little distance above the fort, put the people on shore, and sent Captain Smidt, with a drummer, to the fort to demand the surrender of our property. The Commandant desired leave to consult Governor Rising, which was refused. In the meantime the road to Christina was occupied by fifty men, and the Commandant, Sven Schute, sent a messenger to ask a parley with us. But we advised him not to wait for a salute from our guns, lest the shedding of blood should be charged upon him. He again desired to confer with us, which was granted, and took place in a valley about half way between the battery, which we were commencing, and the fort. He insisted that he should send an open letter to his Governor, which was denied him. Then he went away dissatisfied. Our troops advanced down into the valley, and our works began to rise up above the bushes. The last summons was delivered, and then the Commandant desired a delay until the next day, which was granted him, inasmuch as we could not have our batteries ready before that time.

"On Saturday morning the Commandant came out and capitulated at discretion. At noon our troops marched into the fort.

"Sunday. To-day our first public divine service was held, and an imperfect thanksgiving.

"Yesterday came one Factor Elswyk from Christina, and in a polite manner, in the name of the Governor, asked for the reason of our coming, and our superior's instructions. Our answer was: to take back that which was our own, and keep it. He suggested to us to be satisfied with that which had been taken, and not go any further — upon which he insisted with polite representations and arguments, with the threat finally introduced: *Hodie mihi, cras tibi.*

"In one or two days our troops shall march thither; but we shall march slowly, so that our people may not be fatigued, and that we may have time to receive your orders. In the meantime we shall advance, taking counsel with Mr. Sille[1] and Captain Coningh, according to the best of our understanding, etc.

"PET. STUYVESANT.

"P. S. — There are thirty Swedes who have surrendered to us, and desire to settle in Manathaan, whom you may expect. It seems that many others may follow them."

9. CAPITULATION AT FORT TRINITY OR FORT CASIMIR.

The following is the capitulation made at Fort Casimir between the Commandant Sven Schute and Director-General Peter Stuyvesant:

1. The Commandant shall have liberty, if he desires it, to take back to Sweden by ship, either of the Crown or others, the cannon which belong to the Crown, both small and great, which, according to said Commandant's report, consist of four iron guns

---

[1] [Nicasius de Sille was in 1653. appointed by the Directors of the West India Comp. "First Counselor to the Director," at a salary of 100 florins ($40) per month. O'Callaghan, II., 236.]

of fourteen lis-pounds[1] and five field-pieces; of these latter, four large and one small one.

2. He shall also march out with twelve men fully armed, as his life-guard, and with the flags of the Crown; the others with their side-arms only; the muskets of the Crown shall stand to the Commandant's account, but shall remain in the fort until they take them away, or send an order for them.

3. The Commandant shall be secure in his person and individual property, either to take it away, or to let it remain until further orders. The same shall be the case in regard to the property of all the other officers.

4. All this shall be kept inviolate, provided said Commandant shall immediately surrender into the Director-General's hands Fort Casimir, with all its pieces, ammunition, materials, and other goods belonging to the aforesaid West India Company.

Given, done, and signed by the contracting parties, September 16, 1665, on the ship *Waegh*, at Fort Casimir.

PETER STUYVESANT.
SVEN SCHUTE, *Engineer.*

10. FORT CHRISTINA CAPTURED.

But the matter did not rest here. The evil undertaking was continued by a march to Fort Christina. The road taken was not directly overland from Sandhuk, which would have been about a Swedish mile, and would have brought them directly in front of the fort, but around over the creek, where the Christina bridge now is, which was two and a half Swedish miles, and they thus attacked the fort in its rear, placing their camp in the field which was fenced off in front of Christina harbor. No great trouble was taken in forming the siege. The time, which was only a few days, was mostly occupied with negotiations, without a single shot being fired, or a single Hollander's blood shed.

11. THE CAPITULATION.

The capitulation was made between the brave and noble[2] Director John Rising, Governor of New Sweden, on the one

---

[1] [The Swedish lis-pound is equal to twenty pounds avoirdupois.]

[2] [There is a spice of sly irony in this characterization of the "high and mighty" contracting parties.]

side, and the brave and noble Director Peter Stuyvesant, Governor-General of New Netherlands, on the other side:

" 1. That all cannon, ammunition, provisions, and supplies, together with other things belonging to the Crown of Sweden, which are in and around the Fort Christina, shall belong to and be preserved as the property of the Swedish Crown and the Southern Company, and shall be under the power of said Governor, to take it away or to deliver it to Governor Stuyvesant, with the proviso that it shall be given up upon order.

" 2. Governor John Rising, his superior and inferior officers, his officials and soldiers, shall march out of the fort with drums and trumpets playing, flags flying, matches burning, with hand and side-arms, and balls in their mouths. They shall first be conducted to Tinnecuck[1] Island, to which they shall be taken in safety and placed in the fort which is there, until the Governor sets sail upon the ship *Waegh*, upon which said Governor Rising, his people and property, shall be conducted to Sandy Huck, situated five Holland miles the other side of New York, under safe conduct, within at least fourteen days. Also the Governor and Factor Elswyk shall in the meantime have allowed them four or five servants for attending to their business, whilst the others are lodged in the fortress.

" 3. All writings, letters, instructions, and acts belonging to the Crown of Sweden, the Southern Company, or private persons, which are found in Fort Christina, shall remain in the Governor's hands, to take away at his pleasure, without being searched or examined.

" 4. None of the Crown's or Company's officers, soldiers, officials, or private persons shall be detained here against their wishes, but shall be allowed to go, without molestation, along with the Governor, if they so desire.

" 5. That all the officers, soldiers, and officials of the Crown and of the Southern Company, and also all private persons, shall retain their goods unmolested.

" 6. If some officials and freemen desire to depart, but are not able to go with the Governor and his party, they shall be allowed the time of one year and six weeks in which to sell their land

---

[1] [Tinnakong or Tinicum.]

and goods, provided that they do not take the oath of allegiance for the period that they remain.

"7. If any of the Swedes or Finns are not disposed to go away, Governor Rising may take measures to induce them to do so; and if they are so persuaded, they shall not be forcibly detained. Those who choose to remain shall have the liberty of adhering to their own Augsburg Confession,[1] as also to support a minister for their instruction.

"8. Governor Rising, Factor Elswyk, and other superior and inferior officers, soldiers, and freemen, with all their property which they wish to take away, shall be provided by the Governor-General with a sound ship, which shall receive them at Sandy Huck, and convey them to Texel,[2] and thence immediately by a coaster, galliote, or other suitable vessel, to Götheborg, without charge; with the proviso, that said coaster, galliote, or other vessel shall not be detained, for which the said Governor Rising shall be answerable.

"9. In case Governor Rising, Factor Elswyk, or any other official belonging to the Swedish Crown or the South Company, has incurred any debts on account of the Crown or of the Company, they shall not be detained therefor within the jurisdiction of the Governor-General.

"10. Governor Rising has full freedom to make himself acquainted with the conduct of Commandant Schute and that of his officers and soldiers in regard to the surrender of Sandhuk Fort (Fort Casimir).

"11. Governor Rising promises that between the 15th and 25th of September he will withdraw his people from Fort Christina, and deliver it up to the Governor-General.

"Done and signed the 15–25th of September, 1655, on the parade between Fort Christina and the Governor-General's camp.

PETER STUYVESANT.
JOHN RISING, <i>Director of New Sweden.</i>"</div>

---

[1] [The Swedes and Finns were Lutherans, and adhered to the Augsburg Confession; the Hollanders were Calvinists, adhering to the Heidelberg Catechism, Canons of Dordt, etc.]

[2] [Texel or Tessel is a small island off the west coast of Holland, at the entrance of the Zuyder Zee.]

Secret Article.

"It is further capitulated that the Captain who is to convey
Governor John Rising and the Factor Henry Elswyk shall be
expressly commanded and ordered to put the aforesaid Governor
Rising and the Factor Elswyk on shore, either in England or in
France; and that the Director-General shall lend to Governor
Rising, either in money or bills of exchange, the sum of three
hundred pounds Flemish, which the said Governor Rising
engages to repay to the Governor-General, or his order, in Amsterdam, within six months after the receipt. In the meantime
he leaves as a pledge and equivalent the property of the Crown
and Southern Company now given up. Hereof we give two
copies signed by the contracting parties.

Concluded September 15–25 on the parade between Fort Christina and Governor-General Stuyvesant's camp.

PETER STUYVESANT
JOHN RISING."

12. THE OATH OF ALLEGIANCE.

Thereupon all who had a desire to remain in the country
were called together by a proclamation to take the oath of allegiance, and be allowed to remain in the country as a free people.
All others were to depart, with liberty either to carry off their
property, or to sell it.

The form of the oath of allegiance was as follows:

"I, the undersigned, do promise and swear, as in the presence
of the omniscient and almighty God, that I will remain faithful
and obedient to' the States-General of the United Netherlands,
to the Director-General and his Council, now, or hereafter appointed. And I will remain so without giving aid or assistance,
by word or deed, to any hostile undertaking or commotion; but
will conduct myself as an obedient and faithful subject so long
as I remain in the country of the South river in the New Netherlands. So help me Almighty God."

13. THE AMMUNITION OF THE CROWN PLEDGED FOR TRAVEL-
LING EXPENSES.

The noble-minded Director Rising now found himself in very
unpleasant circumstances, when he saw all his worthy purposes

and honest undertakings, as well as the Swedish government in America, coming to so lamentable an end; and that which was most grievous, that he was compelled to put in pledge the arms and ammunition of the Crown for his travelling expenses home. The only consolation was in the hope that it might be repaid at home in a double measure. Stuyvesant's orders upon Cornelius Jacob Steewyk to supply Rising with eight hundred guilders for the articles pledged, were dated on the 2d of November, 1655. In his quittance of three hundred pounds Flemish, Rising was obligated to redeem the pledged articles within six months, or to consent to their sale. Herewith it came no further than that each held what he had. The Swedish cannon thus sold are still to be seen[1] in Fort St. George in New York. Director Rising did not immediately set out on his voyage to Sweden. The Report[2] about New Sweden, which he published in order to encourage his victorious King to reconquer New Sweden, was dated at Elbingen, June 3, 1656.

14. THE TYRANNY OF THE HOLLANDERS.

The terrible tyranny to which the Swedes were at that time subjected cannot be fully described. The flower of the Swedish male population were at once torn away and sent over to New Amsterdam, though everything was done as though it were with their free consent. The men were taken by force and placed on shipboard; the women at home in their houses were abused, their property carried off, and their cattle slaughtered. Then it was the right time to send out a proclamation and call the people to take the oath of allegiance. Those who withheld themselves were had in continual suspicion and disfavor. Further proofs of this are the testimonials which Director Rising furnished to those who were in the midst of the fire. Several of these are found in their originals of the same date and import, of which it is sufficient to adduce the following:

---

[1] [Namely, in 1756, when Acrelius left the country.]

[2] [A translation of this Report of Gov. Rising, by the Hon. Geo. P. Marsh, now Minister of the U. S. to the Kingdom of Italy, may be found in the "New York Historical Collection," New Series, Vol. I., pp. 443–448.]

"His Royal Majesty, my Most Gracious King's most humble and faithful servant and Director of New Sweden:

"Hereby witnesseth, that inasmuch as the bearer of this letter, the upright and intelligent Nils Matsson, freeman, of Herring Island, in the troubles of these times here in New Sweden, wherein we Swedes have been unexpectedly involved by the hostility of the Hollanders, cannot remove from this country so hastily, but on account of his property must remain here until a more convenient season, and therefore desires a testimonial from me, which I cannot justly withhold from him; I therefore herewith testify that during the whole period of my residence in this country, he has conducted himself as an honorable and faithful subject of the Crown, and willingly assisted in the repair and building of the fort, as well as in other service of the Crown, and now lately in the war for the defence of the country voluntarily went down to Fort Trinity, but was taken prisoner on the way and conveyed on shipboard, where, during the space of three weeks, he encountered much contumely and reproach. (Meanwhile the enemy was robbing his house and stripping his wife of everything at their home.) Through all this he conducted himself as a good subject ought to do. The truth of all this I confirm with my own hand and seal.

"Done at Fort Christina, September 24, 1655.

[L. S.]   JOHN RISING."

15. THE COUNTRY BELONGED TO THE CROWN OF SWEDEN, AND NOT TO ANY TRADING COMPANY.

The Hollanders vainly seek to cover up their violence by giving out that the country had never been subject to the Crown of Sweden, but only to a private company, which sought merely its own advantage. But that is far from the truth. It is true that the place was settled for a trading company; but it was all under the protection of the Swedish Crown. The Indians concluded the contract for the purchase of the land with the Queen of Sweden. The government was conducted under the Royal direction, the officials were sent out with Royal commissions and orders, and the ships and people with Royal equipments and at the Royal expense. That Queen Christina understood herself to have a right to the country, and full power to rule over it, may be concluded from the following deed:

"WE, CHRISTINA, by the grace of God, Queen of the Swedes, the Goths and the Wends, etc., hereby make known that we, out of our grace and favor, as also for the zealous and faithful service which our faithful servant and Captain, *Hans Asmundson Besk*, has honorably and manfully shown and performed for us and our Crown, and which hereafter, so long as he lives and is able, he binds himself to show and perform for our sake, have given and granted, as we herewith and in these our Letters Patent do confirm, grant, and give to him, his wife, and heirs forever, a piece of land situated in New Sweden, called Marcus Huck, which extends into Upland's Kihl, that, together with all things pertaining and belonging to it on land and water, by whatever name they may be called, without any exception of those now therewith connected, and formerly so connected, which rightly belong thereto, or may hereafter fall to or be gained by legal decision; to enjoy, use, and retain as an indisputable property forever. All herewith concerned shall conduct themselves in a manner thereto concordant; not doing to the said BESK, his wife, or heirs, any hindrance hereto, nor any manner of wrong or injury, either now or in time to come. For further confirmation, etc., etc., etc. Stockholm, August 20, 1653.

"CHRISTINA.[1]

"N. TUNGELL."

"The foregoing copy is of like import with the record which is to be found in the Archives of Her Royal Majesty and of the Realm, witnessed in the usual form of Her Royal Majesty's and the Realm's Chancelry.

"M. V. HERMANSON,
Secretary of the R. R. Chancelry.

"PETR SCHYLLBERG,
Secretary of the R. R. Swed. Archives."

"We, Christina, by the grace of God, Queen of the Swedes, the Goths and the Wends, Grandduchess of Finland, Duchess

---

[1] This deed is in the collections of the Historical Society.

of Esthonia, Carelia, Brehmen, Vehrden, Stedtin, Pomerania, Cassuben, and Vaenden, Princess of Rügen, Lady of Ingria and Vissmar, etc., hereby make known that we, of our grace and favor, as also for true and brave service hitherto honorably and manfully done and performed unto us and the Crown of Sweden by our faithful servant and Lieutenant, SVEN SCHUTE, and to be hereafter done and performed so long as he may live and is able, and to be bound to be and to show himself faithful to us and to the Crown of Sweden: We have granted, given, and bestowed, as we do herewith in virtue of these our Letters Patent grant, give, and bestow upon him, his wife, and heirs forever, a certain piece of land in New Sweden, to wit, Morkorhutting's Kijl, Achara-kong, Kinsesingh, and Aronamex Kijl, all as far as the river, with its adjacent small islands, namely, the islands of Kjäringe and Kinsesingh, together with Passyungk, and all things belonging and pertaining to the same on land and water, whatever other name they may have, without exception of any that now belongs thereto, or may formerly have belonged, ought rightfully to belong, or may hereafter belong or be gained by legal right and decision; to enjoy, use, and hold as his indisputable property forever.   All whom it may concern are to regulate themselves accordingly; not causing to the aforesaid Sven Schute, his wife, and heirs, any manner of hindrance, wrong, or injury, either now or hereafter.   For further confirmation we have subscribed this with our own hand, and so empowered our Secretary.

"Given at Stockholm, August 20, 1653.

"CHRISTINA.

"N. TUNGELL."

16. CAUSES OF THE SWEDES' WEAKNESS.

The Hollanders had no difficulty in showing their bravery in conquering the country.   They had Menahades their New Am-sterdam, from which they frequently drew reinforcements.   On the contrary, Sweden was so far out of the way, and was at that time involved in the long German and Polish war.   The voyage was insecure, inasmuch as the Spaniards now sought to pick up the Swedish ships, as they were in alliance with the Emperor and Poland, against whom the Swedish Crown waged various bitter wars, especially under King Charles X. A part of the blame was laid upon Governor Printz, for conducting himself too severely towards the people — making slaves of the Swedes, keeping them at work upon the fortresses, as also upon his estate at Tenakongh. And although that is still talked of, yet it cannot but be looked upon as groundless. It is, however, probable that the Swedes, after they came into that Canaan and obtained a taste of a good hitherto unknown, were now disgusted with such labors as were nothing but what was usual at home, and so conceived an unfounded hatred of their Governor. It may also be possible that, if Director Rising had not upon his arrival stirred up the Hollanders anew, both races might have lived many years together, and by their common forces have kept out the English.

17. That the Hollanders had no Right whatever to the Country.

But how little right the Hollanders had to call the country theirs, and on that ground take it by force, is shown by this, that neither before the arrival of the Swedes, nor during the Swedish administration, did they possess any land upon the Delaware, which the Swedes claimed for themselves, and much less did they establish any colony there. The purchases of land which the Hollanders professed to have made, to which they asserted their right, and their mode of procedure therein, are the following:

Sam. Goodijn and Sam. Blœmart purchased for themselves Cape May, of ten Indians, and called the bay, Goodyn's Bay. The land was four miles from the cape, and its sea-side was out in the bay south, running four miles inland, and so was sixteen square miles. The purchase was made May 5, 1630, and was confirmed by the Holland Governor and his Council on January 3d, 1631.[1]

On the 10th of August, 1646, Abr. Plank, Simon Ruth,

---

[1] [This was De Vries colony of Zwanendal, which he established in 1631, but having been absent from it a year, on his return, in 1632, found all his colonists massacred, and never again attempted a settlement there.]

Jan Andriessen, and Peter Hermansson, took possession of one hundred (100) morgens of land on the west side of the South river, directly opposite to Fogelsand, on condition of settling thereon four farms within a year, under the penalty of losing their title, if they failed so to do. They were also to hold allegiance to the West India Company, under their High Mightinesses, the States-General, together with such rent as might be imposed upon them. They were also promised more land than they required, provided they would build upon it. If they left the place, all their rights were forfeited. But they never came upon the land thus designated. On the 9th of April, 1649, Simon Ruth, Cornelius Mauritzen, Peter Hermansson, Andries Hudde, Alexander Boyer, and David Davids purchased the land from Ancocus Kihl up to Tenekong, to the east of Fort Nassau, and received a deed therefor, with the proviso that if the Company would pay the purchase-money, they should relinquish their rights.

And. Hudde, Commandant at Fort Nassau, informs Stuyvesant about this, and also that there were no funds in the Company's treasury for any purchase. They must have some way out, as the Swedes had taken such extensive possession of the country. Stuyvesant laments the state of affairs, and promises to send money to purchase the country from Narraticon's, or Raccoon's Kihl, down to the bay, May 13, 1649. But this was never done.

The Holland Company purchased the land for Fort Casimir on the 19th of July, 1651. That land lay between the river and Mingues Kihl (Christina creek), from its mouth to Canarasse (Bambo Huck).

These are all the purchases of land which the Hollanders made before that time, and from this it can be seen what rights they had. The question is, How the West India Company and the States-General could give a title for that which private individuals had bought, in direct opposition to all the laws and usages of nations? How could they authorize the purchase of land to which they had no right? How could they give the investiture of land which they themselves purchased thirteen years afterwards? How could they buy land which the Swedes had bought before? But this is nothing strange to those who have seen how that people forced themselves into other parts of the world.

18. DESTITUTION OF MINISTERS.

The Christian work which had been aimed at by the sending out of five ministers, at the same time received a lamentable check. The Rev. Reorus Torkillus, of east Gothland, who came over with Commandant Menewe, ended his days in Fort Christina, on the 7th of September, 1643. The Rev. John Campanius Holmensis only remained six years, during which time, however, he was very zealous in learning the nature of the country and the language of its heathen inhabitants. During all this time he had constant intercourse with the wild people, for there is still a tradition that he travelled up into the interior among them, and so went by land home to Sweden.[1] From his journal, it is seen that he sailed from Elfsborg, in New Sweden, on the 18th of May, and reached Stockholm on the 3d of July, 1648, an uncommonly quick voyage. The Rev. Israel Holgh and the Rev. Peter followed some years after. The Rev. Lars Lock was the only one who remained in the country, and took care of the poor and scattered Swedes, preaching at Tenakong and Fort Christina until the day of his death, which occurred in the year 1688.

19. THE DESTITUTION OF THE TENACON CHURCH.

Vice-Governor John Papegoija's wife was a daughter of Governor Printz. She resided for many years upon her father's place at Tenacongh, and preferred calling herself Armegot Printz rather than Madame Papegoija.[2] They still tell of the lady at Tenacong, how haughty she was, and how she oppressed the poor when she was in prosperity, although it is uncertain whether or not she deserved these reproaches. It is, however, true that she, for a considerable time before her return to Sweden,

---

[1] [A tradition which shows how soon the well-known and well-established facts of history may be forgotten.]

[2] [The history of Printz's son-in-law, Papegoija, is quite obscure; we have no other notice of him than that given above by Acrelius, nor do we know why his wife continued to reside in America after her husband's return to Sweden.]

enjoyed a pension from the Holland Government. It is reported that, out of contempt for the Swedes, she sold along with her farm the church which was built upon it, as also the bell, to a Hollander. However that may be, they had to buy their bell back again by two days' reaping in harvest time, after Madame Armegot had gone away. The church was used without hindrance until 1700. Perhaps the bell was not excepted in the bill of sale, although the following obligation was given:

[Copy.]   " LAUS DEO,[1] May 24, 1673.[2]

" I, the undersigned, Armegot Printz, acknowledge to have transferred to the congregation of the adherents of the Augsburg Confession in this place, the bell that has been on Tennakong, that they may do therewith what pleases them, and promise to keep them free from all claims that are made. Before the undersigned witnesses. Given as above.

ARMEGOT PRINTZ."

" His mark,
   P. K.
PETER KOCK.

His mark,
   ✕
JONAS NILSSON."

The English, during these changes, had not relinquished their pretensions to the country, but were in the way of coming to an understanding with Sweden in regard to the trade with America, which now, by the intervention of the Hollanders, was entirely broken off.[3]   Finally it came to pass that the Crown of Sweden

---

[1] [I am not sure whether this is intended to denote a locality, or is only a religious expression, equivalent to " Thank God."]

[2] [There is probably an error in this date, as it is not likely that she remained so long in the country (nineteen years) after her husband's departure.]

[3] Treaty of Commerce between Queen Christina and the Protector Oliver Cromwell, concluded at Upsala, on the 11th of April, 1654. § 16. " De commercio in Americam faciendo, item de piscationis commoditatibus, etc., statuetur pröut in posterum peculiari Tractatu vel Contractu invicem conveniet." " In regard to the carrying on of commerce with America, also in regard to rights to fisheries, etc., it shall be determined as shall be hereafter mutually agreed upon in a special treaty, or agreement."

had to relinquish[1] its West India trade entirely to the English, from which it was concluded that they did not at that time think of leaving the Hollanders much longer upon the Delaware. In like manner, also, arrangements for peace were made with the Republic of Holland, after which the Swedish flag was never again seen upon the coast of America. And thus it happened that Sweden was never satisfied for her lamentable losses upon the Delaware.[2]

---

[1] Fœdus Anglicum cum Svecia, ... Actum Westmonasteriis d. 17 Julii, 1656. § 9. Quoad commercium in America habendum, id quidem lege disserte cautum est, ne cujusvis praeterea Reipublicae Subditis sine peculiari licentia commercium illic promiscue habendi potestas fiat; Si quis autem Subditorum Sereniss: Regis Sueciæ ejusdem Literis Commendatitiis munitus, hanc sibi licentiam privatim, ad eas quaslibet Colonias petiverit, Dominus Protector, quoad rerum et Reipublicae status pro tempore permiserit, haud invitus hac in parte Serenissimae R: ae Maj.'s Sveciae desiderio satis fiat." " As regards trade in America, it has been distinctly provided by law, that it shall be allowed to none, except the subjects of the Republic, to traffic there generally, without a special license. But if any of the subjects of Her Most Serene Majesty of Sweden, provided with her Letters Commendatory, shall separately ask permission to go to said Colonies, the Lord Protector, so far as the condition of the Republic shall at the time allow, will very willingly meet the wishes of Her Most Serene Majesty of Sweden in so far as the case and circumstance will admit."

[2] Treaty between Sweden and Holland, Haag, 18th July, 1667. § V. Regarding the Swedish trade to the coast of Africa, as also the ship Christina, which had been seized, it was agreed:—1st. That the King of Sweden and its West India Company withdraw all claims upon the coast of Guinea and Cabo Corso, etc. Whereupon the High and Mighty States, and their West India Company, withdraw all claims against the Swedish West India Company. 2d. That the King and Company withdraw all claims to the Fort at Cabo Corso, and to all forts, harbors, and settlements in Guinea, so that the Swedish flag shall no more come thither, and no foreign flag be protected there by the Swedes. 3d. Hereupon one hundred and forty thousand R. Dol. shall be paid them by the Bank of Amsterdam. § VI. "As to the controversies which have taken place between the Swedish American Company and the Holland West India Company, in regard to the damages said to have been inflicted upon each other in America, it is decided and ordered that they shall, so soon as possible, be examined by His Royal Majesty's Ambassador at the Haag, according to the principles of right and justice, and satisfaction shall then immediately, and without any delay, be given to the injured party."

Part Second.

OF THE HOLLAND ADMINISTRATION.

CHAPTER I.

THE ADMINISTRATION UNDER GOVERNOR PAUL JAQUET.

1. ESTABLISHMENT OF THE GOVERNMENT.

THE country on both sides of the river was now in the power of the Hollanders. They had now more right than before to count it a part of their New Netherlands. The river was called the South river. The General-Governor, Peter Stuyvesant, resided at Manathan, or New Amsterdam; his authority extended over all matters, military, commercial, and judicial. All officers received their commissions from him, and were accountable to him. When, after the conquest, he left the country, he appointed Captain Deryk Smidt Commissary, or Commandant *ad interim* on the river. Immediately upon his return to New Amsterdam, he prepared a commission dated November 29, 1655, for John Paul Jaquet as Vice-Governor, with directions to make arrangements for trade, and keep order among the people. He fixed his residence at Fort Casimir. And. Hudde was made his Counsel; Almerhausen Klein, Secretary, etc.

2. DIVISION OF THE COUNTRY.

The country on the west side of the river was divided into two colonies. From Christina Kihl down to Bomtie's, or Bambo Huck, also between the river and Christina Kihl, together with Christina Fort and the piece of land around it, was "the Com-

pany's Colony." The other land, on the north side of Christina Kihl and along the river upward, belonged to the city of
Amsterdam, was governed by the Burgomaster and council
through Peter Stuyvesant, their General-Governor, and his council, and was called "the City's Colony." The occasion for this
was given when Fort Casimir was built; but the project was disturbed for some years by the predominance of the Swedes. Before this all transactions were in the name of the States-General
and the West India Company; but now they acted separately.
Deeds for land were issued in Amsterdam by the Burgomasters
and Council upon the land of the city, but by the Directors and
Commissaries for the Company upon its land. A little town was
laid out near Fort Casimir on Sandhook, and was called Newer
Amstel; but Christina took the name of Altona. Some Holland Jews desired liberty to settle here, and carry on trade on
the river, only two of whom were permitted to do so.[1]

3. The Condition of the Swedes.

Of the Swedes there were not more than nineteen men who
took the oath of allegiance at the capitulation. Swen Schute
and Anders Jurgen, a Finn, were among them. The others who
still remained had their abodes within the colony of the city, to
the north of Christina, and along the river. Over them was
placed Göran van Dyke as *Schout Fiscal*, or Magistrate. Under
him was Anders Jurgen, the Finn, at Karakung, or Alkarakung.
The sixth article of the Governor's Instructions was as follows:
"That the Swedes should not be permitted to remain in the
forts over night;" and the twelfth, "That a watchful eye should
always be kept upon the Swedes. If any were found disorderly,
they should be immediately taken to New Amsterdam."[2] Some
Swedish freemen, who settled at other points, desired to have
the time prolonged, so that, instead of one year and six weeks,
they might have one year and six months to get ready for their
departure; but this was granted with the proviso that they should
remove into the new town and live there, but not otherwise.[3]
Others were suspected of secret plottings with the Indians, as

---

[1] The Gen. Index, Lib. C., p. 176.   [2] The Gen. Index, Lib. C., p. 185.
[3] Ibid., Lib. O., p. 17.

they frequently came to the houses of the Swedes, and were, as usual, received in a friendly manner. On that account Swen Schute and Jacob Swenske were denounced by name. It was immediately determined that they should be arrested and sent to New Amsterdam, — a trick which the Government of Holland constantly practised. It seemed as if they were afraid of their own shadows.

4. THE FOURTH SWEDISH COLONY.

The friendship of the Indians to the Swedes continued equally strong even after the change of government. The proof of this was given in the year 1656, March 24, when the Swedish ship *Mercury* came up into the river without knowing that the country was under a foreign government. The Swedish preacher Matthias was in this ship together with Anders Bengtson, a native of Stockholm, who was still living in the year 1703, when he gave with his own mouth this narrative: That the Hollanders forbade said ship to ascend the river, she having on board a large number of people. But the Indians, who were fond of the Swedes, united together, went on board the ship, and, in defiance of the Hollanders, conducted the ship past Sandhook, or Fort Casimir, without its daring to fire a shot, and conveyed it up to Christina. It was then determined that the ship should be set free, first going to New Amsterdam to take in provisions, and then to make the voyage home to Sweden. The Rev. Mr. Matthias[1] immediately returned to Sweden, where he became pastor in Helsingland. But Anders Bengtson remained in the country, and became the ancestor of an honorable and wealthy family.[2]

5. THE HOLLANDERS' FIRST COLONY.

It was now for the first time that the Hollanders could be said to introduce a colony, although that of their own people was very weak. Here and there, indeed, some few small families had settled themselves, but they cultivated scarcely more land than a vegetable garden, or the like. Up to that time no deed for land had been given by their boastful Governor, except for such as no one would either cultivate or

---

[1] Rudman's MSS. Also, The Gen. Index, Lib. C., p. 347.
[2] [Who now have the name of Bankson.]

build upon. Besides, they were in constant fear of being driven out either by the heathen or the Swedes. But as soon as the winter was over and the sea opened to navigation, in the year 1656, various parties came over from New Amsterdam to settle in this place. Then there were distributed by the Governor-General and his council, first, eleven deeds for land, then fifty-six, and finally, by the end of August, eighteen. These pieces of land were all quite small, most of them nothing more than building-lots in New Amstel. The Hollanders were not much given to agriculture. A small patch was enough for most of them, as no laborers were to be obtained. Moreover, an order was issued, for the sake of security, that twenty or thirty households should settle together, although this was done scarcely anywhere else than at Sandhook. For every *morgon* an annual rent of about twelve stivers was paid. A *morgon* is about one acre. Within the land occupied by the Swedes there was no enfeoffment at that time. But upon every Swedish or Finnish family a yearly rent of five or six guilders was assessed, according to the decision of the Schout.

6. MONEY.

The current money of the Hollanders in the New Netherlands was in guilders or florins, as follows: one Holland guilder passed here for five (5); and so it continued until about the year 1700. After that one (1) for six (6); but it was unsettled after English coin came in. Traffic with the Indians was carried on in their wampum, as already described.[1] Wampum was by the Hollanders called *Sewant*.

7. THE DEMANDS OF THE INDIANS IN REGARD TO TRADE.

The Indians came to Governor Jaquet and demanded good order and uprightness in trade; that the Hollanders should buy of them as many peltries as they could bring; also, that payments should be so regulated that one beaver should sell for two deer-skins. But the Governor answered that he had not received orders to make any treaty of commerce. Still, presents were made to them by contributions of the colonists, among whom some few Swedes also gave their share.[2]

---

[1] See above, p. 42.　　　　　　　　[2] Ubi supra, O.

8. Laws.

Various other regulations were made for the occupation of
the country.   On the 26th of February, 1656, it was resolved in
council[1] that all the inhabitants should inclose their farms and
lots by the middle of March, under a penalty of six (6)
guilders; that all who had goats should keep herdsmen, or be
answerable for damages; that no one should come into the fort
either by land or water without first announcing himself; that
no places for building should be granted between Sandhook and
Christina; that the forests should be preserved for the use of the
fort and of the town.   And on the 22d of May, that all owners
of swine should put yokes on them within twenty-four hours,
or have them shot down by soldiers.

9. Jaquet's Departure.

Governor Jaquet's administration was brief, lasting scarcely
over a year.   Many complaints were made against him, which,
however, his successor declared to have proceeded rather from
hatred than from truth.   Notwithstanding this, the Governor-
General and his council sent Jaquet his recall on account of his
incompetency, with which he was reproached in a letter of the
20th of April, 1657.

CHAPTER II.

THE ADMINISTRATION UNDER GOVERNORS ALRICH AND BECKMAN.

1. Two Governors.

IN Jaquet's place came Jacob Alrich, appointed in Holland by
the Burgomasters and Council of Amsterdam, as Governor
of that city's colony.   His commission was given to him in the
capital city of Amsterdam on the 19th of December, 1656, and
renewed in Fort Amsterdam in the New Netherlands on the

---

[1] Lib. O.

12th of April, 1657. His residence was at New Amstel, or Sandhook. The Swedes were still ruled by a Schout, or Commissary. Upon Schout Goeran van Dyke's representation the Governor-General directed them to come together and build a town at Upland, or Passaijung, or Finland, or Kingsessing, or wherever they pleased. This was dated June 12, 1657. But the people did not find it convenient to do so.[1] On the 15th of June, 1657, Abe Claesson, formerly a sea-captain, presented a petition to Governor-General Stuyvesant that he might receive three hundred and seventy-seven florins, the arrears of his pay in the Swedish service under Governor Printz — September 1, 1653, to September 1, 1655 — to be paid out of the Swedish property left behind by Governor Rising. Hind. Hyger, who was Commissary at the same time, gave his testimony in the case, and the debt was paid.[2] The following year, October 28, 1658, William Beckman, Alderman in Amsterdam, was appointed Vice-Governor of the Company's colony, and was to have his residence at Altona, from which all his letters are dated. He managed the Company's trade, commanded the garrison, received the duties of ships coming into New Amstel, and had the Swedes under his supervision. Andrew Hudde, on account of his thirty-one years' service, and his poverty caused by robberies committed by the Indians, became Beckman's secretary, and also sexton of the Altona Church, in June, 1660.[3] Although the two had each his separate government, yet they for the most part acted together, so Beckman had transactions in the city's colony, and Alrich gave deeds for lands sold by the Company. A long time passed before the Hollanders settled themselves among the Swedes. Two farms near Altona were all that the Hollanders gave deeds for among the Swedes, as also for a mill which was built upon Skyllpot Kihl, which was to grind free of toll for the garrison.

2. ORDERS TO EXTEND THE LIMITS OF THE COMPANY'S COLONY.

Beckman received orders to extend the Company's colony from Bomties Hook to Cape Hinlopen. He was to take advice of Alrich, and inquire of others which of the Indians were the

---

[1] Lib. E.   [2] Ibidem.   [3] Lib. G.

rightful owners, and also to ascertain what price was proper to pay. In like manner Alrich had orders to secure the land at Hore. Kihl. Alrich, in his answer to Governor Stuyvesant, presented several difficulties in the way of this, such as, that there were neither people nor means for erecting or taking care of fortifications ; that such a fortification would be of no account so long as the country all around it was wild and desolate. The few agriculturists who were here had suffered a severe failure of their crops that year, so that they could scarcely support themselves. Beckman saw that Alrich was a capricious man, who only wasted time, and therefore himself made a journey to Hore Kihl, with Lieutenant Hinoyosa in his company, made the purchase there of the Indians on the 23d of March, 1659, and also took a deed of purchase for it, threw up a fortification there, and put in it as many soldiers as he could get. Trade was carried on by Alrich at Sandhook, by Pet. Alrich at Hore Kihl, and by Israel Helm at Passayungh. Duties were levied as well upon exports as imports.

3. Fear of the English.

The reason of that undertaking was that two vessels with fourteen English persons from Virginia came to settle themselves there, and were attacked by the Indians, but rescued by Alrich. That greater numbers might not come over and forestall them, it was found necessary to have the land secured.

4. Claims by Maryland.

Herewith came a report that the English from Maryland were thinking of making an attack and taking the country. My Lord Baltimore,[1] its proprietor, was inquiring about the boundaries which were not yet settled. He maintained that his right extended to within two miles of New Amstel, and gave various deeds upon land to that point His Governor, Josiah Fendal, sent Colonel Utie, with five other gentlemen, to New Amstel to report their claims. They were admitted into the fort, and were

---

[1] [Cecil Calvert, Lord Baltimore, commenced his colony of Maryland by landing at St. George's (now St. Mary's), the Indian village of Yoacomoco, on the 27th of March, 1634.]

there for four nights. During this time each party urged its claims, and Beckman was called to the conference. The meeting was closed with hard words and dissatisfaction upon both sides; but Stuyvesant did not approve of these first friendly advances, but complained of Alrich to the Company for having received and harbored such dangerous strangers within his jurisdiction.[1]

5. THE COLONY WEAKENED.

Alrich's administration was on the way to dissolution. His severity and selfishness caused many Holland families to remove to Maryland, and some soldiers also fled in the same direction. Finally, there were not more than ten soldiers in Fort Casimir, and half as many at Hore Kihl. The inhabited part of the Company's colony did not extend more than two Holland miles, at the close of the year 1659. Stuyvesant, in his letter of September of the same year, represented to the West India Company the probability that England, with the aid of Sweden, would soon take possession of the country, while Holland was in disquiet. He urged them to send expelled Poles, Lithuanians, Prussian and Flemish peasants to settle the country. Still further, in the year 1660, March 4, he sent out one Andries Lawrenson to recruit for the garrisons among the Swedes and Finns, and offered them from eight to ten or twelve guilders recruiting money. Those who had fled to Maryland and Virginia on account of debt were promised three or four years' security against their creditors, together with a free pass; but little was accomplished thereby.[2]

6. FEAR OF THE SWEDES.

The suspicion that the Swedes and Finns were favorably disposed towards the English, but unfriendly to the Hollanders, was deeply seated in the mind of the Governor-General Stuyvesant. Although the Swedish families were not now more than one hundred and thirty (130) in number, according to the account given of them by the Schout, yet they still formed the strongest

---

[1] [See this controversy between Maryland and the Dutch well presented in O'Callaghan's Hist. of New Neth., II., pp. 377 to 388.]

[2] Lib. G., p. 116.

part of the people in the country, and thus kept the government in fear. Therefore his former advice was changed into a command that all the Swedes should remove together into small towns, where less danger seemed to be feared from them. Passayung was proposed for this plan as a very pleasant place, with good land. Beckman, who was to put that plan in operation, was very zealous in trying to convince them of its advantages; but was not able to do so. Neither was there a sufficient force to compel them. In his answer to Stuyvesant he represents to him that it would be unmerciful to drive the people from their homes, which they had established, and put them to new labor and expense. Some of the Swedes had removed from the Company's colony into that of the City, where Hinoyosa had given them better privileges. Others again had gone to Sassafras river,[1] but, disturbed by the savages, had returned to their former homes, all of whom it would be very difficult to compel. On this account Beckman desired Stuyvesant to recall his order, and also to provide the Swedes with Holland books, by which they might become more united with the Hollanders. He had suggested this before, but received none.

7. LADY ARMGOT PRINTZ.

Lady Armgot Printz still dwelt at Tenakongh, the residence which had belonged to her father, Governor Printz. When she was told to remove, she set forth all the difficulty, as so fine a house and property as she had in possession could not be obtained elsewhere but at great expense, to say nothing of her having here a church in her own house. But although the situation was fine, and the soil rich, she was not able to gain her support upon it. She could neither obtain servants, nor rent the farm to any one, since every man who was able and willing to work owned more land than he needed. Whether from sympathy, or on account of some debt owing to her, she received a support from the Holland Government. This, for some time, consisted of one fat ox, some fatted swine, and a sufficient

---

[1] [The Sassafras rises in Delaware and empties into Chesapeake Bay, forming the boundary between the counties of Cecil and Kent, on the eastern shore of Maryland. It was into this part of Maryland that the Swedes went.]

supply of grain.   Finally, she returned home to Sweden.   Israel Helm followed her, but immediately came back, and became a member of the Council in the city's colony.[1]

8. DEATH OF GOVERNOR ALRICH.

On the 30th of December, 1659, Governor Jacob Alrich died, and Lieutenant Alex. Hinoyosa was appointed his successor *pro tempore*, with Gert van Gizet as his Secretary.   Hinoyosa immediately sequestrated all the papers of his predecessor, and took extracts from them.   The next day he called together his Council and showed that Alrich had acted contrary to his instructions in thirty or forty points, and so had forfeited both life and property, if he had lived longer.   But he did not find many who sustained him in these views.

CHAPTER III.

THE ADMINISTRATION UNDER GOVERNOR ALEXANDER HINO-YOSA, AND VICE-GOVERNOR W. BECKMAN.

1. THE COMPANY SURRENDERS ITS COLONY TO THE CITY.

THE Trading Company had found but little advantage in its trade.   It scarcely met the expenses of service, war, and expenditures on the Indians.   The servants showed themselves altogether selfish.   The superiors were more strict in forbidding all individual traffic than the inferiors were in obeying their orders.   The English upon Long Island carried on here an uninterrupted smuggling.   On this account the Company, on the

---

[1] [In the "journal of a voyage to New York in 1679–80," published in the first volume of the "Memoirs of the Long Island Historical Society," on pp. 177–180, is a very full and interesting account of Tinicum Island, and also of a lawsuit growing out of its sale. Madame Armgot there has her proper name of Popegay, or Papegoia, given to her. It is also there stated that she finally sold her property to Mr. Otto Knif (Otto Ernest Koch, or Kock), for one thousand five hundred guilders, and then returned to Sweden, where her two brothers were still living — probably about the year 1673.]

7th of February, 1663, gave up all its rights to the city's colony, when it was agreed: that Fort Christina should also belong to it, with the proviso, that the settlers around it should continue to possess their privileges; the city should send another garrison, and relieve that which belonged to the Company, so that the colony might be defended against the Indians and the English; that a mile of land should be cleared and settled every year; that the agents of the city should never be allowed to transfer that land to any one else, either in whole or in part, on the penalty of forfeiting all their right, etc.

2. HINOYOSA GOVERNOR.

Hereupon the South river was wholly and entirely given over to Governor Hinoyosa, by Patent of the Governor-General Stuyvesant and his Council, dated December 22, 1663, — but with the proviso that it should be governed entirely by the prescribed laws of the States-General and their West India Company, and to their advantage. But before this came about, he, associated with Beckman, presided over the government for three years, after Alrich's death. John Crato, Secretary, Van Sweringe,[1] Schout, Mr. William, Army Surgeon, and Hans Block, Constable, were his Council on the 25th of January, 1660.[2]

3. CONTROVERSY ABOUT JACOB ALRICH.

Great disturbance arose about Hinoyosa's complaints against his predecessor Jacob Alrich, and his sequestration of his papers and property. Cornelius van Gizel petitioned Stuyvesant to release the property, and treat it according to the will. Various examinations and correspondence were held about the matter. Finally, Hinoyosa received orders to desist from all opposition on pain of disgrace.[3]

4. TRADE.

Trade was at that time conducted with the Indians in peltries, and with Virginia in tobacco. A good understanding between

---

[1] [The ancestor, in all probability, of the family of Swearingens in Maryland.]
[2] Lib. R.
[3] Lib. G.

the Hollanders and English was now promised as Stuyvesant sent the Governor of Virginia presents of French wine, and the like.[1] Peter Alrich was appointed by Hinoyosa Commandant at Hore Kihl Fort, with the exclusive privilege of all traffic with the Indians from Bomties Hook down to Cape Hinlopen, whereat the Swedes grumbled dreadfully.[2]

5. FEAR OF THE INDIANS.

In the year 1663 they lived in great fear of the Indians, called Senecas.[3] Some parties of these came down from the interior and committed terrible murders. The Mynquesses,[4] who took part with the Christians, did, indeed, make a stand against them, but were not strong enough to repel them. Fort Christina was greatly decayed, and entirely without ammunition, having no more than ten or twelve musket-balls, and no flints. That year the small-pox raged terribly among the Indians, a disease not uncommon among them. Ill-disposed people advised them to leap into the river and bathe themselves, whereby many perished.

6. BECKMAN'S DISSATISFACTION AND COMPLAINTS.

William Beckman also had a hand in the government, as long as there were two colonies here, but had little to say, and was scarcely regarded. This occasioned him to have, as well, constant correspondence with Stuyvesant, as disputes with Hinoyosa. He used his most zealous endeavors to construe everything that he could to his disadvantage, and complained of his haughtiness. It was especially alleged that Hinoyosa had burnt the palisades of the fort under his brew-kettle; sold muskets to the Indians; the city's millstones to Maryland, for tobacco, and even a kettle of the Company! — all of which he proved by testimony. But as Hinoyosa was of higher authority and esteem, nothing was thereby effected. When, then, it was ascertained that the Company had transferred its colony to the city, and that Hinoyosa was to rule over all, Beckman was compelled to petition Stuy-

---

[1] Lib. G.   [2] Lib. R.
[3] [One of the tribes of the Iroquois, or Five Nations.]
[4] [A tribe of the Lenni Lennape. This must have been one of the last struggles of the Delawares with their Iroquois conquerors.]

vesant, that he might not be sent away at an inconvenient season, and in the winter, as unprovided with a situation, he should be compelled to go to Maryland, which he well knew would be displeasing to the Holland Government.[1]

7. THE SAME.

Stuyvesant directed Beckman to remain at Altona (Christina), cultivate land, and have five or six servants there.   But he saw himself without any means for this, as no freeman had the right to trade either with the Indians or with the English.   But he had already made known that Hinoyosa had asserted a right to half the land and traffic.   Fifty laborers had landed in the last year, who were at the same time farmers and soldiers, receiving one hundred guilders pay per year, also six or seven girls who were to keep house for them.   These women had engaged themselves in Holland to serve for a term of years in the colony for the expenses of their voyage.   But Hinoyosa had hired out some of them for his own profit, at the yearly wages of sixty, seventy, or eighty guilders.   He also had thoughts of taking up his residence at Apoquiminy, establishing a metropolis there, and getting into his own hands all the English trade.   All these complaints may have been untimely, as nothing was effected by them.[2]   For the rest, he may have understood that among the Swedes there was a report current, that Queen Christina had given to one Captain Amund Besk a deed for all the land which lies between Marikiens Huck (Marcus Hook), and Upland Kihl, to which Besk's son-in-law, Hullengren, now asserted his right. He should investigate the matter, and give further information about it.   Finally, Beckman was removed to Hudson's river, and appointed Commissary or Schout at Arosapha, or Esopus, on the 4th of July, 1664.

8. LOCK'S MISFORTUNE.

The Holland Government, during all its continuance, took very little trouble about public worship.   At Sandhook there

---

[1] See his letter, dated Altona, December 6, 1663.
[2] His letter, dated December 2, 1663.

stood for a time a little wooden Church, but without regular service. The Swede, the Rev. Lars Lokenius, was the only clergyman in the country, and ministered to both Swedes and Hollanders. He met with the misfortune that his unfaithful wife fled from him in a canoe with one Jacob Yung, a depraved character; whereupon an express was sent to the Governor of Maryland, as also to the Officers of the Crown at Sassafras river to arrest him, for Yung stood in debt to both Hinoyosa and Beckman.[1] The Rev. Lars, who had several children and a large household, was in need of another wife, and thought that all that was necessary was to find one, but he did not think any tribunal necessary to give judgment in his case. Then, quite too hastily, and ¬vithin nine months, he entered into another marriage, whereby he drew upon·himself the severe animadversion of the presiding Governor and his Commissary, who required him to intermit his ministry for some time. Meantime a divorce was procured for him from Stuyvesant, whereby his former marriage was annulled, and the last confirmed, and the Rev. Lars was again invested with his gown.[2]

9. ABELIUS SELSKOORN.

A person—a student—by the name of Abelius Selskoorn came to the country, and for some time performed divine service at Sandhook, went to New Amsterdam, and received a call from Governor-General Stuyvesant, together with a recommendation to the vestry of the Augsburg Confession to ordain him to the ministerial office, and also to promise him like support with Dominie Larse.[3] He was reported to have already taken upon himself to baptize children; but Beckman's testimony acquitted him of this. However that was, he never presided over any congregation on the South river as an ordained minister.

---

[1] Lib. A, Beckman's letter to Stuyvesant, dated August 17, 1661.
[2] Do., April 14, 1661.
[3] [The Reverend Lars (Lock).]

PART THIRD.

THE ENGLISH ADMINISTRATION.

CHAPTER I.

THE GOVERNMENT UNDER THE DUKE OF YORK.

1. THE COLONIZATION OF NORTH AMERICA.

ORTH AMERICA was first discovered by Sebastian Cabot in the year 1497, in consequence of which some Englishmen take to themselves the honor that the whole of America was discovered by them first of all Christian nations, inasmuch as Christopher Columbus did not go beyond the Gulf of Mexico until the year 1498 to take possession of the country, although he visited some of its islands in 1492. Nevertheless more than a hundred years passed before the foundation of any colonies was laid. A charter was granted by King James I., in the year 1606, for two united Companies from London and Bristol[1] to all that land which lies between 34° and 45° of north latitude on the Atlantic Ocean, and for one hundred miles into the interior, and all this so far as it was not occupied by any Christian nation. But these Companies did not find as great advantage in this as they had anticipated, for in the year 1635 they surrendered their charter to the Crown.[2] In the

---

[1] [The London Company's Patent extended from Cape Fear to the southern limit of Maryland, that is to say, from 34° to 38° north; the Bristol Company from 41° to 45° north.]

[2] [The first alteration of the Charter or Patent took place in 1609. See Bancroft's Hist. of U. S., I., p. 136. It was the Charter of "The Council of Plymouth," granted in 1620, that was surrendered in 1635. Bancroft, ubi sup., pp. 271 and 408.]

beginning of the reign of King Charles I. a new charter was again granted for New England; but as the government was at that time in great disorder, the first colonies did not keep very strictly to the laws prescribed for them, but settled, dwelt, and lived as they pleased, or as they could. When King Charles II. was reëstablished upon the throne, new charters were granted, as was desired, and these are still in force.[1]

2. PRETENSIONS OF THE ENGLISH.

The right which the English asserted to the Delaware, as well from their discovery of the coast as from the charter granted thereupon before any Christian power had taken possession of it, they did not forget under either the Swedish or the Holland Government. In consequence of this, at three different times, some families came in from Virginia to settle upon the river, which was not permitted them. The difficulties and disquiet in England during the reign of King Charles I., and during Cromwell's administration, did not contribute much to the strength of the colonies.

3. THE CAPTURE OF THE COUNTRY.

But when those internal disorders had subsided, and out of revenge against the Hollanders who had intruded upon the supposed rights of the English in Africa, India, and elsewhere, King Charles II. sent four Commissioners over to Virginia to reduce the colonies within certain limits, as they had encroached upon each other. They came with a squadron three hundred men strong before Manahates, captured New Amsterdam and its fortress on the 6th of September, 1664, and expelled its Governor-General, Peter Stuyvesant, who was there lame, and used a silver limb. Thirteen days later Sir Robert Carr anchored before the town and Fort of Aurania (Oranien = Orange[2]), then twelve days later before Arosapha (Esopus), and made himself master of them. The colony of New Amsterdam at that time extended westward three Dutch miles from the Delaware, and on the other side ten English miles east of the North river. The

---

[1] The Present State of North America, London, 1755, pp. 10, 11, 12.
[2] Now Albany.

conquest was extended to the Delaware and the only fortified place on it, Fort Casimir, whose garrison consisted of Hollanders and Swedes. Thus the Englishman within a few days triumphed over four towns and an equal number of forts without meeting with any resistance, and without the loss of a single life, for the conquest was made by an unexpected surrender, and completed by a capitulation. In this agreement the officers and servants of the Company were not included, but only the people. These last took the oath of allegiance to the King of England, and remained undisturbed in their houses and property. It was likewise determined that the Swedes should remain undisturbed in their religion as Lutherans, and in the public service of God, as they particularly insisted. New Amsterdam was thenceforward called New York; Aurania, Albany; and Fort Casimir, New Castle upon Delaware,[1] although there has never been any "castle" in it to the present day.

4. EXCHANGED FOR SURINAM.

The Hollanders had taken Surinam[2] from the English, and never relinquished their claims upon the New Netherlands until, to settle the matter, it was concluded by the peace of Breda[3] (July 31, 1667) that from that day the New Netherlands should belong to the English, and Surinam to the Hollanders. The third article of said treaty declares, "That each party respectively should retain the places that they had taken by arms or other-wise, and had in possession on the 20th of May last past." Thus the English had to pay dearly enough for the land to which they declared themselves to have so indisputable a right.

5. RECONQUERED BY THE HOLLANDERS, BUT AGAIN SURRENDERED.

But the quarrel did not rest here. Another fierce war arose, which England, in league with France, declared against the States-General of Holland. At home the Hollanders were severely pressed; but abroad they had a victorious fleet under

---

[1] [Probably suggested by the name of New Castle upon Tyne, and a faint resemblance of the name "Casimir."]

[2] [Surinam, now Dutch Guiana, in South America.]

[3] [A town of Holland, in North Brabant.]

their Admiral, the younger Evertse,[1] who destroyed nearly the whole of the French and English marine from New Foundland to Barbadoes, and in August,[2] 1673, stormed New York, and took it without a capitulation. The existing council of war carried their right of conquest as far as the rights of the Hollanders had formerly extended, and so compelled both the civil and military officers within the same limits to take the oath of allegiance to the States and the Prince of Orange. Thereupon Anthony Colve was appointed Governor-General of New York and its adjacent territories. He again appointed Peter Alrich as Schout, or Commandant, over the South river or Delaware, but under the superintendence of the Governor-General, and Walter Warton was Surveyor.[3] Peter Alrich made his official oath, and took the oath of allegiance of the inhabitants. The first article of his instructions read as follows: " He shall uphold the true Christian doctrine, in accordance with the Decrees of the Synod of Dordt, and admit of no other doctrine in conflict therewith." [4] Thus the proposition was at this time made to expel the Augsburg Confession from the country. But that administration endured for but a short time, and was terminated by the Peace of Westminster on the 19th of February, 1674,[5] in the tenth article of which it was concluded, "that whatever countries, towns, fortresses, etc., had been captured on either side since the beginning of the war, should be restored to their former lord and owner." In consequence of this New York was restored to the English on the 31st of October, 1674.

6. THE DUKE OF YORK'S GOVERNMENT.

The province of New York now embraced all the country lying between New England and the Delaware river, of which

---

[1] [Usually written " Evertsen " in English. See Bancroft's Hist. of U. S., Vol. II., p. 322.]

[2] Bancroft, ubi sup., gives July 30 as the date.

[3] In the Record of Upland, Memoir of the Society, Vol. VII., p. 180, is a foot-note regarding Walter Wharton, " Surveyor-General, on the west side of the Delaware."

[4] [This proves that Mr. Bancroft is not quite correct when, in his Hist. of the U. S., Vol. II., p. 322, he says, "the counties on the Delaware, recovering greater privileges than they had enjoyed, cheerfully followed the example."]

[5] [The original has the date of 1684, which is evidently a slip of the pen or a typographical error. The Dutch government at this time lasted about fifteen months.]

James, the Duke of York, became the proprietor, as a mark of honor for his heroism with the English fleet, which he commanded against the Hollanders during the aforesaid war. He also had what were called the "Three Lower Counties" on the other side of the Delaware, namely, New Castle, Kent, and Sussex, by an especial grant. The government was conducted by a Governor in the name of the Duke of York, for that Prince never came personally to the country. To the government of New York also belonged all the inhabited country on the west side of the Delaware, which was sometimes called New Virginia, but mostly "The Places upon the Delaware." There the Swedish and Holland families had their abodes, for there were as yet no residents upon the east side of the river, which was afterwards called Jersey,[1] which was a poor, sandy, and abominable country, notwithstanding which West Jersey received some inhabitants under the government of the Duke of York.

7. THE OCCUPATION OF THE COUNTRY.

Under the Swedish government no deeds were given for the land; at least there are no signs of any, those excepted which were given as fiefs by Queen Christina. The Hollanders, indeed, made out quite a mass of deeds in 1656, but most of them were upon building-lots at Sandhook. Meanwhile no rents were imposed. The land was uncleared, the inhabitants lazy, so that the income was scarcely more than was necessary for their sustenance. But when the English administration came, all were summoned to take out new deeds for their land in New York, which they had already taken, or supposed that they had taken. These were issued in the name of the Duke of York. The rent was a bushel of wheat for every hundred acres, if so demanded. A part took the deeds; but others did not trouble themselves about them, but only agreed with the Indians for a piece of land for which they gave a gun, a kettle, a fur coat, or the like, and they sold them again to others for the same, for the land was superabundant, the inhabitants few, and the government not strict. Hence it comes that in law-

---

[1] [Acrelius invariably writes this word "Yersey."]

suits for land people still appeal to "*Indian rights,*" which are valid when they can be proved. The deeds which were given to the Swedes contained the proviso, "so far as they remain faithful to the government." Many who took deeds upon large tracts of land were in great distress about their rents, which, however, were very light, if people cultivated the lands, but heavy enough when they made no use of them; and they therefore transferred the greater part of them to others—which their descendants now lament. Some few English families came in, and were the only ones that would pay anything for a piece of land. But the Indians looked upon them as another race of people, showed less friendship for them, as they were less acquainted with them; which often produced great disorders. The people lived in great quiet, but in still greater idleness. There was no agriculture, no traffic, or no more than was required by absolute necessity. The Duke of York had very little more from it than the name; but no wonder, for the disorders in England continued, and the question of the succession to the throne kept him in the greatest anxiety.

CHAPTER II.

THE ESTABLISHMENT OF THE GOVERNMENT UNDER THE PROPRIETOR WILLIAM PENN.

I. THE CHARTER.

WHEN England was in her highest delirium, under the direction of her Protector, or, to speak more correctly, her Usurper, Oliver Cromwell, there arose among other sects that of the Quakers, opposed alike to the Crown and to the Church. In this sect William Penn was a mighty hero. He expressed his desire to conduct a colony to the country upon the Delaware, to extend the English power, and promote such interests as were most useful to the realm; to bring the wild heathen by peaceful and serviceable means into civil society, and to the doctrines of Christ, but not the less to hold his own brotherhood together. In regard to which, as also on account of the great services of his father, who was the deceased Sir William Penn, who, in the year 1665, as Admiral under Prince James, the Duke of York, had gained a victory over the Dutch fleet commanded by Van Updam, King Charles II. granted the country to him with a charter dated March 4, 1681.[1]

2. PENN'S GRANT FROM THE KING.

This grant embraces all that country in America, with the islands adjacent thereto, which has the Delaware river to the east of it, taking its beginning "from twelve miles distance northwards of New Castle town unto the three and fortieth degree of northern latitude, if the said river doth extend so far northward, but if the said river shall not extend so far northward, then by the said river so far as it doth extend; and from the head of the said river the eastern bounds are to be determined by a meridian line to be drawn from the head of said river unto said forty-third degree. The said lands to extend westward five degrees in longitude, to be computed from the said eastern bounds; and the said lands to be bounded on the north by the beginning of the three and fortieth degree of northern latitude, and, on the south, by a circle drawn at twelve miles distance from New Castle northward and westward unto the beginning of the forty-third[2] degree of northern latitude; and then by a straight line westward to the limits of longitude above mentioned."[3]

3.

In virtue of said Charter, William Penn and his heirs and successors by inheritance, or purchase, became absolute proprietors of the aforesaid country, the king's rights as king being premised, "saving always to us, our heirs and successors, the faith and allegiance of the said William Penn, his heirs and assigns, and of all other proprietaries . . . . yielding and paying

---

[1] "The Royal Charter granted to William Penn, Esq., Preamble." [We quote the Charter as given in Proud's "History of Pennsylvania," Vol. I., pp. 171-187, where it is called "*The Charter of Charles the Second,*" etc.]

[2] This is clearly erroneous. Acrélius certainly meant the fortieth degree.

[3] "*The Charter of Charles II.,*" Sect. I.

therefor to us, our heirs and successors, *two Beaver skins*, to be delivered at our Castle of Windsor, on the first day of January in every year; and also the fifth part of all gold and silver ore, which shall from time to time happen to be found within the limits aforesaid, clear of all charge. . . And we do hereby erect the aforesaid country and islands into a province and signiory, and do call it *Pensilvania*,[1] and so from henceforth will have it called."[2]

4.

He shall have power, "to make laws with the approbation of his freemen of said country, or the greater part of them, or of their delegates or deputies . . . . to appoint and establish at his discretion judges and justices, magistrates and other officers for the probates of wills . . . . to remit, release, pardon, at his discretion either before or after judgment, all crimes and offences whatsoever, committed within the said country, against the laws (treason, and wilful and malicious murder only excepted, and, in those cases, to grant reprieves until our pleasure may be known therein); to regulate courts and processes of law, 'provided, nevertheless, that the same laws be consonant to reason, and not repugnant to the laws and statutes, and rights of England;' and that every man shall have the right of appeal to the king.[3] Also that a copy of every law shall, within five years after the making thereof, be transmitted to the King, and if any law shall, within six months after its transmission, be disapproved, it shall be null and void; otherwise it shall remain, and stand in full force."[4]

5.

The Proprietor shall be answerable for every offence committed by him against the laws of England, relative to trade and navigation, and shall pay all damages assessed against him in the courts of the realm, within one year. Otherwise the king may resume the government of the Province, until all such damages are paid; yet so that no individual shall be disturbed in his rights

---

[1] [We write the word as it stands in Proud, *ubi sup.*]

[2] Section III. of Charter.

[3] Section V.

[4] Section VII.

of property.[1]   He shall not hold friendship with the enemies of
the Crown, nor make war upon its friends.[2]   He shall appoint a
Captain-General, who shall make war against the enemies of the
country by land and sea, and pursue them even beyond the Province, and do all and everything which belongs to the office of
a Captain-General.[3]   Neither the king nor Parliament shall have
power to impose upon the inhabitants any taxes or subsidies,
without the consent of the proprietor, or their own.[4]   If any
doubts arise in regard to the true sense and meaning of any part
of this Charter, the matter shall be so adjudged as shall be most
favorable to the interests of the proprietor.[5]

6. PRIVILEGES GRANTED TO THE COUNTRY BY W. PENN.

After this Charter had been confirmed, William Penn made
his plan known throughout all England, and as encouragement
for those who were disposed to emigrate, published certain
articles in regard to the settlement of the country under this
title : " Certain conditions, or concessions, agreed upon by William Penn, proprietary and Governor of the province of Pennsylvania ; and those who are the adventurers and purchasers in the
same province, the 11th of July, 1681."[6]   In the same spirit also
he drew up a form of government, the best that he could devise,
dated, April 29, 1682.   Then, when many of his people gave
their names for emigration, it was also thought necessary to
provide certain laws, so that everything might be in order at the
time of their arrival in the country, in consequence of which a
Constitution was drawn up in forty articles, assented to by those
present, and signed on the 5th of May, 1682.[7]

7. TWO OTHER GRANTS.

Hereupon followed two other deeds of gift, though called
sales, which Prince James, Duke of York, made to William Penn,
on the same side of the Delaware, of that land which had been
granted to him by his brother, King Charles II., and of which

---

[1] Section XIV.   [2] Section XV.   [3] Section XVI.   [4] Section XX.
[5] Section XXIII.
[6] [See Appendix, No. I., in Proud's History, Vol. II.]
[7] [Proud's History, Vol. II.   Appendix, No. II., p. 5.]

he was the actual proprietor. The former, dated August 24, 1682, gave him the town of New Castle, upon the Delaware river, with all that land which lies within a circle of twelve miles, drawn from and to the river. The purchase money was ten shillings, and a rent of five ditto, to be paid yearly, on Michaelmas day, to the Duke, his heirs, or to whomsoever he might appoint assigns.

The latter, of the same day and year, gave all that land upon the Delaware Bay and river, beginning twelve miles south of the town of New Castle, and extending to Hore Kihl, or Cape Henlopen. The purchase money was ten shillings. The yearly rent demanded by the Duke was one rose, to be presented on Michaelmas day, if so demanded. But Penn bound himself to pay annually to the Duke and his heirs, to those whom they might rightfully appoint, one-half of all the rents, income and resources which might accrue from the land. In the event that either a part or the whole of the rents should be in arrears for twenty years, the land should revert to the Duke, his heirs, etc., until the whole was paid.

8. PENN'S ARRIVAL.

William Penn made his preparations to take possession of his new country. He encouraged everybody to take part in the venture, and even offered them a free passage, where they had not the means to pay for it. Especially did the Quakers, from all parts of England and Wales, associate themselves with him — a society that the realm could very well spare. With these on his first[1] voyage he filled twenty ships, expecting many more soon to follow, and arrived on the 24th of October, 1682.[2] The Swedes[3] received their new fellow-citizens with great friendliness, carried up their goods and furniture from the ships, and entertained them in their houses without charge — as many aged Quakers still relate with great pleasure.

9. CHANGE IN THE FORM OF GOVERNMENT.

The new Government was to be erected immediately, and under it, by the donation of James, Duke of York, the three

---

[1] [His nephew, W. Markham, preceded Penn, with three ships.]
[2] Campanius, p. 82.   [3] [Penn landed first at New Castle, and then at Upland.]

10

lower counties had fallen. A general meeting was held in Chester, where Penn's *"Frame of Government"* [1] was laid before the inhabitants of Pennsylvania, and the subject districts, in 1682. But in this there were found some points that were impracticable, as, for instance, that the Provincial Council should consist of *seventy* men, and the Assembly of *two hundred*, as there was not that number in the country at that time, who knew what a Government was. On this account the form of government was so far changed.[2] Next year another form of government was established, nearly like the first, wherein the same number of the Council and Assembly were introduced, as it was hoped that the people would multiply, and that all would soon become statesmen.[3]

10. THE LAYING OUT OF PHILADELPHIA.

On the river at Wicacoa, a high, dry, and pleasant place, the city of Philadelphia was laid out. The land for it, consisting of three hundred and sixty acres, was given by three brothers of the Swaenson family, upon condition that two hundred acres should be given to each of them in another place in the city, in what are now called the "Northern Liberties" of the city, with a yearly rent of one-half bushel of wheat for each one hundred acres. Those who bought land in the country had building-lots given to them in the city. Its first Charter was given in 1682, and its so called "Liberties" extended three English miles beyond the city, between two navigable streams, the Delaware and the Schuylkill. Within the first year the city contained eighty houses, and after twenty years was amazed at its own strength and greatness. Its beautiful situation, deep harbors, regular streets, expensive buildings, important commerce, and rapid improvement, are a wonder to the world, and may become hereafter, even greater.

---

[1] See this in Proud's History, Vol. II. Appendix, No. III.

[2] "An Act of settlement, made at Chester, 1682."

[3] "The Frame of the Government of the province of Pennsylvania," etc. [Article III. See Proud II. Appendix, No. III.]

11. THE DIVISION OF THE PROVINCE.

The inhabited country was divided into six counties, viz.,
Philadelphia, Buckingham, or Bucks, and Chester. These belonged to the province within which the Quakers took up their
abode. The other three were New Castle, Kent, and Sussex,
which were called the "lower counties," it being still uncertain
whether they should form a government for themselves. In all
of them together there were not as yet more than four thousand
souls.[1]

12. LAWS.

Two general assemblies or parliaments were held within the
first year, and that with such unanimity that within three weeks
seventy laws were enacted. But nearly one-half of them met
with the misfortune of being disapproved in England, some of
which received the reproach that they led people into Quakerism,
e. g., a statute to change the names of the months and days of
the week. Instead of Sunday, Monday, Tuesday, etc., they were
to say "the first day," "the second day," "the third day," etc.
So, also, instead of January, February, March, etc., they were
to be called "the first month," "the second month," "the third
month," etc. In like manner a statute "against the drinking
of healths," etc.

13. COURTS.

For the better governing of the country courts and court-
houses, judges and officers were appointed for every district, and
sessions were to be held every month. But to prevent expensive
lawsuits three justices of the peace were appointed in every
county, chosen by each county court, as pacificators. In autumn
and spring, courts were to be held for widows and orphans, to
regulate their inheritance in every county.

14. DIVISION OF HOMESTEADS.

Land was set off and surveyed for homesteads or farms. The
proprietary let it be seen that it was not his intention to acquire
wealth in this way. Each one received as much as he could use,

---

[1] Penn's "Letter from Pennsylvania," in 1683.

provided he would pay for the deed and survey of the land.
But, in order to uphold the government, a yearly rent of one
penny sterling was laid upon every acre of land.[1] The Swedes
and Hollanders, who had obtained the titles to their lands from
the Duke of York, paid one bushel of wheat for every hundred
acres of land, which is much less, and is fixed upon them for all
time. Seven years of undisputed possession were to be held as
an unquestionable title.[2]

15. TREATIES WITH THE INDIANS.

The Proprietor ingratiated himself with the Indians. The
Swedes acted as his interpreters, especially Captain Lars Kock,[3]
who was a great favorite among the Indians. He was sent to
New York to buy goods suitable for traffic. He did all that he
could to give them a good opinion of their new ruler. Penn
then made them presents, and so bought of them one tract of
land after another, the Indians still removing further and further
into the interior of the country. He also associated a great deal
with them, and made himself acquainted with their mode of
living and their language, so that he might treat with them
without an interpreter. Hereby he also gained a high reputation among them, which is still held in remembrance by their
old men.

16. FRIENDSHIP BETWEEN THE PROPRIETOR AND THE SWEDES.

The Swedes were especially agreeable to him, as he has himself related. "They are," says he,[4] "a plain, strong, industrious
people, yet have made no great progress in the culture or propagation of fruit trees, as if they desired to have enough rather
than a superfluity." "They kindly received me, not less so

---

[1] According to English usage a *homestead* or farm is assessed according to the
number of its acres of land. The extent of each acre is the same as that of two Swedish *spanland*, or *skäppoland*.

[2] "Laws agreed upon in England," etc., § XVI.; also various other Constitutions.
[Proud, II., Appendix, p. 17.]

[3] [Called by Proud, in his "Hist. of Pa.," I., 206, "*Lacy Cock*." Lars is the
contraction of Lawrence.]

[4] See Proud, *ubi supra*, I., 260.

than the English, who were few before the people concerned with me came among them. I must needs commend their respect to authority, and kind behavior to the English. They do not degenerate from the old friendship between both kingdoms. As they are a people proper and strong of body, so have they fine children, and almost every house full; rare to find one of them without three or four boys, and as many girls; some six, seven, and eight sons. And I must do them that right — I see few young men more sober and industrious."[1] The Swedes had a place both in the General Assembly and in the Governor's Council. Mr. Penn also, immediately after his return to London, applied to the Swedish Envoy Extraordinary for his assistance in obtaining for them clergymen and books from Sweden, assuring him that he would take care to have them forwarded from London. He himself sent them a box of Catechisms and other books,[2] together with a Bible in folio, for use in the church, though all in English.[3]

17. THE PROPRIETOR'S TROUBLE AND EXPENSE.

After a year's sojourn in America, Mr. Penn returned to England, having appointed William Markham as Vice-Governor. So far as we know, it can be safely judged that Proprietor Penn, in the establishment of that colony, was actuated by good intentions towards all men. Especially in the beginning did he look more after the interests of his brethren than of himself. For, to obtain a right to the country, to transport the people over the sea, and put everything in order, cost him, in the first place, a donation to the English Crown of £50,000 sterling, which was owing to his father, Sir W. Penn; then the loss in Ireland of £2000 of yearly income; another in England of £1000; also another of £500. So it happened that he, although the owner of such an immense territory, was for some time compelled to keep out of the sight of his creditors.

---

[1] See "William Penn's Information about Pennsylvania, August 16, 1683." [First published under the title of "A Letter from William Penn, Proprietor, etc., to the Company of the Free Society."]

[2] Post-Master John Thelin's Letter from Götheborg, November 16, 1692.

[3] Rudman's MSS., in Wicacoa Church.

18. Uproar among the Swedes.

About that time It happened that an impostor by the name of Köningsmark came among the Swedes, who made a great disturbance, and found many followers, especially among the Finns. He was apprehended, properly punished, and banished from the country. They who supported him forfeited their homes, and suffered heavy loss. He had also wellnigh brought his countrymen, who were innocent, into evil report and suspicion, had not the honesty of these people in general been well known by so many proofs before.[1]

CHAPTER III.

OF CHANGES IN THE GOVERNMENT, AND ITS PRESENT CONDITION.

1. Dissatisfaction with the Form of Government.

AFTER the lapse of seventeen years Penn saw his colony remarkably advanced. But the trouble which they had with the government seemed to those simple people too burdensome; most official positions received but little pay, and few of them were educated as rulers. Moreover, Penn came to the afterthought that he had stood for the first and heaviest expenditures, whilst his income now seemed to be very scanty. He had also given all offices into the hands of the people, to fill them by election, which cut off from him both power and income. By the desire of the people, no less than of his own prudence, he again, in the year 1700, undertook a journey to Pennsylvania, and there changed the government in many respects.

---

[1] [Köningsmark is called by Proud (Vol. I., p. 128,) "Conningsmark." His real name was Marcus Jacobsson, as he himself confessed to Peter Koch, by whom his falsehood and machinations were discovered. There is a very graphic and interesting account of this affair preserved in MSS. in the Royal Library at Stockholm, a copy of which has been brought to this country by Mr. Jos. J. Mickley, and which it is to be hoped he will translate and publish in some suitable place.]

2. NEW PRIVILEGES.

On the 28th of October, 1701, another Charter, or form of government, was issued, consisting of eight articles, the first of which declares that, " no person or persons inhabiting this province or territories, who shall confess and acknowledge one Almighty God, the Creator, Upholder and Ruler of the world; and profess . . . . to live quietly under the civil government, shall be, in any case, molested or prejudiced . . . . because of his or their conscientious persuasion, or practice, nor be compelled to frequent, or maintain, any religious worship, place, or ministry, contrary to his or their mind, or to do or suffer any other act, or thing, contrary to their religious persuasion.   And that all persons who also profess to believe in *Jesus Christ*, the Saviour of the world, shall be capable . . . . to serve this government in any capacity, both legislatively and executively, he, or they, solemnly promising, when lawfully required, allegiance to the king, as sovereign, and fidelity to the proprietary and Governor, and taking the attests as now established by law." [1]

3.

The government has ever since remained in the hands of the proprietor as Governor-in-Chief, and in the Assembly, or Parliament of the country.   William Penn's two sons, Thomas and Richard Penn,[2] the present proprietors, preside over the government through their Deputy Governor, as did their father before them.

4. POWER OF THE DEPUTY GOVERNOR.

The Deputy Governor, appointed by the proprietor, and confirmed by the king, is invested with all the powers which belong to a Governor-in-Chief, such as; to appoint judges, magistrates, officers of the army, civil officers, etc., to pardon all offences against the laws, either before or after trial (treason and murder aforethought excepted), with the proviso, that appeals may be made to the king in all cases; also, to sign all laws made by the

---

[1] [See "*the Charter of Privileges*, granted by William Penn, Esquire, to the inhabitants of Pennsylvania and territories."]

[2] [In 1759.]

Assembly, provided that they are not in conflict, but so far as possible, accordant with the laws of England; to grant privileges for towns and trade; to establish markets and harbors; also to grant charters to all sorts of associations. He is the generalissimo, can declare war against any not in alliance with the king of Great Britain, and can try and punish robbers, pirates, and traitors according to the articles of war, or, at his pleasure, pardon them; he can conclude peace, and perform all acts of a Commander-in-Chief.

5. Duties of the Deputy Governor.

The Deputy Governor shall receive his instructions from the King and the Board of Trade, to suppress manufactures which are prejudicial to those of Great Britain, and subversive of the rights of the Crown. He also receives instructions from the proprietors to guard their interests, and moreover gives his bond for five thousand pounds penalty, if he violate his instructions. These instructions are often in conflict with the popular wish, and give the Governor a great deal of trouble in his office. If he displeases the proprietor, he is in danger of having his commission revoked; and if he displeases the Assembly, to lose his pay, which is in their power, when and how to give it, and how much. Some Governors, after getting into controversy with the Assembly, have found out a way of sustaining themselves in another manner, deposing magistrates who side with the Assembly, and putting their own creatures in their place. These recommend great numbers for keeping taverns and dramshops, for which one pound is paid annually to the Governor, so that one need not wonder at the increase of vice and crime of late years.

6. The Governor's Council.

As a relief in the discharge of his office the Governor has a number of intelligent and experienced men to give him advice in weighty matters, and these are called the Governor's Council. He calls and dismisses them at his own pleasure. Their number is not fixed, but generally consists of ten or twelve. They are his Privy Council generally, during the continuance of his administration.

7. The Government — President of Council.

In case of the Governor's death, or deposition, and until some successor is appointed, the oldest member of the Council becomes its President. He, with his Council, four, at least, in number, has the right to act in all things as a Governor, the signing of laws alone excepted.

8. The Assembly or Parliament.

The General Assembly, or House of Representatives, consists of thirty-six members, as follows:

For Philadelphia County	....	8
" Chester "	....	8
" Bucks "	....	8
" Lancaster "	....	4
" York "	....	2
" Cumberland "	....	2
" Berks "	....	1
" North Hampton "	....	1
" Philadelphia City	....	2

The Assembly is elected annually on the 1st of October, and meets in Philadelphia on the 14th of the same month. The usage is this: each County is divided into eight Districts, each consisting of several Townships. The Constable of each Township, on the 25th of September next preceding, holds an election, in which he is assisted by two residents of the Township. Then all the residents in the same Township elect one man who is regarded as best acquainted with the condition of the inhabitants, to act as an *Inspector* in the approaching County election. There is thus appointed an Inspector for each Township, and so many Inspectors for each District, as there are Townships.

The grand election is held in the court-house of each County, and is conducted by the Sheriff. He receives from every Constable the name of him who has been elected Inspector for his Township. The Inspectors for each District are placed together in a closed room. An impartial man takes out one name from each room, and these eight persons become the Inspectors of election for that occasion.

The settled residents, who own fifty acres of land, properly located, and twelve of these under cultivation, or who own property to the value of fifty pounds of provincial currency, and have lived two years within the province, have the right to vote, when they give into the Inspectors a folded piece of paper, upon which are the names of so many persons as are to be elected as the Representatives of the County. If the person who gives in his vote is well known to the Inspector, as possessed of the required property, he immediately puts his vote into a box with a hole in its lid. In the other case he who is doubted about has immediately to make his oath that he owns property to the value of fifty pounds. There are also Clerks, who record the names of those who present their votes. When all the votes are given in within the allotted time, the votes are counted, and the number of votes for each candidate; whereupon the Sheriff at the court-house door calls out the names of those who have been elected. These names are placed upon two lists, the upper corners of which are placed one within the other, and cut in a crooked line, so that when they are placed together they coincide. The lists are arranged by the Sheriff and six settlers; one of these is taken to the Governor, and the other to the Assembly.

The Assembly meets on the 14th of October, and after they are mutually sworn, they elect their Speaker. A committee of members is sent to the Governor to inform him that they are assembled, and prepared to present their Speaker. A time is appointed, when the whole House proceeds to wait upon the Governor; and when that is done, and the Speaker is presented, he reminds the Governor of certain privileges belonging to the House, as, especially, free access to the Governor when the public business demands it; freedom of speech in their proceedings; that the Governor is not to make any corrections in their proceedings until they have passed their resolutions; and that the members of the House are free from arrest during the time of their session.

The House appoints its Notary or Secretary, Keeper of the Seal, Doorkeeper, and Agent for the province at the Court of Great Britain. In later times Deputations (Committees) have been established for special occasions, such as grievances or complaints, correspondence, the supervision of accounts, etc., all which is done in the first meeting.

The Governor never comes into the House, but sends his messages in writing through his Secretary, and they send back their answer by two Deputies, who are members. The Governor is always spoken to in the third person:[1] "*May it please the Governor;*" or, "*With the Governor's permission.*"

In public matters they give their vote *viva voce;* in private matters, in writing (by ballot). In their proceedings for the passage of bills, resolutions, etc., they follow as closely as possible the usages of the Lower House of the British Parliament. After bills have been passed in the House they are usually all taken together at the close of the session and presented to the Governor. If they meet with his approbation the Provincial seal is placed upon them, and they are recorded, proclaimed in the court-house, and printed. But it is very common for them not to meet with approval.

At the end of the year the Speaker gives to each member a certificate of the time that he has sat in the House, with an order to the Provincial Treasurer to pay five shillings a day. And although they often separate, return home, and are called back again during the year, yet they never have mileage paid them for more than their first journey to and from the Legislature.

What most distinguishes this assembly from any other of the kind in the English colonies in America is, that they meet at a certain time in the year, and sit as long as they please. They also have the control of the public income, just as the House itself resolves. But to determine the pay of the members requires a law in which the Governor has a hand. Also, that the Governor's Council has nothing to do with legislation, as is usual in the other colonies.

Although the Assembly adjourns at its own pleasure, yet they still show the Governor the courtesy of making known their intention to him, and inquiring whether he has anything to suggest to the contrary. But it seldom happens that he detains them.

---

[1] [Original, "*tertia persona.*"]

If anything special should occur during the time that they are at home, which is very common in disturbed times, the Governor, through the Sheriffs and written orders, again calls the Assembly together to convene at Philadelphia on a designated day. When they have been thus convened they may adjourn again whenever they please.

At their last session for the year, by a Committee of Deputies they set forth the public accounts, which are then annually printed along with their proceedings. Their annual election contributes greatly to the upright official conduct of the members.

The Assembly decides in the case of disputed elections, punishes the Sheriffs and other officers for embezzlement or neglect of duty, and also prosecutes those guilty of misdemeanors, as criminals, just as is done by the Lower House of the British Parliament.

9. COLONIAL FINANCES.

The business of the Proprietor is managed in three offices: first, the Secretary's; second, the General-Treasurer's; and third, the Surveyor-General's.

When any one desires to take up a piece of vacant land anywhere within the province, he presents himself to the Secretary to get an order for its survey. The price of land bought from the Proprietor is, at the present time, fifteen pounds ten shillings, Provincial currency,[1] for one hundred acres. Five pounds upon every hundred acres is paid at once before the orders are issued, and six months' credit is given for the remainder.

The Secretary gives orders to the Surveyor-General, who preserves these orders in his office, sending copies to his Deputy-Surveyors in the place where the land is situated. After the survey has been made the Deputy-Surveyor sends back a map to the Surveyor-General's office; there it remains until the purchaser applies for further rights in the Secretary's office. In the meantime he may build, cultivate, and use the land, or sell it along with the right that he now possesses. Many thousand farms have of late years been taken up by poor people in the back country, and also sold with no better right than this, which are now in a great measure laid desolate by the Indians.

---

[1] [The Pennsylvania shilling was then worth about eight pence sterling.]

The Surveyor-General examines the calculations of his Deputy, and makes out a perfect description of the land, which he sends to the Secretary's office. The Secretary, upon being shown a receipt for the payment of the remainder of the purchase-money from the Treasurer-General's office, gives the purchaser a title confirmed by the Provincial seal, a copy of which is thereafter kept in the Archives (Records). And although a copy of the same is also kept in the Secretary's office and also in the Treasurer's, and many transactions are also therewith connected, yet all the expenses for two or three hundred acres of land seldom exceed two pounds sterling, or three pounds if the land amounted to one thousand acres.

The Treasurer-General appoints in certain places certain times for the payment of rents. In later times a remarkable mildness is employed in this respect, so that people may have almost as long credit as they please. It is seldom heard of that any one is distressed for rent; but the majority let the debt run for many years. Especially is indulgence granted to those who live in the most remote districts, which are but newly settled.

10. The Three Lower Counties Separated.

At the erection of the government under Proprietor Penn the three Lower Counties, New Castle, Kent, and Sussex, were subject to Pennsylvania. But when Penn was in the country for the second time, and changed the form of government of Pennsylvania, the three Lower Counties insisted upon their right to be a separate government, inasmuch as such had been the case under the Duke of York. Penn was strongly opposed to this, but had to give way, as the first charters had been surrendered. He offered them new charters under his new government; but they opposed this in the Assembly held at New Castle in 1700, where the representatives from Pennsylvania separated themselves from the representatives of the three Lower Counties as violent enemies, in the presence of their Proprietor.

11. An Independent Government.

Since that time these three Lower Counties have formed a government by themselves, and have their own Assembly, which is annually chosen, for the most part, in the same form and manner as that of Pennsylvania. They also recognize the Governor in Philadelphia, who comes down annually to their meeting at New Castle on the 20th of October. This is called the Lower Government.[1] They make their own laws, which always meet with the Governor's approval, without the least hostility. They adhere to the charter of Pennsylvania, and the same form of government, so far as their own laws have not made any change therein. They have great doubts as to whether the Penn family has any rights over them or not. Their reasons for this are, first, because the grant made to Penn by James, the Duke of York, for the three Lower Counties, was never confirmed by King Charles II. on account of his death thereupon immediately following, nor by King James himself upon his succession to the throne, on account of his expulsion, which so speedily followed. Already from the death of William Penn, forty years since, there has been pending a suit in law between Lord Baltimore's family in Maryland and the Penn family in Pennsylvania in regard to the proper boundary between them, which runs through these Lower Counties, owing, probably, to the variation of the magnet, which was not noticed in former times. In consequence of this, some have their deeds from the Duke of York, which are safe enough. Another party holds from Penn, another from Lord Baltimore, and some from both. Meanwhile no land-rents have been paid since the year 1715, nor have they been demanded. How it will go in this matter when the long suit comes to an end, there are many conjectures. It is their object, if possible, to push themselves forward into the condition of a Royal Government.

12. LIST OF GOVERNORS.

William Penn, as absolute Proprietor, was also himself Governor in 1681 and 1682, when his government was first introduced. After he had put everything in order, as far as was possible, and had returned to England, he sent William Markham to the country as Vice-Governor. William Penn returned

---

[1] [Now the State of Delaware.]

in 1700, and under the changed government himself presided over the government the second time. The Vice-Governors since that time have been the following: John Evans,[1] 1704; Charles Gookin, 1708; William Keith, Baronet,[2] 1717; Patrick Gordon, 1726; George Thomas, 1738; James Hamilton, 1748; Robert Hunter Morris, 1754.

CHAPTER IV.

MISUNDERSTANDING BETWEEN PROPRIETOR PENN AND THE SWEDES IN REGARD TO RIGHTS TO THEIR LANDS.

1. NEW IMPOSITION OF TAXES.

ON the 14th of June, 1683, Proprietor Penn, under his own hand and the seal of the Province, issued an order to all the old inhabitants of the Province, who had not yet received deeds for their lands, but only the Surveyor's certificate to make their surveys, according to orders from the Governor of New York, to send in these certificates, and take out deeds for the same. Also, that those who had deeds from the Duke of York should present themselves, and hand in their old deeds. The good and simple people, who did not know what that meant, generally handed in their certificates and deeds. Immediately

---

[1] Governor Evans was a native of Wales. In the year 1705, May 16, there came a report that some French cruisers were at Cape Inlopen, and intended to visit Philadelphia, as war existed at the time. The Governor had some fortifications thrown up on Society Hill, planted cannon on them, and commanded the soldiers to be on the watch. As the wind and tide were favorable, the arrival of the enemy was fully expected. Thereupon there was consternation among the Quakers in the city. Some of them fled into the woods, others down into the marshes. Some hid their property in secure places, or sunk it down into wells. But afterwards, when no enemy came, it was regarded as a trick of the Governor to try what the Quakers would do under such circumstances, as they condemned him who resorts to arms even for defending himself.

[2] This gentleman was a Scottish Baron of high mental qualities, but of weak decision in sustaining his dignity. His son was General Keith, who commanded the Russian army in Finland in 1743, and in the following year was quartered with the Russian troops in Stockholm.

thereupon Penn directed his Assembly to enact a law that all old homesteads (farms) should be resurveyed, and then large lots were found in excess of what the deeds covered, as they were not so particular about land in former times. Upon the river and creeks (kihl) there were large tracts of swamp-lands which stood under water at flood-tide, but were dry at the ebb,[1] and were useful for pasturage of cattle, but were not formerly embraced in the deeds. Some thousands of acres were, therefore, at this time, taken away from those who had hitherto possessed them, and sold to others, notwithstanding it was fixed by law that seven years of undisputed possession should give a clear title. Those who had given in their certificates and deeds never received them back again, and when they took out new ones were laid under three or fourfold rents. Those who did not pay of their own accord were sued. But those who did not give up their old deeds, both held what they had and were exempt from increased rents.

2. The Quakers to Blame for this.

The principal cause of this was the Quakers' dissatisfaction with the Swedes, who were the holders of the land along the navigable waters. They had hoped to have a fruitful land, but most of it cost great labor before they began to eat its fruits. They were also slow in settling in the interior of the country, from fear of the heathen, and therefore sought by craft, or for a small price, to smuggle themselves into the property of the Swedes, or in the manner just mentioned to compel them thereto, although the Swedes had now for twenty years been the faithful subjects of the British Crown. When Penn came to the country the second time, he offered the Swedes ten thousand acres of land in Manathanim,[2] sixty miles higher up in the country, with one bushel of wheat yearly rent for one hundred acres, under the pretext that they might there have more room, and live together. But the upshot was to get their homes for his Quakers, and few, therefore, accepted of the offer. In this the government

---

[1] ["*Fluxus et refluxus maris*," in the text.]
[2] [Manatawny, now in Montgomery county.]

Secretary, James Logan, had his hand especially. He was a stiff Quaker, and the object was both the oppression of the Swedes and the advantage of the Penn family.

3. The English the Source of the Troubles.

As long as the Swedes themselves were in possession of their homes, this dissatisfaction was scarcely anything more than a secret grumbling. But as some of them had sold their titles to other Englishmen, who were still less friendly to the Quakers, a public outcry was raised about the matter. They represented to the Swedes that they were the King's subjects, that the rents belonged to the King, and that Penn was Proprietor only of that land which was unsettled when he came in — a misinterpretation, by some, of the first article of his charter. They who bought the Swedes' lands stood up for the rights of the Swedes, and used them as the instruments of a general disturbance.

4. Complaints.

Finally these complaints burst forth in a petition to the Assembly in the year 1709, with the request that James Logan might be empowered to restore to them their old deeds, together with the excess of rents which he had wrongfully taken. The complaints were sent over to Proprietor Penn, who did not omit to communicate them to Count Charles Gyllenberg, who was at the time the Swedish minister resident in London. Whereupon His Excellency, the Count, brought the affair to the notice of the Royal Swedish Council, from which an earnest admonition was despatched to the members generally of the Swedish congregations upon the Delaware in America, to conduct themselves in obedience to the laws of the country, and of the English Court, as well as to Penn, the lord and proprietor of the country, if they expected hereafter from Sweden any services for their spiritual edification.[1] This was taken very hard by our Swedes, that they should be represented in London as disorderly, and still more so with regard to the government in Sweden; as they believed that

---

[1] Given at Stockholm, June 23, 1711, by *E. Wrede, G. Falkenberg, M. Stromberg, Knut Posse, C. G. Frölick, Arvesson Spens,* and *A. Leyonstedt.*

11

they were only demanding a manifest right.   Wherefore, in order
to bring their innocency to light before the whole world, they
presented a petition to the Assembly of 1713, demanding their
good testimony, that during the whole time that the country had
been under the English Government, and even to the present
time, they had conducted themselves as quiet and loyal subjects;
and also desired that this might be so represented to the Royal
Swedish and English Courts, and that this testimony might be
sent over to England and Sweden by Provost Björk.   Herewith
also followed a statement of the petitioners to the Resident
Count Gyllenberg, in which they set forth their grievances at
length, with various statements, which do not seem to be con-
sistent with justice on the side of the proprietor.

5. COMPLAINTS RENEWED.

The complaints were discontinued for some time, but Penn's
Commissioners continued to question the Swedish titles through
the Duke of York, to clip off pieces from their lands, to put on
higher rents, and to withhold their old deeds.   On this account
many others took part in this matter.   The first English inhabitants,
together with those who had bought Swedish titles, all united in
the complaints.   They presented a petition to the Assembly in
the year 1722, in which the chief complaint was, that the Proprietor by his Commissioners, and especially within the last five
years, had interfered with the Swedes' lands, as also with the
lands of those who had the same titles, or were the oldest English inhabitants in the country, and had their rights to the land
not only from the English authorities before Penn's time, but
these also, afterwards, still further confirmed by the fundamental laws of the country, namely, that seven years' undisputed
possession of property should become a good title.

6. THE GOVERNOR'S OPINION.

The Assembly communicated the complaint to William Keith,
the Governor for the time being, for his consideration, together
with the explanations of the Commissioners in the matter, which
they had called for, with the assurance also that they well knew
that he would not allow any one to be disturbed in his just

rights, although he did not approve that any of the inhabitants, as a peculiar people, should separate themselves from the others under the name of Swedes.

7. THE SWEDES DECLARED INNOCENT.

Richard Hill, Isaac Norris, and James Logan, the Commissioners at the time answered: that the titles which people had of the Duke of York had never been called in question; that the Swedes had no cause for their complaints, considering the high favor in which they stood with the Proprietor, who, although they were aliens in the English Government, and were in possession of the best lands upon the Delaware at the time of Penn's arrival, were yet confirmed in their possessions, without any further investigation, and this, be it observed,[1] to the great injury of those who had ventured their life and property upon the sea, to people the country,[2] etc. But that these complaints had their origin in another cause, this, namely: that evil-minded people who dwelt among them, and stood in closer connection with the English Crown, had already in the former unhappy times, in order to disturb the public, used the Swedes as instruments and means, in which they have the greater claims to be excused, as they are totally unacquainted with such matters. That these Englishmen may be properly regarded as the same disturbers, to whom all differences, which arise anywhere, are to be ascribed. That the Swedes in the country have never been disturbed by the Proprietor, nor by any one under him, but that they are badly dealt with by those who, from time to time, abuse their hands and names, to push forward plans that require such a cloak. That the Swedes, as they are descended from a race renowned for its submission and obedience to civil authorities, are of themselves, when not misled by others, quiet and honest men, etc. But as the Proprietor is now deceased, the matter could not be further investigated.[3] From that time no more was heard of the matter.

---

[1] [The original here has merely N. B.]

[2] [As though the Swedes had not done the same a century before.]

[3] Richard Hill's, etc., answer to Governor Keith, 1722. [A very specious mode of smothering the investigation, and covering up an ugly business.]

8. ATTEMPT TO INTRODUCE QUAKERISM.

Under a continued misunderstanding, the Quaker Assembly sought to establish by law, that every one, of whatever religious views he might be, who could not conscientiously make oath in the form and manner that was done in Britain, should have liberty to make his affirmation in the Quaker manner, that is to say, that when any one is by law called upon to assume any office, or to testify in any matter, that that shall not be demanded as in the presence of Almighty God, according to the teachings of the Holy Evangelists, and by kissing the Bible, but only by a "yea," or a little inclination of the head. A new plan to lead others into Quakerism. To this end a law was thereupon made in Philadelphia in 1710, but was disapproved in England the same year. The same law was again revived here in 1714, when everybody was afraid that it might be established. The Swedes sent in a petition against it to Queen Anne, and their clergymen recommended the subject to the Bishop of London, which petitions, etc., Provost Björk presented upon his journey home. Other churches also labored against it, so that the law was again revoked in the following year, under King George's government. An attempt was again made with some modification, but without effect. In the year 1717 an act was passed in regard to legal process, and its service. In this was inserted this point: that those who call themselves Quakers may make their affirmation, as has been established by Act of Parliament for Quakers in Great Britain. That remained in force.

CHAPTER V.

MISUNDERSTANDING BETWEEN THE PROPRIETORS AND THE PROVINCE IN LATER TIMES.

1. THE PROPRIETORS ILL RECEIVED.

IN consequence of William Penn's will, his three sons, John, Thomas, and Richard, became the Proprietors of Pennsylvania. After their death the proprietary right is expected to fall to him who is the head of the family. John Penn came to the country to take the oversight of matters in 1730,[1] but immediately went back, and not long after departed this life. Thomas Penn came in 1733 to visit his country, and examine into its resources. But as he and his brother Richard had entirely fallen away from the Quaker connection, and he inquired more about the government than the upholding of Quakerism, he was met by his father's old friends with uncommon disesteem, and after six or seven years' intercourse with them, instead of any other token of honor, had a gallows erected for him on the side of the road along which he travelled.

2. THE CAUSES OF THIS.

The Vice-Governor always has secret instructions from his principals : much depended upon their rights, which are impugned in the highest degree. For some thirty years the Assembly has stood, as it were, in opposition, and often opposes the most reasonable matters, merely to disoblige the Proprietor. Their Vice-Governor, whose hands are bound, is disgusted with an administration in which, within nine years' time, three, one after another, have resigned their commissions long before their time had expired. Some subjects may be mentioned, which, in later years, have created grievous misunderstandings, and which clearly show upon what uncertain ground the government stands.

3. MATTER FOR DISPUTE ABOUT EXPENDITURES FOR THE INDIANS.

In the year 1751 a dispute arose in regard to expenditures for the Indians, to keep them in alliance with the Province. The Proprietors up to that time had purchased of them great tracts of land, as often as the Province could be extended by the increase of its inhabitants; for these they had paid out of their own pockets. But the Provincial Assembly had also expended heavily in

---

[1] [Gordon, in his " History of Pennsylvania," p. 216, says that John Penn visited the country in 1734? He also declares that both he and his brother Thomas Penn " were received affectionately by the people."]

gifts to the Indians, at their councils, to retain their friendship for trade, as also to guard against the French and their Indians, in the event of war. To this also belong the salaries of the interpreters, agents and commissioners on both sides, so often required, and various other expenditures, now within four years amounting to five thousand pounds. In these the Assembly maintained that their Proprietors ought to bear a share, inasmuch as their property was thereby secured, as much as that of any other inhabitant; not to say that the Indians sold their land to the Proprietors at a low rate, as they were always so liberally paid at the expense of the Province. Hereupon a written representation was presented by the Assembly to the Proprietor, since, as they said, their representations, made time and again, to the Vice-Governor, had had no influence whatever. The Proprietors answered that the Assembly should keep themselves to their Vice-Governor, through whom they had already received answer; that the Board of Trade in London had given its opinion; that the Province itself ought to be responsible for these expenditures; that if the expenses of the Province should exceed its income, there was no occasion for that occurrence; but it was the fact that the income was double of these, and, therefore, their murmurs could not be regarded in any other way than as a means of gratifying the multitude, rather then as resting upon justice; that the Proprietors' reserved lands could not be laid under contributions; notwithstanding all this, they had always, for their part, contributed more than could be demanded of them, and so forth. For the rest, they recommended to them courtesy, good-will, and better conduct towards their Proprietor. The Assembly, which was thus refused all further correspondence with its Proprietors, still found it necessary to make its defence as to these points through some of its deputies, which defence was appended to every point in the Proprietor's letter, and thus afterwards inserted among its Acts, and made known in print in the year 1754. The whole affair shows nothing else but the highest contempt, and an excessive disposition to quarrel, in which some restless spirits found their pleasure, and also stirred up others to play upon the same string.

4. ANOTHER ABOUT A HOSPITAL.

The second cause of controversy was the establishment of a hospital. After suitable preparation, on the 23d of January, 1751, a proposition for this was passed into a law by the Assembly, and confirmed by the Governor, that when two thousand pounds had been collected by voluntary contributions for this purpose, an equal amount should be given from the tax receipts of the Province. As soon as the law was published the work was at once favored by donations from private individuals, which far exceeded the proposed amount. Directors and a Treasurer were chosen for the institution. Three of the best physicians in the city agreed to attend upon it for three years without any charge for their services. A lot outside of the city, belonging to the Proprietors, seemed to be the most suitable location. With this view, application was made to them to favor an undertaking of a character so necessary and so Christian-like by contributing to it a piece of ground for its buildings. The lot that appeared most suitable for the purpose was indicated by those who presented the application. Further, it was stated that if the Honorable Proprietors were disposed to aid the undertaking by good advice, it would be very thankfully received. After some consideration the Proprietors sent orders to their Vice-Governor·to give the Directors of that Province a charter for a hospital. But instead of the proposed lot they gave them another, which was regarded as equally good and serviceable. This was done with the proviso that when that arrangement for a hospital should cease, the ground given for it should revert to the Proprietors, etc. The Directors immediately let it be understood that they could make no use of such benevolence. They had already received so good a charter from their Assembly that no better could be given. Moreover, the worst possible construction was placed upon the Proprietors' expressions, as though the whole property should revert to them when the institution should cease to be supported by contributions, inasmuch as the work was completed when no further contributions were needed. Further, that the lot offered was more suitable for a graveyard than for a place of health. They renewed their request for the lot first proposed — that they might either buy it or rent it. But the

Administrator of Thomas Penn refused to make any change in his conclusion.[1]

5. Another in Regard to the Defence of the Country. Whether the War was Right or Wrong.

The third cause relates to the defence of the country. The Ohio is a river which flows upon the boundaries of Pennsylvania and Virginia, is a branch of the famous Mississippi, and gives opportunity for communication with the Gulf of St. Lawrence. The surrounding lands are very fertile, adapted to grain and forests, tar and hunting. The French in Canada have long been anxious to possess it, and in the year 1753 erected several forts there. When the English Court[2] thought that its neighbors had gone too far, orders were sent through the English Secretary of State, the Earl of Holderness,[3] to all their Governors in North America, that in the event of any foreign power intruding upon them, they should each and all drive them out of their Province, and also aid each other in driving out the enemy. James Hamilton, Esq., at that time Governor of Pennsylvania, laid these Royal orders before his Assembly, which always consisted, in the greater part, of Quakers; set forth their duty to take up arms, and declared himself willing to take the field if they would properly equip him. Thereupon there were various discussions as to whether the Ohio belonged to the English or to the French. Further, when it was agreed that the French forts stood upon English ground, a new controversy arose as to whether the land was within the limits of Virginia or Pennsylvania? In the meantime it was cast up to the Governor that his only object was to disquiet the people, and himself lead such an expedition.

6. War Supplies Refused.

The valorous Virginians made a stand against the French, but were defeated in May, 1754.[4] It was manifest that the enemy

---

[1] " Some Account of the Pennsylvania Hospital from its first rise to the beginning of the Fifth Month, called May, 1754," p. 4, etc.

[2] [Under New Castle's administration.]

[3] [" The inefficient Holdernesse," as he is called by Bancroft's Hist. U. S., IV., p. 160.]

[4] [Washington defeated Jumonville on the 25th of May, 1754, but was himself

stood not only upon English ground, but also within the limits of Pennsylvania.   The Assembly should therefore express itself, whether they would defend the country or not?   Money was demanded for this purpose, and it was moved in the Assembly by some well-disposed members, that twenty thousand pounds should be voted for this purpose; but this was voted down by the majority.   Another vote was taken upon a grant of fifteen thousand pounds; but this also was refused.   Then, again, ten thousand pounds; but it was negatived.   Once more a vote was taken upon five thousand pounds, when there was only a majority of *two* against the use of this amount for the defence of the country.   Governor Hamilton saw that he could do nothing with such a wrong-headed Assembly in times of such peril, and therefore resigned.

7. Demand for Making Paper-Money.

In his stead, at the close of 1754, came, as Lieutenant-Governor, *Robert* Hunter Morris,[1] a gentleman gifted with such qualities as are not only highly necessary, but also most ornamental to a Governor.   But the misfortune was that he was already known as a hater of everything that is or is called Quakerism.   When he made his public entrance, a sharp-sighted Quaker declared the day to be the darkest that Philadelphia had ever seen.   The work of defence was now to be laid hold of with zeal.   The Governor set forth His Majesty's orders, and the extreme danger of the country.

The Assembly agreed to grant twenty thousand pounds, with the proviso that they should be printed in the usual paper-money. The Governor reminded them that two years before His Majesty had forbidden the Eastern Colonies to issue any more paper-money, inasmuch as great disorder had thereby been produced in trade with England; but yet he would agree to do so if they would raise the same amount upon excise within five years' time.

---

compelled to capitulate and retire from Fort Necessity on the 4th of July following. See Sargent's Hist. of Braddock's Expedition, Vol. V. of Memoirs of the Hist. Soc. Pa. pp. 43–57.]

[1] [Son of Lewis Morris, a former Governor of New Jersey.   He retired from the government of Pennsylvania in 1756, and returned to New Jersey, where he died as Chief-Justice in 1764.]

The Assembly objected, and alleged that the prohibition related to the Eastern Colonies, but not to Pennsylvania; also, that so large a sum could not be raised within five years without ruining the inhabitants. The Governor showed that the prohibition affected that Colony at least indirectly, the others directly, whereupon he exhibited corresponding opinions from England; also suggested a certain method of raising the amount within five years, which could not injure the country, inasmuch as its income far exceeded its expenditures. But all this was interpreted by the Assembly and common people, who formed its party, in the sense that the Proprietor, by the instructions which he had given, prohibited the introduction of a sufficient amount of current money into the country, because he himself kept a bank here, and loaned money upon real estate, and drew to himself the people's money, so as to convert into mere tenants at will those who were now free owners of their lands. The Governor received information from Mr. Robinson,[1] the Secretary of State, that His Majesty was sending over General Braddock[2] with troops from England, who should make an expedition to the Ohio; whereupon followed an order to furnish them with provisions, baggage-wagons, workmen, and the like. He laid his orders before the Assembly, and called upon it to aid him in carrying them out, and proposed impressing wagons and laborers, should that be necessary.

The Assembly promised to furnish the provisions so soon as the Governor would allow them to strike off paper-money for the purpose. But as regarded the impressment, they could not believe that such was His Majesty's order, as it was in conflict with the charter of the country. Finally, the matter was sent over to England, for the King's consideration, about the close of the year 1754.

8. WAR MATERIAL EMPLOYED ACCORDING TO THEIR OWN IDEAS.

The Assembly did not wish to appear as opposing the Royal orders; would contribute their share in aid of the war; but it

---

[1] [Sir Thomas Robinson, created Baron Grantham in 1761.]

[2] [Gen. Braddock arrived in America Jan. 14, 1755, but received his instructions for his campaign in America Nov. 25, 1754. See Sargent's Braddock's Ex., pp. 393–400.]

must be done in a manner agreeable to their own notions and peaceable character. Bonds were, therefore, issued to the amount of fifteen thousand pounds, to be valid in business and trade, and to be redeemed by their Treasurer at the expiration of a year. From this amount ten thousand pounds of provisions were given to General Braddock's army, and five thousand pounds of the same to General Shirley's in New England. All this was done by their own counsel and resolutions. General Braddock was utterly routed in July, 1755; his remaining troops took another route to Oswego, and Pennsylvania was left open to any attacks of the enemy.[1]

9. New Quarrels about Land Taxes.

Governor Morris called his Assembly together, and laid before them the extreme danger of the country. They offered fifty thousand pounds, to be raised by taxes upon real and personal property in the country. This aroused a new quarrel, because they were thus aiming at the large tracts of unoccupied land which the Proprietors had retained for themselves in the valuable country still unsettled, that they might be assessed along with all the rents derived from the Province. The Governor did not find himself authorized to agree to anything of this kind, and so the time was wasted in violent interchange of correspondence, in which the Assembly charged the Proprietors with the design of putting every one under burthens like those of the German peasants, and at the same time assailed their Governor with very low expressions, to their own deep disgrace.

10. The Country Miserably Laid Waste.

The enemy well knew how to take advantage of this internal dissension and want of protection for the country. They stirred up the Delawares, Minnesinks, Shawanees, and other Indian tribes who had always before been the friends of the English, inducing them to fall upon the people in the back country. The attack was made by various roving parties, seldom more than

---

[1] [It is interesting to remember that these are the opinions of an eye-witness of those exciting events.]

three or four in a body. This was also done in the month of November of the year last named, to the great terror of the country, with murdering, burning, and carrying off into a horrible captivity. Men, women, and children, horses and cattle, all met the same fate. In Gnadenhütten, a place of the Herrnhutters, the brotherhood were sitting at their evening meal, when the wild heathen, like so many spirits of darkness, crept into the house, murdered the people, and tore off their scalps, and then let all things ascend in smoke, among the rest horses and sixty head of fine cattle designed for the brotherhood in Bethlehem. On the following morning only a wretched-appearance of their mingled and charred remains was to be seen. In other places the remains of men were found scattered over the ground, torn asunder and scarcely to be distinguished from those of brute animals. . . . Brutalities too horrible to mention. A mother weltering in her blood, and her new-born infant placed as a pillow beneath her head. The father was upon the ground with his entrails torn out. In another place was a woman with a sucking child, who, when she saw an Indian, fell upon her face in order to shield her child with her own body. The hell-hound rushed forward from his lurking-place, dashed his hatchet, or *tomahawk*, into her head, tore off the scalp, and then immediately withdrew — perhaps scared off. Some time afterwards the infant was found still alive under its dead mother. These and similar examples are a sufficient testimony to the lamentable desolation of Pennsylvania at that time.[1]

Yet all this had no stronger influence than that an investigation was ordered as to how far the Proprietor's Commissioner had or had not dealt fairly with the Indians in their purchases of land? A question which, now at least, was not only ill-timed, but also one which gave no immediate satisfaction. But this could not remedy the present injuries, nor prevent those that were coming. All right-minded persons complained, and severely attacked the Quakers for such proceedings. The people back in the country prayed for help, at the same time threatening to come down in great crowds, and cut both the Governor and the Assembly limb from limb, if measures were not speedily

[1] [See Gordon's Hist. of Pennsylvania, p. 312 et seq., and Note O 2, pp. 614–620.]

taken for the defence of the country. They also sent down some of the murdered bodies to Philadelphia, and laid them at the door of the State-house. But the nearer it drew to a resolution to defend the country, the more zealously did they preach in the Quaker meeting-houses, where the preachers are mostly old women, that they should "*not fear them that kill the body*," etc., and the more did the elders show themselves zealous in threatening all those, who advised or aided in the defence, with being expelled from their Society. To act more uprightly than ever before, the chief men of the Quakers presented a petition to the Assembly, in which they altogether dissuaded from all defence which should result in bloodshed, but urged them to employ other means whereby the enemy might be pacified.[1]

11. UPROAR.

All this could give no satisfaction to those who were the greatest sufferers. A body of four hundred men, mostly Germans, came down from the country, but in a friendly manner, and without any weapons. They first called on the Governor, and did not ask for anything but protection. The Governor thanked them for the assistance that they were giving in the objects for which he had so long labored, and promised to sign any bill that the Assembly might lay before him, if only there were any defence in it. He also showed them a letter which had arrived two days before from the Proprietors, wherein they presented five thousand pounds for the defence of the country. Thereupon there was heard a loud hurrah, with good wishes for the Governor. The same body continued its march and visited the Assembly in their house. After a loud knocking the door was opened. There the blame was laid upon the Governor; but the people, or those who acted as their spokesmen, would not enter into these quarrels, but insisted upon the defence of the country. They were asked whether they were willing that the Assembly should give up their liberties? To which it was answered, that their liberties were of no use when the enemy was taking their

---

[1] [Comp. Gordon's Hist. of Pennsylvania, pp. 321–322. An extract from the petition is found in the same author, Appendix, p. 620, Note Q 2. See, also, "Woolman's Journal" (Whittier's Ed., 1871), pp. 124–132.]

life and property. The conclusion was that their demands should be granted.

On the same day, which was the 24th of November, 1755, one act was passed in regard to the contribution of sixty thousand pounds for the defence of the country; another for the collection of a military force in the Province — the most ridiculous thing the world ever saw, as the upshot was that those who were disposed to take arms, and unite together in companies and regiments, and serve at their own expense, should have liberty to do so, but should be governed by the usual articles of war. That this act might not be nothing more than scorn and mockery, some Commissioners were placed over the military funds that they might be applied to the best advantage. These Commissioners immediately organized two regiments of regular troops in the pay of the Province, and placed them on the frontiers in some small forts. But as the boundaries are of vast length amid wild forests, and the bush-fighting of the Indians entirely unlike that of Europeans in the open field, so all this labor and expense were in vain.[1]

12. RECONCILIATION.

The controversies which were sent over to the King were by him remitted to the consideration of the Board of Trade, and decided to the honor of the Governor. Parliament took the subject into closer consideration, and was greatly dissatisfied with the conduct of the Quakers. It was just upon the point of excluding them from the Assembly, and from all public positions for all time to come; but some of their responsible heads in England gave the assurance that they should never again in time of war form the majority in the Assembly, whereupon six of them immediately vacated their seats in that body.[2] And as sufficient promptness in the defence of the country can never be expected from Pennsylvania as long as its original

---

[1] [See Gordon, ubi supra, pp. 319 and 320. Benjamin Franklin was at the head of these arrangements for the defence of Pennsylvania, which were more effective than our author here declares.]

[2] [Gordon, ubi sup., pp. 325 and 326, gives a very different account of these resignations; but Acrelius, being on the ground, and writing contemporaneously with the event, was probably correct. Gordon, probably, gives the *professed* reasons for the resignation.]

charter remains undisturbed, so Parliament has found it advisable to order the establishment of a regiment, called the Royal
American, composed of four battallions, with one thousand men
in each.

CHAPTER VI.

OF THE TOWNS AND THEIR TRADE.

I. IN PHILADELPHIA COUNTY.

PHILADELPHIA is the chief city in Pennsylvania.   It is
situated on the west side of the Delaware river, standing
upon a high, dry, and pleasant plain.   The city is laid out on a
square parallelogram, two miles in length and one in breadth,
extending on the east to the river Delaware, and on the west to
the Schuylkill.[1]   The streets are all parallel and at right angles
to each other — none of them less than fifty feet, and the widest
one hundred feet broad.   All the houses, built of bricks, are
from two to three or four stories high.   The building of the city
commenced on the bank of the Delaware, and stretches to a
great distance on the north and south beyond the ground as it
was at first laid out for it, so that now it has two suburbs — one
on the north and the other on the south; but the city buildings
do not yet extend more than half-way from the Delaware to the
centre of the city's ground which is on the west.   The streets,
which extend from north to south along the Delaware, are very
conveniently named — first, Water Street, then Front Street or
First Street, Second Street, Third Street, etc.   The streets which
run across these from east to west, or from the Delaware to the
Schuylkill, have various names, such as Market Street, Chestnut
Street, Mulberry Street, etc.   The harbor is quite secure and
convenient, where ships of the heaviest burthen may lie quite
securely in water of from seven to eight fathoms at the lowest
ebb tide, and unload at the bridges without the least danger.   And

---

[1] [" Skullkihl (Skörkihl)," in the text.]

as this harbor is, at least, thirty miles from the salt water, so must it also be free from ship-worms. The ebb and flood here rises and falls from seven to eight feet, and runs up thirty miles above the city. The great distance of the city from the ocean greatly contributes to its security, inasmuch as the ship-channel in the river is long and difficult to find, and so serves as a natural fortification, which, together with a battery a little below the city, provided with twenty-seven heavy guns, is regarded as a sufficient protection against any attack from the sea side. This flourishing city was founded by William Penn, the first Proprietor of Pennsylvania, in the year 1682, and has had such a rapid growth that in 1753 the number of dwelling-houses was reckoned at 2300. The city is governed by a Mayor, Recorder, Aldermen, and Council ; is full of inhabitants, and has a commerce so widely extended that in the month of October, 1754, there were 117 large sailing-vessels in the harbor at the same time. Its exports from December 25, 1751, to the same day in 1752, were, according to the accounts of the custom-house, as follows :

Wheat, .	.	86,550 bushels.	Iron rods, .	.	189 tons.
Flour (wheat),		125,960 barrels.	Pig-iron, .	.	205 tons.
Indian corn, .		90,743 bushels.	Ginseng root,	.	57 boxes.
Wheat biscuits,		599 hogsheads.	"	.	112 tons.
"		812 tierces.	"	.	6 cases.
"		28,338 tuns.	Deerskins and furs,		305 boxes.
"		7,888 quarter tuns.	" "		32 half boxes.
"		249 skeppund (tuns).	" "		15 quarter boxes.
Beef, .	.	925 tons.	Flaxseed, .	.	9,865 hogsheads.
Bacon, .	.	3,431 tons.	"	.	454 half hhds.
Staves, .	.	4,812,943 pieces.	"	.	39 third hhds.
Bar-iron,	.	4,491 tons.	"	.	221 tuns.

The imports into Philadelphia from England for three years, from December 25, 1748, to December 25, 1751, amounted to £647,267 8s. 9d., of which £478,282 5s. 5d. were the produce of the manufactures of Great Britain.

The principal public buildings are —

1. The English Church ; 2. The Swedish Lutheran Church ; 3. The German Lutheran Church ; 4. The German Calvinist Church ; 5. The Old Presbyterian Church ; 6. The New Presbyterian Church ; 7. Two Quaker Meeting-Houses ; 8. Anabaptist's

Meeting-House; 9. The State-House; 10. The Academy; 11. The Court-House.

Kensington, a little suburb of Philadelphia, is engaged in ship-building.

Germantown, six miles north of Philadelphia, is three miles long. It has one principal street, which is a public wagon-road, and 350 houses. The inhabitants are generally German mechanics.

2. CHESTER COUNTY.

Chester, the county-town,[1] on the Delaware, is sixteen miles below Philadelphia, and has 120 houses.

Marcus Hook, eighteen miles from Philadelphia, is engaged in ship-building.

Derby, seven miles from Philadelphia, has some public houses or taverns.

3. LANCASTER COUNTY.

Lancaster, the county-town of Lancaster county, is sixty-two miles west of Philadelphia, and has 500 houses. The inhabitants are for the most part German laborers, who trade a great deal with Maryland. It is regarded as the largest interior town in America. The owner of the ground is Mr. James Hamilton.

4. VARIOUS COUNTIES.

Bristol, in Bucks county, twenty miles from Philadelphia, on the Delaware, has 90 houses.

New Town, the county-place of Bucks county, has a few houses.

York, county-town of York county, twenty miles from Lancaster, has 190 houses. The inhabitants are mostly Germans, who traffic with Maryland.

Reading, the county-town of Berks[2] county, is fifty miles from Philadelphia, has 60 houses, and the inhabitants are mostly Germans.

Carlisle,[3] the county-town of Cumberland county, is one hun-

---

[1] *County-town*, or *county-place*, is that where all matters relating to the same canton, or county, are transacted. There are the seat of justice, court-house, land-office, jail, workhouse, place of execution, etc.

[2] [Acrelius has here written *"Reading county"* instead of Berks county.]

[3] [Acrelius writes the name *Carl-Isle*.]

12

dred and twenty miles from Philadelphia, has a few houses, and the inhabitants are mostly Irish.[1]

Easton, the county-town of Northampton[2] county, sixty miles from Philadelphia, has a few houses.

Bethlehem, a town and community of Herrnhutters,[3] is fifty miles from Philadelphia. The buildings consist of large stone houses for the Brothers and Sisters separately.

5. In the Lower Government.

New Castle, county-town of New Castle county, on the Delaware, thirty-five miles below Philadelphia, has 240 houses.

Willmington,[4] thirty miles from Philadelphia, at the mouth of Christina creek, on the Delaware, has 260 houses.

Newport and Christina Bridge are small places on Christina creek, having each 70 or 80 houses.

Noxentown is a market-town on the Apoquiminy.

Dover,[5] county-town of Kent county, ninety miles from Philadelphia, has 100 houses.

Lewis-Town, county-town of Sussex county, one hundred and twenty-eight miles from Philadelphia, on Cape Henlopen, has 100 houses, and its inhabitants are mostly pilots.

6. In New Jersey.

Burlington, the county-town of Burlington county, eighteen miles from Philadelphia, has 130 houses, and has a ferry.

Bordentown, twenty-eight miles from Philadelphia, has 60 houses. The last-named places have post-boats to and from Philadelphia, with post-coaches to Amboy for travellers to and from New York, making the route twice a week.

Trenton, thirty miles above Philadelphia, with 130 houses, lies at the falls of the Delaware, and has a ferry. Near to this lie the valuable copper mines, for the use of one-third of which Governor

---

[1] [Scotch-Irish, from the north of Ireland.]
[2] [He also writes this word " *North-Hamptons*."]
[3] [The Moravians were so called from Hernnhut, in Lausatia, fifty miles east of Dresden, in Saxony.]
[4] [The spelling is according to Acrelius.]
[5] [The text writes Dower, the Swedes pronouncing w as v.]

Morris, within eighteen months, in 1755, paid five thousand pounds.

Gloucester, county-town in Gloucester county, three miles below Philadelphia, has 30 houses and a ferry.

Salem, the county-town of Salem county, twenty miles below Philadelphia, lying upon Salem creek, has 120 houses.

7. COMMERCE.

All these small towns and places, upon both sides of the Delaware river, carry on trade with Philadelphia and the country people, with the exception of Wilmington, which always keeps its own sea-going vessels. Salem also has one or two, at times. But when these are in foreign ports they are all regarded as Philadelphia vessels.

Their commerce is based chiefly upon the following exports and imports :

To the West India Islands are sent wheat flour, bread, Indian corn or maize, beef, bacon, cheese, butter, staves, bar-iron, and cedar shingles. There is brought thence rum, Muscovado sugar, syrup, Spanish gold or silver coin, and exchange upon England.

To North Carolina are sent wheat flour, bread, and cheese ; and thence are brought tar, pitch, turpentine, hides, and tallow.

To the Bay of Honduras are sent all kinds of provisions, and thence are brought various kinds of wood — mahogany, lignum-vitæ, logwood, and Brazil-wood. The same trade is also prosecuted along the coast of the Gulf of Mexico, called the Musqueto Shore, from which also buffalo hides are brought.

To London, Bristol, and Liverpool are sent raw hides, deer-skins, and peltries, rum, sugar, and syrup; various woods from the Bay of Honduras, staves, boards of walnut and oak, tar, pitch, turpentine, pig and bar iron, and copper ore. Thence are brought all kinds of English manufactures, and even bottled liquors. But as this commerce is carried on with a very heavy balance against it, this must be made up by bills of exchange, and by money in Spanish and Portuguese coin.

To Ireland are sent staves, ship-timber, walnut boards, tar, turpentine, pitch, iron, together with a great quantity of flax-seed, cash, and bills of exchange. Thence are brought linen —

white, striped, and checked — servants, and emigrants. All else is prohibited.

To Lisbon are sent wheat, ship-bread, and wax; and thence are brought wine, salt, olive-oil, silk, satin, tea, spices, and coin, but by smuggling. The same trade is also carried on with Madeira and the Canary Islands.

With Rotterdam has sprung up a very profitable commerce in the transportation of German and Swiss emigrants. The ships go to South Carolina,[1] where a cargo of rice is taken in, and duty paid to England; after which they go to Rotterdam. Thence the people are conveyed to Philadelphia. Each person has to pay about three hundred and fifty dollars (copper coin) for the passage. Those who have no means of payment are sold to service for three, four, or five years.

CHAPTER VII.

OF AGRICULTURE.

I. OF THE SOIL.

THE soil in Pennsylvania is generally either white or reddish clay, sandy or gravelly; but the gravel is a gray sandstone, which contains some iron, and is found to be good for wheat-land. Some large tracts on the Susquehanna river have so strong a black mould that it is of use only for hemp and maize, but not for wheat and other small grains. This soil has been found twenty feet deep upon high hills. The reddish soil is in some places light, where it is regarded as a marl; in others dark, where it is complained of as poor land. The farms which were first cultivated have by constant use become impoverished, so that they are now considered of but little value. The people cleared the land, which was new and strong, but did not think of manuring and clearing meadows until of later years. For those who do not keep their animals in stables have no other manure than

---

[1] [The text has "Lartina," which is, no doubt, a typographical error.]

this: that they place a few hay-stacks on a field, on which the animals are fed during the winter, when they trample as much under their feet as they eat, whereby the manure becomes alike unequal and insufficient. That Pennsylvania is regarded as the best grain country in America arises more from the excellence of the climate than the fertility of the soil.

2. NEW CLEARINGS.

Yet most of the farms are newly cleared. Some miles up in the country but few places are to be seen where the stumps do not still stand thick upon the ground. Not one-half of the forests are cleared off as they ought to be. The clearing is not made by the destructive burning of the trees, whereby the fertile soil is converted into ashes and carried away by the winds. Some stocks or stumps may be thus burned so as to put them almost entirely out of the way. As labor is very high, so sometimes only the bushes and undergrowth are removed; but the large trees are still left standing. But around these a score is cut, and they thus dry up within the first year, and thus soon fall down; so that one may often see fields filled with dry trees, and a heavy crop of grain growing under them.[1]

3. THE IMPLEMENTS OF AGRICULTURE.

The implements of agriculture are the plow and the harrow. The plow is so made that from the share two pieces ascend with a handle upon each, about an ell and a half apart from each other. It is put together with screws; light, and easy to handle. The plowman holds each handle with one hand, and throws up the field into high "lands," plowing first on the one side and then on the other side of a "land," so that the earth is thrown up high. Immediately before the plow, a pair of oxen draw, or a pair of horses, which are guided by some little boy either leading or riding on them.[2]

---

[1] [This mode of treating large trees was called "girdling," and widely practised in the heavily-timbered regions of the United States.]

[2] Agriculture would undoubtedly be lightened in Sweden of one-third of its labor if the same modes were employed there. It is well known how the stumps of trees cover the ground with lumps, so that there is often no end of turning and twisting and beating about. But the plow turns the stubs down and the earth up, and so the turf is sooner rotted, and the field kept free from weeds.

The harrow is three-cornered and heavy. The traces are fastened to it with a link, which makes a convenience in turning. A pair of horses before the harrow, and a boy on the horse's back, smooths the field into fine and even pieces without any great trouble. Sometimes two harrows are fastened together after the same team.[1]

The beam of the plow does not come forward between the draught animals. Under the end of the beam is a strong clamp with a link, on which is fastened a double-tree back of both the animals. At each end of this double-tree is another shorter one (single-tree) provided with a link for each animal. From these single-trees there go upon both sides of the draught animals ropes or chains forward to the hames, which are held together by a broad strap above and below. In place of ropes or chains, most farmers use straps of raw deer-skins — twined and twisted together, and so dried — which do not chafe the sides of the horses. Out of these, also, the whole of the harness is made.[2]

4. THE KINDS OF GRAIN.

Flax is sown in the beginning of March. The ground is plowed for it some days before, and new or good ground is required. It is pulled in July,[3] and much used.

Oats are sown at the same time, mostly on good ground, which is plowed some days before. But if the plowing is done in the autumn before — in November or December — and then again just before the sowing, the oats themselves pay for it, according to the common saying. It is cut in July. It is used a great deal, but only for horses, and is of the thin and white kind.

Wheat is the land's chief product. It is sown in the beginning of September, after three plowings preceding — the first in May,

---

[1] A four-cornered harrow is not so easily turned. They have to change the draught from one end of the clamp to the other, at the ends of the fields. But a three-cornered harrow, with a link to it, is easily turned, and when a boy does the work, the laborer is spared a great deal of trouble.

[2] That the draught animals work easier in hames than in yokes, also in rope and straps than in heavy and stiff yokes for the belly, and the like, which chafe and bruise the animal, can be easily understood.

[3] The original has June.

then in July, and the last just before the sowing, but always according to the moisture and quality of the soil. As the autumn is long and warm, the sprouts grow so strong that all kinds of cattle are fed on them during the winter. Strong ground is not required for wheat; the middling is good enough. Harvesting is performed in July, in the hottest season. Sickles are used, with the edge sharpened like a file. The stalk is cut just about half its length, so that the stubble is quite high; the sheaves, short and small, are counted in dozens, and a bushel is expected from each dozen.

Rye is sown in November, mostly upon some field that has borne another crop during the same summer, and one plowing is usually regarded as sufficient. If the shoots only come up before winter, there is hope of a good harvest. Where the sowing is made early, there is a supply for pasturage during the winter. It is cut at the same time and in the same manner as wheat.

Buckwheat is sown at the end of July. For this is taken some ground which has just before borne rye or wheat. Poor ground and one plowing does very well for it. It ripens in October, and is mostly used for horses and swine. Turnips are not in general use. The seed is sown in the beginning of August; for this is taken either a piece of newly-cleared land or swamp. Those who have neither of these prefer letting it alone. The leaves are often exposed to the ravages of small flies, which destroy the whole crop.

5. PLANTINGS.

Maize is planted at the end of April or the beginning of May. Four furrows are plowed close to one another, and then five or six steps from these four other furrows; and so over the whole field. The plowing is done in the month of March. For the planting is used a broad hoe, wherewith the earth is opened to the depth of three or four inches, into which are cast five grains of corn, which are then covered with the hoe. Sometimes also they add two Turkish beans, which thrive very well with the maize, and run up its stalks. Each place thus planted is called a *hill*. An equal distance is kept between each hill, so that the

rows may be straight either lengthwise or crosswise. As soon
as the young plant comes up it is plowed over, and even harrowed, so that it may be free from weeds. When the plants are
half an ell[1] high, the ground is hoed up around them; and again
when they are two ells high. In the month of September, when
the maize has obtained its greatest growth, although not ripe,
the strongest blades are cut off for fodder. They then plow
between the rows of corn, sow wheat, and harrow it in; and
this, in the next year, gives a full crop. By the end of October
the ears are ripe, pulled off on the field, and carried home. The
stocks and roots are torn up during the winter, when the ground
is loose, to make the fields clean. Maize is the principal food
of the Indians, and it has hence been called "Indian corn."

Potatoes are quite common, of two kinds — the Irish and the
Maryland. The Irish are also of two kinds: the first round,
knotty, whitish, mealy, somewhat porous. They are planted
thus: upon a smooth and hard ground a bed of dung is formed.
Portions of this are thrown upon the potatoes, which are then
covered with ground of even the poorest kind. When the stalks
have come up about four ells high, they are again hilled up with
the same kind of earth, in order to strengthen the roots, which
are thus considerably increased in number. The other kind is
long, branching, thick, reddish, juicy, and more porous. For
these a long ditch, the depth of a spade, is dug; the bottom of
which is covered with manure, set with pieces of potatoes, and
covered over with earth. When the stalks come up, they are
treated as those above mentioned.

Maryland potatoes[2] are long, thick, juicy, sweet, and yellow.
They are planted from sprouts in hills, or round heaps of good
earth. When the stalks come up, they are hoed around. These
are also wonderfully prolific, so that everywhere around and
between the hills the fruit is dug up.

Cabbage is planted two or three times a year, but seldom
thrives well until towards autumn. Crisped colewort stands

---

[1] [The Swedish ell (*aln*) is equal to nearly two English feet; but it can scarcely
be so much as here used by our author, as is evident from what he says of the height
of potatoes (four ells) when hilled.] He no doubt means inches.

[2] [Sweet potatoes.]

through the whole winter.   On cabbage-stocks, which stand through the winter, new leaves come out in the spring, which are used for greens.

Tobacco is planted in almost every garden, but not more than for domestic use.   It is universal among the Indians.   When the leaves are ripe, they are cut, cured, and twined together like twists of flax, and are used, without any further preparation, by the country people for chewing and smoking.   The trade in tobacco is permitted only for Maryland and Virginia; although its exportation is almost yearly diminished, as its production is increased in Europe.

6. VEGETABLE GARDENS.

Vegetable gardens are kept for almost every house.   There are generally cultivated beets, parsnips, onions, parsley, radishes, Turkish beans, large beans, peppergrass, red peppers, lettuce, head-lettuce, German lettuce, and scurvy grass.   Anything else is regarded as a rarity.   Common herbs for domestic remedies are wormwood, rue, sage, thyme, chamomile, etc.

Pease are also grown in gardens, as they can be eaten whilst still green.   When dry, a worm grows in them, which comes out a fly in the spring.   And although the pea then seems destroyed, yet it still serves as seed for a new growth.   That sort is like field pease.   Sugar pease are also used, and are free from that evil.

7. ORCHARDS.

Orchards may be regarded as among the highest advantages of the country.   But the fruit consists mostly of three sorts — cherries, peaches, and apples.   Pears are rare.

Cherry-trees are generally planted here and there around houses and roads, away from the gardens.   The berries are generally of the common kind, bright and sour; some black, and more juicy.   The better sorts are rare, and lately introduced. They bloom in April and ripen in June.

Peach-trees[1] stand within an inclosure by themselves; grow even in the stoniest places without culture.   The fruit is the most

---

[1] [It is interesting to find this region still retaining its early success in the culture of the peach.]

delightful that the mouth can taste, and is often allowable in fevers. One kind, called clingstones, are considered the best; in these the stones are not loose from the fruit as in the others. Many have peach orchards chiefly for the purpose of feeding their swine, which are not allowed to run at large. They first bloom in March, the flowers coming out before the leaves, and are often injured by the frosts; they are ripe towards the close of August. This fruit is regarded as indigenous, like maize and tobacco; for as far as any Indians have been seen in the interior of the country, these plants are found to extend.[1]

Apple-trees make the finest orchards, planted in straight rows with intervals of twelve or fifteen paces. The best kind is called the Van der Veer, as a Hollander of that name introduced it; it serves either for cider or apple-brandy. Another sort is the house-apple, which is good for winter fruit. For apple orchards not less than two or three acres are taken; some have five or six. The cultivation consists in grafting and pruning in the spring, and plowing the ground every five or six years, when either maize is planted, or rye or oats sowed in the orchard.

CHAPTER VIII.

OF STOCK RAISING.

1. HORSES.

THE horses are real ponies, and are seldom found over sixteen hands high. He who has a good riding-horse never employs him for draught, which is also the less necessary, as journeys are, for the most part, made on horseback. It must be the result of this, more than of any particular breed in the horses, that the country excels in fast horses, so that horse-races

---

[1] [We have no evidence that the peach is a native of this continent; but it was evidently introduced at an early period. As it grows readily from the seed, and yields its fruit in three or four years, there would be no difficulty in its growing from seed imported from Spain or Italy.]

are often made for very high stakes. A good horse will go more than a Swedish mile (six and three-quarter English miles) in an hour, and is not to be bought for less than six hundred dollars copper coinage.[1]

2. CATTLE.

The cattle are also of a middling sort, but whence they were first introduced no one can well tell. Where the pasture is fair, a cow does not give less than two quarts of milk at a time—that is, twice a day. The calf is not taken from the cow until it is four weeks old—that is, as long as she can keep it fat, in case it is to be slaughtered; otherwise, two or three weeks are regarded as sufficient. And as animals are not kept in the house during winter, so it sometimes happens that calves are caught in the snow, and are none the worse for it. There is no such thing heard of here as calves dying.

3. SHEEP.

The sheep are of the large English sort. They are washed whenever convenient, and then immediately shorn, once a year, towards the end of April. Their wool is regarded as better for stockings than the English. The flesh is generally very strong in its taste, especially in old sheep. Some persons are unable to eat it.

4. PASTURAGE.

When the Christians first came to the country, the grass was up to the flanks of animals, and was good for pasture and hay-making. But as soon as the country has been settled, the grass has died out from the roots, so that scarcely anything but black earth is left in the forests. Back in the country, where the people have not yet settled, the same grass is found, and is called wild-rye. The pasture in the forests, therefore, consists mostly of leaves, but also of the grass which grows along watercourses. Until pasture comes in the stubble-fields and meadows, the best is in the orchards. Early in the spring there springs up a strong grass-leek (wild garlic), especially on poor ground, which

---

[1] [That is, about $60.00 of our U. S. money.]

makes the milk and butter unpleasant to the taste. But afterwards the fields are covered with clover, red and white, and make excellent pasture. Some sow clover-seed after they have harrowed in their wheat, to make the crop stronger. Back in the country, where horses and cattle are pastured in the wild woods, they become wild, and so live in great numbers.

5. Upland Meadows.

The clearing for meadows has advanced very slowly, as there was so much new land suitable for cultivation. Upland pastures are scarcely advantageous, unless they are frequently plowed, manured, sown with good grass-seed along with other seed, and also irrigated. They conduct the water from streams and ditches, so far as it is possible to do this, with dams, to irrigate the meadows when the drought increases, which must be done in the night time, when the air is cool.

6. Swamp Meadows.

Along the Delaware river and the streams which fall into it, there are large tracts of swamp, which, within the last fifteen years, to the extent of many thousand acres, have been improved into good meadows, but at a very great expense. The mode of procedure is to inclose a certain amount of swamp with a bank thrown up quite high, so as to keep out the water (the ebb and the flood), or tides. This bank commonly rises as high as five feet; sometimes ten feet. Also to make a ditch to carry off the water which comes on it from the land, and at the same time to place drains in the bank to let the water out; and then, again, by a gate upon the drains, to prevent it from running in. When dry, the earth is plowed, some kind of grain is sown in it, and then it is afterwards sown with clover and other English hay-seeds. When people saw the success of such work, their minds were so taken with it, that, in the year 1751, the price of an acre of swamp meadow advanced to six hundred dollars copper coin. But just at the same time it also happened that some high tides came up from the sea and swept away the embankments. Numerous muskrats live in these embankments, and make them leaky; also a kind of crabs, called "*fiddlers*," dig into them, and make the banks like a sieve. Then the ditches were found not to be rightly built so as to answer their purpose. Thus the grass and grain were destroyed, the land returned again to its wild nature, and there was no end of patching and mending. Then the price of the land fell to half its value, and he thought himself best off who had none of it. Again, in 1755, there came a great drought; no grass nor pasture was to be found, and, as no other plan could be devised, then the price of these lands rose again. The conclusion was that swamp land, as well as high land, has its advantages as well as disadvantages. Experience has taught that upland earth improves the swamp land, and swamp land the upland; also, that the vermin flee from the embankments when upland earth is found in them.

7. STABLES AND CATTLE-SHEDS.

Stables and cow-houses are seldom seen on a farm. The first Swedish inhabitants kept their animals under shelter during winter; but it was then said that they were exposed to vermin and other diseases, which have not been heard of since. Then people went into another extreme — that of letting the animals endure the severity of the winter, which, along with rain, frost, and snow, is sometimes intolerable. A good housekeeper has a stable with thin sides for the horses, and sheds for the cattle and sheep built near the barn, and standing out in the stable-yard, so that they may be protected there when the weather is severe. In milder weather all the cattle run out in the inclosure, and are foddered with hay or straw stacks, which are set up there. They also graze on the land around, in the swamps, or on the sowed ground, which is mostly used for young cattle. The sheep especially feed themselves on ferns and the young grass which grows up under the snow in warm weather. The lambs skip about in the snow, and stand in danger of being buried under it, for want of proper care. The man-servant takes care of the foddering of the cattle, whilst the housewife and women-folks roast themselves by the kitchen-fire, doubting whether any one can do that better than themselves. Hay alone, even of the best kind, is not sufficient to keep any horse or cow well; a considerable amount of grain, such as oats, maize, and buckwheat, is used for horses, and wheat-bran for milch cows.

8. The Fruitfulness of the Country.

The country is undeniably fruitful, as may be judged from the following examples:

Joseph Cobern, in Chester, twenty years ago, had the blessing to have his wife have twins, his cow two calves, and his ewe two lambs, all on one night in the month of March. All continued to live.

Olle Tossa (Thoresson), in Brandywine Hundred,[1] in 1742, had a cow which, in the month of March, had one calf; at her next calving, she had three; the third time, five — altogether, *nine* calves within two years. Three continued to live, but five died — two males and three heifers.

Thomas Bird, of the same place, had a ewe that yeaned four lambs within as many days, only one dying.

CHAPTER IX.

THE MANNERS AND CUSTOMS OF THE PEOPLE GENERALLY.

1. The Land as First Peopled.

THE land is so settled that each one has his ground separate, and, for the most part, fenced in. So far as was possible, the people have taken up their abodes by navigable streams, so that the farms stretch from the water, in small strips, up into the land. No country in the world can be richer in streams than Pennsylvania is in rivers, creeks, rivulets, and good springs.

2. The Houses.

The houses are built of bricks, after the English fashion, without coating, every other brick glazed; or they are of sandstone,

---

[1] [In Delaware.]

granite, etc., as is mostly the case in the country. Sometimes
also they build of oak planks five inches thick. To build of
wood is not regarded as economy, after everything is paid for.
The roof is of cedar shingles. Within, the walls and ceilings
are plastered, and whitewashed once a year. Straw carpets
have lately been introduced in the towns. But the inconvenience of this is that they must soon be cleansed from fly-
spots, and a multitude of vermin, which harbor in such things,
and from the kitchen smoke, which is universal. The windows
are large, divided into two pieces, the upper and lower; the
latter is opened by raising, and shut by lowering. The wood-
work is painted, or it does not last long.

3. FURNITURE.

The furniture of the house is usually made of the woods of the
country, and consists of a dining-table, tea-table, supper-table,
bureaus, cabinets, and chairs, which are made of walnut, mahogany, maple, wild cherry, or sweet-gum. All these trees are the
growth of the country, except mahogany, which is brought from
South America.

4. FASHION OF CLOTHES.

The articles of dress are very little different among city and
country people, except that the former procure them from the
merchants' shops, and the latter make them for themselves, and
usually of coarser stuff. Wool, weaving, and fulling-mills are
not used for manufacturing broadcloth, camelot, and other
woollen cloths, which might be finer, if more carefully attended to.
The coloring of certain stuffs is very inferior. Silks are rare
even in the towns. Plush is general, and satin is very widely
used all over the country. Calicoes and cottons are used for
women's dresses. Handsome linen is the finest stuff sought by
men, as the heat is great and of long continuance. By their
dress most people are known, whether of Irish or German birth.

5. ORDER OF MEALS.

The meals are cleanly, and do not consist of a great variety
of food. Ham, beef, tongue, roast beef, fowls, with cabbage set

round about, make one meal. Roast mutton or veal, with potatoes or turnips, form another. Another, still, is formed by a
pasty of chickens, or partridges, or lamb. Beef-steak, veal-
cutlets, mutton-chops, or turkey, goose, or fowls, with potatoes
set around, with stewed green pease, or Turkish beans, or some
other beans, are another meal. Pies of apples, peaches, cherries,
or cranberries, etc., form another course. When cheese and
butter are added, one has an ordinary meal.

The breakfast is tea or coffee. Along with these are eaten
long and thin slices of bread, with thin slices of smoked beef, in
summer. In winter, bread roasted, soaked in milk and butter,
and called toast; or pancakes of buckwheat, so light that one
can scarcely hold them between his fingers, are also used. The
afternoon meal (" four o'clock piece "), taken at four o'clock, is
usually the same. Suppers are not much in use. Where one is
so invited, chocolate is the most reliable. Whole pots of it are
sometimes made. but little or no milk in it, chiefly of water.

Of these articles of food more or less is used in the country,
according to the ability or the luxury of the people. Tea, coffee,
and chocolate are so general as to be found in the most remote
cabins, if not for daily use, yet for visitors, mixed with Muscovado, or raw sugar. Fresh fish for a meal is found nowhere
either with high or low. Of soup they think in the same manner.
It serves only for ordinary household fare. Salt and dried fish are
seldom seen : as few have eaten them, they are almost unknown.

The arrangement of meals among country people is usually
this : for breakfast, in summer, cold milk and bread, rice, milk-
pudding, cheese, and butter, cold meat. In winter, mush[1] and
milk, and milk-porridge, hominy[2] and milk. The same also
serves for supper, if so desired.

For noon, in summer, soup (såppa),[3] fresh meat, dried beef, and

---

[1] Mush is made of corn-meal, boiled in water; it is of a bright-yellow color; eaten
with milk, cider, or syrup.

[2] Hominy (Swedish, *håmene,*) is the grains of maize; the grains are first laid in a
steep to loosen the hull; then it is pounded in the section of a stock of a tree that has
been dug out, and thus the hull comes off. Then the kernel is mixed with Turkish
beans. From this is made såppa, mixed with flesh in winter time, and with milk in
summer.

[3] *Såppa* (soup) is a thin broth of meat, in which bread is crumbled; sometimes

bacon, with cabbage, apples, potatoes, Turkish beans, large beans, all kinds of roots, mashed turnips, pumpkins, cashaws,[1] and squashes.   One or more of these are distributed around the dish. Also boiled or baked pudding,[2] dumplings,[3] bacon and eggs,[4] pies [5] of apples, cherries, peaches, etc.

In winter, hominy-soup is cooked with salt beef and bacon. Then, also, pasties of lamb or chicken are used, and can keep cold a whole week; also pancakes of wheat flour or of buck-wheat-meal.

Bread is baked once a week or oftener.   It is in large loaves, mostly of wheat flour; seldom of rye.   The wheat flour, which is used in the towns for bread or table use, is beautiful, like the finest powder.   The flour in the country is dark and coarse.

---

it is drunk, and sometimes it is eaten with a spoon out of tin cups with handles, each person having one by himself.

[1] The cashaw is a kind of pumpkin, reddish within, more firm and fleshy than the common sort; it makes a stiff pap when mixed with the fat taken off of meat broth. Squashes are a smaller kind, about as large as a man's fist, whitish within, sweetish, growing in various forms, and are prepared in the same manner.   These are native American vegetables.

[2] Boiled pudding is made of light dough, mixed with fat; it is placed in a linen bag and boiled in meat broth.   When the dough is made of good flour, eggs, raisins, or dried peaches, it is called "a fine pudding."   Baked puddings are the young people's pancakes, and are eaten with a sauce of butter and sugar, like the last named.

[3] Dumplings are lumps as big as a fist, made of dough in which fresh apples are inclosed; it is boiled in meat broth, and eaten with prepared sauces.   Puddings and dumplings are called "Quakers' food."

[4] The bacon is fried in a pan with the yolks of eggs whole — a common dish in poor places of entertainment.

[5] A pie is a tart made of the fruits named in the text.   Apple-pie is used through the whole year, and when fresh apples are no longer to be had, dried ones are used. It is the evening meal of children.   House-pie, in country places, is made of apples neither peeled nor freed from their cores, and its crust is not broken if a wagon-wheel goes over it!

13

CHAPTER X.

DRINKS USED IN NORTH AMERICA.

1. French wine.
2. Frontegnac.[1]
3. Pontac.[2]
4. Port a Port.
5. Lisbon wine.
6. Phial[3] wine.
7. Sherry.
8. Madeira wine, which is altogether the most used.[4]
9. Sangaree is made of wine, water, sugar, a dash of nutmeg, with some leaves of balm put in.

10. Hot wine, warmed wine, is drunk warm, with sugar, cardamoms, and cinnamon in it. Sometimes, also, it has in it the yolks of eggs beaten up together, and grains of allspice, and then it is called mulled wine.

11. Cherry wine. The berries are pressed, the juice strained from them, Muscovado or raw sugar is put in; then it ferments, and, after some months, becomes clear.

12, 13. Currant wine, or black raspberry wine, is made in the same manner.

14. Apple-wine[5] (cider). Apples are ground up in a wooden mill, which is worked by a horse. Then they are placed under a press until the juice is run off, which is then put in a barrel, where it ferments, and after some time becomes clear.

When the apples are not of a good sort, decayed or fallen off too soon, the cider is boiled, and a few pounds of ground ginger is put into it, and it becomes more wholesome and better for

---

[1] ["Fronteniac," in the original.]

[2] [A species of claret.]

[3] [Our "Fayal."]

[4] [These are the common English wines, and show the predominance of English habits at that time.]

[5] [I have retained the idiom of the original, although the term "apple-wine" is s rictly synonymous with cider.]

cooking; it keeps longer and does not ferment so soon, but its taste is not so fresh as when it is unboiled.

The fault with cider in that country is that, for the most part, the good and the bad are mixed together. The cider is drunk too fresh and too soon; thus it has come into great disesteem, so that many persons refuse to taste it. The strong acid[1] which it contains produces rust and verdigris, and frightens some from its use, by the fear that it may have the same effect in the body. This liquor is usually unwholesome, causes ague when it is fresh, and colic when it is too old. The common people damask the drink, mix ground ginger with it, or heat it with a red-hot iron.

15. Cider Royal is so called when some quarts of brandy are thrown into a barrel of cider along with several pounds of Muscovado sugar, whereby it becomes stronger and tastes better. If it is then left alone for a year or so, or taken over the sea, then drawn off into bottles, with some raisins put in, it may deserve the name of apple-wine.

16. Cider Royal of another kind, in which one-half is cider and the other mead, both freshly fermented together.

17. Mulled cider is warmed, with sugar in it, with yolks of eggs and grains of allspice. Sometimes, also, some rum is put in to give it greater strength.

18. Rum, or sugar-brandy. This is made at the sugar plantations in the West India Islands. It is in quality like French brandy, but has no unpleasant odor. It makes up a large part of the English and French commerce with the West India Islands. The strongest comes from Jamaica, is called Jamaica spirits, and is the favorite article for punch. Next in quality to this is the rum from Barbadoes, then that from Antiguas, Montserrat, Nevis, St. Christopher's, etc. The heaviest consumption is in harvest-time, when the laborers most frequently take a sup, and then immediately a drink of water, from which the body performs its work more easily and perspires better than when rye whiskey or malt liquors are used.

---

[1] [It is rather remarkable that our author does not employ the term "vinegar" — ättika — in Swedish.]

19. Raw dram, raw rum, is a drink of rum unmixed with anything.

20. Egg dram, eggnog. The yolk of an egg is beaten up, and during the beating rum and sugar poured in.

21. Cherry bounce[1] is a drink made of the cherry juice with a quantity of rum in it.

22. Bilberry dram is made in the same way.

23. Punch is made of fresh spring-water, sugar, lemon-juice, and Jamaica spirits. Instead of lemons, a West India fruit called limes, or its juice, which is imported in flasks, is used. Punch is always drunk cold; but sometimes a slice of bread is toasted and placed in it warm to moderate the cold in winter-time, or it is heated with a red-hot iron. Punch is mostly used just before dinner, and is called "a meridian."

24. *Mämm*, made of water, sugar, and rum, is the most common drink in the interior of the country, and has set up many a tavern-keeper.

25. Manatham is made of small beer with rum and sugar.

26. Tiff, or flipp, is made of small beer, rum, and sugar, with a slice of bread toasted and buttered.

27. Hot rum,[2] warmed with sugar and grains of allspice; customary at funerals.

28. Mulled rum, warmed with egg-yolks and allspice.

29. Hotch pot,[3] warmed beer with rum in it.

30. Sampson is warmed cider with rum in it.

31. Grog is water and rum.

32. Sling, or long sup, half water and half rum, with sugar in it.

33. Mintwater, distilled from mint, mixed in the rum, to make a drink for strengthening the stomach.

34. Egg punch, of yolks of eggs, rum, sugar, and warm water.

35. Milk punch, of milk, rum, sugar, and grated nutmeg over it; is much used in the summer-time, and is considered good for dysentery and loose bowels.

36. Sillibub is made of milkwarm milk, wine, and sugar, not

---

[1] [Literally, "Cherry Dram" — "*Körsbärs Dramm.*"]

[2] ["*Stufwad Råmm*" is the original. I am not sure about the English that it is intended to represent.]

[3] ["Hått Pått" is the Swedish word; perhaps meant for "Hot Pot."]

unlike our Oelost.[1] It is used in summer-time as a cooling beverage.

37. Milk and water is the common drink of the people.

38. Still liquor, brandy made of peaches or apples, without the addition of any grain, is not regarded as good as rum.

39. Whisky[2] is brandy made of grain.   It is used far up in the interior of the country, where rum is very dear on account of the transportation.

40. Beer is brewed in the towns, is brown, thick, and unpalatable.   Is drunk by the common people.

41. Small beer from molasses.   When the water is warmed, the molasses is poured in with a little malt or wheat-bran, and is well shaken together.   Afterwards a lay of hops and yeast is added, and then it is put in a keg, where it ferments, and the next day is clear and ready for use.   It is more wholesome, pleasanter to the taste, and milder to the stomach than any small beer of malt.

42. Spruce beer is a kind of small beer, which is called in Swedish "*lärda tidningarne*" (learned newspapers).   The twigs of spruce-pine are boiled in the malt so as to give it a pleasant taste, and then molasses is used as in the preceding.   The Swedish pine is thought to be serviceable in the same way.

43. Table beer made of persimmons.   The persimmon is a fruit like our egg-plum.[3]   When these have been well frosted, they are pounded along with their seeds, mixed up with wheat-bran, made into large loaves, and baked in the oven.   Then, whenever desired, pieces of this are taken and moistened, and with these the drink is brewed.

44. Mead is made of honey and water boiled together, which ferments of itself in the cask.   The stronger it is of honey, the longer it takes to ferment.   Drunk in this country too soon, it causes sickness of the stomach and headache.

45. Besides these they also use the liqueurs called cordials, such as anise-water, cinnamon-water, appelcin-water, and others

---

[1] [The Swedish *Oelost* is made by mixing warm milk and beer.]

[2] [The text has " Wiskey;" but that may be an error of the press, or a slip of the pen.]

[3] [Prunus institia (Dalin).]

scarcely to be enumerated, as also drops to pour into wine and brandy almost without end.

46. *Tea*[1] is a drink very generally used. No one is so high as to despise it, nor any one so low as not to think himself worthy of it. It is not drunk oftener than twice a day. It is always drunk by the common people with raw sugar in it. Brandy in tea is called *lese*.[2]

47. Coffee[3] comes from Martinica, St. Domingo, and Surinam; is sold in large quantities, and used for breakfast.

48. Chocolate[4] is in general use for breakfast and supper. It is drunk with a spoon. Sometimes prepared with a little milk, but mostly only with water.

CHAPTER XI.

NOTICES OF IRON-WORKS IN PENNSYLVANIA AND THE ADJACENT ENGLISH COLONIES.

PENNSYLVANIA, in regard to its iron-works, is the most advanced of all the American colonies. When New Jersey is added to it, one can safely say that from the Delaware the greatest part of the iron in America is taken. Herewith, however, the provinces of Maryland, Virginia, and New York deserve to be mentioned. No iron-works are, as yet, erected in Nova Scotia, which is only in a small degree inhabited. The inhabitants, for the most part, keep themselves within fortified places for fear of the savages, who, incited by the French, are very hostile to the English settlements.

1. IRON-WORKS IN PENNSYLVANIA.

1. Cornwall, or Grubb's iron-works, in Lancaster[5] county. The mine is rich and abundant, forty feet deep, commencing two feet under the earth's surface. The ore is somewhat mixed

----

[1] [Sw., "*Thée*."]   [2] [Lazy ?]   [3] [Sw., "*Kaffe*."]
[4] [Sw., "*Chocolad*."]   [5] Now Lebanon county.

with sulphur and copper.   Peter Grubb was its discoverer.   Here there is a furnace which makes twenty-four tons of iron a week, and keeps six forges regularly at work — two of his own, two belonging to Germans in the neighborhood, and two in Maryland.   The pig-iron is carried to the Susquehanna river, thence to Maryland, and finally to England.   The bar-iron is sold mostly in the country and in the interior towns; the remainder in Philadelphia.   It belongs to the heirs of the Grubb estate, but is now rented to Gurrit & Co.

2. French [1] creek, in Chester county, near the Schuylkill. The mine is rich and abundant, from ten to twelve feet deep, commencing on the surface.   Its discoverer is Mr. Nutt, who afterwards took Mr. Branz [2] into partnership.   They both went to England, brought workmen back with them, and continued together.   Each has his own furnace — Branz at Reading, Nutt in Warwick.   Each also has his own forges — Branz in Windsor. Nutt supplies four forges besides his own in Chester county.

3. Sarum belongs to Taylor's heirs; has three stacks, and is in full blast.

4. Crum creek belongs to Peter Dicks; has two stacks, is worked sluggishly, and has ruined Crosby's family.

5. Two others are in Great Valley.

6. Durham, in Bucks county.   The mine, situated upon a high hill, is rich in good ore, and forty feet deep.   _. furnace at the foot of the hill receives the ore.   It may be regarded as the best iron-works in the country; has a rich supply of ore, wood, water, sand, limestone, etc.   The ore is so near to the furnace, and the furnace so near to the forges, that there is not one-eighth of a Swedish mile (three-quarters English mile) of hauling about the works.   It is only one-fourth of a mile (Swedish) from the forges to the station upon the Delaware river, whence the iron is conveyed by water to Philadelphia.   The owners are William Logan and Anthony Morris.

7. Manathanim, [3] or Rutter's works, sometimes called Loesher's, is in Berks county.   The mine is rich, but of red, broken ore, and is used chiefly for castings.   It has a furnace; also a

---

[1] Acrelius incorrectly calls this Friend's creek.   It never bore that name, but as early as 1729 was called French creek.   Its Indian name is Sankanac.

[2] Branson.   [3] [Now " Manatawny " creek.]

forge, which is used after the addition of ore from French creek.

8. Dixon's works, in York county. The mine has been lately discovered by its owner, Peter Dicks.

2. WORKS IN NEW JERSEY.

1. Union iron-works. Here is a tract of land of twelve thousand acres belonging to William Allen and Thomas Turner, Esqs. They have two mines distant one and a half miles from each other. The iron is of good quality in both. In the one which is most used, and twenty feet deep, iron appears mixed with sulphur and copper. But below the surface, good and pure ore is found all along, that can be used in all sorts of ways. Of the mine that has been less used, only small experience has been had, and not much has been smelted — only about forty tons, which, however, appears to be of a good quality.

Here are two furnaces and two forges, each with two stacks. Also a trip-hammer and a flatting-hammer.

2. Besides these there are four other furnaces : Oxford, Sterling, Ogden's,[1] and Mount Holly — each with its mines. The last yields brittle bog-ore in gravel, and is only serviceable for castings.

3. IN MARYLAND.

Maryland has several iron-works, such as *Sippi*,[2] which is regarded as the best in America. Snowden's, or North-East, belongs to a company in England, and is worked by Mr. Baxter with great success. There the ore and pig-iron are transported on the rivers many miles very profitably. The Maryland iron is not regarded as being so good as that from Pennsylvania. The ore is like a scaly gravel stone, and is usually found upon the shores of navigable streams, and yields a very tough iron.

4. IN NEW ENGLAND.

In New England there are two furnaces which yield a brittle iron, with some forges, which mostly purchase their pig-iron

---

[1] [The original has " Oyden's ; " but this is evidently a misprint for " Ogden's," as I am assured by the Hon. W. B. Ogden, of Chicago, that his family was for many years in possession of the property, which was situated near Newton, in Sussex county. The Ogdens settled in East Jersey about the year 1664.]

[2] Principio, in Cecil county.

from Pennsylvania.   The ore is here found in some places on the sea-shore, like sand.

5. The General Qualities of American Iron.

The American iron is generally soft and tough, and is regarded as most suitable for house- and ship-building, for which also it is employed; but for use in horse-shoes and wagon-tires it is far inferior to the Swedish iron.   But good iron can also be smelted at many points, whereof edge-tools, and all sorts of implements, are made in the country, such as axes, scythes, sickles with file-like edges for reaping, spades, shovels, hoes, plows, with other articles, all of which are obtained in the country better made than they could be brought from England.   No one is allowed to make nails.   The trip-hammers which were erected some years since, were condemned on account of their interference with the importation from England.

The custom of making bar-iron immediately out of the ore, which is, perhaps, called, in Swedish, "*Rännsmide*," is in use in some places, and is called "bloomery;" but is not regarded as good.   Such was at first Manathanim furnace; so also is Dixon's at the present time.   In New Jersey there are four, and in New York five or six, bloomeries in full blast.

6. Steel-Works.

At French creek, or Branz's works, there is a steel-furnace, built with a draught-hole, and called an "*air oven.*"   In this, iron bars are set at the distance of an inch apart. Between them are scattered horn, coal-dust, ashes, etc.   The iron bars are thus covered with blisters, and this is called "blister-steel."   It serves as the best steel to put upon edge-tools.   These steel-works are now said to be out of operation.

7. The Yield of Iron.

The no less honorable than wealthy Supreme Judge, William Allen, Esq., informs me that at his "Union Iron-Works," and also at Durham, one and a half tons of ore give one ton of pig-iron, and that a good furnace yields from twenty to twenty-five tons weekly, on an average, for the whole time they are in blast.

Also, that in the year 1753 Reading Forge gave eight hundred and fifty tons, and Warwick seven hundred and twenty tons of bar-iron.

One forge, with three hearths in good condition, and well attended to, is expected to give two tons a week, and a clear profit of £6 12s. 8d. sterling.

8. THE WORKMEN.

The workmen are partly English and partly Irish, with some few Germans, though the work is carried on after the English method. The pig-iron is smelted into "geese" ("gösar"), and is cast from five to six feet long and a half foot broad, for convenience of forging, which is in the Walloon style. The pigs are first operated upon by the finers (smelters). Then the chiffery, or hammer-men, take it back again into their hands, and beat out the long bars. The finers are paid 30s. a ton, the hammer-men 23s. 9d. per ton, that is to say, both together, £2 13s. 9d. People are so generally acquainted with the process of making iron that it is not necessary to describe it here.

The laborers are generally composed partly of negroes (slaves), partly of servants from Germany or Ireland bought for a term of years. A good negro is bought for from £30 to £40 sterling, which is equal to 1500 or 2000 of our dollars koppar mynt. Their clothing may amount to 75 dollars k. mt., their food 325 ditto — very little, indeed, for the year. The negroes are better treated in Pennsylvania than anywhere else in America. A white servant costs 350 dollars k. mt., and his food is estimated at 325 dollars more, of the same coinage.

For four months in summer, when the heat is most oppressive, all labor is suspended at the furnaces and forges.

The wood in the country is very abundant, and will not be readily exhausted, as it grows rapidly; although it does not live long. Charcoal from the hickory is used as the best; next to this, that of ash and white oak; but still more of black oak, as that is most abundant, and can be best spared. The country is everywhere cut through by running streams, which are in many places navigable, and waterfalls are not difficult of passage.

Iron ore in Pennsylvania is more abundant than the people

will ever make use of. On the best ground for farming are found
stones which contain some iron, of which the rain washes out
particles, which are seen in long streaks along the public high-
roads. The Delaware river, which receives so much running
water, throws up, during storms, black iron sands upon its
strands, so that a great quantity of it can be gathered up, which
is attracted by the magnet, and is only used as writing-sand.

Pig-iron is sold at the furnaces for from £3 6s. 8d. to £3 10s.
per ton. Bar-iron at the forge brings £20 per ton, or 20s. per
100 pounds. It is sold dear, for six months' credit is given.
Pig-iron is sold in Philadelphia at £5 per ton; bar-iron, in large
quantities, at from £14 to £16 per ton. It certainly seems
remarkable that the price is diminished after the long transportation to the city; but in this people find their profit.

The iron-works of Pennsylvania lie mostly within forty miles
of Philadelphia. The carriage for such a distance does not exceed twenty shillings sterling per ton. As a set-off to this is
reckoned the return-freight upon goods serviceable for the storehouse of the works.

Mr. Allen's calculation of expenses is: Pay for labor for the
manufacture of the iron from pig-iron into bar-iron £2 8s. per
ton. Pig-iron at the furnace cannot cost the proprietor of the
works more than £2 per ton. Bar-iron costs at the forge
£10 per ton. Bar-iron is sold in country places at from £19
6s. 8d. to £20 per ton. In Philadelphia at £15 per ton. In
London at from £16 to £17 per ton. In the West India Islands
at from £17 to £18 per ton. Pig-iron is sold in Philadelphia at
£5 per ton.

Moulded goods, or castings of kettles, stoves, etc., are sold at the
furnace for £5 6s. 8d. per ton; in Philadelphia for £7 6s. 8d. per ton.

Pennsylvania, New Jersey, and Maryland supply more iron
than their inhabitants need. From Maryland some pig-iron is
carried to Philadelphia in exchange for West India goods, as
Maryland has but little commerce with the Islands, and no other
off-set against Philadelphia. The export is made to London, the
West India Islands, and other English colonies on the continent
of America.

London, with the exclusive privilege of the trade, has received, in exchange for her exportations thither, American iron, which, both as pig-iron and bar-iron, serves as ballast for ships, and is admitted free of duty. But in the month of March, 1757, the English Parliament gave the same freedom from duties to other English ports, of which Bristol and Liverpool are preparing to avail themselves. But perhaps only a few vessels, with a full cargo of iron, will be sent over to England, it being too heavy a freight for the high sea; and, perhaps, that exclusive privilege will not, for some years, be any injury to the iron trade of Sweden.

9. COPPER MINES.

Copper ore has been found at several points in Pennsylvania. In Cornwall [1] a small vein has been found, but the source of it has not yet been reached. The mine is rich, but does not reach any great depth, lying but three or four feet under the surface. The first stratum is a whitish earth, the second a vein of copper three feet thick, and the third a red clay. In this ore pure copper is found. Samples of this may be seen in the cabinet of the Chancellor Charles de Geer. The progress of that work has been arrested by the death of its discoverer and proprietor, Peter Grubb.

Another place, in Bucks county, belonging to William Plumstead, Esq., has lately furnished rich specimens, and is now under examination.

At Rocky Hill, in New Jersey, a mine was discovered some eight years since. Some small veins have shown native gold, specimens of which are to be seen in De Geer's cabinet. Other pieces of ore, where the gold was not visible, have still yielded two pennyworths of gold to the pound of ore. This mine, three years ago, was so highly valued that Governor Robert Hunter Morris paid two thousand pounds sterling for an interest of one-eighth for only eighteen months; but immediately after that the mine began to fall off in its yield.

Schuyler's mine, in East Jersey, at Shrewsbury,[2] is rich and productive, being now worked for thirty years. The ore is sent to London.

---

[1] [In Lebanon county, Pa.]

[2] The Schuyler mine was not at Shrewsbury, but was near Belleville, on the left bank of the Passaic. Not long prior to the Revolution, Mr. Schuyler was offered, but declined, £100,000 for the mine.

At Pipe creek, near the Potomac, in Maryland, a rich copper mine has been found, which gives fair hopes of success in its working.

It has been reported that silver ore has been discovered in Pennsylvania. Mr. Allen says that lead ore has been found, and that lumps of it have yielded silver to the amount of one hundred and twenty-four ounces per ton.

CHAPTER XII.

THE MOST REMARKABLE KINDS OF TREES IN PENNSYLVANIA.

1. White oak (hvit ek) grows in good soil. Light bark. The leaves long, grass-green, blunt-pointed. The acorn is small, long, with a short cup. The wood white. Is used for ship-timber, planks, staves for hogsheads, or wine-pipes for spirituous liquors, but not for molasses. There is a heavy exportation of it to England, Ireland, France, and the West Indies, in the form of boards and staves. It is also used for posts, with boards, and clapboards around fields and gardens. It burns well, and makes good ashes. White oak growing upon low land and in swamps is considered more reliable for ship-building than that which is found upon high ground.

2. Black oak (svart-ek) grows upon any kind of soil. Bark dark. Leaf dark green, very blunt-pointed. The acorn large, with short cup. The wood, when split green, is of a reddish-brown color; when dry, darker. It is used for staves of molasses hogsheads, or barrels for dry goods, such as wheat flour, sugar, Muscovado; also for piles or palings built in water, but rots on land within three or four years. Does not burn well, but dissolves into smoke and poor ashes. The bark is used in tanning.

3. Spanish oak (Spanisk ek) also grows everywhere. Bark gray. Leaf small, sharp-pointed, light green. The acorns, which are gall-nuts, are serviceable for ink. The wood whitish, with spots like the beech-tree, is used as black oak, and is con-

sidered better. The bark is the best for tanning, and yields a yellowish color. There are several species of Spanish oak, which are distinguished by their leaves, but are the same for fuel, bark, and use.

4. Red oak (rŏd-ek) usually grows upon low land. Bark gray. Leaf broad, pointed, with saw-like teeth towards the stalk. The wood, when fresh, reddish; when dry, whitish. Is used as black and Spanish oak.

Black, Spanish, and red oaks are porous and loose in structure, so that if one takes a piece of their wood three feet long, wets the one end, and blows into the other, bubbles come out. All these species are usually spoken of under the name of black or red oak. Few natives of the country know how to distinguish them all correctly.

5. Swamp oak, water oak, peach-leaf oak, live oak (kărr ek, watn ek, svamp ek) grow in swampy places. Not common. High trees. Bark dark gray. Leaf long as the fingers, narrow, with one point. Wood gray, but the hardest of all oak. Is seldom used for anything but cog-stocks in cider-mills.

6. Walnut-tree, black walnut (valnŏtträd, svartnŏtbom), grows in dry ground. Bark dark gray. A high tree. The leaf in pairs on a stalk. The nuts black, large as apples, rough, and sharp on the outside, covered with a thick green skin. The shell hard enough to break with a hammer. The kernel very oily; fit for oil for fine paintings. The wood brown, and quite firm when the tree grows in free air and good soil, also valuable; but insignificant and of little value when it is surrounded by thick and close woods. It is used for furniture of houses, tables, chairs, bureaus, etc. Boards of it are exported in large quantities.

7. Hickory (hvit nŏtbom) grows in a rich soil. The leaves arranged in pairs along the branches, with teeth serrated at the edges. The nuts white, flat, pointed, large as the cultivated walnuts. Grows within a thick green hull, which when ripened, in the month of October, opens itself in four clefts, and pushes out the nut. Has a division within, as a walnut, but is hard as a bone. The kernel has a pleasant taste, and from it the Indians, as it is said, press an oil for winter use. The wood is tough, white on the outside, brown in the heart; that of young trees is used

for hoops; that of old ones for agricultural implements and wagons, but chiefly for fuel, and makes the best fires, with the finest ashes.

8. Chestnut-tree (castanie träd) grows in dry soil, high, straight, and thick. The bark ash-gray. The leaf oblong, pointed, with serrated teeth at the points. The shell double; the outer one large as an apple, externally like a burdock-bur, internally with a woolly down; when ripe naturally opens itself in four clefts, and throws out the nut, of which there are usually two, round upon one side and flat upon the other. If three grow together, they are mostly poor, and the middle nut is flat on both sides, the other two of the ordinary shape. Sometimes seven nuts are found together, and then none of them are good. The chestnut-tree, surrounded by thick woods, bears neither large nor numerous nuts; but where they are found in abundance, the swine have an excellent food. The wood is ash-gray, is used for posts or rails, but for nothing else, except fuel.

9. Poplar (poppel träd) grows indiscriminately. High, straight, and rich in foliage. Bark of a greenish-gray. The seed in pods. The leaf broad, single, scalloped. The wood yellowish, brittle, but hard. Used in carpenters' work for door and window-frames, also for boards. Is cut out for canoes; is turned for wooden vessels, such as pails, dishes, boxes, and the like.

10. Sassafras grows in rich soil. Low trees and bushes. The bark is dark green, smooth, with a yellow juice. The leaves unlike, even on the same tree; oblong, with one, two, or three stumpy points. The wood yellowish, especially the root, which, as well as the bark, has the smell and taste of saffron. It is used for planks and gate-posts, also for palings on the Susquehanna.

11. Cedar grows chiefly in swamps, or low, sandy ground. In smell and bark like the juniper-tree. Its needle-shaped leaves are long and tender. Red cedar is dark red, hard, used for planks and posts, and in New England for cabinet-work; on the Bermuda Isles for ship-timber. White cedar is a soft wood. Used for house-timber, boards, palings, and shingles.

12. Maple (lönn) grows in dry ground, high and straight. The bark a gray-green. The leaf small, three-pointed, serrated at the points. The wood whitish, spotted. Used for furniture

in houses, tables, chairs, etc. Is exported from the country in the form of boards.

13. Sweet gum (sötgämm) grows in low lands. The bark gray, smooth. The leaves five-pointed, with serrated edges. The wood yellowish, spotted, warps easily when it is wrought. Used for furniture and cabinet-work.

14. Sour gum (surgämm, fiskare) grows everywhere. The bark dark, sharp. The leaf oblong, one-pointed. The wood white, cross-grained, does not admit of splitting, and is used for wheel naves or hubs.

15. Locust grows in dry, rich soil, as a high tree. The bark greenish. The seed in long pods, the kernel large, sweet, edible. The leaf upon a long stalk, the leaves long, one-pointed, in pairs, like the mountain ash. The wood bright, hard, used for pegs in ship-building, for trundles and cogs in mills. The streets in New York are planted with locusts.

16. Dogwood (hundträ) grows in dry ground, seldom more than four inches in diameter. The flowers white, the berries red and small. The wood yellowish, hard, like boxwood, does not burn well. It is used for little else than carpenters' tools.

17. Wild cherry (wildt körsbärsträd) grows in good land, not high, but thick. The bark and leaf, like those of the cultivated cherry-tree, but the berry smaller, sweeter, with seed and no kernel. The wood reddish; is used for cabinet-work.

18. Persimmon (mispel) grows in good dry ground. Scarcely more than a foot thick. The bark rough and sharp. The leaf single, oblong, one-pointed, dark green. The berry like the wild plum; when frosted it is used for brewing table-beer. The fruit and its seed are pounded together, kneaded up with wheat-bran, baked in large loaves in a stove; pieces of it are then taken at pleasure, and from these the drink is brewed, which becomes quite palatable. The wood is white, hard, and used for carpenters' tools.

19. The button-tree (knappträ) grows wild, but is planted before the doors of houses. The bark greenish-gray, smooth. The seed-pods, round and large as marbles, hang upon long stems, which, when ripe, and one strikes them, all at once separate into small pieces, as if one were to throw a handful of

down into the air. The leaf is quite large, broad, single, five-cornered, sharp-pointed. The wood is brittle. Its greatest use is for shading houses from the great heat of the sun.

20. Spice-wood grows in dry and sandy soil as a bush. The flowers yellow. The berry red, small, mostly single upon the stalks. The leaves are oblong and one-pointed. The bark is green, has the taste of cinnamon when it is chewed; would probably serve as a medicine.

21. Pine is planted near houses as an ornament. Boards of it are introduced from other places, where it grows in a poor, sandy soil. Beech, hazel, and birch are rare. Alder is found abundantly in the marshes.

14

PART FOURTH.

THE STATE OF THE CHURCH FROM 1655–1696.

CHAPTER I.

THE CHURCHES FALL INTO A DECLINE.

1. THE FIRST SWEDISH CHURCHES.

FTER the Swedish government had been expelled, the Swedes and Hollanders, through intermarriages with each other and living together, coalesced into one church-association. The Hollanders had no Minister, nor did they, during their whole time, build a single church. Tenakong Church was in good condition, and was ordinarily used. The church at Christina usually held its services in Christina Fort; but for greater convenience, a small wooden church was, in 1667, erected at Tranhook, at the distance of one-fourth of a Swedish mile (one and three-quarters of a mile English) from the fort on the creek; this was more suitable for the Hollanders who dwelt at Sandhook. On the strand at Wicacoa stood a block-house, which some years after was changed into a church, so that service was held here and at Tenakong alternately. A block-house answered the purpose very well, for the churches generally were of the same material. The Indians were not always to be depended upon that they would not make an incursion, fall upon the Christians, and capture the whole flock. It was, therefore, necessary for them to have their religious houses as a place of defence for the body as well as for the soul. The churches were so built that, "after a suitable elevation, like any other house, a projection was made some courses

176

higher, out of which they could shoot, so that if the heathen fell upon them, which could not be done without their coming up to the house, then the Swedes could shoot down upon them continually, and the heathen, who used only bows and arrows, could do them little or no injury." [1]

2. PASTOR LARS LOCK CRIPPLED.

The Rev. Lars Lock, who came into the country in Governor Printz's time, and remained there, was certainly an instrument in the hands of God for sustaining these Swedish churches for so long a time.   He alone took care of both the congregations, Tenakong and Christina, for twenty-two years; [2] but finally kept himself chiefly with the latter, which was called Tranhook.   In a deed of division, which he drew up between Paul Jön's widow and her children, dated at Tranhook on the 14th of April, 1664, he calls himself Pastor Loci, although the church was not erected for three years after that time.   His old age was burthened with many troubles.   Finally, he became too lame to help himself, and still less the churches, and therefore he did no service for some years, until his death ended all his sorrows in 1688.   He has left behind him many of his name in Rapapo, all Swedish men, honest in word and deed, who brought up their children in the Lutheran doctrine, and within the Swedish Church.

3. PASTOR JACOB FABRITIUS BLIND.

His fellow-laborer was the Rev. Jacob Fabritius, by birth a German, or, as some have thought, a Pole.   He was called from New York, where he was without any assured position.   He preached mostly in Dutch, but so far mastered the Swedish language as that he could intelligibly hold service in it.   His first sermon was delivered at Wicacoa on Trinity Sunday of the year 1677.   Five years afterwards he had the misfortune to become blind, and continued so until the time of his death, which was

---

[1] Rudman's Mscr. [in Wicacoa Church].

[2] [As he came in the time of Governor Printz, who left the country in 1652, he must have been associated with Israel Holgh until 1655 at least, as that would be required to complete the twenty-two years of his unassisted service, until the arrival of Fabritius in 1677.   But as the elder Campanius left in 1648, it is probable that Pastor Lock was in America about that time.]

nine years later.[1] Nevertheless he watched over his congregations according to his ability. He resided above Philadelphia,
in the place called Kensington, and by the aid of a canoe went to
Wicacoa, yea, even down to Tranhook Church, about four Swedish
miles, in the same manner, and what is more also down into
Maryland. When he walked, he was led by some one who went
before him with a staff. From this it may be concluded that,
although there were two ministers in the churches, yet their infirmities made them hardly equal to one.

4. His Salary.

How it went with his pay can be judged from the following
letter:

"We, the undersigned Church-Wardens of Wicacoa parish,
greet the brethren of our parish, and herewith inform them that
our preacher, the well-learned and Reverend Jacobus Fabritius,
has now completed his service for the time agreed upon, and his
year is now out. It is, therefore, our friendly request to all and
each that they will voluntarily, through our duly appointed
agent, Jacob Yung, without any objection or excuse, discharge
their bounden duty to the aforesaid Rev. Jacobus Fabritius, so
that we be not obliged to resort to other means, and thereby
incur unnecessary expenses, which will all fall upon those who
shall give occasion for the same. We further request, and it is
our earnest desire, that all those who are willing longer to retain
the said Rev. Jacobus Fabritius, if that be possible, should here-
unto subscribe their names or marks, and what they will voluntarily give for his salary and support. Given at Wicacoa on the
10th of August, A. D. 1684."

It is found that the subscriptions for the same year amounted
to ten hundred and seventy-seven guilders of Holland — a salary
which, together with other small perquisites at churchings, marriages, administering the holy sacrament to the sick, burials, etc.,
all of which were fixed, is thought to have been sufficient for his

---

[1] [The time of his ministrations was, therefore, fourteen years — that is to say,
from 1677 to 1691, which leaves an interval of five years until the arrival of the
Missionaries Rudman and Björck, in 1696. But Springer, in his letter to Thelin,
written in 1693 (see J. W., below), speaks of Fabritius as still living at that time,
which would prolong his services two years.]

support, if the engagements were met by giving him what was promised, which, however, admits of some doubt, as the old gentleman, towards the close of his life, lived in great distress.

5. WANT OF CLERGYMEN.

The Rev. Mr. Fabritius became aged and lame, and a lamentable condition of the church seemed to be at hand. The right-minded were heartily desirous of relief, but they did not know whither they should direct themselves. Nothing was heard from Sweden: no ship came thence. Sweden had no advantage from the country, and those who were here could not expect any advantage from Sweden. They had no acquaintances in England who could further their affairs. The old Swedes, who had themselves made the long voyage, regarded it as quite incredible that any Swedish clergyman would come to them. And yet, at two different times, they made the attempt to write home for clergymen. But either the letters were lost upon the way, or those to whom they were sent had not sufficient intelligence and influence to place them before the proper persons; so no answer ever came back to them. Nevertheless they remained firm in their determination to obtain a clergyman from Sweden, and had recourse to another plan. There were in New York merchants who regularly traded with Amsterdam. Through them an appeal was made to the Lutheran Consistory of that city to obtain some Swedish clergymen, either one there known as being without charge, or some one from Sweden, through the recommendation of the Consistory above-named. To this end the following letter was dispatched in the year 1691:

6. A LETTER TO THE LUTHERAN CONSISTORY OF AMSTERDAM; TRANSLATED FROM THE HOLLAND LANGUAGE.[1]

"The grace of God through Jesus Christ, first of all. Very reverend, most honorable, and highly-learned gentlemen of the Consistory of the Unaltered Augsburg Confession in Amsterdam; most gracious and most learned gentlemen, our partakers

---

[1] [We translate from the Swedish, only a few lines of the Holland original of the letter being given.]

in a common faith: With a cordial and respectful salutation, we of the Swedish nation dwelling here in America (formerly called the South river, but now Pennsylvania) notify you, reverend and highly-esteemed gentlemen, that since the arrival of the reverend, highly-learned Magister Jacobus Fabritius, whom, in the year 1677, we called from New York as our preacher, who also by God's help, and the aid of the Most Honorable Sir Edmund Andros (at that time Governor of New York, Albany, and the South river), came to us, and delivered his first sermon on the 9th of June, being Trinity Sunday; the said Fabritius has ever since continued to discharge his duty as a minister of the Gospel, and to administer the Holy Sacraments. He did this for five years, whilst he had his sight; but with the new year he became blind, and so continues to this time. Yet he has faithfully and zealously taken care of us in accordance with the teachings of the Unaltered Augsburg Confession, in pure doctrine and an exemplary life. But now, considering his advanced age, his blindness, and his infirmities, he has notified us that he must necessarily lay down his office as a minister of the Gospel. Meanwhile we must fall into and remain in a most deserted condition in regard to our holy religion: yea, we shall be as chickens without the hen, as sheep without a shepherd, as sick without a physician — verily, in the greatest danger, as your reverences, our most highly-esteemed lords, can yourselves judge.

"Your reverences, most highly-esteemed gentlemen, cannot, therefore, blame us that we thus have recourse to you. We present, therefore, our most humble petition that your reverences would be pleased, in view of these great dangers, as well as in regard to our blessed fellowship in the Lutheran religion, to provide us with a suitable Swedish minister, inasmuch as we know that in Amsterdam persons of various nations are to be found, and especially students of theology, who are waiting for appointments as clergymen.

"And inasmuch as it is right that a laborer is worthy of his hire, we do therefore herewith promise the preacher who shall come to us, according to our present circumstances, the yearly salary of one hundred rix-dollars, with a house and glebe for his support, along with a regular call.

"As all that is herein requested tends to the honor of God, the advancement of the Gospel ministry, the continuance of our Christian faith, and the spiritual refreshment alike of the old and of the young for their eternal salvation, we therefore hope for the speedier aid and a friendly answer, with an earnest prayer to your reverences, our most highly-esteemed lords, that if no Swedish clergyman is to be found in Amsterdam, your reverences and our highly-esteemed lords would kindly aid us by correspondence with some one in Sweden,"[1] etc.

7. Nothing Effected.

Yet nothing was effected hereby. The letter was dispatched. The people waited, but no clergyman came. All the church service they now had was that an old man, Anders Bengtson by name, sat and read out of Möller's Postilla[2] in Tenakong Church; but at Tranhook, Charles Springer was the reader. The people were not very anxious to hear these things. The youth who came were fonder of riding races than of attending Divine service. There was no order, no reverence among the people. It was time for God to help them, for all human help had failed. Such have always been the ways of the Lord: to let all human counsel, wisdom, and greatness first come to nought, so that He may then accomplish great things by small and despised instrumentalities.

8. Anders Printz and John Thelin.

A man, a native of Sweden, named Anders Printz, came hither in an English ship. He said that he was a nephew of Governor John Printz. He became at once acquainted with the Swedes, his countrymen, and was heartily welcomed by them. A newly-arrived Swede was then a rare bird in the country, for then the Swedes knew no more of their mother-country than what they heard through traditions. This Printz thus became informed as to their condition, and then returned to Stockholm. There, in a conversation with John Thelin, secretary and postmaster at Götheborg, he told about the Swedes in America — their condi-

---

[1] [We have retained, as far as possible, the peculiarities, and even the grammatical inaccuracies of this letter, as characteristic of the writers and their circumstances.]

[2] [Sermons on the Gospels.]

tion, manner of life, and their sore need of spiritual guides. God thus awakened in the pious man, Thelin, a sincere zeal for the church of God and for his countrymen who were suffering such destitution, so that he was emboldened to present to His Royal Majesty,[1] King Charles XI., an account of the same. He was informed, in return, that his action was graciously received by His Majesty; and he, therefore, without any delay, at once wrote a letter to the Swedes in America,— which, for safety, was sent off by two different routes, — to let them know what he had heard about them and done for them, and what was now required of them, as can be further gathered from the following copy of his letter:

9. THELIN'S LETTER TO AMERICA.

"Highly-esteemed friends and countrymen: The occasion which gives me the honor of writing to you is, that during the past year I was in Stockholm, where I fell into the company of one Andrew Printz, who told me, and others also in the city, that he had been in an English ship to the West Indies, which I knew to be the fact. I was very glad of his arrival, and inquired if he had had a prosperous voyage. Whereupon he answered, thanking God, that he had there found not only a fine country, but also the old Swedes in good condition; and further, that they were heartily rejoiced to see him, as he was a Swede; that they had taken the occasion to inquire what was now the state of affairs in Sweden, their own foster-land, and who was now the reigning king in Sweden? Also that you, my good friends, had that confidence in His Majesty as to believe that if some one would lay before His Majesty your want of ministers and books, you had no doubt that His Majesty, out of his feeling and Christian heart, for the sake of your salvation, and for the up-holding of the Evangelical religion among both Swedes and Finns, would send you assistance. It is told us that both nations have lost their ministers: that the Finnish congregation lost their minister some years since, and that their church is now deserted; but that Divine service is still held in the Swedish

---

[1] [Charles XI. ascended the Swedish throne in 1660, when he was only five years of age, and died in 1697, at the age of forty-two, after a very prosperous reign.

church, though chiefly by the son of the deceased minister, in
such a way that hymns are sung, and the Gospels for the day
are read, but without the hearing of any sermon, and without the
reception of the Lord's Supper. Also, that you are in great need
of Bibles, hymn-books, and other books of devotion; and that
you would willingly pay for them if they were sent to you upon
the first opportunity. In truth, this goes to my heart, and to
that of many others; and as I had some good friends in the
Royal court, I related this before a distinguished lord, and he,
again, presented it to His Majesty. Our most gracious King
thereupon gave it his especial attention. I was immediately
commanded to present in a written communication everything
that I had learned concerning you. In consequence of which
His Majesty did most graciously resolve not only to send you
ministers, but also all sorts of religious books in both languages.
He would also willingly have employed in this work the man
who had presented this, as a guide and spokesman for the
ministers, but the Lord only knows whither he has now gone;
he has not since been seen nor heard of, so that no further information could be obtained from him.

"On this account I take the liberty of inquiring your names,
which are all unknown to us. An elderly woman, who lives
here in the city, relates that she has a brother there by the name
of Peter Gunnarsson Rambo, and desires me now to write a letter
to him, wherever he may be found, if he be still in this life, as
well as to some other good, honest men and old countrymen,
and thus to let us know whether you will still be called honest,
upright, and true Swedes, so that we may become acquainted
with you. Also, if it is truly so, as the man relates, and if you
do really wish such a favor from His Majesty, and how you
would arrange that these ministers may be sent and conveyed to
you. Whereupon I also will assure you that His Majesty would
not send ministers upon so long and difficult a journey for nothing.
For, as the old proverb has it, ' *He who goes unbidden to a feast
meets with no welcome.*'

"In reference to which it is my earnest desire that you would,
by the first and speediest opportunity, inform me circumstantially,
promptly, with truth and certainty, how you, His Majesty's old,

faithful, and honest subjects, are employed and situated. You may honestly tell me all this, for I am His Majesty's loyal and real subject, as also postmaster here in Götheborg. Let your letter be forwarded to a merchant in London by the name of Peter Grefve, who carries on a large business here in Götheborg, and who will surely send it to me whenever your letter reaches London in safety.

" For the rest, as regards your life and conduct, what means of support you have, whether agriculture or commerce, His Majesty will be greatly pleased to understand, as also that you are all prospering. Only inform us of every particular of your condition, in the least as well as in the greatest. The person above named also told me that you live well and in love to one another; that you, in all things, follow Swedish customs in eating, drinking, and farming, as well as in other forms of labor, which it was very welcome to His Majesty to learn; and it deeply affected his heart thus unexpectedly to hear of his old and faithful subjects, as he still has for them the same royal grace as for his own subjects here in his own realm. In consequence of which you have reason to congratulate yourselves upon His Majesty's great and especial grace and affection for you. For as he stands in close friendship and alliance with His Majesty of England, so it may be taken for a certain token that the Almighty, who hath the hearts of kings in His hands, will also direct this work. Take this as encouragement to send back your answer as speedily as possible and without any delay, as this may lead to your souls' welfare and salvation. But, above all things, let us know how many ministers and books you desire ; also, how large your congregations are, and how many churches you have. Eight or ten years since, Governor William Penn communicated to the Swedish Envoy Extraordinary in London his desire, on your behalf, to have ministers and books forwarded to you, saying that he would take care to send them to you. In regard to which I do not know what was the result, but believe that nothing was effected. If anything was actually done, let us know of it. Be not negligent in the matter which pertains to your eternal welfare, for you can certainly see that the great God doth just as speedily help through lowly friends as through the great. For the rest, commending

you to the gracious care and protection of Almighty God, I shall
be in daily expectation of hearing from you by the first possible
opportunity, and remain

"Your most loving friend and servant,

"JOHN THELIN.

"GÖTHEBORG, Nov. 16, 1692."

This letter arrived safely and occasioned great joy. And that
this undertaking might not occasion any misunderstanding with
the government, the letter was translated into English, and communicated to William Markham, who was at that time the
Governor of Pennsylvania, who expressed a like satisfaction with
it. He bade them, in God's name, to write their answer, and not
delay therewith, promising also his recommendation to the Proprietor, Mr. Penn, as also to the Swedish Secretary of Legation
in London, M. Leyoncrona.

10. CHARLES SPRINGER CONDUCTS THE CORRESPONDENCE IN AMERICA.

Great assistance in these arrangements was given by a Swede
of the name of Charles Springer,[1] who had come into the country
a short time before. He was born in Sweden, and had subsequently been in service with the Swedish Minister, John Leyon-
berg, in London. It happened, one evening, when he was going
home in a carriage, that he was seized and carried off to a
merchant's ship in the river Thames, and so sent off to America.
The ship landed in Virginia, where he was sold as a servant for
five years, during which time he worked on a tobacco plantation.
After some time he heard them speak of his countrymen, the
Swedes in Pennsylvania, and therefore, as soon as he was set
free, he went to them. God's gracious providence showed itself
remarkably therein. This man was now the most suitable among
them to write Swedish, and to read Swedish writing. He was
also, in regard to his education, a very intelligent man, had been
appointed a magistrate among the Swedes at Christina, and but

---

[1] [Dr. Anjou, in the last volume of his "Svenska Kirkans Hist.," p. 378 (note),
mentions a circumstance we have not noticed elsewhere: "A letter from Springer to
his mother, who was nurse with the Queen, informs her of his adventures."]

few things were done in which he did not aid either by his writing or his advice. He was a pious and God-fearing man, who spared neither labor nor expense for the establishment of the Swedish Church in the American wilderness. In the first place, he had translated Postmaster Thelin's letter into English, to be presented to the Governor. Now he was also urged to write an answer to the same, which had been translated for the reasons above mentioned, in which it may be believed that he used his greatest diligence. The contents of the letter are as follows:

11. Springer's Letter to Postmaster Thelin.

"Highly-esteemed, loving, and most trusty friend, Mr. John Thelin, His Royal Majesty's faithful servant and postmaster in the great mercantile city of Götheborg: We wish you grace from God Almighty, with all temporal and eternal blessings. Your most excellent and welcome letter reached us on the 23d of May, A. D. 1693, bearing the date of Götheborg, November 16, 1692, by the welcome arrival of which we are all most heartily rejoiced and refreshed. We have, from this your letter and writing, been made to understand how that Almighty God has deigned to awaken a young man by the name of Anders Printz, who was here among us in the West Indies, and saw our circumstances, in one thing and another, and that he has reported them in our fatherland much as they happened; but partly through misunderstanding he stated some things which did not occur, and which we in our simple manner will circumstantially and truthfully relate. By this we perceive how that His Royal Majesty has, upon the information given by the person aforesaid, been drawn to us as his old and faithful subjects, and still cherishes a Royal grace and care for our eternal salvation and welfare, and for the upholding of the pure and uncorrupted Lutheran religion, and is also concerned as to how we may obtain for ourselves over here clergymen and godly books. For which great care and Royal grace we all in common most heartily and most humbly thank His Royal Majesty, wishing His Royal Majesty much happiness, prosperity,

---

[1] "This letter, with various others from different individuals, is still preserved in the Clerical Archives (prestestes arkif): (Eccl. 5, 181–189.)" L. A. Anjou "Svenska Kirkans Historia," Vol. II., p. 377, Note 2.

and blessing, both spiritual and temporal. So also do we all most humbly desire that since it has entered into the mind of His Majesty to deign to order that ministers and books may be sent to us with all possible expedition and haste, if we so answer your highly-esteemed letter which has now reached us : we, therefore, beg that there may be sent to us two Swedish ministers, who are well learned and well exercised in the Holy Scriptures, and who may well defend both themselves and us against all the false teachers and strange sects by whom we are surrounded, or who may oppose us on account of our true, pure, and uncorrupted service to God and the Lutheran religion, which we shall now confess before God and all the world, so that if it should so happen, which, however, may God avert, we are ready to seal this with our own blood. We beg also that these ministers may be such as live a sedate and sober life, so that we and our children, led by the example of their godly conversation, may also lead lives godly and well pleasing to God. It is also our humble request that we may have sent to us twelve Bibles, three copies of Sermons, forty-two Manuals, one hundred Hand-books and Spiritual Meditations, two hundred Catechisms, two hundred A B C books, for which, when we obtain them, we will pay and make satisfaction in all honesty and uprightness, as may be desired and demanded for them, as we shall also send payment for them to such place as may be designated by you. And to these ministers we promise for their support, and most solemnly bind ourselves, that we will pay them yearly and maintain them according to our ability. And when this our humble letter has been dispatched, we will provide for the church and for the ministers a piece of land whereon they may dwell.

" Now, as regards our general condition in this country, we are almost universally farmers, who plow and sow and practise agriculture, and live according to the laudable old Swedish customs in meat and drink. This country is also a very rich and fertile land in all kinds of grain, so that, God be praised, it bears richly and abundantly whatever we sow and plant in it, so that we have plentifully our support in meat and drink, and it has every year sent out through this river to most parts of the adjacent islands both flour, grain, bread, and beer. There is here also a great abundance of all kinds of wild animals, birds, and fish. Our wives and daughters also busy themselves much in spinning both wool and flax, many also with weaving, so that we have great reason to thank Almighty God for the support of our daily life. God grant that we may also obtain faithful Pastors and watchmen for our souls, who may also feed us with that spiritual food, which is the preaching of God's Word, and the administration of the Holy Sacraments in their proper form.

"We live in great amity with the Indians, who have not done us any harm for many years. It has also been told you, as your letter informs us, that the sons of the Swedish minister perform divine service in the Swedish church. But that is not so, for in that congregation we had a Swedish clergyman, whose name was *Laurentius Caroli Lockenius*, who came to the country in Governor Printz's time, and within five years past, in the coming September, fell asleep in the Lord. In the other Swedish congregation, also, we had a clergyman, M. Jacobus Fabritius by name, who is a German, and preaches for us in the German (Holland) language. Him we have had now about sixteen years. He is also an admirable preacher, but, God's blessing on him, he is so aged, and has lost his sight for so long a time ; yet is he one who has taught us God's pure and true word, and administered the Holy Sacraments among us. As to the other congregation, they assist themselves with a lay-reader, who is a Swede, born in Stockholm, who performs Divine service with hymns and prayers, and by reading sermons out of a Swedish Postilla. As for a Finnish minister, we have never had, nor do we need one, for we all in common understand Swedish.

"It is further his Royal Majesty's desire to know how we are and have been treated in this country — we therefore acknowledge and truly declare that both by the Hollanders, and under his Royal Majesty of England, our most gracious King, we have been well treated. For the Swedes have been faithful to them in thought and deed, as they still are to this day; and we have thus always had a good and gracious government, and we live with each other in mutual confidence and unity.

"And as we all now hereby most humbly and respectfully desire that this our earnest prayer and request may now, upon the

receipt of this our most simple writing in our fatherland, be
hastened to the immediate accomplishment of the work, of which
with all our heart we wish for the most desirable progress and termination, and so we shall always bear this in mind in our prayers
and petitions to Almighty God, that the great God, who, we
verily and in our hearts believe, has and will continue to have
His hand in the completion of this work which has been begun
in so Christian a manner, will graciously complete it.   For we
do not believe that God will forsake us, although we are in a
strange and heathen land, far away from our own dear fatherland.   Therefore we hope that those ministers and books may
come to us as soon as possible, although we have already on
two occasions written to the authorities of our fatherland for
ministers, and obtained no answer, as the letters were, without
doubt, miscarried.   Therefore, we beseech you, Mr. John Thelin,
that you will do your best for us in this matter, for which we
shall make you the most grateful return.   Nothing more at this
time, except that we all most heartily commend you to the gracious and merciful care and protection of the Almighty and
merciful God, for both soul and body ; and we remain in longing
desire and hope for the much wished for accomplishment of the
work.   And we remain, most highly esteemed friend,

        " Your friends, servants, and countrymen,

" Dated and written in Penn-   ERICH COCK,
   sylvania, Delaware river,   PETER GUNNASSON RAMBO,
   May 31, A. D. 1693.   MICHEL LAIKAN,
             PETER COCK,
             PETER RAMBO, junior.

  " Carl Göstaffson, Eric Molica, Sven Svenson, Anders Vieler,
Anders Bonde, Otto Ernst Cock, Hans Laikan, Casper Fisk.
Anders Bengtson, Lars Bure, Hans Georgen, Capt. Lars Cock,
Gunnar Rambo, Israel Helgh, John Hoppman, Broor Hinneke,
Mårten Mårtenson, Jerta Ferdig, Jesper Wallrawen, Peter Johan-
son, Johan Stille, Mårten Mårtenson, junior, Hans Nilsson, Otto
Thomasson, Peter Matson.

  " P. S.—In the event that it should so happen that the above-
mentioned books which we have engaged to take should meet
with some unfortunate accident on the way, we do yet give the

assurance, and bind ourselves, even then, honestly to pay for them. Our gracious Lord, the Lieutenant-Governor, William Markham, has also promised to send to our fatherland a letter of recommendation for us."

"Mr. John Thelin:

"Here is Capt. Lasse Cock, who was not present at the closing of our letter, but was with the Governor and Council, but he now respectfully requests that you will send him, for which he will pay, two Swedish Postillor, containing both the Epistles and the Gospels, and a Bible, and I remain

"Your most obedient servant,

"Carl Christopherson Springer.

"P. S.—We send this letter in duplicate, so that in the event of its miscarrying, the one or the other may reach you."

Hereupon followed a list of the Swedes then living in the country, accompanied by the number of persons found in each household.

12.

No. I.—An exact list and roll of all the men, women, and children which are found and still live in New Sweden, now called Pennsylvania, on the Delaware river.

Names.	No.	Names.	No.
Hindrich Anderson	5	Jacob Clemsson	1
Johan Andersson	9	Eric Cock	9
Johan Andersson	7	Gabriel Cock	7
Joran Anderson	5	Johan Cock	7
John Arian	6	Capt. Lasse Cock	11
Joran Bagman	3	Mans Cock	8
Anders Bengston	9	Otto Ernst Cock	5
Bengt Bengston	2	Hindrich Collman	1
Anders Bonde	11	Conrad Constantine	6
Johan Bonde	1	Johan von Culen	5
Sven Bonde	5	Otto Dahlbo	7
Lars Bure	8	Peter Dahlbo	9
William Cabb	6	Hindric Danielsson	5
Christian Classon	7	Thomas Dennis	6
Jacob Classon	6	Anders Didricsson	1

Names.	No.	Names.	No.
Olle Diricksson	7	Anders Jonsson	4
Staphan Ekhorn	5	Jon Jonsson	2
Eric Ericsson	1	Måns Jonsson	3
Göran Ericsson	1	Nils Jonsson	6
Matte Ericsson	3	Thomas Jonsson	1
Hindrich Faske	5	Christiern Jöransson	1
Casper Fisk	10	Hans Joransson	11
Mathias de Foff	6	Joran Jöransson	1
Anders Frende	4	Staphan Joransson	5
Nils Frendēs (Widow)	7	Lasse Kempe	6
Olle Fransson	7	Frederic König	6
Eric Gästenberg	7	Mårten Knutsson	6
Nils Gästenberg	3	Olle Kuckow	6
Eric Göransson	2	Hans Kyn's (Widow)	5
Brita Göstafsson	6	Jonas Kyn	8
Göstaf Göstafson	8	Matts Kyn	3
Hans Göstafsson	7	Nils Laican	5
Jons Göstafsson	3	And. Persson Longåker	7
Måns Göstafson	2	Hindrich Larsson	6
Johan Grantrum	3	Lars Larsson	7
Lars Halling	1	Lars Larsson	1
Måns Hallton	9	Anders Lock	1
Israel Helm	5	Måns Lock	1
Johan Hindersson, junior	3	Antonij Long	3
Anders Hindricksson	4	Robert Longhorn	4
David Hindricsson	7	Hans Lucasson	1
Jacob Hindricsson	5	Lucas Lucasson	1
Johan Hindricsson	6	Peter Lucasson	1
Johan Hindricsson	5	Johan Månsson	5
Matts Hollsten	7	Peter Månsson	3
Anders Homman	9	Mårten Mårtensson, junior	10
Anders Hoppman	7	Mårten Mårtensson, senior	3
Frederic Hoppman	7	Mats Martenson	4
Johan Hoppman	7	Johan Mattson	11
Nicholas Hoppman	5	Nils Mattsson	3
Hindrich Iwarsson	9	Christopher Meyer	7
Hindrich Jacob	1	Paul Mink	5
Matts Jacob	1	Eric Molica	8
Hindrich Jacobsson	4	Anders Nilsson	3
Peter Joccom	9	Jonas Nilsson	4
Didrich Johansson	5	Michael Nilsson	11
Lars Johansson	6	Hans Olsson	5
Simon Johansson	10	Johan Ommerson	5

Names.	No.	Names.	No.
Lorentz Ostersson	2	Carl Springer	5
Hindrich Parchon	4	Måns Staake	1
Bengt Paulsson	5	Chierstin Stalcop	3
Göstaf Paulsson	6	Johan Stalcop	6
Olle Paulsson	9	Peter Stalcop	6
Peter Pålsson	5	Israel Stark	1
Lars Pehrsson	1	Matts Stark	3
Olle Pehrsson	6	Adam Stedham	8
Brita Petersson	8	Asmund Stedham	5
Carl Petersson	5	Benjamin Stedham	7
Hans Petersson	7	Lucas Stedham	7
Hans Petersson	5	Lyloff Stedham	9
Lars Petersson	1	Johan Stille	8
Paul Peterson	3	Johan Stillman	5
Peter Petersson	3	Jonas Stillman	4
Peter Stake, alias Petersson	3	Peter Stillman	4
Reiner Petersson	2	Olle Stobey	3
Anders Rambo	9	Gunnar Svenson	5
Gunnar Rambo	6	Johan Svenson	9
Johan Rambo	6	William Talley	7
Peter Rambo, junior	6	Elias Tay	4
Peter Rambo, senior	2	Christiern Thomo's (Widow)	6
Matts Repott	3	Olle Thomasson	9
Nils Repott	3	Olle Thorsson	4
Olle Resse	5	Hindrich Tossa	5
Anders Robertsson	3	Johan Tossa	4
Paul Sahlunge	3	Lars Tossa	1
Isaac Savoy	7	Matts Tossa	1
Johan Schrage	6	Cornelius van der Weer	7
Johan Scute	4	Jacob van der Weer	7
Anders Seneca	5	Jacob van der Weer	3
Broor Seneca	7	William van der Weer	1
Jonas Skagge's (Widow)	6	Jesper Wallraven	7
Johan Skrika	1	Jonas Wallraven	1
Matts Skrika	3	Anders Weinom	4
Hindrich Slobey	2	Anders Wihler	4

NOTE.—This roll of 188 Swedish families, comprising 942 persons, living on the Delaware river in 1693, is invaluable to the student of the early history of Pennsylvania, New Jersey, and Delaware. At the court held under the Duke of York, at Upland, on the 13th of November, 1677, a return was made of the names of the Tydable persons, 136 in number, living at Tacony, Carkoens Hook, Upland, Marcus Hook, and the Eastern Shore. Record of Upland, pp. 77–80. It is important to consult both lists.

No. II. A list of those still living and born in Sweden.

Peter Rambo, ⎱ Have been here
Anders Bonde, ⎰ fifty-four years.
Anders Bengtsson.
Sven Svenson.
Michel Nilsson.
Måns Staake.
Mårten Mårtenson, senior.
Carl Christ. Springer.
Hindric Jacobson.
Jacob Clemsson.
Olof Rosse.
Hindric Andersson.
Hindric Iwarsson.
Simon Johansson.
Paul Mink.
Olof Paulsson.
Olof Petersson.
Mårten Mårtenson, junior.
Eric Mollicka.
Nils Mattson.

Antony Long.
Israel Helm.
Anders Homan.
Olle Dedricsson.
Hans Petersson.
Hindric Collman.
Jöns Göstafsson.
Måns Hallton.
Hans Olofsson.
Anders Seneca.
Broor Seneca.
Eskil Andersson.
Matts de Voss.
Johan Hindricsson.
Anders Weinom.
Staphan Jöransson.
Olof Kinkovo.
Anders Didricsson.
Anders Mink.

Among the members of these congregations in the above list many Hollanders were also intermingled,[1] inasmuch as they now regarded themselves as one people. Many others afterwards added themselves in the same manner, after the congregations got into better order; not only Hollanders, but also English, Scotch, Irish, and German families, all using the Swedish language. To whom many Swedish families also came in later times, such as Colsberg, Hulling, Hesselius, Brunberg, Smidt, Tranberg, Bary, Degner.[2]

---

[1] [Most probably by intermarriage.]

[2] The Swedish names were greatly changed in after times. Names were introduced into public documents according to the English pronunciation; in consequence of which the people afterwards, both in writing and speaking, generally called themselves in accordance with said change. Thus, *Bengtsson* was changed to *Bancksson* (Bankson); *Hulling* to *Fulling*; *Göstafsson* to *Justis* or *Justisson*; *Kyn* to *Keen* (Kean?); *Coln* to *Culen*; *Hesselius* to *Issilis*; *Colsberg* to *Colsbery*; *van Neman* to *Vannimman*; *Didricsson* to *Derecksson*; *Cock* to *Koch* (Cook); *Hindricsson* to *Hendersson*.*

* [Quite a number of changes may be added to the above. Thus, *Mårten* naturally becomes *Mor-*

No. III. "A list of the Bibles and Manuals for which we, the undersigned, send to our fatherland, for which we hereby give the assurance of our handwriting that we will honorably and honestly pay for the same when we obtain them.

Anders Bengtsson,	1 Bible, 2 Manuals.[1]
Caspar Fisk,	1 " 1 "
Peter Rambo, jr.,	1 " 1 "
Anders Langhorn,	1 Postilla.
Otto Ernst Cock,	1 Manual.
Lars Bure,	1 Bible, 1 Postilla, 3 Manuals.
Jonas Fooin,	2 Bibles.
Peter Yrm,	2 Manuals.
Eric Cock,	1 Bible, 1 Manual.
Gabriel Cock,	1 Manual.
Michel Nilsson,	2 Manuals.
Johan Stille,	1 Postilla, 1 Manual.
Göstaf Göstafsson,	1 Bible.
Johan Schute,	1 "
Måns Göstafsson,	1 "
Johan Svensson,	1 "
Hans Loican,	1 " 1 Manual.
Mårten Mårtenson, jr.,	2 Manuals.
Anders Wiler,	1 "
Charles Springer,	1 Bible, 1 Manual.
Olof Thomsson,	1 "

"We, the undersigned, acknowledge and confirm that the books which we have expressly ordered are, three Postillor, thirteen Bibles, twenty-one Manuals; and if any accident should happen to these books aforesaid, yet we obligate ourselves to pay for them honorably."

14. THE LETTER ARRIVED SAFELY.

The letter arrived safely and promptly, together with the lists, and Thelin sent them all over directly to the Royal Chan-

---

ton; *Iwarson, Ivarson; Joccom, Yocum; Swån* and *Swånson, Swen* and *Swenson;* and, according to Mr. Clay's statement ("Annals," p. 147), *Bonde* has become *Boon; Cock, Cox; Jonasson, Jones; Hoppman, Hoffman; Von Colen, Colin; Wihler, Wheeler."* Christian names of one language are naturally exchanged for those of another.]

[1] [Probably the "*Manuale Sveticum*" mentioned in Chapter II., of the Seventh Book of this History.]

cery.   But various obstacles intervened, especially the death of Her Royal Majesty, Queen Ulrica Eleanora, the wife of King Charles XI., which occurred just at that time.   Hence the American Mission was delayed for some time.

CHAPTER II.

REVIVAL OF THE MISSION.

1. King Charles XI. takes Counsel of Dr. Svedberg.

THE business of the Mission was again taken up.   His Majesty was pleased to call to him at the castle, *Dr. Jesper Swedberg*,[1] who was at that time Provost of the Cathedral (Dom-Probsten) in Upsala, gave him the lettter to read, and asked him what should be done?   That great light of the Church immediately recalled to mind the conversation which, during his travels, he had had with the Licentiate of Theology, Ezardi, in Hamburg.   In one of their conversations in regard to the conversion of the Jews, Dr. Ezardi had stated how the early Christians in that place had in their wills devised considerable property for the conversion of the heathen ; that a large part of this had at the present time come into the hands of the Swedish Crown, among the property held by Sweden at Stade, in Bremen ; that the income of this property had been converted into stipends to pay the travelling expenses of the nobility ; as, also, that some who enjoyed the benefit of this abused the trust, of which a dissolute nobleman, who was then in Hamburg, travelling upon this stipend, was an undeniable example ; that thus they who had the benefit of it converted no heathen, and so the property was expended in direct contrariety to the contents of the will.   It would therefore be much more becoming, as there were no heathen in the neighborhood, to apply it to the conversion of

----

[1] [Dr. Svedberg (father of Emmanuel Svedberg, commonly called Swedenberg) became an army chaplain in 1682; Court preacher in 1689; Pastor at Vingåker in 1690; Professor of Theology at Upsala in 1692; Provost of the Cathedral in the same place in 1695; Bishop of Skara in 1702; died in 1735.]

the Jews. This now came to Dr. Svedberg's mind, and gave him occasion to answer: "In America, most gracious Sovereign, where there are many Swedes who now need and desire Ministers, Bibles, Hymn-books, and various other works of devotion, there is now a good opportunity to convert the heathen, yea, to see to it that the children of Sweden do not become heathen as they dwell among them. Thus can those means be used in accordance with the wills of the deceased; otherwise, His Majesty would find it hard to answer to God for the violation of those wills."

The King answered: "We shall find the means thereto, and provide them with Ministers, God's word, and the necessary books, so that there shall be no lack of the same. Therefore provide suitable Ministers for me."

Hereupon the worthy Doctor suggested to His Majesty to put the matter into the hands of the Archbishop, *Dr. Olaus Suebilius*,[1] which was accordingly done by an order, as follows:

2. THE KING'S LETTER TO ARCHBISHOP SUEBILIUS.

"Charles, by the grace of God, King of Sweden, etc. Our faithful and well-beloved Archbishop: We herewith send you a copy of a letter, written by the Swedish Colony on the South river in America, to John Thelin, the Postmaster at Götheborg, which he has delivered to our Cancellie,[2] from which we have seen, with great pleasure, that this people have a very pious zeal for the preservation to themselves and their children of the pure evangelical doctrine, and we are thus moved to grant them aid in the matter. And as regards their desire to obtain two clergymen, it is our gracious will that you zealously exert yourself to seek out and provide them with such learned and godly men as they desire; it being our will that, so soon as we are informed by you that they are ready, proper arrangements shall be made for their

---

[1] [Dr. Olaus (Òlof) Suebilius succeeded the younger Bàazius as Archbishop of Sweden in the year 1681. He was the author of the well-known exposition of Luther's Shorter Catechism, which was the established book for the religious instruction of the youth of Sweden until the beginning of the present century.]

[2] [Sw., "*Cancellie*," for which we have no corresponding term, but it is substantially our "*Department of State*."]

journey, and also to provide them with money for the same. The Bibles, Postils, Hymn-books, Catechisms, and A B C books which they desire, we will have provided, and make them a donation of the same, so that the Ministers may take the same along with them. We doubt not that you will, in God's name, feel it to be your bounden duty, according to what has already been communicated to you, to procure faithful laborers for that vineyard of the Lord, whereby you will do that which is our most gracious pleasure.   And we graciously commend you to the favor of Almighty God.

"At Stockholm, the 18th of February, A. D. 1696.

"CAROLUS.

"C. PIPER."

3. THE CANDIDATE AND. RUDMAN CALLED.

The Archbishop laid his instructions before the Consistory, and there the matter was considered. Dr. Jesper Svedberg engaged in the deliberations with great zeal. He had previously, in his *"Homiletical Association"* [1] trained a number of students for the active duties of the ministry, and therefore he had no difficulty in proposing the most suitable candidates. The first one called was Andrew Rudman of Gestricia,[2] candidate for the Degree in Philosophy, who was encouraged to enter upon this duty by the most pressing reasons. Taken by surprise at first, he knew not what answer to give, but, after some days' reflection, consented. But foreseeing the great difficulties of the undertaking, he desired and received from His Majesty a rescript, assuring him that after some time he should have leave to return home, and then receive suitable promotion in his native land. This was done by a Royal Brief of His most gracious Majesty, which is still to be read among the Patents.[3]

---

[1] [A meeting of students of the University of Upsala for practical instruction in preaching and the duties of the ministry, conducted by Dr. Svedberg.]

[2] [Gestricia is a district in the province of Norrland.]

[3] [" *Privilegia*," which we have translated by the word " Patents," includes not only patents of nobility, but charters and all special grants made by the King in favor of any person or corporation. They were, of course, recorded.]

4. Eric Björk and Jonas Aurén called.

It was then left to the Rev. Mr. Rudman to select for himself a fellow-laborer in his office, and for this Dr. Svedberg, who was well acquainted with him, proposed Mr. Eric Björk of West-mania,[1] who was then in the Doctor's house, at his desk, being tutor for the sons of his brother, Assessor Schönström. To these two clergymen a third was also added by the King's command, namely, Mr. Jonas Aurén of Wermeland.[2] It was to be his chief errand to make a map of the country, with a description of its character and the condition of its inhabitants; then to come home immediately, and to communicate it to His Majesty. Yet, that he might accomplish the more good, he was also ordained along with Mr. Björk in Upsala, Mr. Rudman having been previously installed.

5. Their Outfit.

Upon the Archbishop's recommendation, the King appropriated for their outfit thirteen hundred dollars copper-mynt, five hundred dollars of which were given to the Rev. Rudman, as he still had something to pay for his academic degree, which was then immediately conferred. The others received each four hundred dollars.

The King called all three of the clergymen to himself in his cabinet, and there commanded them to come directly to himself, and to see no one else if they needed anything, or if there was any obstacle placed in their way. When the books, of which the King made a present, were ready, the following orders were issued :

"It is the gracious will of His Majesty that the three clergymen, Andrew Rudman, Eric Björk, and Jonas Aurén, chosen by the Archbishop of Upsala to travel to the Swedish congregations in Pennsylvania in America, shall take with them the religious books specified in the annexed catalogue, and deliver them to the officers of those congregations as a gracious donation from His Royal Majesty to said congregation, and therewith assure

---

[1] [Westmania, or Westmanland, is in the province of Sweden, having Örebro for its chief city.]

[2] [Wermeland is also a province of Sweden, and has Carlstad as its principal city.]

them that it gives especial gratification to His Majesty to hear
of the well-being of said congregations, and of their zeal and
constancy in the pure and evangelical doctrine.   Given at Stockholm, July 15, A. D. 1696.

"C. PIPER."

"CAROLUS.

Among these books were five hundred copies of Luther's
Catechism translated into the American Virginian [1] language,
upon which, as also upon the Bibles, Postils, and Church books,
the King's name (initials) was stamped in gilt letters.

6. THEIR LEAVE-TAKING WITH THE KING.

Thereupon His Majesty commanded that one hundred dollars
silver-mynt should be paid to each one for his expenses of travel.
The Custom-house Director received orders to engage their passage to London in a good ship, and to direct the captain to pay
these persons the kindest attentions.   Orders were also sent to
Mr. Leyoncrona, Secretary of the Swedish Embassy in London,
to assist in their voyage from that place.   Thus all three took
their leave most respectfully, and with the deepest gratitude to
the kind King, who, extending his hand to them, said, "Go, now,
in the name of the Lord, to the place to which I send you. God
be with you, and make your undertaking successful.   If any
opposition is made, or any injury done you, return. I will remember you."   Then, turning himself to Mr. Aurén particularly,
having often been in his father's house, the King, clapping him
upon the shoulder, said to him, "You are to come back at once.
Greet your parents from me." [2]   This was a token of especial
favor.   Mr. Aurén went by land to Götheborg, to join his companions in London.   The others went on shipboard at Dalarön,
on the 4th of Aug. 1696.

---

[1] [I have seen two copies of this book, which bears the title, "Lutheri Catechismus
översatt på American Virginske språket, Stockholm, tryckt uthi thet af Kongl.
Maytt. privileg.   Burchardi tryckeri, af J. J. Genath f. anno MDCXCVI." One of
these is in the archives of Zion's Luth. Church, Philadelphia, the other in the library
of the Lutheran Historical Society, Gettysburg, Pa.   See also the Ev. Review, Vol.
I., No. 1, p. 172, note, for a fuller account of it.]

[2] Rudman's Mscr.

7. THE VOYAGE COMMENCED.

In their company on board the ship also went Anders Printz, who had brought over the first message from America to Sweden in regard to their desire for ministers, whom the King had appointed for their guide, as has been already mentioned. It was now his intention to accompany them to America, and settle there. At the Scagen,[1] in the North Sea, they were in danger of being driven ashore by a violent wind. The ship also struck several times on the Onion, at the mouth of the Channel,[2] but without serious injury. On the 10th of October they arrived in London. Secretary Leyoncrona, in accordance with his instructions, announced them to the Royal English Court, and requested permission for the continuance of their voyage; which, at first, seemed as though it might be denied, but was afterwards accorded in respect for the Christian work which they had undertaken. Their passport was given by the King[3] himself, as follows:

" WILLIAM R.

" To all our Admirals, Vice-Admirals, Commanders, Captains, Governors, Mayors, Sheriffs, Justices of peace, Constables, Customers, Comptrollers, Searchers, and all others whom it may concern, greeting: These are to will and require you to permit and suffer the bearers hereof, Andreas Rudman, Ericus Björk, and Jonas Aurén, with their goods and necessaries, freely and quietly to embark at any port of this our Kingdom, and pass over to Pennsylvania in the West Indies, without any let, hindrance, or molestation whatsoever. Given at our Court at Kensington, 22d day of November, 1696, in the eighth year of our reign.

" By His Majesty's command,
" WILLIAM TRUMBULL.[4]

" [L. S.] WILLIAM R."

---

[1] [The Skagen, or Skan (as it is now written), is a cape forming the north point of Jutland. The channel called Skager Rack, connecting the Cattegat with the North Sea, is north and west of this point.]

[2] [The English Channel.]

[3] William of Orange, King of England.

[4] [Sir William Trumbull was at this time the English Secretary of State.]

8. Voyage continued from England.

It was a piece of great good fortune to them that there was delay in obtaining the passport. The ship in which they had engaged their passage, called *The Happy Union*, left them, and went to sea without them, and soon after lost its sails, masts, and rudder, and with great difficulty reached a port in Portugal. It was nearly a year after the arrival of the Missionaries in Pennsylvania that this ship, having been repaired, reached the same place. In the meantime they lost their good friend Anders Printz, and never knew what had become of him, but supposed that he had been pressed by some ship of war.[1] In his place came another Swede, Jonas Bjurström, who became their attendant in common. On the 4th of February, 1697, they left London and went to sea with a convoy, for fear of the enemy during the prevailing war. They were ten weeks at sea before they obtained sight of land in America, where they first landed in Virginia, and then went up to Maryland, whither the ship was bound. Then, after the Governor of Maryland, Francis Nicholson, Esq., had hospitably entertained them for two weeks, and made them a donation of twenty rix-dollars for their travelling expenses, they continued their journey on a yacht to Elk river, and there they landed on midsummer's day (June 24). Some Swedes dwelt in that place, who welcomed their countrymen most heartily, and immediately sent word to their brethren in Pennsylvania, who came without delay, and with tears of joy conducted their much longed-for countrymen overland to their homes.

9. The Arrival.

Their first act was to collect the congregations together, and show their passport, the brief and commission from the King and Archbishop. That was done first at Wicacoa, in the church, on the 30th of June, and next at Tranhook on the 8th of July, 1697. It is usual for congregations to choose their teachers, but here the teachers chose their congregations. The agreement

---

[1] [The wars growing out of the expulsion of the Stuarts from England and the accession of William of Orange to the throne were still raging.]

was as follows: As the Rev. Rudman had been first called and chosen, so he was to have the liberty first to name his congregation.   He selected Wicacoa, and Mr. Björk then took Tranhook.   Then they separated with thanksgivings, prayers, and tears, and each one remained with his own flock, which he must now gather up, as it were, out of the wilderness.   Mr. Aurén remained for some time with the Rev. Rudman before he entered upon his travels over the country.

PART FIFTH.

OF THE WICACOA CONGREGATION.

CHAPTER I.

OF RUDMAN'S TIME.

1. THE WICACOA CONGREGATION.

HE parish of Wicacoa is in the Province of Pennsylvania, and its members live partly in the city of Philadelphia, and partly in various surrounding districts,— Wicacoa,[1] Moyamenzing,[2] Passayungh, a district along the Schuylkill, Kingsess, Bond's Island,[3] and Pennypack, in

---

[1] Wicacoa is an Indian word, derived from *Wickhing, dwelling*, and *Chåo*, a *fir-tree*. Its correct pronunciation, according to common use now, is *Wickackåå*. Probably there was in former times at that place a fir, or a collection of firs, where the Indians had their abode. *Cohakyn*, a place in West Jersey, is from *Chåo, fir*, and *Haking, forest*. Many places in the country retain their original Indian names; and all of these are significant, partly of the nature or situation of the place, partly of some transaction which took place there, to trace out all of which is now almost impossible, as the Indian language is quite unknown among the Christians, and no sufficient accounts have been given to posterity. Upon the shore by Wicacoa was a place which was formerly called *Puttalasutti*, which means " Robbers' Hole." The reason of that was that some Indians, who had engaged in robbery, had dug a cave in a hill by the river, and there concealed themselves. When other Indians went along there upon the strand to fish or hunt, these robbers attacked, seized, and murdered them. The Indians around there missed their people from time to time, and did not know what had become of them. Finally, they discovered the robbers' nest. The entrance was well fortified; so they dug a hole through the roof on the hill and smoked them. Those who were besieged resolved to die in their stronghold; but although they could not save themselves, they would not give up their booty to others: they broke up their *Scevan* or *Wampum* by pounding it between stones, which was heard by those outside. From that time the place was called *Puttalasutti*.

[2] *Moyamensing* signifies an unclean place, or dung heap. At one time great flocks of pigeons had their roost in the forest, and made the place unclean for the Indians, from which it received its name.

[3] Bond's Island was so called from the *Bonde* family, which was settled there.

Philadelphia county; Kalkonhook,[1] Amasland,[2] and Matzong in Chester county. Of these Bond's Island is distant from the church about 1¼ Swedish miles; Pennypack, 1¾; Kalkonhook, 1½; Matzong, 2½ and over, where they still have their grave-yard, but seldom visit it. Formerly there also belonged to Wicacoa, Nitshamene, in Philadelphia county, and Manathanim, in Berks county, which now have but few Swedes, or are turned aside to another faith.

2. THE SITUATION OF WICACOA.

Wicacoa is a level, and also an excellent piece of land, lying on the west side of the Delaware, and on the south side of Phila-delphia. It is now a suburb, but not densely inhabited, though divided into city lots. On it stands Wicacoa Church, with its parsonage close by, just upon the banks of the Delaware, and having a very fine prospect.

3. NEW CHURCH BUILT.

When Mr. Rudman came into the country, all the Swedish people dwelling in the places just named united themselves into one parish, to which also belonged those who dwelt on the other side of the Delaware in New Jersey, who lived and had their houses from Raccoon's Kill,[3] and thence up along the river. Those that dwelt on the other side of the Schuylkill called them-selves " *the lower settlers*," the others " *the upper settlers*." Wicacoa and Tenakong Churches were still standing, but in a very ruinous condition, so that service was held in them alter-nately, and then only in case of necessity. All, therefore, not only regarded it as good, but insisted upon it that a new Mother Church should be built. For this £400 sterling were promised by subscriptions, for commencing the work.

---

[1] *Kalkonhuken,* so called from the *wild turkeys* that formerly harbored there in great numbers. These birds are now quite rare, since the country has been so cleared up and settled. They are in appearance like tame turkeys, of a dark gray species, but more delicate in taste.

[2] Amasland was at first called Ammansland. A midwife formerly lived at the place where Archard's farm now is; hence that place, and subsequently the whole tract around it, received the name of *Amman's Land,* now *Amas Land.*

[3] [Or Narraticon creek, on which Swedesboro' is now situated.]

4. CONTROVERSY AS TO THE LOCATION.

But when at last they were prepared to begin, a terrible controversy arose as to the place upon which the church should be built. At Passayungh, some years before, the congregation had bought a piece of land for a parsonage and glebe. There also the "settlers below" wished to have the church built, as being nearer and more convenient for them. The "upper settlers" wished to have it again at Wicacoa, upon the same ground on which the old church stood, as more convenient for themselves, and nearer to Philadelphia, so that if more land should be purchased for it, and the city extended itself further, the church should, in the future, be benefited by it. A third proposition was also made, namely, that as Tenakong was the oldest church in the country, it should be kept up as long as possible, and then another one should be afterwards erected at the same place. · In this all those united who dwelt at Marcus Hook, Raccoon's Kill, Rapapo Kill, Crum Kill, Amas Land, and Kalkonhook, in all 57 (fifty-seven) families. All this was established in "resolutions," but not in fulfilment. There were strong reasons on both sides, which made the parties more determined, but at the same time more lukewarm in the Christian work. The Minister was hindered in his Christian work, and at the same time distressed in mind. Whilst the congregation at Christina was erecting its costly church, the others were disputing about the place where they should build. The Rev. A. Rudman had, by a letter to Prof. Jacob Arrhenius, of the 20th of October, 1697, the first sent hither, declared that he did not know of any place in the world where a Christian Minister could live happier, or more beloved than here; but before the first twelve months had fairly elapsed, he was compelled to declare that he would not live another year among them, if they would not put an end to their offensive quarrels; and in a short time thereafter entirely gave up the care of the congregation, with the intention of immediately returning to Sweden, and, in the meantime, betook himself to Christina.

5. RECONCILIATION.

How far he was really in earnest, or whether he was only using that as a means of frightening the turbulent, cannot be very well determined. Yet, as he saw that he could not accomplish anything more with them, he called to his assistance his faithful fellow-laborer, Mr. Eric Björk, from Christina, who first, on the Tenth Sunday after Trinity, 1697, delivered before them a sermon on " *The Tears of Christ,*" with a direct reference to the congregation. And as a part of them were not present, he presently put his admonitions and reproofs into a written form, which was sent around through the congregations for them to read. The effect of this was all that could be desired. They all became humbled and penitent on account of their folly, and bound themselves to commit the matter wholly and entirely to the judgment of the three Ministers, Rudman, Björk, and Aurén, as well in regard to the choice of the place, as to the plan and cost of the church edifice; and also agreed that there should be a fine of £10 imposed upon any of those who should find fault with what was done therein. To this conclusion Governor William Markham was requested to give his approval. Both parties, "the upper settlers" and "the lower settlers," also gave a written pledge that they would adhere to their old subscriptions to the church edifice, whether that was placed at Wicacoa or at Passayungh, and also to send down their representatives to Christina, to beg their teacher's forgiveness, and beseech him that he would not forsake them.

6. The Position for the New Church.

The conclusion finally reached by the decision of the Ministers Rudman and Björk was this: that the new church should be built at Wicacoa, close by the old one, for which the family of Swän Swänson[1] gave the ground, and increased the same by an acre on the 19th of September, 1697. The reasons for this were: that the same place had once already been selected for this purpose by the casting of lots, on the arising of disputes: that a graveyard was already arranged there, along with the church: that the name of the Swedes would ever be held in remembrance, as their church thus stood in view of vessels as they

---

[1] [Or Svän Svänson, or Svén Svenson, the Swedes now substituting *v* for *w*, and long *e* being nearly equivalent to *ä*. The same from whom William Penn obtained the land upon which he laid out Philadelphia. See above, Part III., Ch. II., § 10.]

sailed upon the river: that the church and congregation would increase the value of their property by its proximity to the city: and that building materials could be thus most conveniently brought together.   As regarded the glebe at Passayungh, it was to be kept as such forever.   Still, as there was not yet any convenient building thereon, the Minister was to be at liberty to reside in his own place on Society Hill, consisting of twelve and a half acres of ground which he had received from his brother-in-law, Valentine Cock, and where he was also near at hand to superintend the building of the church, and to attend to its management.   The difficulty experienced by the lower settlers in coming over the Schuylkill should be relieved by a flat-boat, which the congregation should maintain at its own expense, and to which the Church-Wardens should keep the key.   This was set forth in a document of eleven sections, and subscribed at the glebe, at Passayungh, on the 18th of September, 1698.

7. The Church Building Completed.

The building of the church was now prosecuted with the greatest zeal.   The masons and carpenters who had finished the building of Christina church came up to put their hands to Wicacoa. The work was prosecuted with such zeal that Mr. Rudman often let the best articles go out of his house in pledge for money, when money for the building did not come in as promptly as it was required.   Thus in the course of the year the church was nearly completed.   Upon the west end a cross wall was intentionally left unfinished, until it could be seen whether some bells could not be obtained from Sweden, and so a belfry be afterwards built.   The size of the church is sixty feet in length, thirty feet in breadth, and twenty feet in height.   The corners are flat upon the east side, the foundation of stone, the walls of brick, every other one glazed.   The dedication was celebrated on the first Sunday after Trinity, that is to say, the 2d of July, 1700, and was performed by Pastor Eric Björk.   The text for the occasion was 2 Sam. 7 : 29.   The name given to the church was *Gloria Dei*.[1]   The dedication was performed in the presence

---

[1] [" *God's glory.*"   The occasion of the name is not given.]
16

of a numerous assembly, a part of whom were English people from Philadelphia, on whose account the conclusion of the address was translated into English, that they might briefly understand its contents.

8. RUDMAN SUCCEEDED BY SANDEL.

Mr. Rudman had not been three years in the country before he found himself in a declining condition. He was naturally inclined to disease of the lungs, which was all the more rapidly developed by the strange climate, by his exhausting labors, and by incessant riding early and late. By letters to his friends and well-wishers in Sweden, he several times gave them to understand that he desired an assistant to preside over the congregation for some time, and then, if it so suited, to give up his place to him as his successor. Especially did he exhort his good old friend, Mr. Andrew Sandel, then studying at the University of Upsala, to come in this direction. He promised to provide him a free passage from London, so that he might the better fulfil his desire. At that time the chair of the Archbishop was vacant, and the matter was therefore brought before the Consistory at Upsala, and it was considered entirely reasonable, as Mr. Rudman's industry and zeal hitherto were so well known. But Sweden was now engaged in a severe war with Russia and Poland; His Majesty King Charles XII.[1] was abroad in Poland, and involved in a protracted war, so that it was not found advisable, at that juncture, to ask assistance from the funds of the Crown. For that reason the Consistory, after having regularly called the student Andrew Sandel, of Upsala, to take upon himself that mission, and he having agreed thereto, he did not object to making the journey at his own expense, especially as Mr. Rudman had promised him his assistance therein, thereupon wrote the following letter to the King:

" Most mighty and most gracious King: Your Royal Majesty permits the Consistory herewith most humbly to represent, how that one of the clergymen, who, some five years since, was sent

---

[1] [Charles XII. commenced his reign in 1697, when seventeen years of age, and was shot during the siege of Fredericshall, in Norway, in 1718. His reign was distinguished by its numerous wars, brilliant victories, and severe reverses.]

hence to the Swedish Colony in America, according to sundry
of his letters to his relatives and friends here at home in the
kingdom, has desired that they would prevail upon some good
and suitable person to incur the labor of travelling over to that
country to assist him in his numerous labors amid those widely
scattered congregations ; inasmuch as he alone, especially as
regards the instruction which ought to be given to the young, in the
the Catechism and doctrines of Christianity cannot so fully serve
the congregation as is necessary, as it is weakened by being so
widely scattered, and ought therefore to be more carefully sought
out and attended to.   And inasmuch as Mr. Andrew Sandel, a
student of theology, has conceived a special desire to undertake
this toilsome journey, and has also, in the examination to which
he was subjected, been found possessed of that learning which is
regarded as necessary for those who would serve such a congregation to their edification, and as he has also received good
testimonials that he has led a quiet, humble, sober, and godly
life ; therefore, as he is disposed in God's name to enter upon this
journey so soon as he is *ordained*, supposing that he can make
the same of his own means and at his own expense, and the
Consistory also think it necessary that, in the event of the sickness or death of the clergyman now there, another should be at
hand who might immediately occupy the same place, so that the
congregation might not have to suffer any inconvenience before
another clergyman could be obtained from this place ; therefore
it is the most humble petition of the Consistory, in his behalf,
that he may be provided with the passport necessary for his
journey to the place aforesaid, inasmuch as he cannot enter
upon so perilous a journey without it.   We remain, in accordance with our most humble obligations of loyalty, so long as we
shall live,

    " Most mighty and most gracious King,
        " Your Royal Majesty's most humble servants,
            " JESPERUS SVEDBERG,   ERICUS LJUNG,
            LAURENT NORMANNUS,   DANIEL DJURBERG."

Answer was made through the Royal Department of State to
the Consistory that Mr. Sandel should be ordained, and that a

passport should be given to him by the King's command. The
Ordination was performed on the 18th of July, 1701, by the
Archbishop, Dr. Eric Benzelius.[1] Upon the same day he was
provided with the Archbishop's recommendation to the congregation, and started on his journey to Stockholm, where he
further received the recommendation of the Royal Department
of State to Mr. Leyoncrona, the Swedish Minister Resident in
London, as follows:

"Most noble Resident: It has been requested of the Archbishop and the Ecclesiastical Consistory in Upsala, by letters
received from the clergymen who, over five years since, were
sent to the Swedish Colony in America, that some good and
suitable clergyman might be sent to them who would take upon
himself the labor of travelling over there to aid them in their
severe labors, so as also to be at hand in case of sickness or
death among these clergymen, and that the congregation there
may not suffer any inconvenience. And inasmuch as the student,
Àndrew Sandel, is inclined thereto, and has been ordained as a
minister, and is minded to enter upon this journey at his own
expense, going first to England, and then further, therefore this
Department, as well upon the request of the Archbishop and
the Consistory as upon that of Mr. Sandel himself, desiring a
passport for the accomplishment of his purpose, has agreed, and
doth herewith recommend Mr. Sandel to His Excellency, the
Resident, in the highest terms, so that the Resident will be
pleased, upon his arrival in London, to give him his good
advice, and inform him in what manner he may, without any
delay or hindrance, in safety and with all possible convenience,
accomplish the journey aforesaid; and also provide him with
such a passport and recommendation from England as may be
serviceable to him in the premises. We have been of the opinion
that it is not necessary for him on his journey to make himself
known as a clergyman. But we submit this to the good judgment of His Excellency the Resident, who can best decide what
may possibly befall him to the hindrance of his journey and
undertaking. Herewith we commend your Noble Excellency

---

[1] [Benzelius, after having been the Bishop of Strengnäs, was, in 1700, elected as
Archbishop, and successor of Swebelius.]

to the care of Almighty God.   At Stockholm, Aug. 15, A. D. 1701.

"In behalf of the Royal Department of State,
> "BENGT OXENSTIERNA,
> J. BERGENHIELM,
> S. ÅKERHJELM."

9. SANDEL'S DEPARTURE.

After seven weeks' travel from Stockholm, and exposure to violent and contrary winds in the Baltic, Mr. A. Sandel arrived in London on the 17th of October.   He was there received very kindly by the Resident, Mr. Leyoncrona, who always untiringly served the Swedish missionaries to America, besides faithfully forwarding their letters both to and from Sweden, as also their books and other articles, so now did he afford all the aid desired.   King William of England was at that time in Holland; but his Privy Counsellor, C. Heelge, gave the passport on the part of the King.   A letter was written to the Proprietor, William Penn, recommending Mr. Sandel to him.   Through a Swedish merchant in London, Mr. John Oriott, always eager to serve the Swedish Mission, a ship was engaged for him, which was going to Maryland; for at that time ships seldom sailed for Pennsylvania.

10. HIS ARRIVAL.

On the 13th of November, 1701, he went on board the ship *Josiah* from London, experienced very unfavorable weather, so that it was past the 7th of December before they could get clear of the English coast.   Afterwards they were at sea until the 21st of February, 1702, before they had any sight of land.   The first coast they saw was that of Virginia; after which they ran into the harbor of Herring Bay,[1] for which the ship was chartered. That was in the worst season of the year, when seafarers are not only exposed to severe storms at sea, but are also in great danger upon the coasts.   The journey was concluded in smaller vessels

---

[1] [Herring Bay is an inlet of the Chesapeake Bay, on its northwest side, in Calvert county, Maryland.]

—first to Bohemia,[1] then to Appoquimini[2] and Christina, and finally to Philadelphia, which was reached on the 18th of March, 1702.

11. LARS TOLLSTADIUS INTRUDES INTO THE CONGREGATION.

Whilst Mr. Sandel was getting ready to go to America, there was a clergyman in Stockholm by the name of Lars Tollstadius, who was anxious to follow him, even at his own expense. Such high ideas had been formed of that country in Sweden, as though no evil were to be found there, and that no account was taken of expense in getting there. This his desire he announced to the Consistory of Upsala, who were at first particularly glad to hear it. But just at the same time a bad report was spread about him, which, it was supposed, was the reason of his wishing to get out of the way, and his journey was therefore stopped, and he was declared unsuitable for the position. When he understood this, he had the boldness to go to the place without either passport, authority, or recommendation; and so hastened in the matter, that, before the real Missionary could get ready, he had already, in November, 1701, arrived in Philadelphia. There he gave himself out as the one that was to come. His language was very suspicious, especially as Mr. Rudman had already received a letter from Mr. John Thelin, in Götheborg, to the effect that Mr. Sandel had been ordained upon his request, and was to come out and take his place. Moreover, Mr. Tollstadius had no evidence wherewith to legitimate his person. But he gave out that Mr. Sandel had, indeed, been called, but afterwards could not come, and was not to be expected; also that he had forgotten his papers in New York, where he first landed, and that his effects had not yet come on. Notwithstanding all this, he was allowed to perform service in the congregation for some time, upon trial, until full certainty could be obtained. In consequence of sickness, Mr. Rudman was often detained from the duties of his office for a long time, and when he was temporarily better, the Hollanders in New York, and also the English in Pennsyl-

---

[1] [A small place, on a creek or river of the same name, on the eastern shore of Maryland.]

[2] [Appoquimini is on the Appoquimink creek, in New Castle county, Delaware.]

vania, came and urged him strongly to give them his assistance, as he had now obtained a fellow-laborer for his own people. Hence it happened that the congregation of Wicacoa was at once given into the hands of Mr. Tollstadius, as Mr. Rudman was, besides all this, intending to return to Sweden the next summer. What happened? Mr. Sandel, who was the properly called and commissioned teacher, came, and at once showed his papers. Mr. Rudman joyfully received him as his old and trusted friend, and yet not without a shock. He could not deny that he had too hastily given up his congregation to a man who had no further proof of his honesty than his own word. But thus was Tollstadius exposed and shown in his true character, and so dis-missed from the service of the congregation.

12. Rudman's Return Home Arrested.

Mr. Rudman had now received the commission and character of a Superintendent, together with leave to return home when-ever he saw fit so to do. It was also his intention not to remain here long; but as no suitable ship was at that time offered for his voyage, the Holland Lutherans in New York very pertinaciously insisted that he should become their teacher, in regard to which he was for some time in doubt. But when some others, who lived sixty miles higher up the river in Albany,[1] also called him to their assistance, he determined to spend some time there, and so delivered his farewell sermon in Wicacoa Church on the seventh Sunday after Trinity (July 19), 1702, and then departed with his family to New York. The undertaking was hard to carry out, on account of his want of health and strength. His return home with his wife and children was considered a ques-tionable step as long as no improvement appeared in his health. His family were natives of Pennsylvania, had there their inherit-ance and property, relatives and friends, which it was hard to leave and go to a strange land, to which no colony ever went hence, but from which many came hither. For these reasons he again, together with his wife and children, returned back to Phila-delphia.

---

[1] [There was a Holland Lutheran church in Albany as early as the year 1680. See the "Albany Ann. Register" for 1849. By J. Mansell, pp. 122–124.

13. Justus Falkner Ordained in Wicacoa.

In his place in New York and Albany he appointed the Rev. *Justus Falkner*. This gentleman had come over from Germany as a student,[1] had fled from his father's house in order to escape from the ministry, which his parents and friends desired him to enter. But after his arrival in America, he voluntarily assumed its duties, and so was ordained by the Pastors Rudman, Björk, and Sandel, which was done in Wicacoa Church, in the year 1703. At first he had a congregation of Germans in Falkner's Swamp, in Philadelphia county,[2] which received its name from him. Afterwards he went up to New York and Albany, where, as a faithful teacher, he ministered to many people.[3]

14. Conclusion of Mr. Rudman's Labors, and his Death.

Mr. Rudman was still thinking of a return home, and was himself strongly disposed thereto, yet he had to be regulated by circumstances within his own house. He did not allow the time to pass idly, so far as his strength permitted him. He presided over the English Church at Frankfurt, or, as it is now called, Oxford, for some years; also over the English Church in Philadelphia, during a long vacancy, both until the day of his death, which occurred on the 17th of September, 1708. On the following day he was attended to his last resting-place, in Wicacoa Church, by a long procession of English and Swedes, and was buried by his dear brother and fellow-laborer, Pastor Björk, who delivered a sermon in English upon the text, Ps. 73 : 24, which he had himself chosen for his funeral. He had lived in America eleven years, and in the world not quite forty years, and left behind him his wife, who was of the Mattson family, and two daughters, Gertrude and Anna Catharina Rudman.

---

[1] [That is, he had just finished his course in the University.]

[2] [Now Montgomery county, Pennsylvania, around New Hanover.]

[3] [This is the first ordination of a Lutheran minister in what are now the United States. He also organized the first German Lutheran congregation in Pennsylvania, preceding Dr. H. M. Mühlenberg about forty years.]

CHAPTER II.

OF MR. SANDEL'S TIME.

1. The Duties of Church-Wardens and Vestrymen.

IMMEDIATELY upon his arrival, Pastor Sandel entered upon his duties in the congregation, which took place on Palm Sunday, the 29th of March, 1702.   Thereupon he held a Parish meeting, installed new Church-Wardens and Vestrymen, and at the same time explained to each of these their duties.   Thus, 1. The Vestrymen were to have the oversight of the church and Minister's house and glebe, for their repair and preservation. 2. That each one in his turn should look after the life of the people, and if any one should conduct himself improperly, give timely notice of it to the Pastor, so that with his concurrence and advice, and according to the circumstances of the persons and their deeds, they might be brought before the Vestry, and either admonished, placed upon trial, or excluded from the congregation, etc.   The duties of the Church-Wardens were: 1. To collect and pay over the Minister's salary twice a year, viz., on the 16th of May and the 16th of November: 2. To take up the Sunday collections in the church, and the other church dues, as for marriages, the churching of women, burials, etc.: 3. To take care of the poor members of the church: 4. To keep the accounts of the church in good order, and exhibit them annually on the 1st of May: 5. To provide the pay for the Sexton, &c.

2. Inventory and Salary.

The congregation was also advised to prepare an inventory of the parsonage, which each Minister should be bound to hand over to his successor, either in kind or its value.   Also, that for three years the people should give days' work at the parsonage, for keeping it in order, in this wise, that each one should give three days' work for the first year, two for the second, and one for the third.   That the Minister's salary should be £60, and that of the Sexton £8, which might be increased afterwards, according to their ability.

3. Agreement in Regard to Times of Service.

Inasmuch as the congregation had had various changes of Ministers in a few years, it was asked, Whether their present Pastor was minded to remain with them until his death, or only for some years? It was answered, That if they would conduct themselves as obedient hearers, with whom he could promote God's glory and their own eternal interests; if his health and strength were sufficient for ministering to a parish so widely extended, and also if he could be settled, and find a support for his household, then he would never leave them until death. In any other event, he could not but return to Sweden; yet not so as to leave them until they were provided with a suitable teacher from his native land and Bishop, yet so that it might not involve them in any heavy expense. That promise was also kept. His best powers were spent in seventeen years' service at Wicacoa. He was a beloved teacher, who secured for himself both respect and affection, and is still spoken of by children and children's children.

4. Building and Repairs.

In the year 1704, the church walls seemed to be giving way under the weight of the roof and the weakness of the walls. Thereupon a sacristry was placed against the church on its north side, and a vestibule was erected on the south side over the great door, where the wall was left only half finished at its first erection. At the parsonage, a stable and barn were erected the year before, and a study for the Minister three years later.

5. Pew Regulations.

As yet there were no regulations for pews in the church. These were arranged as follows: As long as any heir is upon his father's farm, or if that is sold and the heir resides within the bounds of the congregation, he owns the right to his father's pew. Others must buy their own pews. Those who remove from the congregation, so as to be unable to attend service there, shall have no right either in the church or in the graveyard.   If any one who has removed, or his heirs, return, he shall receive either his own former pew or some other, without purchase.

6. Church Discipline.

The Pastor showed himself sufficiently zealous in church discipline.   He exhorted his congregation to place fines upon certain transgressions, which, after some years' experience, he found were to be apprehended.   If any one came to the church in a state of drunkenness, he was to pay forty shillings, and do penance publicly.   If any one made sport of God's Word or Sacraments, he should pay five pounds, and undergo church-penance.   If any one made a disturbance in the church, he was to be proceeded with according to circumstances.   For untimely singing, six shillings.   It was further observed that some, when they were reproved, admonished, or punished, gave up the church, and conceived a hatred against their Teachers.   It was, therefore, resolved that those who conducted themselves in this manner, and would not submit to a proper church discipline, should be entirely excluded from the society of the church, and not have the right to any of its privileges, neither to the graveyard, nor to burial, unless a reformation took place.   In betrothals great precaution was used, of which we have the following example:

7. Christopher Lidijn.

In the spring of the year 1714, there came to the country a man named Christopher Lidijn, who had been an ensign in the Swedish army.   He was an open-hearted fellow, and took lodgings at Moyamensing with John Stillé, courted his daughter Brita, and obtained her consent, as well as that of her parents, for marriage.   He was a fortune-hunter, and impressed them with the idea that he himself was rich, and so commenced quite merrily and pleasantly.   But after notice had been twice given, it was made known by a seaman, who was his comrade, that he had murdered his captain, and then taken to flight; that he had no money, but was practising rascalities and thievery.   For these reasons the engagement was broken off, and thereupon a divorce was issued, with the consent of both parties, according to Chap. 16, § 2, of the Church Law.

8. Order of Divine Service.

Divine service was performed in the following order: On Sundays there were two sermons delivered. The first[1] was between the first and second ringing of the bells, when a morning hymn was sung, or "*O God vi lofve tig*" ("*We praise Thee, O God*"), etc. Then a sermon was preached upon a portion of the Catechism, and the service was ended with a prayer and a hymn. The second bell was then rung for the second sermon,[2] when the Teacher went through the aisles and repeated his sermon, and also examined the people upon what had been said before. This was done in summer-time. In winter, when the days were short and the congregation could not come together so generally, in the morning service one chapter of the Old and one of the New Testament was read and explained. High Mass[2] was performed according to the Church Ordinance. The catechization was at first performed in the church; but afterwards, for greater convenience, in private houses, for which purpose the congregation was divided into certain sections.[3] The Parish was of such wide extent that the old and infirm could not come very regularly to church, and the preacher had therefore at times to visit his hearers and preach in their houses; as also sometimes, during the winter, in Penipeiok (Pennypack); occasionally, during the year, in Amasland and Kalkonhook, and in those places especially on the fourth days of holy days; at Manathanim two or three times a year, and once at Egg Harbor. That part of the Parish which was on the east side of the river, and which fell off through the machinations of Mr. Tollstadius, was still at times visited by Mr. Sandel at their request.

---

[1] [Called below Ottesången, which might be translated "*Matins*."]

[2] [Called "*Högmässan*," or "High Mass;" corresponding to the principal morning service in the Episcopal Church.]

[3] ["Rotar," which we have translated "*Sections*," is the established usage of Sweden, and is thus explained by Wiggers in his "Kirchliche Statistik," Vol. II., p. 410: "The whole congregation is examined by the preacher on the contents of the sermon. Annually, also, at appointed times, house examinations take place, in which the clergyman has an opportunity of investigating the moral and spiritual condition of each individual member of his church, and thus to be brought into a close personal relation to him. With this view the congregation is divided into sections (*rotar*), each of which consists of about one hundred persons, young and old."]

9. Arvid Hernbom, School-Master.

A young man from the Gymnasium at Skara, named Arvid Hernbom, who first went out with Mr. Anders Silvius, Chaplain to the Embassy with Consul de Beche at Lisbon, came to the country, at his own prompting, in the year 1713, but provided with good testimonials as to his learning and ability. He was employed as a school-master in that congregation for some years. When he seemed to be qualified for the ministerial office, he was, upon recommendation of the Pastor, invested with license to preach by Bishop Svedberg. In the year 1714, three years afterwards, upon Mr. Sandel's recall home, there also came an order from the Bishop for him, as Provost for the time being, to ordain Arvid Hernbom to the priesthood, so that he might serve the congregation after his departure until another appointment was made. But the man excused himself from the office. The other clergymen having examined him did not think that he would answer for the position, and the Provost remained with his congregation until the arrival of his successor.

10. The English Congregation in Philadelphia holds its Service in Wicacoa.

The exhortation which the Bishop, Dr. Svedberg, gave to his Presbyters in America, to hold cordial intercourse with the English clergy, was especially heeded at that time. The confidence shown by the English missionaries in return was marked by the following example, which also shows that the English Church is more disposed to affiliate with the Lutheran than with the Scotch or Presbyterian Church. In the year 1710 the English Established Church in Philadelphia was enlarged, and then its Minister and people requested permission to hold their services in the meantime in Wicacoa, which was granted. The English Presbyterians had offered them their meeting-house, but they declined it. The Swedish service was closed at 11 o'clock in the morning, and after that the English service was begun, during which a Swedish hymn was sung as a stronger token of unity. This was done for three Sundays in succession.

11. Preaching at the State-House.

The same mutual confidence continued afterwards. In the year 1715 the English Minister, Francis Phillips, had made unguarded and gross charges against Mr. Trent's wife and Mr. Moore's daughter, although they were of the most respectable families in his congregation. His charges were not proved, and he was therefore thrown into prison. Then the English again requested Provost Sandel to allow them to hold their services in Wicacoa. They would not go to the Presbyterian house. The Governor gave his approval of this. The English clergy requested it, and the Swedes consented. English service was again held after the Swedish, and Provost Sandel preached for them, except when some English Ministers occasionally came in from the country to his assistance. But as Mr. Phillips also had some followers, and various inconveniences resulted, the holding of this service in the Swedish church was discontinued at the end of two months. In recognition of this kindness, the English made a present of altar linen to the Wicacoa Church, as this article had some time before been stolen from that church. Their services were afterwards held at the Provincial Hall[1] in Philadelphia, where Provost Sandel preached for them alternately with the English clergy. Finally came an order from the Bishop of London excluding the said Mr. Phillips from the Church, and forbidding him to preach any more within the Province. Low pasquinades, in which no one was spared, were put forth by both parties.

12. The Consecration of Oxford Church.

When any English church was consecrated, the Swedish Ministers were invited thereto. But, according to English custom, that was nothing more than a church opening, inasmuch as they hold that no one but a Bishop can consecrate a church. In the year 1713 both Björk and Sandel were on that errand at Oxford Church, eight miles from Philadelphia, in company with the English clergy. No other ceremonies than such as are customary were used on the occasion, except that, in place of a chapter of the Old Testament, Solomon's prayer was used. The sermons were suitable to the occasion, and, after preaching, some

---

[1] This venerable building was in Market Street at Second, and the courts sat there.

suitable prayers were read. The church was named the "Church of the Holy Trinity."

13. THE LAYING OF A CORNER-STONE.

But something peculiar is to be seen among the English at the laying of the foundation of a church. On the 9th of May, 1715, Pastor Sandel was invited to attend the laying of the foundation of Radnor Church, sixteen miles from Philadelphia. First, a service with preaching was held in a private house; then they went in procession to the place where the church was to be built. There a prayer was made; after which each one of the clergymen laid a stone according to the direction of the master mason.

14. THE SUPPORT OF THE CLERGY.

The support of the clergyman at that time came from subscriptions, marriages, burials, etc., upon which every year there was a considerable amount standing back. But it was never heard of that any misunderstanding arose between him and his hearers on this account. They lived together as in a golden age. The glebe at Passayungh was rented for the benefit of the Minister. The house thereon was consumed by fire on the 7th of August, 1717, which happened from the careless handling of fire. Thereupon another house was immediately erected at the expense of the congregation; but no better than was required for a peasant. By prudent housekeeping and a fortunate marriage, the Pastor had come into the possession of a house of his own at the Schuylkill ferry, in a fine situation, at the present time worth several thousand rix-dollars.

15. PROVOST SANDEL RECALLED TO SWEDEN.

In the year 1718 Provost Sandel received his recall home, together with the investiture of the Pastorate of Hedmora, from King Charles XII, dated at Lund, in Skåne, on the 11th of November, 1717. The church was to be entered upon immediately, as there was no "year of grace"[1] connected with it. But the

---

[1] [The church remaining vacant for a year after the death of its incumbent, and the salary going to his widow.]

Provost could not get ready so soon with his family. Meanwhile he attended to his congregation with the same zeal as ever, and, as regarded the welfare of the church in this his last year, he did more than ever before.

16. PURCHASE OF LAND FOR WICACOA CHURCH.

Some of Swensson's heirs had determined to sell the land which lies upon both sides of the church. To prevent strangers from coming into it, and so, either by building too near it or by a ship-yard on the strand, endangering it, it was thought necessary to buy a piece of land all around it for the congregation. The first difficulty in the matter was to induce all the members of the congregation to agree to this; next, to agree with Miss Märta, to whose share it belonged; further, to get men learned in the law to show whether she had, or had not, the right to sell; still further, to find good men to go security for a minor heiress, who seemed to have no share in the matter, that she would not object to the sale when she came to be of age; and finally, to collect the money for this purpose from among the congregation, to survey the land, and get the proper writings and a deed for it. Then came other branches of the family asserting their right to the same ground, but unable to prove any such right. When, now, they had got so far that the deed of purchase was to be signed, the girl Märta refused to sell as much as had at first been promised, and had not, in some way, as much as was included in the deed, and would not receive payment in three terms, as was at first agreed. Then all the writings had to be changed (they were all done on parchment), and payment had to be made at once in full. Other papers of the same kind were prepared instead of the first; but the girl's securities were often sick, and so the affair was protracted for a long time. Finally, when they were all to come together on the same day to terminate the affair, Miss Märta was not to be found, because others were enticing her to deal with them. Thereupon she was hunted up and reproved for such trifling, and finally consented to sign the deed of purchase. When it came to the signing of the deed for the land, which she also had to do, difficulty was again made about the times of payment. The conclusion was that twelve

and a half acres were sold for ninety pounds — half the payment
down, the other half payable within six months afterwards. That
is the ground by which the church of Wicacoa is now chiefly supported. And it is thus seen with what toil and labor the good
Provost Sandel completed the business by means of which the
church of Wicacoa is now happily endowed, but from which he
himself did not expect the slightest advantage.

17. The Voyage Home.

On the 7th of May, 1719, the last Parish meeting was held,
where, among other things, it was decided that the parsonage at
Passayungh should have its roof, windows, and walls repaired
and put in order for the coming successor of the late Rector.
At the same time the church accounts for the whole of Provost
Sandel's time were reviewed and approved. It was further asked,
What the Parish proposed to do with the inventory which had
been delivered to the Provost upon his arrival in the country?
Sixty pounds had in the first instance been promised as his
annual salary; but in the end not more than fifty pounds were
realized by him.   Then concessions were made upon both sides,
and the inventory was given as an offset to the unpaid salary.
Finally, arrangements were made for the continuance of Divine
service until some regular Pastor should come into the place.
The Pastors Hesselius and Lidenius agreed to visit the congregation alternately once a month to administer the Lord's Supper,
christen children, and visit the sick.   On the other Sundays Mr.
Arvid Hernbom was to preach ; and twenty-five pounds a year
were promised him for his trouble, or proportionately if a regular
clergyman should come sooner.   Provost Sandel took his leave
on the 25th of June, 1719, and set out on his voyage homeward,
together with his beloved wife, Maria Dahlbo, and his children,
Magdalena and Peter, by whom an honorable Minister's household was afterwards formed in the town of Hedemora.[1]

---

[1] [Hedemora is a town of Sweden Proper, on the river Dahl, in the old province
of Dalecarlia, northwest of Stockholm.]

17

CHAPTER III.

OF LIDMAN'S TIME.

1. MR. LIDMAN'S CALL AND SENDING.

HIS Royal Majesty, King Charles XII., had, by a Royal Commission, given at Lund, in Skåne, on the 23d of December, 1717, appointed the Rev. Samuel Hesselius of Dalecarlia to be a regular Minister in Pennsylvania, in some of the Swedish congregations there; and he was called by the Bishop, Dr. Svedberg, as the successor of the Rev. Provost Andrew Sandel in Wicacoa congregation, and thereupon ordained in the Cathedral of Skara on the 27th of April, 1718. At this time the coinage[1] in Sweden was greatly disordered, so that it was very difficult to obtain a bill of exchange suitable for travelling expenses. His departure was on this account delayed for over a year. And as it was considered necessary that the congregation should be supplied with an Assistant Minister who could aid in all kinds of Parish work, so also was Mr. Jonas Lidman of West Gothland[2] to accept of a call to the same. But inasmuch as Mr. Lidman was said to be further advanced in service, although younger in years, the order was so far changed that he, who was called later, should be appointed as the regular Pastor, but Mr. Samuel Hesselius, who was at first named as regular Pastor, should become the Assistant Minister; yet with the assurance that he should soon be promoted to the place of his brother, the Provost And. Hesselius, in the congregation at Christina, as he was to be recalled home. On this account Mr. J. Lidman, in

---

[1] Financial embarrassment in Sweden was relieved for a time by a scheme proposed by Baron Görtz, on whose recommendation copper coins stamped "1 Daller, S. M," (one dollar, silver mint,) were struck during a period of five years, and by order of the King were current at the rate designated. Twelve varieties of this coin, all of which are in Mr. Mickley's cabinet, were issued between the years 1715 to 1719, both inclusive. For thus assisting his unfortunate master, Charles XII., Baron Görtz, immediately on that monarch's death, was arrested on the charge of corrupting the currency, and was beheaded. — M. and W.

[2] [Gothland is the southeastern part of Sweden.]

his commission from Queen Ulrica Eleanora,[1] was appointed as Preacher in some of the congregations in Pennsylvania, but afterwards placed by Bishop Svedberg's Letter of Ordination as the Minister in Wicacoa congregation. He was the first who brought a wife with him from Sweden to this country.

2. INSTALLATION IN WICACOA.

Before the year 1719 had passed, the congregation saw its new Pastor. The installation was performed on the first Sunday in Advent by the Provost, Mr. And. Hesselius, who was then there, and in his sermon, in the first place, exhorted the people to true godliness and Christian thankfulness for the spiritual care bestowed upon them. After that was read the letter of Queen Ulrica Eleanora to the congregations at large, which, upon her accession to the government, at the request of the Bishop, Dr. Svedberg, was sent at the same time, as follows: [2]

"ULRICA ELEANORA, Queen of the Swedes, the Goths, and the Wends.

"Our favor and gracious benignity, and the blessing of God Almighty be with you. Beloved, and our dear Swedish people dwelling in Pennsylvania, we have with sincere pleasure heard both of your steadfastness in your faith and your godly Christianity, as well as of your loyalty and love towards us and your fatherland. We are therefore moved to give you graciously to understand, through this our letter, that almost from the very beginning of our reign we have had you in gracious remembrance, and have also determined, according to the old custom, to promote and sustain your prosperity and happiness. In the meantime we have commanded Bishop Svedberg again to present you with some devotional books through two clergymen, whom, upon our gracious command, he will send thither to minister to you for your Christian edification. And we herewith

---

[1] [Ulrica Eleanor, sister of Charles XII., succeeded him upon his death in 1718, and in 1720 procured the election as King of Sweden of her husband, Frederic, Prince of Hesse-Cassel. She was a most amiable and exemplary Sovereign.]

[2] [It is almost impossible to reproduce in a translation the peculiar quaintness of this curious old letter. I have somewhat curtailed its prolixity, but otherwise given it as literally as I thought would be intelligible.]

graciously commend you to the grace of Almighty God.   Given
at Stockholm, on the 15th of April, 1719.

"ULRICA ELEANORA.
"D. HÖPKEN."

Thereupon followed King Charles XII.'s Commission to Mr.
Hesselius, Her Majesty the Queen's Commission for Mr. Lid-
man, Bishop Svedberg's letter to the Bishop of London, D.
Robinson, and the Society,[1] his general letter to his Swedish
congregations in America, and finally the special one to the
Wicacoa congregation.

3. SAM. HESSELIUS, PASTOR EXTRAORDINARY.

Wicacoa had now received two Pastors, one ordinary and the
other extraordinary, and was glad to have them both.   But when
the question was asked, How both were to be supported? various
difficulties arose.   As a beginning, the plan was adopted that Mr.
Sam. Hesselius should preach in Kalkonhook and Nitshamene,
places distant two or three Swedish miles from Wicacoa.   That
was done only for a few months; for when it was found that these
congregations would be thus separated from Wicacoa, the members themselves brought the matter before the Provost, and
desired a change.   Then the plan was adopted, that, as Kalkonhook lay nearer to the church, the people there might be served
by the Pastor Ordinary.   But Nitshamene[2] and Manathanim,[3]
which were still farther distant, were more in need of that assist-

---

[1] [The Society for the Propagation of the Gospel in Foreign Parts.]

[2] [Nitshamene, Neshaminy, is on a stream of the same name in Bucks co., twenty
miles from Philadelphia.]

[3] Manathanim was the name applied to the region, as is most probable, between
the Schuylkill river and Manatawny creek, which latter, rising in Berks county, runs
through the northwest corner of Montgomery county and falls into the former just
above Pottstown.   Owing to the course of these streams this region is not of great
width, and while occupied by the scattered farmers seems to have borne the name
of the stream, Manatawny.   There is reason to suppose that the place where the
church building was situated came to be called Molatton, and that it was where
Douglassville now is.   In 1760-2 George Douglass was one of the Vestry.   Letters
from and concerning the church at Molatton are to be found in that treasure-house
of inestimable value, "The Historical Collections Relating to the American Colonial
Church," by Wm. Stevens Perry.   Vol. II., Pennsylvania, pp. 289, 345-47, 383, 388,
and 389. — T. W.

ance. At the Parish meeting on Laetare [1] Sunday, 1720, many attendants at Manathanim were present, who represented that they had always held to Wicacoa congregation, and had contributed their share to the building of the church and for the support of the Minister and church, and that they now, therefore, as well in regard to that their right, as to their destitute condition, with tears besought Mr. Samuel Hesselius to dwell among them, and exercise there his office for their spiritual edification. Thereupon he removed up to them, and preached alternately at Nitshamene. The following year he complained that his hearers were few, and unable to support him, and so Matzong was also given into his charge.

4. GOOD ORDER CAREFULLY PRESERVED.

Pastor Lidman lived with his congregation in great amity and love. His labors, as well within his church as out among his people, secured him universal esteem. But he had the advantage of coming to a congregation where good discipline was established. Yet his reputation was well deserved, as he upheld all the regulations carefully, and wherever anything got out of order, it was restored as soon as possible. Among other things, and one of the first that occupied his attention, was how the children's school should be kept up, as Arvid Hernbom, who had hitherto kept it, had become weary, and given it up entirely. Nothing else could be done but to exhort the parents themselves to teach their children, and the older ones those that were younger.

5. THE IMPROVEMENT OF THE CHURCH.

In his time the church was improved, as follows:

The pulpit, doors, windows, dormer-windows, and gates were painted. The roof which was decayed on the south side was replaced with cedar shingles. The doors of the vestibule had new frames and sills put in them. The windows, especially that at the altar, and the dormer-windows upon the north side, were repaired. Also, the gable on the west side, which had sprung out, was put in better shape.

---

[1] Laetare Sunday is the third Sunday before Easter. In 1720 it fell on the 27th of March.

6. Improvements in Pew Arrangements, and the Fencing of the Graveyard.

About that time many had deceased in the congregation, who had also been the oldest people at the building of the church, and had held the front pews in the church, whereby this space became vacant. On the other hand, the young who had seats in the church became more numerous, and thronged forward, whereby disorder was created, even during service. Therefore, those who were then the oldest sought out and moved up into the foremost pews. Another disorder also crept in, namely, that of burying their dead upon the graves of others, which had arisen from a new staking out of various lots in the graveyard. The fencing of the church-yard was set for a certain time in the year; then the fencing was divided in this way: The share of Passayungh was on the east side; that of Nitshamene on the north side; Cobb's Kill and Amasland on the west side; Matzong[1] on the south side. Those who did not live just within these districts should keep up the fence with either the one or the other of these.

7. The Minister's Salary.

The Minister's salary was raised by subscriptions within the Parish, as had been customary. Upon his accession, it was asked, whether the congregation was in favor of making the subscription in the form of a note upon which the Church-Wardens could seek judgment from a civil magistrate, and compel them faithfully to pay that which they had promised. This was now usual in Christina and Racoon congregations, and was found very necessary. But the congregation would not agree to this, but promised to keep its word of its own free will. But although the people paid honestly at the time, yet whether the Minister's contentment with his portion was to blame for it or not, still there was never heard from him any complaint of parsimony, or that his just dues were withheld.

8. The Church Glebe.

The parsonage at Passayungh was not so far restored after its burning as to be habitable when Mr. Lidman came into the

---

[1] Matson's Ford is on the Schuylkill, where the bridge at Conshohocken crosses.

country. He therefore bought for himself a house of his own, with a little ground belonging to it, at Moyamensing, and lived there during his time. To assist him, the congregation lent him £30, the income from the land which had been sold in Provost Sandel's time at Polskungs Hook.[1] He offered security[2] for his debt, but no one cared about it. The interest was applied to his salary, and there was no doubt about the capital. But he did not so secure himself as to neglect his successors. He often reminded the congregation to put the house upon the church glebe in better order, and, to promote the work, he advanced money upon the wall and carpenters' work, after it had long stood only roofed in. Afterwards the glebe was rented. A well was required for the house. A great deal of labor and money was expended upon this, but in vain. The soil was so loose that they tried in three different places by digging and walling, but the work would not stand.

9. The Improvement of the Church Land.

To pay for the land purchased at Wicacoa, money was collected in the congregation, and a good deed was secured for it. But in order that this, as well as the farm-land at Passayungh, might be made use of, they were cleared and fenced in for pasture, for they were covered with timber, which would not so well pay for itself, and was not so serviceable near the city. The land at Passa-yungh was first cleared and divided into two portions. About seventy good trees were reserved on it for occasional use. Afterwards these pieces of land were hired out to the people of the city for pasturage for cattle. The timber was sold to great advantage for the benefit of the congregation. Although that was a prudent and careful economy, yet, in later times, ungrateful people have undertaken to say that the woodland of the Parish was destroyed, and the timber sold for the benefit of the clergy-man.

10. His Voyage Home.

After the lapse of nine years came Bishop Svedberg's letter of recall for Mr. Lidman. It was dated at Brunsbo, January 5,

---

[1] [This place is not found either on the map of Campanius, or on that of Björck.]
[2] [Orig., " *Caution.*"]

1728; also His Majesty's gracious assent to the same, together with the assurance of suitable preferment at home. This was delayed so long upon the way, as also the answer thereto, that the Bishop renewed this recall on two different occasions, namely, on the 29th of May, 1729, and on the 22d of November of the same year. The administration of the property of the congregation had been entrusted to him along with the Vestry, and the deeds for the Parish lands were in his hands, of which, at his departure, he delivered up no less than *nine* separate ones of grounds belonging to Wicacoa and Passayungh, as also other documents therewith connected. His debt he discharged in full through Lars Bure, a Vestryman of the congregation, who went his security. Then, when he had delivered over the care of his congregation to Mr. John Eneberg, who was then preaching for the Germans,[1] and had no particular charge, and had also been honored with a most excellent testimony by his beloved congregation, he returned home to his native land on the 14th of November, 1730. His dear wife, Anna Jern, who was his companion in his voyages both to and from the country, blessed his marriage[2] with four children born in America — Margaretta, Sarah, Maria, and Jonas; and on their return to Sweden their married life was continued at the pastorate of Ekesjö in the Diocese of Linköping.

* * *

CHAPTER IV.

OF MR. FALK'S TIME.

1. HIS COMMISSION.

IT was something singular that Mr. Lidman's return home should be so hastened without any other special appointment of a successor. For it was not before two years afterwards that Mr. Gabriel Falk of West Gothland came to his congregation.

---

[1] [Probably in Philadelphia and other points around. This was some two years before the letter of the German Lutherans to Dr. Ziegenhagen, in London, and ten years before the arrival of Dr. H. M. Mühlenberg.]

[2] [In the original, "*saw his marriage blessed with four*," etc.]

He was the last Swedish Minister whom Bishop Svedberg sent to America. He was ordained by the Bishop in the Skara Cathedral, provided with the Royal Commission of King Frederick I.;[1] also with a letter to the Bishop of London and the Society for the Propagation of the Gospel;[2] and also with a letter to the congregation of Wicacoa. The high opinion the Bishop had of this man, not less than the affection which he bore for the people whom he was to serve, can be understood from his letter of recommendation, in which he tells of his sending, and desires that they would receive him as an angel of the Lord of Hosts. The voyage was prosperous until they reached Cape Inlopen, or the entrance of the Delaware; but there they lost their ship. The passengers saved their lives with difficulty, and Mr. Falk and his servant lost everything but their lives.

2. His Arrival.

He was received with great kindness by all on the first Sunday after the Epiphany, which was the 7th of January, 1733. Mr. John Eneberg was then ministering to the congregation, and had been receiving full salary as Pastor for two years past; but room was not only immediately made for Mr. Falk, but he was supplied with clothes and other necessaries, so that he was well provided for, in accordance with the recommendation sent with him by the Bishop. His ministerial gifts were edifying; his manner zealous. The good discipline which had been already introduced he preserved with strictness, and immediately upon his arrival began to visit the people in their houses for the purposes of catechization.

3. The Building of a Parsonage.

The congregation, which was greatly attached to its Teacher, immediately thought of building him a new house. This was placed upon the banks of the river on the Wicacoa land. The house was built of brick, two stories high, and two rooms upon each floor, with a convenient kitchen and garret besides. In

---

[1] [Frederick I. reigned from 1720 to 1751.]

[2] [The "Society for the Propagation of the Gospel in Foreign Parts" was organized in 1647–1667.]

regard to its arrangement, work, and admirable situation, it is an excellent house.

4. PETER JONSSON'S TROUBLE THEREWITH.

Peter Jonsson, a well-to-do farmer, and a Vestryman of the Parish, was for many years much honored by the congregation. A more honorable Swede never set his foot in America. None of his countrymen, and especially no stranger, ever made known his wants to him in vain. That man undertook the building of the Minister's house, and in a short time had it completed. But the money for the building was not so soon supplied by the congregation, and he had therefore to make the expenditures out of his own means. He had patience with this for a long time, and many accounts were still unpaid. Those who had furnished the materials, or done the work, applied to him for their pay. He urged the people to have patience, but was threatened with arrest. Finally, he voluntarily allowed himself to be taken to prison, and found this to be his best plan, for never did the laggards in the congregation pay more promptly what they had promised than when they did it to deliver Peter Jonsson, who was sitting in prison for the parsonage.

5. FALK'S LAWSUIT.

Pastor Falk's good time continued only for a few months before a lamentable change took place. One of the elders of the congregation, also a Vestryman, an honorable and wealthy man fell under his suspicion of having had incestuous intercourse with his own daughter. As this report was widely spread, Mr. Falk was called upon to prove an assertion that no one but himself believed. The man (Jacob Bengtson) would have very properly preferred to keep silence, if Mr. Falk had not incessantly pressed the matter. The congregation was deeply grieved thereby, and all right-thinking people were greatly scandalized. For these reasons the matter was taken to the court-house. Mr. Falk pretended that as a Minister he was the best judge in the matter; that the other Ministers were aware of the fact, but were unwilling to come out with the truth, and so forth. But he could not prove his charge, and he was therefore condemned to pay five hundred pounds damages, and was driven from Wicacoa.

6. THE DESTITUTION OF THE CONGREGATION.

Our Swedish congregations were now in a declining condition, and seemed not far from their final dissolution. Their faithful Bishop, Dr. Svedberg, had arrived at extreme old age; his vital energies were prostrated; he was disturbed by many troubles from the same source, and sad from an unfortunate mission. Neither were those whom it most concerned sufficiently careful in giving their Bishop the requisite information in regard to the congregation's present misfortune, so that all correspondence with Sweden was, for a time, broken off. No Provost was appointed for the mission, and thus it happened that there was not the same co-operation as formerly. No meetings of the clergy were held for mutual edification. There was no prudent promptness in promoting the good and in preventing and stemming the evil.

CHAPTER V.

OF MR. DYLANDER'S TIME.

1. APPLICATION TO BOTH THE KING AND THE BISHOP.

WHEN the church of Wicacoa, towards the end of the year 1733, thus unfortunately lost its spiritual watchman, its members did, indeed, in the beginning of the following year, send over to King Frederick I. their humble petition that they might be again supplied with a teacher. But the letter miscarried, and never reached its destination. When their hope was thus disappointed, many were discouraged, and either resorted to the English congregation, or wandered around like straying sheep that had no shepherd. Some, however, were more free in expressing their mind, renewed their petition to the King of Sweden, and, at the same time, urged the then Archbishop, Dr. John Steuchius,[1] to take upon himself the superintendence of the Swedish American Church in the place of Bishop Svedberg, who had now departed this life. This was done on the 26th of June, 1736. This letter, which did not arrive until

---

[1] [Succeeded his brother, Mathias Steuchius, as Archbishop of Sweden in 1730, and died in 1742.]

the beginning of the next year, His Majesty saw fit, on the 1st of March, 1737, to communicate to His Grace the Archbishop, and at the same time to direct him to take the proper care of said congregations. In consequence of this, Mr. John Dylander, who was then Adjunct in the church of Börstil, was called as Pastor to Wicacoa, and at the same time provided with the Royal Commission bearing the date of May 17, 1737, which, with other matters, is set forth in the following letter:

" To the Christian and honorable members of the Evangelical Swedish Church in Philadelphia, we herewith send grace and peace from God our Father, and the Lord Jesus Christ!

"Inasmuch as the Christian and honorable members of the congregation have requested, not only by their humble petition of the 29th of June to His Royal Majesty, that some one might be appointed, in the place of the departed Bishop, Dr. Jesper Svedberg, to take charge of the interests of said congregation, as well in regard to the appointment of suitable teachers, as also in other matters pertaining to its interests; but have also, both in the same letter, and in others to me, (John Steuchius,) been pleased to express their confidence in me, which is acknowledged by me with all thankfulness and respect; therefore, upon His Majesty's most gracious letter to me of the 21st of March of the current year, wherein He was graciously pleased to demand my humble opinion and advice in regard to the matter aforesaid, after having duly consulted with the Ecclesiastical Consistory, I have submitted it to His Majesty's most gracious pleasure and approbation, that under God's gracious and almighty aid and assistance, so far as in me lies, and according to the extent of my ability, I will honestly serve the Christian and honorable congregations which His Royal Majesty has been graciously pleased to commend to my care; also most humbly suggesting that it might please his Royal Majesty graciously to give to the Ecclesiastical Consistory here in Upsala a share in the management of this work in behalf of those congregations, so that in the event of death taking place, when it shall please the Most High to call me hence, the congregation may not, as is now lamentably the case, be destitute of teachers who watch for their souls, but may, even during vacancies, and on the decease of the

Archbishop, enjoy the support, care, and aid of the Consistory, so far as may be necessary and desirable. And as His Royal Majesty, in His most gracious letter of the 4th of April next following, did graciously entrust both to me and to the Ecclesiastical Consistory, in the manner just stated, the supervision of said congregations; therefore the Consistory has sought out and called to the filling of the vacancy now existing in the ministerial office in Philadelphia, a Clergyman of this Diocese, the Reverend John Dylander, who has been found qualified for the discharge of the duties of the aforesaid office, as well by his learning as by his conduct, and is also willing, under God's gracious guidance, to enter upon this journey, which he has also humbly announced and proposed to His Royal Majesty, in his letter of the 18th of May last. And as His Majesty has, by his Commission of the 27th of May last, graciously appointed the said John Dylander as the Pastor of this Christian and worthy congregation, to which end Mr. Dylander is now, in the name of the Lord, entering upon his journey, the Consistory has herewith not only recommended him to the favor and kindness of the members of said congregation when he arrives, under the firm hope that, by God's gracious aid and assistance, he will, as becomes an upright clergyman and Pastor, duly and with all zeal and fidelity seek to promote the honor of God's most holy name, together with the edification and welfare of His most dearly bought flock; but they also make known that the Christian and worthy congregation may, whenever circumstances call for it, present their desires in writing to this our Ecclesiastical Consistory, which will then to the extent of its ability give them its assistance in all honesty. Finally, the Consistory prays for God's merciful favor and blessing upon the Christian and worthy congregation, and will at all times include the congregation in its prayers to God, that He may bestow upon it all blessings, both spiritual and temporal, remaining ever and unchangeably,

"For all true and willing service,

"Your most obedient, etc.,

"JOHANNES STEUCHIUS.

"OLOF CELSIUS, ER. M. MELANDER, AND. WINBOM, JOHAN WIMAN.

"UPSALA, June 8, 1737."

2. DYLANDER'S DEPARTURE.

He took his departure from Stockholm on the 13th of July, and arrived in Philadelphia on the 2d of November of the same year. The voyage was quick, and did not occupy more than five weeks from Stockholm to London, and seven weeks from London to Philadelphia. His companion was John Malander, of Rosland, a student of theology. He took his passage as a servant, and travelled at Mr. Dylander's expense. He afterwards became a school-master, and assisted in preaching when necessary.

3. HIS ARRIVAL.

Pastor Dylander entered upon his duties in the church on the 6th of November, 1737, that being the 22d Sunday after Trinity, when he, for the first time, preached before a very numerous congregation. The Rev. Peter Tranberg was present, and read His Majesty's Commission, together with the letter of the Venerable Consistory of Upsala to the church. Now there seemed to be a new joy among the people. The new Teacher seemed to be entirely unlike his predecessor, not only in regard to his good gifts for his office, but also in regard to the pleasant manner of his intercourse with his people, which secured for him not only love and respect within the congregation, but also the friendship of all who knew him.

4. THE RENEWAL OF GOOD ORDER.

The good regulations which, it may well be said, lay dormant for seven years, were now again re-established. Especially were the Church-Wardens reminded of their duty ; that each one in his turn was to see to it that the congregation should practise their Christian duties, lead an honorable and Christian life, and keep their children in the same. If any intentional violation of this was noticed, it should be proceeded against according to the grades of warning in the church laws, and, in defect of improvement, such a person should be expelled. The Church-Wardens were to attend to the income and expenditures of the church, and to repairs of the same, as also to the parsonage ; they were also to give an annual account of their expenditures to the

Vestry. The Trustees of the congregation were two, and the deeds for the church lands were made out in their names. They had these documents in their care, but copies of them were entered into a book which was kept with one of them. The lands of the church were at that time found to cover thirteen and a half acres.

5. THE INJURY OF VACANCIES.

One man was found slow in exhibiting the original deed for the land, and thus drew upon himself a grave suspicion of wishing to appropriate the church's land to himself. However that was, the writings were at last produced; but the church-book, which contained the baptisms and burials from Mr. Rudman's time, and likewise in the hands of the same man, has never since been produced, so that great inconvenience was occasioned thereby in after times, especially to old people who wished to know their age.

6. ENJOYED UNIVERSAL LOVE.

The congregation, which was thoroughly pleased with its teacher, was pretty well brought together at the public service. Yet its numbers were greatly reduced as compared with former times, both in consequence of the removal of many families to more remote parts of the country, and from the disturbance in Falk's time. However, the part that still remained were united in their church. At that time the Germans were not supplied with any Minister, although they were pressing into the country in great numbers. So, as Mr. Dylander was well versed in their language, he was able to comply with their request that he would preach for them. He also frequently supplied those who resided in Lancaster with Divine service. He did the same in German-town, where he consecrated a stone church built by the Germans in the year 1730. No less satisfaction was found by the English in their intercourse with that Teacher. He sometimes preached for them, also, to their entire satisfaction, in their State Church.[1] The people now resorted so greatly to this Swedish Minister that the English thought that he was interfering with them, especially as the greatest number of marriages were celebrated in Wicacoa,

---

[1] [That is to say, the Church of England in the colonies.]

from which a most important part of a Minister's income is derived in that country. The Minister of the English Church made complaint to the Governor about this matter, but received no other answer than that he believed that the Minister who was most resorted to by the people, made himself most deserving of it ; for the rest, his power did not extend so far as to regulate the official proceedings of Ministers. Every one had the liberty of employing such a Minister as he pleased. No one can deny to Mr. Dylander the honor which he gained for himself in his ministerial office, in that for more than a year he held morning service (at eight o'clock) in German, High Mass in Swedish, and Vespers in English, in the church at Wicacoa.

7. Improvement of the Church.

During the long vacancies, the church had become quite ruinous in its roof, windows, and doors. The members of the congregation were, indeed, willing to aid by their contributions in making repairs ; but when the expenses amounted to more than was expected, and so the church fell into debt, there was no other plan than to exhort them to a new contribution, to which they also agreed quite willingly, and most of them contributed two pounds apiece. A small, new, and fine organ was put up in the church at the same time.

8. Proposition for a Church at Kalkonhook.

On the 27th of May, 1738, at a Parish meeting then held, the people belonging to the congregation on the west side of the Schuylkill desired that they might be furnished with some assistance in building a church for themselves at Kalkonhook,[1] because the way to church over the ferry was expensive for their children, long and inconvenient to travel in autumn and winter, as well as for funerals in the heats of summer. If their Minister would supply them with public service once a month, they would con-

---

[1] [Kalkonhuken is the name given on Björck's map to what is now called Darby creek, and the name is probably still retained in what is now Hook creek. Ferris, in his map (Hist. of Orig. Settlements), calls it "Karaking, or Water Mill creek," now "Cobb's creek." As Tinicum, Gov. Printz's seat, was at the mouth of this creek, there was of course a large Swedish population in that region.]

tinue to pay their share for the support and repairs of Wicacoa Church. This was agreed to by the others; but as Wicacoa Church was then undergoing repairs, no new building could be undertaken just at that time. It is uncertain whether their Pastor's speedy death, or the poverty of the people afterwards, frustrated the plan. And however much is still talked about a church edifice in that place, which it is now thought would be most conveniently placed in Darby, it is still quite probable that it will never be brought about, as well from the clashing between the Swedes and the English as from the astonishing indifference which there is in the country to true godliness; not to say that such an undertaking would draw after it an entire separation of that part of the congregation from its mother church — Wicacoa.

9. THE MINISTER'S SALARY.

The Minister's salary was still raised by voluntary subscriptions in the congregation. And although the number of attendants was greatly reduced, yet those who remained showed themselves so much the more honorable towards their Teacher, that no misunderstanding ever arose on that account. When he arrived, the parsonage was not yet completed; but in a short time it was put into a very neat and habitable condition, with a fine vegetable garden, and an orchard on two sides of the house. Meanwhile the Pastor dwelt up in the city, where the congregation paid for his boarding and lodging. The church land was not yet rented out so as to bring any larger income than twelve pounds ten shillings a year. But now that suburb of Philadelphia called "*Society Hill*"[1] had stretched itself out to this neighborhood, so that ground was desired from the church lands for making city lots. And as that proposition had already been made in Provost Sandel's time, when that piece of ground was bought, it was now found to considerably increase the income of the church and the salary of the Minister. Now, wealthy men in the congregation

---

[1] ["At the intersection of Pine and Front Streets was a prominent knoll, which took the name of Society Hill from the fact that the lots of the 'Society of Free Traders,' when the city was laid out, extended between Spruce and Pine Streets entirely across from river to river." Day's Historical Collections of the State of Pa., p. 559.]

18

took it upon themselves, for the encouragement of others, to take the lots upon an annual ground-rent, and build handsome stone houses on them, the ground-rents to remain the same forever. Others took large lots for pastures for a term of years. In these arrangements there was not only a cheering unanimity between the Minister and his people, but he also greatly aided the officers of the congregation by his prudent advice.

10. An Earthquake.

On an earthquake, the Rev. Pastor has inserted in the church-book the following remarks: " In the year 1737, on the 7th of December, at eleven o'clock in the evening, an earthquake occurred. The houses shook and the windows clattered. The higher one was up in the house, the more vividly was it felt. A couple of hours before the earthquake there was a terrible rainstorm, with the wind from the southwest, which did not last for more than half an hour. Thereupon the sky cleared up, and the atmosphere became remarkably pure and calm. Just as the clock struck eleven, there began a soughing from the west, which continued to increase, and was heard down in the ground, until the house shook so that those who were lying upon beds thought themselves to be shaken backwards and forwards. Those that were standing on the ground could scarcely keep an upright position. Plates and glass were tumbled down in some houses. This continued in some places for about *one minute*, in others for *two minutes*, but was so universally felt all over the country, that they have felt the same effects from it as far as has been heard from on both sides of the river.

11. Dylander's Death.

The joy now universally felt at the good regulations that were established in Wicacoa, as well in the church as outside of it, the pleasure experienced by the Archbishop and the Ecclesiastical Consistory of Upsala from a frequent interchange of letters with their missionary, and the remarkable esteem that Pastor Dylander had secured over almost the whole country — all this was soon terminated by his death, which occurred on the 2d of November, 1741. His lifeless body was laid out in Wicacoa Church, and honored in a funeral sermon in English by Pastor Peter Tranberg, in the presence of a great multitude of people, as well from the congregation as from the city of Philadelphia, of all forms of religion. All laid this tribute of praise upon his grave — that he was a chosen Teacher for the Church, an ornament of his order, an honor to his countrymen, and an affectionate husband to his widow, the daughter of Peter Kock, of Passayungh.

CHAPTER VI.

OF MR. NAESMAN'S TIME.

I. MESSRS. HEDSTRAND AND NAESMAN.

A LETTER in regard to Pastor Dylander's death was immediately dispatched to Sweden. The year before, the German Lutherans in Lancaster [1] had sent over a petition to His Majesty, Frederick I., begging that, in view of the confidence which they had in the Swedish clergy, as well as the great edification they had already experienced from their ministrations, His Majesty would be pleased to gratify them by sending a Teacher to their congregation. The matter was referred to the Archbishop and Consistory of Upsala, who thereupon provided and called two clergymen to be sent to America, Mr. Gabriel Naesman, of Gestricia, for the Swedish congregation in Philadelphia, and Mr. Hedstrand, of East Gothland, for the German Lutheran congregation in Lancaster. Both were ordained for this purpose in the Cathedral of Upsala, in the month of May, 1742. But when the question arose in regard to the expenses of the journey for Mr. Hedstrand, nothing could be drawn therefor from the Royal Treasury; neither had the congregation of Lancaster sent such a positive obligation for it, that full confidence could be given to it; nor was there any plan for receiving an ad-

---

[1] [This is the first notice of the Lutheran Church in Lancaster, and fixes its origin near the year 1740.]

vance of one thousand dollars silver for this object, even supposing payment to be made at the Minister's arrival. For these reasons Mr. Hedstrand relinquished that call. Mr. Naesman, who had in the meantime waited for his travelling companion, now found the season too far advanced, and so was compelled to remain until the following spring, when he took his departure, having the Royal Commission bearing the date of August 9, 1742. He landed in Philadelphia on the 20th of October, 1743.

2. THE CONGREGATION SCATTERED.

Mr. Naesman found his Parish in an entirely different condition from what he had anticipated. During the existing vacancy of two and a half years, the new sects of Whitfieldites,[1] or " New Lights," and Zinzendorffians[2] which had come in, were most zealously drawing the people to themselves, and obtaining a hold among the Swedes, all the more readily as their church was now standing unused. One part of them went to the English congregation, and did not propose to come back any more, inasmuch as Wicacoa Church, resting on so insecure a footing, was long and frequently empty. Mr. Naesman did, indeed, travel around to every part of the Parish, and exhorted the people to unity. He appointed Parish meetings at five separate times, but so few came together that nothing could be effected. Finally, after he had requested a Parish meeting for four Sundays in succession, a considerable number got together at the appointed time, which was on the 26th of March, 1744.

3. PARISH MEETING.

Upon this occasion he read before them a " memorial," which he had arranged in twenty-three Articles, most of these having

---

[1] [George Whitefield was ordained in England, in 1736, by Bishop Benson of Gloucester, and soon afterwards visited the British Colonies in North America — Boston first in 1740, dying there during his last visit in 1770.]

[2] [Nicholas Louis von Zinzendorf was born at Dresden, May 26, 1700. In 1722 he became acquainted with the Moravian Brethren, at whose head Christian David then stood, and who were fugitives from their native country. Count Zinzendorf established a settlement for them on his estates in Saxony, and called the place Herrnhut, "*The Lord's Care*." He came to America in December, 1741, and departed in January, 1743.]

also their divisions and subdivisions. Of these, eleven (11) treated [1] " of Doctrine, and the manner of teaching it ; " six (6) " of Church government ; " four (4) " of Church discipline ; " two (2) " of the keeping up of the church building and the Pastor's house." He publicly read this writing in the church at two different times, in order to excite an interest in the matter; he found, however, but little good result from it. The greater part of the Parish meeting was devoted to misunderstandings between the parishioners. Those from Kalkonhook and Amas Land insisted that the Minister should visit them every fourth Sunday in the month and preach, otherwise they would not bind themselves for his support. The others opposed this, as the church (at Wicacoa) would thus often be unoccupied, and the congregation scattered. Mr. Naesman offered to preach at Amas Land every other week on some week-day, or upon any holy-day occurring therein. Or, he would be willing to go out on Saturday, preach for them on Sunday morning, and then be at the church at the proper hour. But none of these propositions were agreeable. The answers were : By one week-day they could earn the Minister's pay. Sunday morning was required for feeding their cattle, etc. The conclusion was that on every fourth Sunday afternoon he should go out and preach for them, after the church services were over ; and if he found them united, he would come on the last Sunday in every month in the forenoon.

4. Good Regulations Proposed.

Mr. Naesman undeniably devoted a great deal of labor and care to the restoration of those scattered congregations, although he met with many hindrances. After he had, with a great deal of trouble, brought the Church-Wardens and Vestrymen into order, he time and again made the proposal that the Sermons on the Catechism should be held at Matins (early morning service) from Pentecost to Advent, and immediately afterwards the " Examination " [2] in the aisles; that the people should be as-

---

[1] [Acrelius has these heads in Latin, but does not state whether the whole Essay or Discourse was originally written in that language. Its headings savor strongly of the scholastic style of the preceding century.]

[2] [" *Examen*," in the original. See above.]

sembled several times a year in their sections for the recital of
the Catechism; that they should, in good time and without delay,
present their children for baptism and confirmation;[1] that the
Lord's Supper should be held in proper esteem, and celebrated
in the church at least four or six times a year, together with the
hearing of confession[2] on the Sunday next preceding.   This and
other matters were readily recognized as becoming, as also the
old order of the church, but though frequently proposed in later
years, these things could not be carried out.

5.   VARIOUS SECTS TRYING TO GET INTO THE CHURCH.

It must be admitted that that was a most unfortunate time for
a clergyman in that place.   A clergyman holding to the English Church, Mr. George Whitfield, had established in Philadelphia a congregation of people of every variety of faith, which
association was called " *New Lights*," and had their meetings in
the so-called " New Buildings."   With these many Swedish
families united.   Immediately afterwards came Count Louis von
Zinzendorff with his pernicious sect called Herrnhutters,[3] and
spread out his net to catch all at one time.   In the year 1742,
just before Mr. Naesman's arrival, the Count brought with him
Paul Daniel Bruselius,[4] who at once crept into the Swedish houses,
pretended to be a Swedish Minister, and offered to preach in the
church; which, however, was not permitted.   In the year 1744

---

[1] [" Christendom " is the word here employed in the original; but as " *veta sin
Christendom*," literally, " *to know his Christianity*," means " to be acquainted with
one's Catechism," so we may translate the phrase most intelligibly as in the text.]

[2] [" Skriftermål"—" Confession "—was not private, but public and general, among
the Swedes.]

[3] [So called from their newly established place of Herrnhut.   The opposition to
Zinzendorff's peculiarities was very strong among the great body of orthodox Lutherans in that day; although Zinzendorff himself was examined and licensed as a
Lutheran Candidate of theology at Stralsund and Tübingen in 1734, and his Moravian Brethren distinctly declared their adherence to the Augsburg Confession.]

[4] [Called in the " Pennsylvanische Nachrichten " (Vierte Fortsetz., p. 136: Halle,
1751,) Pyrlaeus — probably a typographical error.   But in the same work (Zehnte
Fortsetz., p. 856: Halle, 1768,) he signs his own name " Paul D. Brycelius," which is
subscribed to his renunciation of Moravianism, after which he was received as a
German Lutheran minister, being also recommended by the Swedish Provost C. von
Wrangel in 1760.   Brycelius arrived in Philadelphia in June, 1742.]

came L. T. Nyberg, who was called from Sweden, and sent to the German Lutheran Congregation in Lancaster; but immediately after his arrival, it was observed that he had already, at home in Sweden, formed a taste for the Zinzendorffian leaven.

6. A UNION BETWEEN THE SWEDISH AND GERMAN LUTHERAN CLERGY PROPOSED.

Already in the year 1733, the German Lutherans in Philadelphia had, by a letter to Mr. Ziegenhagen, the German Court-Preacher[1] at the Royal English Court, and St. James's Chapel in London, and also to Dr. Frank,[2] in Halle, announced their earnest desire to be supplied with a Teacher. This their desire was not, however, gratified before the year 1742, when, in a happy hour, the Pastor, Henry Melchior Myhlenberg,[3] arrived. In the following year, 1743, the German Pastor, Peter Brunholz, followed, and settled in the Philadelphia Congregation, whilst the former (Mühlenberg) took the congregations at Providence and New Hanover in Philadelphia[4] county. Thus were the Germans in Philadelphia supplied with a Pastor of their own, and had no longer need to attend the Wicacoa Church. But their Ministers, who were strangers, and employed in building up new congregations, also daily assailed by Count Zinzendorff and his Herrnhut adherents, needed in their counsels and purposes a firm alliance with the Swedish Ministers, their associates in a common faith, even more than the Swedish Ministers required the same for the security of their congregations. This was strengthened

---

[1] Chaplain. The Court of St. James was at this time (the reign of George II.) decidedly German — the Prince of Wales also being married to a Princess of Saxe-Gotha.

[2] The well-known A. H. Francke of the University and Orphan House at Halle in Germany. Our author seems disposed to give all names, so far as possible, a Swedish form, as is seen more particularly in the one immediately following.

[3] [H. M. Mühlenberg, the great organizer of the German Lutheran Church in the United States. His descendants in the United States have taken the name of *Muhlenberg*, probably from the absence of the German *ü* from the English alphabet. The labors of Mühlenberg and his energetic assistants are given in considerable detail in the "Hallische Nachrichten," which we have already quoted in our notes, which consist of sixteen numbers, and form a volume of over one thousand five hundred pages, which ought long since to have been translated into English.]

[4] [Now Montgomery county.]

by two Philadelphia merchants, Peter Kock, a Swede, and Henry Sleydorn,[1] a German. The proposition was made that they should hold yearly meetings together, and that in these a few of the elders of the congregations, as well Germans as Swedes, should also be included. They should there consult together in regard to the best establishment of each congregation, for the condition of their affairs required that they should shake hands with each other, and fight their common enemy the Zinzendorffers.

7. Various Hindrances thereto.

Mr. L. T. Nyberg,[2] a secret Herrnhutter, declared that he did not know of anything wrong in the Moravian Brotherhood, and advised all others not to say any evil of them. On the contrary, he said that he was well acquainted with the Pietism[3] which had come forth from Halle; and he called the German Ministers "ungodly Hallensians," against whom Archbishop Benzelius[4] had warned him when he was departing from Sweden. Mr. Naesman knew very well the errors of both sects, and suspected the present Ministers of being divided between these two parties, and so would not commit himself to either side. Mr. Tranberg was not sufficiently instructed in these differences, as he had now for a long time been in America, and as regarded his

---

[1] [H. Schleidorn died in 1759, being at the time one of the Elders of the German Lutheran Church in Philadelphia. An interesting notice of his death is to be found in the Pennsylvania Nach., p. 751.]

[2] Laurence Thorstansen Nyberg was intrusted by the Moravians with the care of their congregation in Lancaster in 1745. There was a personal assault upon Bishop Spangenberg, while preaching there in that year. See " Transactions Moravian Historical Society," Vol. I., 383.— W. C. R.

[3] [The well-known Dr. P. J. Spener gave occasion to this new school of Lutheran theology, by his writings and practical activity, about the middle of the seventeenth century. His professed aim was the promotion of "*practical piety;*" hence the name of " Pietists " given to his friends by their opponents. The University of Halle, with such men as Francke, Freylinghausen, Starke, and the like, at its head, becoming the great centre of this movement, also gave origin to the term " Hallensians," used in our text. Both the Pietists and Moravians were treated with great severity in Sweden from 1706, when Charles XII. published an edict against the Pietists, until 1769, when Rutström, the Moravian, was recalled from his banishment. The free exercise of religion was first allowed in Sweden in 1781.]

[4] Erik Benzelius the younger, formerly Bishop of Linköping, created Archbishop in 1742, died in 1743.

present brethren in office, he left each one undisturbed in his own proper place. Mr. Kock elaborated a Church Regulation, which should forever unite the Swedish Ministers with the German, and adapted to the special circumstances of the present time. Mr. Naesman suggested that the Swedish congregations were in an entirely different situation from that of the Germans. The Swedes were possessed of property and land, which should so much the less come under the control of the others, as the one Swedish congregation never troubled itself with the affairs of the other. Such annual Consistories, Synods, or Meetings could not be well arranged, inasmuch as matters there would have to be decided by voting, and the Swedish Ministers were not equal in number[1] to the Germans; also, that it was impossible to induce the Swedish officers to enter into consultations with the Germans, which would also be absurd, as they did not understand each others' language. And however good the proposed Regulation might, in his opinion, be, yet, in many particulars, it diverged widely from the Swedish church-laws, as well as from the Manual[2] for church ceremonies; and, finally, if there were no other obstacle in the way, it was sufficient that the Swedish clergy stood under their Archbishop and the Consistory, without whose approbation they could not enter into such a union.

8. Meeting and Consultation Thereon.

It was thought that the matter might be best arranged by a general meeting. With this view Mr. Kock went down to Christina, and invited the congregation there to send some of its elders to it. But the people did not know what might be the import of such a meeting, and because it was new it seemed dangerous, and therefore no one would come up. The day came, and the meeting was held in Wicacoa Church. The Swedish and German Ministers, with some also of the officers of their congregations, came together. The first question was, Whether the Herrnhutters were also to be regarded as associates in the Augsburg Con-

---

[1] [There may have been half a dozen German Lutheran Ministers in the country at that time (1744-5).]

[2] [The "Manuale Sveticum, Stockholm, 1691," the "Directory for Public Worship," etc., was one of the books sent over from Sweden by the King in 1696.]

fession? [1]   Pastor Nyberg maintained that they were; Pastor
Mühlenberg denied it.   Pastor Naesman declared them both
incompetent to decide the case, and they got no further.   Next
came the question, Whether the proposed Church Regulation
should be adopted?   The Swedish church-usages would have to
be changed before the Lutheran religion could be established in
the country.   Those who opposed this were responsible for it
that a work so useful was hindered.   Pastor Naesman repeated
all the points stated, and brought them out in a good order;
and added thereto that the Germans ought to accept the Swedish
church-usages, inasmuch as the Swedish Church was the oldest
in the country.   Pastor Tranberg had subscribed the plan, but
now withdrew his signature.   In regard to the other projects,
nothing was done.   Mr. Mühlenberg called Nyberg " Moravian,"
and Nyberg called him " Hallensian."   Mr. Naesman received
the name of " Orthodox" and " Scholastic."   And thus the
meeting ended without coming to any conclusion.

9. CAUSES OF THE MISUNDERSTANDING BETWEEN MÜHLENBERG AND NYBERG.

That Mr. Nyberg had taken such an aversion towards Mühlenberg was not surprising, in view of the fact that when Mühlenberg came to the country Count Zinzendorff was in a fair way
to bring under him the whole German population, especially the
Lutherans, to whom he gave out that he had a perfect right in
consequence of a unanimous call, and he represented himself as
their Inspector.   Nowhere could he experience more active
opposition than from Mr. Mühlenberg, to whom the greatest
part of the Germans attached themselves; who also, by the action
of the Magistrates, compelled the Count to give up the church-
book, together with the Communion chalice, which he had got
into his possession through a church-warden.   It was also a
groundless charge to call him a " Hallensian," meaning thereby
that he was a " Pietist," on account of his having been sent from
Halle.   The congregations had asked for Ministers from Halle,
and from Halle they received them.   But they had also studied

---

[1] [The Moravians have repeatedly declared their adherence to the XXI. Doctrinal
Articles of the Augsburg Confession, more particularly in their meeting at Herrnhut
in 1749.]

at other Universities as well as at Halle, namely, Wittenberg, Leipzig, and Jena. Every right-minded person in the place must acknowledge that Mr. Mühlenberg is a pure Evangelical Teacher, and a chosen instrument of God, who, with wisdom, liberality, and zeal, has gathered and built up the Church of Christ in a wild land. That, for the performance of the Lord's work, as a stranger in troublous times, he had to resort to many means and modes which were not the most direct to the end, that may be best left to the judgment of those who have themselves been in like trials.

10. Kock's Untimely Assumption.

Mr. Kock was a wealthy man, helpful to his countrymen, and well disposed towards his church. He was, therefore, after some few years' residence in the place, appointed a Trustee and Vestryman. But the misfortune was that he stretched his authority too far. He had a large trade with the Germans, and was intent on promoting their interests. When he observed that Mr. Naesman either would not or could not at all times concur in his views, he sought to put him out of the way. He encouraged Mr. Naesman to return home to Sweden, and promised him money for his travelling expenses, and a good recommendation ; or he advised him to engage with some German congregation up the country, and convert Wicacoa into a German Orphan House, like the Orphan House at Halle; or he wished him to advise the Swedes to unite themselves with the German congregations, as the number of the Germans was far greater than that of the Swedes. When nothing of this could be effected, he wrote home severe charges against him, desired Mr. Naesman's recall home; also promised free travelling expenses for the Minister that should come, which was already deposited with Mr. Abraham Spalding, in London, of which, however, scarcely any one in the congregation had knowledge.

11. Cause of Misunderstanding on the Part of the Trustees.

The disagreement had its origin chiefly in the management of the landed property of the church. Mr. Kock was appointed a Trustee, and had all the church's deeds for land in his hands, as also in his name and that of three other good men, whom he held pretty much under his control. The laws of England do

not allow any Church, Congregation, or Society to own land.
For this Trustees are appointed, and the deeds are made out in
their name. But the bond[1] which these men in turn have to
give the church, that all the land with which they are entrusted
shall be employed for the support of the church and its Minister,
according to orders, was never executed. The law which thus
assigned the church's land to persons entrusted therewith was
new, and at first excited a great deal of uneasiness in the congregation, by the suspicion that it was the intention of these men
to appropriate the church's land to themselves. That would all
have been prevented, if the Trustees had given their proper
guarantee, or " *Obligation in Trust*." But that was not yet in their
power, as no bond was given, although an Act had already been
published in the country which, indeed, forbade this.[2] Mr.

---

[1] [The original word is "*revers*," a legal and technical term applied to all sorts of
documents to which a personal signature is attached — an official oath.]

[2] The Laws of Pennsylvania, p. 423, Cap. CCCXVI.:

" An Act for the enabling religious societies of Protestants within this Province to
purchase lands for burying-grounds, churches, houses for worship, schools, etc.

" Whereas, sundry religious societies of people of this Province, professing the
Protestant religion, have, at their own respective costs and charges, purchased small
pieces of land within the Province of Pennsylvania, and thereon have erected churches
and other houses of religious worship, school-houses, and almshouses, and inclosed
part of the same lands for burying-grounds : And whereas the said lands were purchased and paid for by the said respective societies in the name or names of persons,
at that time being of, or professing themselves to be of, the same religious persuasion
with the societies who made use of the names of the said persons as trustees for and
in behalf of the said societies : And whereas some of the said trustees, or their heirs,
having afterwards changed their opinions, and joined themselves to other religious
societies of a different persuasion from the people by whom the said persons were at
first entrusted, and upon pretext of their having the fee simple of the lands, so purchased in their names, vested in them, have, contrary to the true intent and meaning
of the first grant or gift, attempted (by granting away the said lands, houses of religious
worship, and burying-grounds) to deprive the society of people in possession of the
same of the right and use of the said houses of worship and burying-grounds, to the
great disquiet and uneasiness of many of the good people of this Province; and
others, being entrusted in the like manner, may hereafter do the same : For remedy
whereof, and for the better securing the several religious societies in the quiet and
peaceful possession of their churches, houses of worship, school-houses, and almshouses, and burying-grounds, within this Province :

" II. *Be it enacted*, That all sales, gifts, or grants made of any lands or tenements
within the Province of Pennsylvania, to any person or persons, in trust, for sites of
churches, houses of religious worship, schools, almshouses, and for burying-grounds,
or for any of them, shall be and are hereby ratified and confirmed to the person or

Kock declared that Mr. Naesman had nothing to do with the matter, which belonged to the congregation. The elders were not very willing to come together so frequently, or had too much respect for Mr. Kock to compel him to this. The other trustees were willing to give the "Obligation of Trust," if Mr. Kock would agree. The injury which resulted was, that when the people inquired after lots for rent, they came to understand that these Trustees had no power to conclude any contract for the church's land before they had given their bond. Thereby the interests of the church and congregation were hindered at the very time when they might have been best promoted.

---

persons to whom the same were sold, given, or granted, their heirs and assigns, in trust nevertheless, and for the use of the respective religious societies for whose use the same were at first sold, given, granted, or purchased, according to the true intent and meaning of such gifts and grants; and that every sale, gift, grant, or devise, of any such trustee or trustees, or any person or persons, in whose name or names the said lands for erecting churches, houses of religious worship, schools, almshouses, or burying-grounds, within this Province, were purchased, taken, or accepted, or the heirs or assigns of such trustees, shall be and are hereby declared to be for the sole use, benefit, and behoof of the said respective societies, who have been in the peaceable possession of the same for the space of twenty-one years, next before the tenth day of June, in the year of our Lord one thousand seven hundred and thirty, or for whose use the same were at first given, granted, or devised, and no other.

"III. *And be it further enacted,* That it shall and may be lawful to and for any religious society of Protestants, within this Province, to purchase, take, and receive, by gift, grant, or otherwise, for burying-grounds, erecting churches, houses of religious worship, schools, and almshouses, for any estate whatsoever, and to hold the same for the uses aforesaid, of the lord of the fee, by the accustomed rents.

"IV. *Provided always, and be it further enacted,* That nothing in this Act contained shall be deemed, taken, or construed to enable any of the said religious societies of people, or any person or persons whatsoever, in trust for them, or to their use, to purchase, take, or receive any lands or tenements, by gift, grant, or otherwise, for or towards the maintenance or support of the said churches, houses of worship, schools, or almshouses, or the people belonging to the same, or for any other use or purpose, save for the uses in this Act before mentioned.

"V. *Provided also,* That this Act, nor anything therein contained, shall be deemed or construed to impeach the just right or title which any person or persons may have to any of the lands or tenements hereinbefore mentioned, so that they prosecute such their right or claim within the space of three years next after the publication of this Act. *Anno regni* Quarto Georgii II. Regis, 4 Jan., 1730." *

* [We copy from the " Laws of the Commonwealth of Pennsylvania," republished by authority of the Legislature in 1810, (John Bioren, Philadelphia,) Vol. I., pp. 191-194, Chap. CCCXX., where it is given as the Act of " Feb. 6, 1730-31."]

12. THE PEOPLE SCATTERED.

A Parish meeting was held in the Wicacoa parsonage twice a year — on the 27th of May and the 27th of November, which are the principal market-days in Philadelphia. As often as they met, Mr. Naesman had some set of Articles in writing to read before them for their union and edification ; but Mr. Kock was thereby offended, and went away, and his friends with him, so that the meeting was no sooner begun than it was ended in displeasure, and thus the people were no longer disposed to come to a Parish meeting. In the same manner the people were scattered from the church. Some complained that the church commenced too late; others, that the sermon was too long; others, that *they* were pointed at in it. But no one could deny that they would certainly be good Christians if they regulated themselves according to the contents of the sermon. However that was, yet, in the end, the number of hearers became very small.

13. MR. NAESMAN'S MANIFOLD LABORS.

As the Swedes were but few, evening service[1] was held in English. At first there were hearers enough present, but rather out of curiosity, for the lawless people thought that his English was not good enough, and so they fell off. Then he made the attempt to preach in French ; but that did not take well after a few times. To show that he had an unquenchable desire to employ his powers in the Lord's vineyard, he extended his labors to remote places, and took this circuit every month. The first Saturday in the month he went over the river and preached in English in a private house with one Thomas Hews,[2] where Presbyterians, Quakers, Whitfieldians, etc., came together. On Sunday he preached in Swedish and English in Racuun,[3] which was vacant, and suffering from the intrusion of the Herrnhutters. On Monday, in English and German, in Cohansy,[4] where the journey

---

1 [" *Aftonsång* " in the original ; the old English, " *Evensong.*"]

2 [Probably " Hughes," according to the common English spelling.]

3 [Now " Racoon."]

4 [This church, upon the head-waters of the Cohanzy and Alloways creeks, is in Salem county, N. J., in a small village called Friesburg. It is one of the oldest German Lutheran churches in the U. S., having been organized in 1738, as appears from the Penn. Nachrichten, where it is frequently noticed under the name of *Cohentzi.*]

out and back again amounted to nearly one hundred English miles. On the next Sunday he preached at home in Swedish and English. Some days in the next week, up in Mazong, in Swedish and English. On the third Sunday he preached in Nitshamene and Pennypack in either Swedish or German, or German and English, on the same day. Changes were here made according to times and circumstances. The last Sunday in the month was appointed for preaching at Amas Land. One Sunday in the month, in later times and during a vacancy there, he went down to Christina, where he served the Swedes, English, and Germans. He was diligent in visiting the sick, attended upon the malefactors condemned to death and lying in the Philadelphia prison — prepared them for their departure, and gave them faithful service until their hour of death. He thus made himself deserving of universal praise.

14. The Support Poor.

The salary was from the beginning small, and finally very wretched. Subscriptions had ceased, and the rented lots were to pay everything. But as the renting of the lots was delayed, so was it also with the income of the rents. Some, who were debtors for many years, entirely refused to pay until they could find out who had the right to receive the money. The Trustees, who collected the rents, had, therefore, presented no account for some years. Meanwhile they gave what they pleased, more or less. The Minister complained; the congregation complained the church and parsonage were running into decay, and everything was in confusion.

15. Mr. Naesman's Recall Home.

In such a condition did the Provost, Mr. Acrelius, find Wicacoa congregation on the 6th of November, 1749, when he arrived, bringing the letter of the Archbishop and of the Venerable Consistory to Mr. Naesman to get ready for his return home, in accordance with the information given to this effect by the Provost, Mr. John Sandin, in his lifetime, as also by the letter of Mr. Kock — a change being found necessary, and a successor already appointed, who was to be expected next spring. This was quite unexpected news to Mr. Naesman, as he had never desired a recall home, and was assured that, as Mr. Kock had died some weeks before, and now two other Swedish Ministers had arrived — one of whom was appointed Provost, the other Assistant in the congregations — everything would soon be brought into good order if he could still remain. The Provost travelled up several times during the winter and preached at Wicacoa, which was also done by Mr. Unander, the Pastor Extraordinary from Racoon, and thus the scattered people were somewhat drawn together. After the Provost had made himself well acquainted with all the circumstances, and perceived among the people generally a great deal of love and good-will, he gave notice that he desired to attend a Parish meeting at Wicacoa on the following Sunday. On the Sunday preceding, when the Provost preached there, he requested the Trustees and Elders to have a separate meeting with him, and there let him know what they had to suggest upon their part, which was also done the day before the Parish meeting.

16. The Meeting.

May 7th, 1750, the Rev. Provost Acrelius, the Rev. Mr. Naesman, and the Rev. Mr. Unander, Pastor Extraordinary, found themselves among a large number of the members of the congregation. The Provost commenced the meeting with a sermon upon 1 John 4 : 16, "*God is love*," whereon he explained — " 1. How God daily displays His love to men; 2. How we ought to show our love to God and our neighbor; 3. The blessings which follow from Christian love; 4. How all uncharitableness is a seed of Satan, which produces tares upon God's fields." That God gave His Spirit and power with the word is concluded, without any doubt, from the love and unity wherewith everything was done ever after.

17. Agreement.

Pastor Naesman had first to suggest what he found necessary for the present time, which was to pay his debts, into which he had fallen during his time of service, and whilst his salary was kept back. Upon the question, How much was required therefor? it was answered that it was something over twenty pounds, and that thirty pounds would be enough. The Trustees gave in a balance of seventy-nine pounds nine shillings. The congregation resolved that all this should be given to their Pastor. Another vote, which greatly affected him, was also given by his desire. The rest went to the Sexton and the repairs of the church. The Trustees promised to give the necessary bond, which was to be ready for the next meeting. Four good men were nominated to take the same. It was left to the Provost to appoint the next meeting at such time as was agreeable to him.

CHAPTER VII.

OF MR. PARLIN'S TIME.

1. The Rev. Mr. Parlin Appointed.

IN the beginning of the year 1749, in consequence of a letter of Mr. Kock and two other Trustees to the Archbishop and the Venerable Consistory of Upsala, in reference to the misunderstandings in the Wicacoa congregation, as a remedy for which another Minister was desired, as also in reference to the fact that the Rev. Mr. Naesman's proposed term of seven years' service was nearly completed, it was decided in the Consistory that the change should be made, and another clergyman sent out. The Rev. Olof Parlin, formerly Chaplain to His Excellency the Royal Counsellor, Count Thure Bielke, Knight, and Member of the Order of His Royal Majesty, together with the Provost Acrelius and the Rev. Mr. Unander, Pastor Extraordinary, were provided with a Commission from His Majesty King Frederick I., bearing the date of May 29, 1749. Whilst preparations were making for the journey, Mr. Parlin fell into a violent intermittent fever, which detained him in Stockholm, to the great grief of his brethren in office when they took their departure. The imprudence of the physician, no less than the burthen of the American mission, threw him into deep melancholy and mental aberration

19

for some months. But a hasty removal from Stockholm to
Arboga, which he made in that condition without any reflection,
cured his sickness by means of great bodily exercise and change
of air. The merciful God thus gave an especial proof of His
healing hand, in the use of insignificant means, to the honor of
His Holy Name, and to the great joy and astonishment of all
who have heard and seen it. "*The counsel and secrets of Kings
and Princes are to be concealed; but the work of God is to be
gloriously praised and made known.*" Tobit 12:7.

2. His Journey.

After Mr. Parlin had thus, in the providence of God, regained
his health, and been provided with a Royal passport dated March
8, 1750, he took his departure, on the 13th of the same month,
from Stockholm to London. There he inquired for the three
thousand dollars, copper coinage, which Mr. Kock had promised
to deposit with Mr. Spalding for the coming Minister. He was
answered that it was, indeed, true that orders had been given to
that effect, but that after his death they had been countermanded
by the executors of his will. How that suited Mr. Parlin, who,
for the past year and during his long sickness, had been living
upon the means of travel supplied him by the King, and was
now embarked upon an expensive voyage, any one may easily
imagine. Had Mr. Kock remained alive, and the sum of money
been paid, it would have been ample; although scarcely any one
in the congregation pretends to know anything about the affair;
neither was there so much to be got out of the treasury of the
church without doing injustice either to the predecessor or the
successor. But what was to be done? Nothing could arrest that
zealous Teacher in the course of his duty. His confidence was
in the Almighty, and his hope did not disappoint him. He arrived
in Philadelphia on the 7th of the July following, after a voyage
of nine weeks from London.

3. His Arrival.

Wicacoa had now two Ministers. The former was, no doubt,
as well satisfied with the place as the latter. But there was only
room for one. Universal joy was visible in the congregation at

the exchange, although scarcely anything was said but what was highly honorable to Mr. Naesman; yet many thought that greater unity might follow the ministry of Mr. Parlin. However, both stood under the order of their gracious King and the ruling authorities — the one to come, and the other to go. On that account the Introduction[1] took place on the sixth Sunday after Trinity, in the presence of a numerous congregation. Immediately before Divine Service was read the letter of the Archbishop, Dr. Henry Benzelius, and the Venerable Consistory, to the congregation; also the letter of recall for Mr. Naesman. Thereupon Mr. Parlin preached. After the sermon, the Introduction was performed by the Provost, Mr. Acrelius, first, by an address upon Matt. 9 : 37, 38, "*The harvest is great, but the laborers are few,*" etc., and then with the usual ritual.

4. MR. NAESMAN'S PAYMENT.

The congregation agreed to contribute £20 for the travelling expenses of Mr. Naesman, and the balance due him on his salary was to be made up as soon as possible. He had leave to stay in the parsonage until he was ready to travel. In the meantime they looked out for a house for Mr. Parlin's abode in the city. But Mr. Naesman's departure seemed to be delayed for a long time. His will was good enough, but circumstances in his family were not convenient for his leaving. He therefore, after some months, removed out of the house, and gave it up to his successor, and then hired for himself another house at his own expense. He also made an agreement with a congregation in New Jersey to preach there every other Sunday, and in the city taught a school in German, French, and Latin. This was protracted into the following year, and he still complained that a considerable part of his salary was as yet unpaid. Upon examination it was found that there was still a balance of £96 13s. 5d. due upon Mr. Naesman's time. From this were taken £51, which consisted chiefly of back interest, which could never be escaped, in part also of necessary expenses for the church and its corporation during the same time, and then there remained

---

[1] ["Installation" would perhaps be the proper word; but I have retained the original as rather more descriptive.]

on hand a balance of £46 13s. 5d., which was given to Mr. Naesman, so that he should not have occasion to complain that he was not paid to the last penny. Thereupon the Trustees gave in their Obligation of Trust, which, after some months, was redeemed.

5. HIS TRAVELS.

But his mind was not immediately turned towards home, although there was no lack of encouraging letters and promises, from Sweden. His journey was taken from Philadelphia to the English island of Antigua in the West Indies, with goods suitable for traffic, in the month of November, 1751. His venture was successful. There he was taken by a wealthy man as tutor for his sons, who had been in attendance at Westminster School in London. He thus had in that expensive place a healthy residence, whilst he was selling his goods to advantage. At the same time he held Divine Service for the Germans, who, with great joy, began to hear preaching in their mother-tongue, which they could not otherwise get in that place. After some months he continued his journey to the Dutch island of St. Eustasia. There he found his intimate friend, Mr. Lawrence Algerus, who made him acquainted with the Germans residing there, who united themselves together in a congregation, took him for their Teacher, and supported him quite honorably. But he could not remain there longer than a few months. His recall home, and the orders of his spiritual superior, lay before him, and were to be obediently followed. In consequence of this, in the month of August, 1752, he turned his course to Amsterdam, after he had so informed his wife, Margaretta Rambo, who had been left behind in Pennsylvania with a little son, named David, requesting them to follow him, and go in his company to Sweden. From Amsterdam, he wrote home that he had got so far upon his return home, but was not able to get any farther for the want of the necessary means of travel, which had also compelled him to leave his wife and child behind him in America. Information of this was laid before the Archbishop, Dr. Henry Benzelius, who, out of Christian compassion, laid his wants before His Majesty, when one thousand five hundred dollars copper coin were sent for his relief, and an equal sum to Pennsylvania for the journey of his wife and children home.   Before this Royal grace was known to him, he could not bear that the time should be spent in vain. He therefore took a journey through the principal places of Holland, where he sought chiefly to gain a knowledge of medicine. The deeper insight he obtained into this, the greater did his pleasure in it become, so that he could not be satisfied until he had spent three months in Paris in the study of the same science, and especially in the department of midwifery.   It was his intention to return to Pennsylvania, and there heal the people both in body and soul.   But just as he had arrived at Rouen, he had placed in his hands the letter of the Archbishop, with the information that the money for his journey had already been sent to Amsterdam, and to London for his wife and child; whereupon he quickly changed his plans and went to Sweden.

6. His Arrival Home.

Upon his arrival at home he was welcomed with great honor, first receiving a present of one thousand two hundred dollars copper coin for every year since he had left his congregation; then he had the character and honor of a Professor bestowed upon him, and finally an appointment to the Pastorate of Christianstad in Skåne.

7. Performance of Duties.

Mr. Parlin had the full confidence of his hearers.   But his prudence was very great in removing everything that might produce a misunderstanding.   All said that their Teacher sought the eternal interests of their souls, and not his own advantage. What they contributed for his support, he received with gratitude.   In his sermons, he adapted himself to the understanding of his hearers.   In his intercourse with them he was no less edifying than agreeable.   In consequence, he saw the number of his hearers continually increasing, and many loving the Church who had for a long time been estranged from her.   He did not neglect, timely and often, to place before them the necessity of attending public worship, as well as the proper use of the Holy Sacraments, and especially of the Lord's Supper, which had come into very great neglect; also, how attached they ought to be to the Swedish language, and to instruct the young in it. At the request of his English neighbors, he sometimes held the evening service in English. Every last Sunday in the month was appointed for Divine Service with the Swedes in Amas Land, where, usually after service, he heard and explained the Catechism. Matzong and Pennipack were supplied with Swedish preaching at certain times during the week.

8. IMPROVED MANAGEMENT OF THE CHURCH PROPERTY.

The Provost, Mr. Acrelius, had advised with the Advocate, Mr. John Moreland, in regard to the management of the church's land and lots, as to the safest and speediest administration of the same. There was a better opportunity of doing this now, as another Trustee was to be elected in Mr. Kock's place. A contract was drawn up to this effect: that the three old Trustees should elect twelve others in their places as their successors; to them, and to their successors forever, they gave up all that right which they, as Trustees, had had to the church's land, grounds, and property, the parts of which were specified, and also the right which the congregation had to them by purchase, upon these terms: 1. That all these pieces of land, with all the rents and use which might be derived from them, shall be forever employed for the support of the Swedish Lutheran Church in Wicacoa, together with the lawfully appointed Teacher in the same. 2. That these twelve Trustees, and their successors in the Trusteeship, should annually, upon the 27th day of May, give an account of their administration to the Elders, or Vestry of the congregation. 3. That no new Trustees should be chosen until their number was diminished to five, when these five surviving Trustees shall have the right, and it shall be their duty, to choose twelve other successors, who are to be members of the congregation, and to establish a like contract with them. That arrangement pleased all, and was established on the 24th of October, 1750. To which, in accordance with Mr. Parlin's views and suggestions, the addition was subsequently made, that two of these twelve should be annually elected as Administrators, who should collect the rents, and give in an account of the same. Thus nothing can be kept concealed which belongs to the rights of the church, the congregation, or the Minister. Every one has free access to examine their affairs, and to make himself familiar with their administration. The administration is conducted so quietly that not the slightest murmur against it is heard.

9. SUPPORT.

For the repair of the organ, the church windows, and the parsonage, as also for the fencing in of the churchyard and parsonage grounds, a contribution was agreed upon, to be taken up in the congregation. For the first year's support of Mr. Parlin, no other way was found than by subscriptions, as the treasury was entirely exhausted by the settlement with Mr. Naesman. In later years the rents amounted to £50, some part of which was always used for the repair of the church and the parsonage. The remainder of the salary comes from burials, which are six shillings, and English marriages, which pay twelve shillings. The last named are not only an uncertain income, but also disagreeable, in consequence of various troubles which follow them. There is good hope that after some years the rents will increase as the old leases expire, and a set of lots can be leased to greater advantage.

10. MR. PARLIN'S DEATH.

In the year 1755, when the Provost, Mr. Acrelius, was recalled home, it was also directed that, in the event of his leaving before an order should come in regard to his successor, he should appoint Mr. Parlin as Provost of the churches. But as this was delayed until the following year, his Commission, in the mean time, came in June, 1756, when he immediately entered upon said office. His course of life ended on the 22d of December, 1757, to the deep sorrow of his wife, Elizabeth Tranberg, and his two children, Peter and Anna Catharina.[1]

---

[1] [The ministers settled in Wicacoa Church since 1757, where Acrelius closes his history, have been the following :

8. (In order of succession) Charles Magnus Wrangel, who arrived in 1759, and returned to Sweden in 1768 — died as Pastor of Sala in 1786.

9. Andrew Goeranson became the Rector in 1768, and officiated until the close of

1779. He had as his Assistant the Rev. Charles Lute (the first minister connected with the Episcopal Church of this country), who entered upon his duties in 1774.

10. Matthias Hultgren commenced his duties in 1780, and returned to Sweden in 1786.

11. Nicholas Collin, of Upsala, first settled at Christina, entered on his duties as the Rector of Wicacoa in 1786, and remained until his death in 1831. He had as his Assistants the following ministers of the American Episcopal Church: The Rev. Joseph Clarkson from 1787 until 1792. The Rev. Slator Clay, appointed in 1792, continued to officiate until his death in 1821. The Rev. Charles M. Dupuy appointed in 1822, continued to officiate until 1828. The Rev. Pierce Connelly succeeded Mr. Dupuy in 1828, and continued to officiate until 1831.

12. Upon the death of Dr. Collin in 1831, the Rev. J. C. Clay, D. D., became the Rector, and continued to occupy that position until his death in 1863. He is the well-known author of "*Annals of the Swedes on the Delaware*," from which I have drawn most of the facts just stated.

13. The Rev. John Leadenham, who had been Dr. Clay's Assistant for some time before his death, succeeded to the Rectorship in 1863, and continued to officiate until 1865.

14. The Rev. John S. Reed was Rector from December, 1865, until September, 1868. He was succeeded by

15. The Rev. Snyder B. Simes, who assumed the Rectorship December 13, 1868, and still occupies that position (1873). I am indebted to his kindness for the list of Rectors from the death of Dr. Clay to the present time.]

PART SIXTH.

OF CHRISTINA CONGREGATION.

CHAPTER I.

OF MR. BJÖRK'S TIME.

1. THE SITUATION OF CHRISTINA PARISH.

HRISTINA Parish is mostly situated on both sides of Christina creek, partly on both sides of Brandywine creek, in New Castle county, and in the Hundreds of New Castle, Christina, and Brandywine. It stretches about two Swedish miles in length and one in breadth. In that place the Swedes dwell more together than in any of the others. The most remote families are not more than one Swedish mile (six and one-half English) distant from the church.

2. THE ORIGIN OF THE NAME.

The place derived its original name from Christina, the Queen of Sweden, of most glorious memory, because the Swedish Colonists, who came over to this country in the time of the same highly-renowned Queen, here first established their abodes. First the creek, and then the fort and Hundreds, with various other places which belonged to the then existing government, were named after the reigning Queen. The fort was erected on a rock near Christina creek, not far from its entrance into the river Delaware, and still nearer to the confluence of the Brandywine with the Christina creek; and it can also command the passage of the Christina ferry. Back of that fort it was the intention to lay out the town of Christina, whereof the Swedish engineer,

Peter Lindström, drew a chart.[1] From the time of the Hollanders until the year 1745, the fort lay in ruins. Spanish cruisers having then threatened to make a landing in the Delaware, all the people began to put themselves in a state of defence. At this time, also, Fort Christina had the fortune to come forward out of its long desolation. In digging there they found a coin of Queen Christina's reign. On the 31st of March, 1755, there was accidentally discovered in the wall of the fort a number of balls, hand-grenades, and the like, which had, probably, been carefully concealed just one hundred years before. Since the peace of Aix-la-Chapelle, that fortification has again fallen into ruins; yet it is in such condition that once a year, on the 20th of October, they can fire a salute for the Governor after the English fashion, that is, with five rounds. This is done when he goes to meet the General Assembly in New Castle. Although the English, since they have got possession of the government, have done their best to root out all Swedish usages, yet the first government still continues in worthy remembrance by the names of Christina Parish, Christina Church, Christina Hundred, Christina Fort, Christina Creek, Christina Ferry, and Christina Bridge, which is the passage over the creek.

3. TRANHOOK CHURCH.

In the year 1697, when Mr. Eric Björk came to the country, there was still standing at Tranhook[2] a wooden church, which had been in use since the year 1667. In the year 1699, the fourth day after Pentecost, Divine Service was held here for the last time. The place is now changed into an orchard; yet the ground still serves as a burial-place for a few families who have there interred their fathers, as also for poor people on that side of the creek who have no fixed residence.

4. A NEW CHURCH BUILT.

On the 28th of May, 1698, the building of a church was commenced at Christina, back of the fort. The ground for it was

---

[1] Th. Campanius, p. 81.

[2] [Now called Cranehook ("trana," in Swedish, meaning "a crane"). The church was on the south side of the Christina, near its mouth.]

given by John Stalcop, who was then a Church-Warden. He gave the ground upon which the church stands, together with two fathoms of ground on the west and south sides for free ingress and egress. But as the English law does not recognize any right to gifts of land, payment must therefore be made, if ever so little. Therefore four pounds, which he had promised to the building of the church, were taken in order therewith to strengthen the gift into a proprietary right. Afterwards he sold one and a half acres of land around it for a church-yard and burial-place, of which only about one-third was at first occupied.

5. MEANS THERETO.

In the year 1699, on Trinity Sunday,[1] the church was conse-crated, and received the name of Trinity Church. The names of Mr. Björk, who was then Pastor, and of the Church-Warden, Mr. Charles Springer, deserve to be held in remembrance for their great labor and expense in the building. The difficulty was great in view of the fact that they had often to go from house to house to obtain both masons and day-laborers. The cost amounted to £800. When the accounts were settled, the con-gregation fell in debt to the Pastor to the amount of £135, which he afterwards made a donation to the church. It is remarked that money was at that time more abundant in the country than for a long time since, which may, indeed, be taken as a strong proof of God's providence. Of this, £320 were borrowed of John Hanson Stillman. But inasmuch as he had taken a note at ten per cent. interest, which was two per cent. more than the law allowed, and so stood in danger of losing £100 in a fine if complaint had been made against him to the Governor, he presented this £100 to the congregation, gave his receipt for the same, and was honored with the front pew in the church, and also with a burial-place. In the year 1704, the first Sunday in Advent, thanks were offered to God, who had moved him to make such a gift, in which also happiness and blessings were invoked upon him and his children. The other £220 were paid at various times, partly upon his own orders, and were

---

[1] [Also in the month of May, about one year after the laying of the corner-stone.]

partly sequestered by the law, as he subsequently got into great difficulties. He had Provost Björk's note for the said £220; but when all was paid, he would neither give the note back nor a general receipt, and also came in the year 1723, October 20th, demanding anew the whole debt, with the accruing interest, although his receipts and assignments were there against him, as they are still, in a good state of preservation. That debt is still frequently spoken of as though it were not yet paid.

6. CHRISTINA CHURCH.

The church is of granite, and is sixty feet long, thirty feet broad, and twenty feet high. The wall is six feet thick in the foundation, and three feet at the windows, as well as above them. In the church there are five large arched windows and three arched doors. In front, on the outside, iron letters are fastened into the church walls, and on the west gable is read this inscription:

1698.

SI. DEO. PRO. NOBIS. QUIS. CONTRA. NOS.

SUB. IMP. REG. D. G. ANG.

WILL. III.

PROPR. WILL. PENN. VICE. GUB. WILL.

MAGNIF. REG. SUEC. NUNC. GLOR. MEMOR.

CAROL. XI.

HUC. ABLEG.

E. T. B.

W. S.

P. L.

That is: "1698. Si Deus pro nobis, quis contra nos. Sub Imperio Regis, Dei Gratia, Anglorum, Guillielmi Tertii. Proprietore Guillielmo Penn. Vice-Gubernatore Guillielmo (Markham). Magnificentissimo Rege Suecorum, nunc gloriosissimæ memoriæ, Carolo Undecimo, huc ablegato Erico Tobiæ Björk Westman, Pastore loci." [1]

---

[1] [" *If God be for us, who can be against us ?* In the reign of William III., by the grace of God, King of England. William Penn being Proprietary; William [Markham], Deputy-Governor. The most illustrious King of the Swedes, Charles XI., now of most glorious memory, having sent hither Eric Tobias Björk of Westmania, the Pastor of the place."]

On the east gable:

LUX L. I. TENEBR. ORIENS EX ALTO.

That is: "Lux lucet in tenebris oriens ex alto."[1]

On the north side:

POLUS N. R. CHRISTUS.[2]

On the south side:

IMMANUEL.

7. THE CONSECRATION OF THE CHURCH.

The consecration of the church was celebrated with all solemnity. The Governor was invited to it, but could not attend. For the dinner, which was given in John Stalcop's house, there had been brought in the preceding week, by the congregation, all sorts of meat and drink, such as wheat, malt, bread, flour, hops, wine, butter, sugar, raisins, eggs, veal, mutton, venison, chickens, turkeys, turnips, etc. Most of the members of the congregation took that meal together. All rejoiced and praised God for His gracious care in raising up His Church in this wild land. The same day, which was Trinity Sunday, was afterwards annually celebrated by an evening service of praise and thanksgiving for a long time after. Matins were held on Christmas, Easter, and Pentecost, as also throughout the summer. Garlanded lights and side lights were made of pine wood, for use in the Christmas service. Bridal pairs came to the services in church with crowns and garlands, and the usual style of hair dressing.[3] A belfry was projected, but never completed. The bell was hung upon a walnut-tree in the church-yard.

8. REGULATION OF PEWS.

The pews in church were distributed in such a manner that those who had helped most in the building of the church were provided with the foremost seats, and so on. The children who possessed their forefathers' homestead likewise inherited their

---

[1] ["The light arising from on high shines in the darkness."]
[2] ["Christ is our pole-star."]
[3] [That is, according to the old Swedish custom.]

pews. Those who are the heirs of their fathers' pews have a right to sell them to whomsoever they please within the congregation. Those of the congregation who have come in subsequently, and purchased a homestead on which the original builders of the church lived, do not own the right to the pew attached to the homestead, unless that is specified in the purchase deed. The right to the pew reverts to the church when any family dies out, or when any one removes without selling his right, or when any one acts disorderly or improperly, or obstinately refuses to support the church and Minister. The same course is pursued with those who in later times have purchased the right to pews.

9. The Church-Yard.

There seems to have been more difficulty in regard to the enclosure of the church-yard than with the building of the church itself. Whilst the church was erected within a year, seven years were not enough to enclose the church-yard with palings or wood-work. Mention was made of it at every Parish meeting, but they never got any farther. At a Parish meeting on the 3d of March, 1705, the Pastor proposed it as a penalty to his hearers, that if they did not have the church-yard enclosed by the following Pentecost, they should not have a sermon. Notwithstanding this, the work was not accomplished until two years afterwards.

10. Land for a Glebe and Rectory.

The famous Pastor Björk, who first gathered a church at Christina, had no sooner seen the church built, and the accounts of its cost put in order, than he devoted his thoughts to a suitable residence for the Minister. It so happened that the same good man, John Stalcop, who had before supplied the ground for the erection of the church and for a church-yard, was still further inclined to supply a good piece of land for the glebe. But this was in the first instance met with this difficulty, that the same man would not sell any land but with the proviso that it should be forever used as a parsonage; whereas, the present Minister and people would not be bound to such conditions, inas-

much as the land was still new, the people were just beginning
to settle there, and they did not know whether the glebe might
not after some time be exchanged or sold to more advantage.
Finally, the words, " As an everlasting possession," being removed, they came to an agreement. The land was sold to the
Parish for the support of the Minister, viz., two hundred and fifty
acres of land for £160, which was done on the 29th of December, 1699. Great prudence was exercised in providing that the
land should have a perfectly good title-deed ; for scarcely any of
the neighbors for many miles around can show so good a right
of ownership to their homesteads.

11. THE PARSONAGE.

The house was now to be built, and a parsonage erected. But
the Parish was still £300 in debt for the building of the church
and purchase of land, as was shown at the Parish meeting on
the 24th of June, 1701. The good Teacher must therefore have
patience, and help himself as well as he could, dwelling in
another's household within the Parish. The building material
was collected and ferried over the Delaware from Pennsneck, for a great many living there belonged to Christina. The
parsonage was begun on the 16th of October, 1701, and was
immediately carried up to the roof, but had advanced no further
than to be half finished on the 20th of January, 1710, when Mr.
Björk and his family moved into it. It had probably reached
its completion in the year 1714, when the accounts for it were
settled. It is certain, that it finally became one of the most
respectable houses that could be met with in that unadorned
land. It was built after the old English style of building, of
wood-work and wainscoted walls, two stories high, two rooms
upon each floor, and a loft overhead, and a frame house on one
side for a kitchen.

12. MR. BJÖRK'S ZEAL FOR THE PARISH.

With admirable zeal did that faithful Pastor converse with his
new congregation, prudently carrying out his purposes with
earnestness, and at times with strictness, operating upon an otherwise free people, and, at the same time, patiently awaiting re-

sults.   Everything that was to be done was done not only with
his counsel and concurrence, but also by himself putting his own
hands to the work, from the beginning to the end, in the purchase
of land, its survey, the drawing of the deeds for land—and their
execution, building, and contracts for building, and the scraping
together of the money to pay for the same, etc.   He was in
much favor with the Proprietor, W. Penn, as also with his Governor for the time being, W. Markham, so that he was thus able
to accomplish so much the more.   He watched over not only
the mother-church, Christina, with his faithful sermons, but also
distributed his labors to those on the other side of the river in
Jersey, as also down in St. George's, below New Castle, where
some Swedish families resided.   At one time he had two Swedish
school-masters, Sven Colsberg, on the Christina side, and Hans
Stålt, on the Jersey side ; which latter on Sunday read for the
people in a Postill,[1] when they were unable to come over to
church.   John Göding also kept school in Christina in his time.
When the books arrived from Sweden, he admonished the people
not only to gratitude and praise to God, but also that each one
should make his church some acknowledgment for each book.
He also encouraged his people to contribute peltry, fox-skins,
raccoon-skins, sables, etc., which were sent home, some to Queen
Ulrica and some to the Bishop of Skara.   Sometimes he discussed their doctrines with the Quakers, and refuted their ideas
in regard to dancing ; representing that a lifeless piece of wood
in a viol, or other musical instrument, can awaken sounds which
promote the praise and glory of God ; that the Scriptures approve of the dance in Eccl. 3, 4 ; Ps. 149, 3 : 150, 4.   All this
was approved and strengthened by the Bishop.   See his *America
Illuminata*, in the large Manuscript, p. 307, 308.[2]

13. Salary.

It has been an old custom to pay Ministers by a contribution
called " subscriptions."   Each one who will identify himself with

---

[1] [A book of sermons on the Gospels and Epistles.]

[2] In Sweden, where ancient manners are well preserved, and where costume of
five centuries ago is still worn, it is still the custom for Ministers to engage in the
festive dance.—T. W.

a congregation, places his name upon a list, with the amount that he will pay annually. That is valid as a legal obligation; but no Minister is willing to take it before a magistrate, as this would be more unfavorably regarded here than elsewhere, especially as the country is full of Quakers, who hate the ministerial office chiefly on account of its pay. It would also soon diminish the number of subscribers. One may, therefore, be well satisfied to call it the half of what is placed upon the subscription lists. Mr. Björk had a subscription the first year of about £100, but some years after he could not get more than £40. The reason was, partly, that the money in the country was reduced in amount; partly, that the people then, as ever afterwards, were willing to make good promises when the Minister first came, but afterwards they fell off. But most of all was this the case after the people on the other side of the river withdrew and established a Parish for themselves. However it was, he complained every year of his poor support, even to the end of his service.

14. His Release.

It pleased His Majesty, King Charles XII., to recall Pastor Björk, and by an order, given at his head-quarters at Smorgonia,[1] in Lithuania, on the 21st of February, 1708, to assure him of respectable promotion at home. Thereupon also followed His Majesty's gracious letter to the congregation in regard to its supply with another clergyman; also, the sending over of Bibles and Hymn-books, given at the same place and of the same year and day. Of this he was promptly informed by the Bishop of Skara, Dr. Jesper Svedberg, in a letter dated April 23, 1708, which, however, did not arrive until January 9, 1709. The state of affairs in Sweden at that time neither allowed of rapid posting for a letter, nor a very speedy discharge for Ministers from their Mission. Notwithstanding this, And. Haquinius, a candidate for the degree in philosophy, was by the Royal Commission appointed as his successor; but he died before he could enter

---

[1] [Smorgonia, or Smorgonie, is now in the Russian province of Wilna, which is a part of the old Polish province of Lithuania. Charles XII. was then in the height of his renown. It was in the following year (1709) that he fought the fatal battle of Pultowa.]

upon his voyage to America. That death, together with the new arrangements to be made with His Majesty, who was in remote regions,[1] and the long voyage across the ocean, protracted the time for four years before the exchange came. But there was nothing lost thereby, for the congregations had watchful shepherds, whose condition had now become tolerably good, so that they had but little desire to return to Sweden. When, on the 1st of May, 1712, the Rev. And. Hesselius and the Rev. Abr. Lidenius arrived, bringing with them the letter[2] of His Royal Majesty aforesaid, together with his Commission,—the former to remain as the successor at Christina, the latter, Assistant at all the congregations, also Dr. Svedberg's letter thereon,—then Mr. Björk still took not less than two years to get himself ready for his departure.

15. Three Ministers in the Parsonage.

For still another year he remained with the congregation. The newly-arrived Ministers assisted in the services on both sides of the Delaware, and in the meantime had free board and lodging in the parsonage. They must, however, have at times been short in supplies of food. There is still heard a story how it happened at one time that the wolves slaughtered a number of sheep for some one in the congregation. As it was summer-time, and it could neither be all eaten fresh nor salted down, so some was carried to the rectory. That is said to have been as opportune for them as was the meat which the ravens carried to Elijah.

16. Pastor Björk, Provost, and Settled at Fahlun.

After the lapse of a year, Mr. Hesselius thought that he had waited long enough for his congregation. He therefore had his Commission read the second time, and let it be understood that he was come as the exchange. Therefore Mr. Björk would no longer withhold his rights from him; but on the 1st of May,

---

[1] [In Turkey, namely.]

[2] [Translations of these letters of Charles XII. and Bishop Svedberg are given in Clay's " Annals," pp. 95–97.]

1713, took his departure alike from the church and the parsonage, removing to his father-in-law's, Peter Stalcop. And as he had desired of his Bishop to stay here another year, that was not only allowed him; but he was, by the brief of August 12th, 1713, appointed Provost of the Swedish Lutheran congregations in America. Immediately afterwards, under the date of the 28th of the same month, came a letter from the aforesaid Bishop, with the information that His Majesty had been graciously pleased to favor him with a Commission to the pastorate of Fahlun, dated[1] at Tamerlash, near Adrianople, June 23d, 1713.

17. THE JOURNEY HOME.

There was now no longer time to delay here. The first opportunity for leaving was regarded as the best; but none was offered before six months thereafter; for at that time London packets were seldom seen in the Delaware. On the 29th of June, 1714, he went to sea with his wife, Christina, the daughter of Peter Stalcop, together with their five children — Tobias,[2] Magdalena, Catharina, Christina, and Maria; also his brother-in-law, John Cornelius van der Weer, and his wife, Maria, the daughter of Peter Stalcop, besides an orphan child, Anna, the daughter of Lulof Stedham. That was the first American family given back to Sweden. His church-book, which he kept with the greatest care, he concluded with these verses:

> " Grant now, O Lord our God, Christina Church Thy blessing,
> That there may never fail souls Thy rich love possessing;
> Her Shepherds grant Thy grace, her Sheep do Thou so guard
> That with Thy flock in Heav'n they have their great reward.

> " I thank Thee, Lord, my God, for all Thy grace me given,
> Sixteen successive years I here for Thee have striven;
> From this place now call'd home, with Fahlun honor'd so,
> (Ah! me, unworthy dust! my worthlessness I know,)

---

[1] [It is remarkable that Charles XII. should, under the discouraging circumstances in which he was then placed, direct his attention to the affairs of these Mission churches in America.]

[2] [The author of the " *Dissertatio Gradualis de Plantatione Ecc. Suec. in America*," who signs himself " *Tobias Eric Biörck*," " Americano-Delcarlus," that is, " an American of Dalecarlia."]

" By God's grace and the King's, and our good Bishop's fitness,
Whose soul-care here we see, the work itself his witness.
My God, all that 's well done is Thine — mine all that 's wrong,
But Christ is all my trust, my everlasting song.
                                    " Ericus Björk."

18. Gift to the Church.

After his arrival in Sweden and Fahlun, which was the place
to which he was promoted, he still continued to hold his Christina
Parish in kind remembrance.   He carried on a correspondence
with the elders of the church, especially with Charles Springer,
who had been his right hand in all his work.   Through him the
Fahlun Mining Company presented to Christina Church a large
Communion-cup, together with a Paten and Wafer-box of silver-
gilt. On the cup was this inscription: Fahlu Bergslags Skenk.
till H. Trefald. Kirkio po Chᴵᴺᴬ i Pensylvanien. A. o. 1718.
Assessor och Bergmästare, Herr Anders Swab.[1]

19. Remembrance.

He loved his American parishioners even until his death, and
was loved by them even after his death, so that the people got
into a habit, which they still retain, of counting their age from
his time — the older ones from his arrival in the country, the
younger ones from his departure.

CHAPTER II.

OF THE REV. AND. HESSELIUS' TIME.

1. The Rev. And. Hesselius.

ON the 1st of May, 1713, the Rev. Andreas Hesselius took
charge of the Parish.   His Commission was issued by the
Royal Council, for the time being, on the 23d of June, 1711.

---

[1] [" The gift of the Fahlun Mining Co. to Holy Trinity Church at Christina in
Pennsylvania. In the year 1718. Assessor and Mine-Master: Mr. Andrew Swab."
Chᴵⁿᵃ is an abbreviation for Christiana. This Communion-set is not only still preserved, but regularly used in the old Christina Church when the Holy Communion
is administered there, as I am informed by the present Rector, the Rev. Dr. Frost.]

Mr. John Abr. Lidenius was sent along with him as his Assistant
in the service of the congregations, as was stated in letters-patent
of the same day and year from the aforesaid Royal Council to
the congregations named.   Both at first acted as Ministers in
the Christina congregation.   Mr. Hesselius, as Ordinary of the
congregation, commenced his accession with a general Parish
meeting, wherein he exhorted the members to adhere to the
Swedish Church ordinances.   He then admonished them to
come early to church; to bring their children promptly to baptism; of the necessity of godfathers, with their proper character;
and that children should in due time be reported to the Minister;
as to the necessity of regular attendance upon the Lord's Supper;
on betrothal and marriage, that these should not be entered into
before a certain fixed age, with the knowledge of parents, without
compulsion, not secretly, nor before the parties have good knowledge of their Christian duties.   These points were again presented
in the following year at another Parish meeting.   Twelve Vestrymen were appointed — seven at Christina, and five from Jersey.
These latter immediately demanded that one of the Ministers
should reside with them, to which they would only agree after
they were informed as to the support which they would give him.

2. THE ESTABLISHMENT OF GOOD REGULATIONS.

From time to time he was diligent in introducing good regulations.   It was arranged that the Minister should keep the church
accounts.   A church-chest was provided, in which the moneys of
the church were placed, and two keys were kept — one by each
Church-Warden.   The moneys of the church were to be paid out
on account of the church upon orders of the Vestry.   The Vestrymen were enjoined to have a strict oversight, each in his
neighborhood, of the lives of the people at home in their houses;
to warn and correct the erring; and, in case this did not help, to
cite such persons before the Vestry, and deal with them according
to circumstances.   The forenamed points, viz., attendance at
church, baptism, sponsorship, the Lord's Supper, betrothals, and
marriage were frequently insisted upon.   He also had, for nearly
two years, John Göding as a school-master at various points in
the Parish, who, under proper supervision, met with very pleasing

success among the children, both in teaching them to read and in giving them a knowledge of Christianity.

3. DISORDERS ABATED.

He also had an eye to the uprooting of bad habits which had from time to time crept in. The laying of money upon the altar-cloth at the distribution of the Lord's Supper, it was found, after some reflection, better to abolish. He took care, by means of church watchmen, to prevent the people from driving around through the church-yard, or sitting as gossipers[1] in the neighboring houses after church-service was begun. It was also ordered that all should kneel in prayer, but stand in singing the Creed and hearing the Gospel[2] read. He had especial regard to propriety in church-singing, in which there was often such discord, as though they intended to call their cows to the church. In opposition to which it was represented that as all those who possessed the gift of praising God with a pleasing voice in psalms and hymns should not stand mute, so, on the other hand, those who were unfitted for this should not with their harsh voices hinder others and make confusion, but, by softly singing after the others, train themselves to correct singing. During the singing, he went around in the church and aided where they failed. By all which he deserved the honor of being called " a man of order " by all after-times.

4. AARON JOHANSSON'S WILL.

In the year 1715 inquiry was made after a testamentary bequest which should fall to Christina Church. A childless Swede, Aaron Johansson, had, on the 20th of November, 1701, bequeathed all his property, real and personal,[3] so that after his and his wife's death it should fall to the church, but a part of it also to Pastor Björk; all this the executors should examine at the proper time. The Church-Wardens in office at the time were appointed executors. The death of the testator took place

---

[1] In Sweden, during the morning church-service, no beverage is permitted to be sold. This was observed by a visitor there in 1871. — T. W.

[2] [According to the ancient usage of the church.]

[3] [" I löst och fast " = " movable and immovable."]

in the year 1707, whereupon Mr. Björk and the Church-Wardens for the time being, Edward Robinson and Matthias Peterson, immediately had the will recorded at the proper place. The time had arrived for Provost Björk to return home to Sweden; but the will was not yet in force, as the widow was still living. But she agreed, and so did the Church-Wardens, that the Provost should take his share in fifty-two acres of land lying separate from the rest, which he immediately sold. The remainder was a valuable homestead, called "Bread and Cheese Island,"[1] which was to be left for the church. He was best off who received his share first, for something else was to follow.

5. AN UNFAITHFUL CHURCH-WARDEN.

Edward Robinson, a Church-Warden, was taken into the Swedish congregation by living among them, and by intermarriage, and was regarded among the church-officers as a Swede, but now showed by his nature that he was Irish. He took the widow home to himself; he called her his mother, and she called him her son; and at the same time he persuaded her to change the will in his favor, and exclude the church; as also to exclude the other Church-Warden from being an executor—all under the pretence that no one else would take care of her, although neither he nor she made any complaint about it either to the congregation or to the Ministers. Mr. And. Hesselius, the present Pastor, saw that the matter was going in a very crooked way, and therefore cited him before a general Parish meeting; but thither he would not come. Thereupon he was visited in his own house by the Pastor and elders with the inquiry, "What he intended to do?" To which he answered outright, "To hold the homestead of 'Bread and Cheese Island' for himself," under the pretext that it was contrary to English law to will land to any church. The Pastor maintained that inasmuch as the will had been received as lawful in the Land Office of New Castle county, it was not to be disputed. To which he again objected that the

---

[1] [Still called by the same name. This island is about five miles southwest of Wilmington, up the Christina. It is formed by the Red Clay and one of its tributaries, called Old Red Clay, which unite a short distance above their junction with the Christina.]

value of the homestead was not greater than was required for
the old lady's support, and she declared that she would not
change the arrangement that she had made in his favor. Inquiry
was made for the accounts for her support, and it was answered
that if justice was done, the homestead would not cover these
bills. For the rest, Robinson promised that he would not do
the church any injustice, but still would hold the property;
they would probably be agreed when the time came, Thus had
the matter to remain during the widow's lifetime.

6. THE MINISTER'S SUPPORT SHORT.

As regarded the support of the Minister in those times, lamentable complaints were made about it, and written upon almost
every page of the church-book, especially on the first. It went as
usual with the subscriptions. Some of them moved away to other
places, without paying what had stood against them for many
years. Some, having incurred the debt of many years' salary,
died, leaving widows and children in poverty. Some were able
enough, but both stingy and slow in paying. The glebe was
considerable, with arable fields, meadow, and woodland — more
than could be managed. It was, in truth, a property upon
which a strong and able farmer could in a few years double his
money.[1] But how should a poor Minister, coming with two
empty hands, set up such a farming, for which one thousand
dollars of silver coinage would not be sufficient? Workmen,
draft-animals, instruments of husbandry were all far dearer than
they now are, although a Swede at the present time, when he
first gets to the country, may be astounded at the dearness of
things. The Minister could scarcely get anything more from
subscriptions than what he paid his workmen for a year's wages.
From which it happened that he who sowed little could reap but
little. Mr. And. Hesselius lamented to his good uncle,[2] Bishop
Svedberg, his condition, and received this consolation: "*Having
food and raiment, let us be therewith content.*" Whereupon he
again inquired, "But when we have not food and raiment, what
then?" He inquired in regard to the imposition of tithes,

---

[1] ["Kunnat göra *alterum tantum*," says the original.]
[2] ["Morbror,"="mother's brother."]

whether that was admissible in the Parish; but was always advised against it. It was thought that it would not work better than any other contribution, as it would still have to be voluntary. Tithes are strongly enough enforced in England, but here they would have no legal protection.

7. Signs in the Sky.

The Bishop, Doct. Svedberg, who, at that time, had an active correspondence with the American clergy, advised them that, among other things, they should pay attention to remarkable occurrences, insert them in their church-books, and also promptly report them to him. Of this sort, Mr. Hesselius reports as follows in one of his letters: "The appearance in the sky, in regard to which the Right Reverend Father writes, was seen on the 6th of March, 1716, and is also written of in the English newspapers, where it is called the *Aurora Borealis*, or 'Northern Lights,'[1] and was such as was never before seen here. But some few Swedes here speak with certainty of an appearance which was seen here about the same time of the year, in the evening sky; but no one remembers the day. It appeared to be like a waving and glittering sword with points hanging down from it, with various flashing and extraordinary streams of light. God grant that it may not betide any evil."

8. Frightful Occurrence.

There is another story in the same letter to this effect: "Last spring there occurred in this country a frightful event. A captain of a ship, well known here in Pennsylvania, in the mouth of the Delaware, on his way home from the West India Islands, was suddenly carried off by the devil, and thrown out of the ship into the bay, in the sight of all the people of the ship, upon whom he vainly called for help. He had been a dreadfully wicked man in his time, and especially he had deceived a young woman under promise of marriage, but had broken his promise, and, no doubt, had a secret compact with the devil. For the same day that he was carried off, he made a settlement with all

---

[1] [" Nordska morgon rådnan " = " the northern morning red."]

the sailors on his ship, and paid them their wages correctly; then he had himself bound firmly in his cabin with a strong rope, and warned all of his approaching doom. The pilot took the Bible to read to him; but the Bible was violently snatched out of his hands and thrown to the ship's mast, without any one being able to see whence this violent action proceeded. Thereupon there arose a terrible storm, which broke upon the ship from every point of the compass. Before any one had any idea of it, the captain was lying in the water, whilst all the knots in the rope were found unopened, and exactly in the same condition as they were when the man stood bound in them. All the people were almost crazed with horror, and some of them had to be kept in fetters of iron lest they should lay violent hands upon themselves. The ship, with all its merchandise, came up to this place in safety by the aid of others. I also saw a part of the goods carried by my house to one of the owners. This narrative is confirmed by the fact that the circumstances have been examined in two places, namely, Philadelphia and New Castle, and found, upon testimony, to be exactly as stated. Christina, Pennsylvania, July 1, 1717." [1]

9. Wonderful Rain.

Another occurrence is recorded in the church-book for October 27, 1715: "Col. French reported to me how, in company with some other gentlemen from New Castle, on the 10th inst., he had seen on the King's way leading to Maryland, about twelve miles from this place, a tree upon which it had rained for a fortnight, whilst the sky was clear and without any sign of rain elsewhere. This tree is a young black-oak, about nineteen inches around at the bottom, over which so much rain falls, both by day and by night, that every one who stands under it becomes wet, as did also the Colonel himself, and yet there was no sign of moisture on the ground below it. For greater certainty as to whether the rain fell from the branches and leaves, or from the atmosphere also, a young man climbed to the top of the tree,

---

[1] [This is taken from Bishop Svedberg's "America Illuminated," as printed in the epitome of 1732.]

and found that the rain descended quite abundantly from the sky. Furthermore, the distinguished Colonel related that that remarkable rain was first noticed on the 3d of October, and continued until the 17th day of the same month, when a thoughtless servant, in his drink, cut the tree down, and so the rain ceased to come from it."

10. A Monstrosity.

Another: "July 10th, 1716, an unusual and wonderful event took place at Lucas Stedham's. A ewe bore a monster so misshapen that the bodies of two lambs' bodies, without any head, were united together, each body having four feet and a tail of its own twining towards each other, just as if there were a head in the middle between them; but no sign of a head was to be found, except a split ear between them on the upper side."

11 Another Wonderful Rain.

Another: "October 17, 1717, the Pastor was called over the Brandywine to John Tossawa's, there to administer the Lord's Supper to Henry Stedham's sick wife. Whilst on the way thither, Henry Stedham showed the Pastor two white-oaks, about two gun-shots apart, both close by the King's highway on its left side, as one goes to Philadelphia, one tree in front of the other on a stony ridge, opposite the land of Hans Petersson, who lives near Skylpot creek. It seemed to rain under these oaks, but nowhere else, whilst the sky was everywhere clear, and the sun shining, without the least cloud that could produce rain. On the day before, being the 16th of October, Henry Stedham, his mother, and Mich'l Meyer, had first noticed the rain; and now, on the 17th of October, when the Pastor came to those trees at mid-day, the day being clear and the sun shining, he saw with astonishment how the rain came dropping down in small drops under the first tree, but not so thickly as under the second. And this rain was so clear to the eye, that one could see every drop upon leaf, hats, and clothes; which although they soon dried, yet one could both observe and taste the moisture, though this taste was not different from that of other rain-water. Towards evening, on my return, ... when the sun was something more than an hour high, I saw still more distinctly this rain opposite to the sun, whilst it was to be seen nowhere else around, although we looked for it quite carefully in various places in the forest. From which we can safely decide that this was a peculiar phenomenon, not unlike that seen some two years since on the King's highway, on the other side of New Castle."

God grant that this may not forebode us any evil. This extraordinary rain has never been seen anywhere else since that day, especially when the sky was cloudy, and with the usual rain, which was very frequently to be seen here in Christina.[1]

12. Aid from the English "Society for the Propagation of the Gospel in Foreign Parts."

Besides the faithful care of his congregation, Mr. Hesselius also extended his labors to the English. In the month of July, 1720, he began to preach for them in the newly-built English church at Hwitler's Kill, which was called St. James'. He did this every third Sunday. In the following year he received this letter:

"London, May 8th, 1721.

" Rev'd Sir:

"The Society for the Propagation of the Gospel in Foreign Parts have received a representation from the Clergy in Pennsylvania, setting forth, among other things, the good services you have done by reading prayers, and preaching in the several vacant churches in Pennsylvania, and have ordered me to acquaint you that, in consideration of your past labors, they have presented you with the sum of ten pounds, for which you may draw on their treasurer. They have also agreed to allow you ten pounds per annum in case you perform Divine Service, and

---

[1] Such rain has never been seen again since the time mentioned above. In the year 1750, when Henry Stedham was still living, the Provost Acrelius asked what he thought of that rain. The answer was, that it might have been a multitude of snails (Skalmatkar) that discharged such drops from themselves. Acrelius bade him to procure such snails, and inform him whether he could see a similar occurrence. He could neither find such snails nor see such a rain, as was noticed in the time of Hesselius. This cause, supposing it to have been produced by insects, does not explain the rain which Col. French found above the tree. And so the matter still remains in equal uncertainty in regard to its efficient cause.

preach in the English language in the several vacant churches in Pennsylvania, at least twenty times in one year, and transmit over hither proper certificates thereof.

"I am, Rev'd Sir,
"Your most humble servant,
"DAVID HUMPHREYS,
"Secretary."

13. HIS UNWEARIED ZEAL.

He also expended a great deal of labor in the conversion of the Indians, who, at that time, were frequently seen among the Swedes. But little was thus accomplished. However, one young boy was induced to spend some time at the Minister's house, was there instructed in English in the principal doctrines of Christianity, and afterwards baptized. But not long after that he again returned to the savages, and lived like them. Of the Quakers, also, none were drawn nearer to the church than that they sometimes came to hear English preaching, but they were "*neither hot nor cold*" for it. He translated into English Bishop Svedberg's book entitled, "*God's Holy Law of Destiny;*"[1] which, however, was never printed. The Rev. And. Hesselius was recalled home by a letter dated June 22, 1722. He took his departure in October, 1723, together with his wife, Sarah Wallrave, who died in London. Their children were, Andrew, Jonas, and Maria Christina. After his coming home, he published a book entitled, "A short Relation of the present Condition of the Swedish Church in America, with impartial thoughts in regard to its further extension. Norköping, 1725."[2] He became the Pastor of Gaguäf in the diocese of Westerås.

---

[1] "*Guds heliga Ödnalog.*"
[2] "*Kort berättelse om den Swenska Kyrkos närwarande tilstand i America, samt oförgripeliga tankar om des widare förkofring.*' *Norköping, Anno* 1725." [A letter of his is also prefixed to the Dissertatio Gradualis of Tobias Eric Björck.

CHAPTER III.

OF THE REV. SAM. HESSELIUS' TIME.

1. HIS ARRIVAL IN THE COUNTRY.

HIS successor was his brother, the Rev. Samuel Hesselius, who arrived in the country December 3, 1719. He was called to relieve the Provost Sandel at Wicacoa, was named thereto in the letter of the Ministers, and also provided with the Royal Commission of King Charles XII. for the same, dated at Lund, December 23, 1717. But, however that was, before his departure some change was made, so that the Rev. Jon. Lidman, who had been appointed as his companion in travel, afterwards received from the Queen, Ulrica Eleanora, a Commission for Wicacoa Church, dated at Stockholm on the 2d of May, 1719, and immediately upon his arrival took charge of that congregation. Mr. Sam. Hesselius in the meantime was content to serve the Swedes in Manathanim upon a small salary, and to add somewhat to it also performed service for those in Matzong.[1]

2. A PART OF THE GLEBE SOLD.

Upon his transfer to Christina, which was done by the order of Bishop Svedberg in October, 1723, the sale of a part of the church's land was ordered, as necessary, and the money received was to be placed out on interest, which should relieve the congregation in the support of the Minister. The land was more than the Minister could cultivate, and so lay unused and unprofitable. Some years before the same proposition had been made ; but then, upon the advice of Provost Sandel, it was judged to be better to rent out this part of the land than to alienate it from the glebe. But now it was found that it could yield but little rent for some years, inasmuch as there was no house upon it, and none of the timber was cleared off. The matter was thus decided : that fifty acres of the land should be sold for £40, which, instead of being put out at interest, was immediately employed for the purchase of a negress as a part of the inventory at the parsonage.

---

[1] This is no doubt Matson's Ford, now Conshohocken.

3. The Bequest to the Church Relinquished.

Before the Provost Hesselius went away from the country, Johansson's widow, who had changed her husband's will from Christina Church to Edward Robinson, had been removed by death. Therefore, as the will now went into effect, and said Robinson persisted in keeping the land for himself, the Provost, with two Elders of the church, went to Philadelphia to make complaint in the matter before the Governor, Sir William Keith. He appointed three Justices of the Peace in the country to examine the affair, and give their opinion in regard to it. These took all the papers presented by both parties, but never gave any decision in the matter. Thus the affair stood at the departure of Provost Hesselius. Some time thereafter his brother and successor, Mr. Sam. Hesselius, wished to see the affair terminated. He admonished the Elders of the congregation to attend to the matter with earnestness, and if nothing else would answer, to apply a legal process to it. But no one was willing to meet the expenses of a suit at law; part of them were on Robinson's side as his debtors, or as his friends and neighbors; and the greatest part, there as elsewhere, did not care which way the matter went. The Pastor complained, partly, that his salary was small, partly, that much of it remained unpaid. The congregation thought that if anything could be got from Robinson to pay their Minister, however little it might be, it would still be well, especially as it would not come out of their purse. Finally, they came to an agreement. Robinson gave £15, in all, for the homestead, which afterwards would not have been sold for £700. For this the congregation relinquished all its claims. The Pastor was the first to sign the agreement, then those who were Robinson's best friends. The rest submitted, and no one said a word against it. This was done on the 30th of January, 1725.

4. Complaint.

On the 29th of May, 1729, the Rev. Sam. Hesselius received a very sharp letter from Provost Björk, in Fahlun, in which he was charged with neglect of duty in his Parish in officiating for the English; also that he had sold a part of the Minister's glebe;

and had also sold the right of the church to "Bread and Cheese Island" to Ed. Robinson, applying all the proceeds to his own use. There also came, on the 11th of June next following, a letter from the Bishop, Dr. Svedberg,[1] to Pastor Hesselius, of the same import, and still stronger admonitions. Both letters came through the hands of Charles Springer, from which it was easy to conclude who had first stirred up that trouble. This induced Mr. Hesselius to request of the then Governor, Patrick Gordon, an investigation of the matter for his justification in the case. In addition to this, Provost Björk and Provost And. Hesselius had jointly written a letter in English to the Governor, complaining against Ed. Robinson for the injustice that he had done Christina congregation by depriving it of the land. They set forth the matter with the proper proofs, and desired his assistance in it. Thereupon an investigation was granted. Three Justices of the Peace were appointed to investigate it. Their meeting was held at Brandywine Ferry on the 6th of September, 1729. The Pastor set forth the circumstances which made him regard Springer as his accuser. He also showed his innocence in the matter charged against him. Springer, who was also a Justice of the Peace in the place, was present with a large number of the members of the congregation, and entirely denied being his accuser, but showed that he was his friend by many acts of kindness that he had done him in time past. Neither did any one else in the congregation accuse him. It may be that Springer would have entered more into the matter, if he had not himself been charged, in the letter from the Provosts Björk and Hesselius to the Governor, as the one who had been engaged with Robinson in the alienation of the land, although he had refused to subscribe the agreement.

5. His Acquittal.

Upon investigation of the complaints, it was found that no other time had been wasted in the congregation than that which

---

[1] [Dr. Rudelbach, in his sketch of Bishop Svedberg, (see his "Christliche Biographie," note 81 to p. 356 of Part V.,) says of this letter (though he says it was addressed to *Andrew* instead of *Samuel* Hesselius): "Svedberg's letter to this missionary, who, he says, 'had rejoiced in good days like the priests of Baal, and caused the name of God to be blasphemed among the heathen,' belongs to the sharpest and plainest that he ever wrote."]

was employed for the English, who were destitute of Ministers, for which he had the approbation of his Bishop, and so that was not considered as neglect. As regarded the sale of the land, it was found that it was done by the advice of the officers of the congregation generally, and so was the congregation's own act, and not the Pastor's. From the proceeds of the one sale, a negress was purchased for the inventory of the parsonage, and so belonged to the congregation. Of the proceeds of the other sale, he had borrowed a part upon his own note, which he had already paid. Thus he was found in all respects innocent.

6. Good Testimonials.

Nevertheless, it will readily be understood what disturbance and misunderstanding there now was on both sides. The Pastor sent over to his Bishop the decision of said Commission in regard to his innocence. Also good testimonials for himself — one from the English Missionary, or Provost, Arch. Cummings, in Philadelphia; another from the whole body of the English clergy; another from the English churches in Chester; and yet another from his own Parish in Christina. But all this could not satisfy him, and he therefore resolved to return home to Sweden without waiting for his recall. The officers of the congregation, and even those also who were regarded as unfavorable to him, prepared an assurance, under their own hands, that if he would still remain, everything should be forgotten, and they would see that he was satisfied. But he was so weary and disgusted with disturbance and disquiet that he would no longer delay. So he was provided anew with a good testimonial from the English clergy in their meeting for the year 1730; also with another from all the English clergymen individually in 1731; also a recommendation from the Swedish congregations both to the King and to the Bishop; and thus, in 1731, made his voyage. His wife, in his first marriage, was Brita Loikan; but his second wife was Gertrude Stillé, who now also took leave of her native place. She died upon the voyage between America and England, and was buried in the ocean. The children, who returned home, were Andrew, Christina, Sarah, and Samuel. This gentleman had no less adverse fortune after his return home. He waited for a

21

Parish for many years, had but little support from the Crown,
until finally he was gratified with the Pastorate of Romfertuna,
in the diocese of Westerås.

<hr />

CHAPTER IV.

OF THE REV. JOHN ENEBERG'S TIME.

1. HIS ARRIVAL.

THE Rev. John Eneberg had come into the country some
years before. On his travels, when he came to London,
he had formed the design of going to the Swedish churches in
America, and offering them his services. He therefore wrote
over to his Bishop, Doct. Svedberg, for permission therefor, and
not only received what he requested, but also orders to Magister
Norborg, who was then there as Pastor of the Swedish church
in London, that he should first ordain him as a Minister. On
his arrival, he first preached for the German people, and then,
after Provost Lidman's departure, presided over Wicacoa Church
for two years, and during the vacancy in Christina came down
to preach one Sunday in every month, in which also the Rev.
Mr. Tranberg from Racoon sometimes gave his assistance.
Finally, he received a Commission as Pastor of Christina from
King Frederick, given at Stockholm on the 4th of July, 1732,
which arrived at the close of the year.

2. HIS ACCESSION.

Accordingly, he entered upon his duties at the commencement
of the year 1733. The former disturbances had, indeed, subsided.
Good order was re-established in the management of the church,
and the church edifice was repaired in its windows and roof.
He kept himself entirely in his own church, and never preached
in English.[1] It was said that he had several times made the

<hr />

[1] [His name, as well as the fact that he first preached to the Germans in Philadelphia and its neighborhood, indicates his German origin. The Swedes seem to
acquire English more readily than the Germans do.]

attempt; but as the language was difficult for him, he soon
desisted.   As regarded his support, he regulated himself very
much by the good pleasure of the people.   He did not, indeed,
gain much by it; but he thought one meal in peace better than
many in disturbance.   He also lived quite sparingly, was never
married, but lived in the houses of other Swedes, whilst his glebe
and parsonage were rented out; but he was not on this account
better served.   The negress who had been purchased, was also
hired out, and as she grew older she also grew worse.

3. A Town Built upon the Church-Glebe.

In the year 1735 it was determined that a town should be built
upon the church-glebe.   Then affairs took another aspect.   A
suitable place for this town was found on Christina creek, which
has a wide extent of water, navigable even for ships of war.
Moreover, some high-roads met there, and a building had already
stood at the place for some time.   One should have thought
that the place back of the fort and the church, where the Swedish
town of Christina was formerly located, would have been much
more convenient in regard to the evenness and situation of the
ground, where also the two navigable streams, Christina and
Brandywine, met.   But whether it was to avoid restoring an old
Swedish settlement, or to avoid such close communion with the
church, the first founders of the town being mostly Quakers, or
for the advantage of fresh air upon the heights on which the
town now stands, cannot be positively said.   It is certain that
the plan adopted was the most useful for Christina Parish, which
would not otherwise have had the town upon its land, as the
church stands some distance off, and has but little of its own land
around it.

4. Agreement thereon.

The principal articles of agreement within the congregation,
in regard to the division of the church-glebe and laying it out in
building-lots, were the following: That inasmuch as the church
had an undoubted right to that land in virtue of its deed, and
also, in accordance with its deed of purchase, had a right to
divide or exchange it according to its own interests, therefore it

was resolved that the present Church-Wardens, together with one of the Elders of the congregation, who should be a Trustee,[1] as also all their successors in the same office, one after another, in the order in which they were elected by a majority of votes in the congregation, should have the power of laying out the land into certain lots, streets, and alleys; to rent out the lots for a term of years or for all time; to give deeds for the same; to receive annual rents; also, to receipt for the same, all in their own name; That the same Trustee and Church-Wardens should be bound, at least once a year, or oftener, if so required, to present an account to the Parish, Minister, and Church-Wardens, as to the lots laid out, and the rents collected and to be collected, and pay over to them the rents collected; That a book shall be kept for the lots laid out, and the rents collected and accruing from the same; That the present Minister and all his legal successors, who minister in Christina Church and congregation in accordance with their ministerial office, shall yearly receive two-thirds of all the rents generally, and of each one severally, paid to them in hand by the Vestry of the church; And that one-third part of the same yearly rents shall be employed by the Vestry for the maintenance of the church and parsonage, together with the other necessary expenses of the church corporation; That said Minister and all his lawful successors shall have the use and benefit of the church parsonage with two lots therewith connected in Wilmington; and that the same house shall be fenced in and repaired out of the third part thereto assigned; that the goldsmith, Edward Followel,[2] shall remain the bookkeeper of the Corporation; also that he and his successors in office shall give a bond in the penalty of five hundred pounds to act honorably and to keep the books and accounts correctly. Passed on the 18th of November, 1736.

5. The Name of the Town Wilmington.

The church-glebe had its front on Christina creek, and was not broader than a few gunshots, where the parsonage still

---

[1] [The English term " Trustee " is given, with the Swedish "Ombudsman " as its equivalent.]

[2] [Called, in Ferris (Original History, etc., p. 212), " Gouldsmith E. Folwell."]

stands. Thence it stretched for about one-fourth of a Swedish mile up into the forest, and became broader the further it went. Adjacent to it there was a similar tract which belonged to an Englishman by the name of Thomas Willing, who had received the property through his Swedish wife, Christina, the daughter of Andrew Göstafsson.[1] That, like the glebe along the creek, was now divided into building-lots, streets, and alleys. The town was commenced upon Willing's land, because he consented to sell his immediately, whilst the church would only rent out those which it held. From this the town was at first called Willing's Town. But as he did not sell his land as rapidly as he spent the money received for it, and exhausted his property before he reached the end of his days, the Governor therefore did not consider it proper that the city should honor his name, which it had received in its charter in 1735, but changed it to that of Wilmington, the name of an English Earl; although it is still called " Willingstown " by the country people.

6. Disorder in Management.

That seemed all to be well and good; but the matter ran into the greatest disorder. The subscriptions were discontinued as soon as the lots began to be laid out. By this is meant the voluntary contributions to which each member of the congregation bound himself for the support of the clergyman. The arable land was changed to town lots, and all expenditures for the church and Minister were to be taken from that rich source. But ignorance and selfishness played into each other's hands, and produced most terrible disorder. Of the Vestrymen and Elders of the Parish there was scarcely any one who could write his own name, much less understand any account. Implicit confidence was placed in the Quaker Followel, their book-keeper and surveyor. He so kept his books, and managed their business, that he himself, in a few years, was the owner of a fine house, and some of the best lots that had belonged to the congregation. On the other hand, he advised the Vestry "never to

---

[1] [Ferris, ubi supra, p. 203, writes this name " Andrew Gustison," and says that Willing was married to his daughter " Christina."]

allow any of their priests to look into their management," for then the whole sum would soon be made away with. This they did so faithfully that they never took counsel with their Ministers in the least, but always with that Quaker. Neither did the Ministers care to trouble themselves about it, for the sake of peace and unity.

7. THE DISORDER INCREASES.

But the disorder increased; the income fell off; and no one could foresee how it was to go in the future. The lots were rented with the proviso that those who did not build upon them within three years thereafter, should lose their rights to them; and so far that was well enough, for every year that they were not built upon, they fell under judgment for back rents. On the other hand, those members of the Parish who wished to take lots for themselves and their children, were not bound by these conditions; had their lots upon three shillings less of yearly rent than was paid by strangers; and also had the right to transfer them to persons not members of the Parish, upon the same terms. Whereby it happened that some of them immediately sold their lots, at a considerable advance, to strangers, as they had so many advantages. They also sold them to unknown people in distant parts of the country, without advising the Parish of it. And then these lots came into third and fourth hands, so that they could neither know the owners, nor get their lots back, nor collect the rents due from the first year. Various lots were also given away, some to the Ministers, some to Vestry-men as a reward for their trouble, which were also immediately sold to strangers at a profit, so that rents could never accrue from them.

8. LAND SOLD TO PAY THE MINISTER'S SALARY.

Now when the ground-rents did not come in at the close of every year as had been expected, but a part remained unpaid for many years, part of them from the very beginning, so it could not but follow that the Corporation must annually fall in debt to the Minister, according to their engagement to him. Had the Vestry agreed with the Minister for a certain amount of yearly salary, according as the rents increased or diminished, they would not have put themselves in the way of unnecessarily falling into debt. And although the ground-rents had come in more regularly in the first year, inasmuch as many lots had not yet found renters, when the Rev. John Eneberg was about to leave the country, he had to demand over £100 as a balance unpaid upon four years' salary, according to their own accounts. The Parish, which had not laid out a penny during all this time for their Minister's salary, had now at once to bring together as much as would meet that debt. But no one would now take upon himself the burthen of paying the Minister; the Corporation would, without doubt, be able to do it when more lots were rented! Therefore the sum of £92 was taken upon interest to pay the debt, and, as it came too heavy to pay the interest yearly accruing thereon, a considerable piece of ground was again sold for its payment.

9. TRANSACTIONS AND CHANGES.

Whilst Mr. Eneberg was with the Parish, the accounts were still kept in pretty good order, so that they knew what went out and what came in. The third part of the rents was employed for the repair of the church; and therewith, in the year 1740, two arches were built on the north side, as a support for the church wall, which was bent outwards by the weight of the roof, and the want of a good foundation. These arches stand over the two church-doors, are like a vestibule, and give the church the appearance of a Roman Catholic edifice. Formerly the bell hung in a walnut-tree near the church, but as the squirrels continually resorted there for the nuts, and built their nests upon the arches of the church, by which the roof was injured, a neat little wooden tower was erected upon one of these outbuildings of the church, and the walnut-tree was cut down. Until that time Matins had been celebrated on Christmas-day, with lights burning in crowns and arms made of wood for the purpose; but as the English people, and especially the Quakers, came in crowds out of the town to gaze at the celebration, and some travelled long distances to gratify their curiosity by staring at it, and also passed unfavorable judgments upon it, it was therefore laid aside, and one now only hears it spoken of as something wonderful. After receiving a recall from the ruling powers at his own desire, Mr. John Eneberg took his departure from the congregation in the year 1742, returned home to Sweden, and spent the remainder of his days upon his own little estate in West Gothland.

CHAPTER V.

OF THE REV. PETER TRANBERG'S TIME.

1. ENTRANCE UPON HIS DUTIES.

ABOUT the same time, 1742, the Rev. Mr. Tranberg had requested a release from Racoon and Pennsneck, with transfer either to Sweden or to Christina. In consequence of which, and in accordance with the proposal of the Archbishop, Dr. John Steuch,[1] by the Commission of King Frederick, dated at Stockholm on the 10th of December, 1739, he was removed over the Delaware to Christina. His Commission came at the same time with Pastor Tranberg's recall home. But as there was war, and the voyage was dangerous, they agreed to delay the exchange for another year. Finally, Mr. Tranberg's accession to his latter congregation took place on the 1st of August, 1742, and that with so much the greater joy in the congregation, as he was naturally so much regretted on the other side of the river. He had already lived fifteen years in the country, and made himself master of the English language, and so he was as much hoped and longed for by the English as by the Swedes. The parsonage was old and ruinous, and so he rented a house in the town. He told his people that if they would give him a lot, he would build a house of his own upon it, as he was determined to remain with them until his death, and should leave a large family behind him. A lot was given him quite near to the old parsonage, and his own house was built upon it, some members of the church

---

[1] [Dr. John Steuchius, or Steuch, succeeded his father, Matthias Steuchius, as Archbishop of Sweden in 1730, and occupied the position until his death in 1742.]

aiding him in it.   It was finished within a year, and was one of the finest brick houses in the town.

2. THE INVENTORY.

The inventory found in the parsonage was of but little value. The negress, who, some years before, had been bought for the price of fifty acres of land, was old and contrary, and being set up at auction was sold for seven shillings.   For the rest, there was one cow, one walnut table, two chairs, some old tin plates and tin spoons, which were turned over to the Pastor.

3. OFFICIAL ACTS.

In regard to Divine Service, the congregation were asked how far they desired English.   Some were as much opposed to it as others were in favor of it.   But inasmuch as they now had so many English around them who would otherwise have no church-service, and some who did not understand Swedish were the descendants of Swedes, therefore it was agreed that English service might be held in the afternoon, when the Swedish was concluded in due time according to the church-law; to which, however, the Pastor was no further bound than might be convenient to himself.   Mr. Tranberg was greatly beloved all over the country, as well for his good gifts in his office as for his exemplary deportment, and the people, therefore, came from many quarters to request his services as a Minister, and also honorably paid him for the same, as money was now, during the war,[1] quite abundant, and circulated freely through the country.   He was sometimes up at the town of Lancaster to preach for the German congregation in that place, and to administer the Lord's Supper.   He officiated at St. James',[2] Folk's Manor, Marlborough, and Concord Churches about once every month — sometimes on week-days, sometimes on Sundays. Some of these places were not less than three or four Swedish miles in the interior of the country.   He often went over the

---

[1] [The war of the " Pragmatic sanction," in regard to the claims of Maria Theresa to the succession of the Austrian empire, from 1744 to 1748.]

[2] [St. James' Church, at Staunton, four miles southwest of Wilmington.   Marlborough is in Pennsylvania, northwest of Wilmington.]

river to preach or to bury their dead, when also a sermon was
delivered. Such constant travelling in frost and heat, in rain
and snow, in storm and tempest, could not but prematurely
destroy his powers and shorten his life, not to say that some
affairs in the Parish could not be equally well watched over.

4. NEW ARRANGEMENT WITH THE CHURCH CORPORATION.

Time and again he complained that that which was destined
for his support came in very irregularly. A great many of the
ground-rents were never paid, for of those who were indebted
some refused to pay, and others could not. Advice was taken
with a lawyer as to whether they could not be compelled thereto
by law. The answer was that no suit could be entered before
their management was set upon a different footing. Two or
three men in the congregation should receive full powers to
manage and act with the church's land as with their own property, under the name of Trustees, or persons put in trust. But
that did not sound well in the ears of many persons, and so
nothing more was done for a time.

5. DELIBERATION ON THE SUBJECT.

The town grew; the inhabitants prospered; the people multi-
plied, and demanded more building-lots. Then the officers of
the congregation were upbraided by the Quaker Followel, their
book-keeper, that they hindered the increase of the town by
refusing to sell lots to those who wished to buy. That they
could thus prevent the irregularities which resulted from the
rents remaining unpaid for so many years. A bank could be
established with the money, which would yield an annual interest; this would also tend to increase the value of the land.
But on the other side it was suggested that land was safer than
money, and that no bank could be made so secure that one
should not be in danger of losing both his capital and his
interest. That so disturbed our old Christina people that for a
time they did not know whether it was better to sell the lots or
not.

6. Trustees, or Managers Appointed.

In 1745, on Ascension day, at a general Parish meeting, they agreed to commit the lands of the church and its town-lots into the hands of two Trustees, to act therewith as they found best, both as regarded the selling and the renting of the lots of a certain tract which lay within the limits of the borough. They were to put out the money at annual interest, collect the interest and rents, and be answerable for the same when the congregation called them to an account. All the deeds and charters of the church were to be put into their hands. All sales and contracts were to be made in their name. Thereupon they also gave their own bond, with a penalty of five hundred pounds, that everything with which they were intrusted should belong to the congregation, and should be employed according to its orders.

7. Management Disordered.

The choice in the congregation fell upon two men who could neither write nor cast accounts, who were to be the Trustees. That exactly suited the Quaker Followel, for all their reliance and confidence were in him. The contracts which were formerly for rents were changed into deeds of sale, which gave him new income, as everything was to pass through his hands. But the management of the church corporation rapidly became worse than ever. He who wished to purchase his lot in fee-simple, when he had no money, was to give his note for an amount so large that it would yield the same interest as the ground-rent had done before, reckoning at six per cent. But security was not demanded for the money either by bond or upon the lots. Whence it came to pass that, as many worthless people took lots in that manner, some of them put the lots in pledge in other places and for other debts, became bankrupt, and then the lots of the congregation went to satisfy the debts of others, whilst the Trustees allowed themselves to be satisfied with a note which was never worth a farthing.

8. Still Greater Disorder.

The management became so much worse that ready money was constantly lent out of the treasury without the least security.

It was thought that it would be impolite to demand such a thing, although that was the general usage in the country. Further, that loans were made in small sums, and those to improper persons, as one often has more trouble to collect the interest of five pounds than of fifty. Money was also lent to unknown persons living many miles out in the country. The one Trustee lent to people whom neither the other Trustee nor any one in the congregation knew. Moreover, the lots that had been set off to members of the congregation, and let at a lower rent, as also those that had been sold by the members of the congregation to strangers at such low rents, were nevertheless now sold by the Trustees far below their value, in view of the moderate rent.

9. No Accounts kept, and more Land given away.

Finally, it is to be remarked that these Trustees never exhibited any correct account of their receipts and expenditures. What was presented as such at their Parish meetings were only receipts for expenditures, or small sheets of paper without any amount carried out on them, still less with *saldo*[1] and balance from the preceding year. But little was said about it, and so the thing was done without any further notice or approval. There was never any inventory of property handed over by one Trustee to the other. The Minister saw that the people were groping along as blind men, but for the sake of peace and unity did not say much about it. But he often complained that he could not live in the way the salary came in. Then they gave him a whole square in the town for himself and his children; but not as a settlement of his back salary, for the balance was afterwards fully drawn out.

10. Tranberg's Death.

Pastor Tranberg was a pious and meek man, who sought to please everybody. During the twenty-two years that he lived in the country, he was blessed with a considerable amount of property on both sides of the river. It would, indeed, have been his desire to see his native land in his old age, had the circum-

---

[1] [*Saldo* is the Italian term for an account closed. Of course, every account should be commenced with the balance of the preceding year.]

stances of his family so allowed.   When he went over the Delaware to Pennsneck, to attend the funeral of a married pair who
had been his old friends and hearers, he was himself, after per-
forming that last service for them, taken deadly sick in the house
of the deceased, and, four days thereafter, fell asleep in the Lord,
in the same place, on the 8th of November, 1748.   His funeral
took place on the 10th of the same month, in Christina Church.
The sermon was preached in English by the English Missionary,
Mr. George Ross, at that time the oldest Minister in the country.
The sermon in Swedish was preached by the Rev. Gab. Naesman, at that time the only Swedish Minister left in the country ;
who also afterwards through the following year, during the
vacancy, came down once a month to hold Divine Service in
Christina.   In the house of the deceased were his widow, Anna
Cath. Rudman, and his children, Andrew, Rebecca, Elizabeth,
and Peter.   The church-book for Mr. Tranberg's time is closed
with the following verses written by his successor.

> So fades one race of men away
> As into darkness changes day ;
> Yet other forms forever rise
> As day again lights up the skies.
> > Forever break eternally
> > Thou ever shifting human sea, —
> > Birth, Life, and Death thy billows roll,
> > But under God's supreme control.
> How happy he who yields his breath,
> Secure of triumph over death,
> Who thro' the faith that Jesus gave
> Can gladly sink into the grave.
> > When the chief Shepherd shall appear,
> > To call him from his labor here,
> > Is he not happier, labor done,
> > Than one whose toil has just begun ?
> Who is just arming for the strife,
> Whose flock demands his care for life ?
> Less gladly he to duty goes
> Than one who sinks in blest repose.
>
> Versified by MALCOLM MACEUEN.

CHAPTER VI.

OF THE REV. ISRAEL ACRELIUS' TIME.

I. ARRIVAL, AND ENTRANCE UPON DUTY.

MR. TRANBERG'S decease became known to the Archbishop[1] and the Consistory of Upsala by a notification thereof from the Parish in the month of May, 1749. The provost, Mr. Israel Acrelius, who had already been called and appointed as Pastor for the Parishes of Racoon and Pennsneck, immediately received a transfer to Christina, in accordance with his own desire, and the approbation of the Archbishop, Dr. Henry Benzelius. King Frederick issued his Commission, which was dated at Stockholm on the 26th of June, 1749. After a speedy and fortunate voyage from Stockholm on the 20th of July, 1749, he reached his Parish at Christina in the month of November following. The officers of the congregation immediately came, one after the other, to welcome their new Teacher to the country. All were heartily glad to find that they were still assisted with Ministers from old Sweden. Tears stood in the eyes of many when they spoke of the grace of the King of Sweden bestowed upon them and their forefathers. They requested the Provost not to be discouraged, if he should at the first find unexpected difficulties. They lamented that they did not speak Swedish as well as they should, and that they had not at once a suitable parsonage for his residence; they assured him that he should not suffer any want among them, and if he wanted money immediately for his travelling expenses, it should be forthcoming. Fifteen pounds were collected to buy him a horse which was to be his own. The joy was so much the greater at his arrival, as he was not expected in the course of the first year; no one was aware that a letter could go to Sweden and a Minis-

---

[1] [Dr. Henry Benzelius, as mentioned below. This family was remarkable for the number of distinguished men it gave to the service of the Church. Erik Benzelius the elder died as Archbishop in 1709, and was succeeded in this office by his three sons, Erik, Jacob, and Henry.]

ter immediately come within a year's time. This was greatly promoted by the fact, that at that time ships began to go more rapidly between London and Philadelphia than was formerly usual, and this has continued ever since. Formerly scarcely more than one a year went, whilst in later years seven or eight have been making that voyage. Hence the people say, that the way between Sweden and America is now shorter than it used to be.[1]

2. ·ORDER AND DISORDER.

The Provost could not but anticipate that he should find many irregularities in a Parish which had stood vacant for a whole year, in a country where restraint was unknown. But, contrary to his expectations, he found that the people came quite unitedly to church, listened to the preaching with much attention, sang their Swedish hymns without a leader,[2] and some of them astonishingly well. Besides, they brought to the church children for baptism, and mothers to be churched. On the other hand, many disorders were observed, such as, that during Divine Service both men and women were going out and coming into the church, under the pretence of some necessity; that children were withheld from baptism for six or seven weeks; that the parents themselves wished to stand as sponsors for their children, did not give in the child's name and age before the time in which it was brought to baptism; that the grave was dug and the body buried without giving notice to the Minister. Sometimes the grave was dug when the people were going to church or during service; the corpse came either during or after service; the greater part of the people were in the procession to the grave, and then desired the service over again. Some sat in church who could very well use a hymn-book, but were silent almost throughout the singing, as well as in the rest of the service. The Minister was to give out the

---

[1] [In the large folio volume of the-church books of Trinity Church, Wilmington, Acrelius has carefully recorded, in a bold English hand, the principal events of his ministry in that church from his call by the Consistory of Upsala until his departure, of which also his successor, Mr. Parlin, gives an account. I am indebted to the politeness of the present Rector, Dr. W. Frost, for the inspection and use of these church-records, perhaps the oldest and best preserved in this country.]

[2] [Or "föresinger," as the original has it.]

hymn before it was commenced, and then the congregation had
to hunt it up in the index, from which it happened that half the
Psalm was often sung before half the congregation was fully
engaged in singing. The hymn-books lay unused and torn in
great heaps in the pews, and sometimes were trampled under
foot. The church was defiled from the roosting of birds in it
for many years; there was dirt and filth in the aisles and pews,
and on the floor.

3. ORDER ESTABLISHED — DISORDERS ABATED.

The Provost went zealously to work, with prudence and earnestness, to bring these things into good order. As often as he
heard allusions to the freedom of the country in this respect, he
answered; "That although people here had freedom of conscience from men, there was no freedom of conscience with God.
His word and commandments were our laws. As regarded external matters and church ordinances, they must be held according to the Swedish church-law, if they were to be and to remain a Swedish church with Swedish Ministers. Without order,
no society, no church, can stand." By God's blessing, this effected
so much, that the disorders above-mentioned within a short time
disappeared, and no one who rightly holds to the congregation
any more speaks of such freedom, but is much rather offended
if any one acts unbecomingly in these respects. For greater
convenience in finding the hymns, two Number Tablets[1] were
arranged—one for Bishop Svedberg's edition, and the other for
the common edition of the hymns. The hymn-books in the
church, the binding of which had been destroyed, were rebound,
and the expense paid by the owner, or any one else who would
procure them for himself. The church was whitewashed, the
pulpit and chancel around the altar polished, whilst the floor and
pews were scoured by the women of the congregation, who now
have the custom of coming together for this purpose one day in
every year. Also, altar-linen was procured, which had not been
the usage for many years.

---

[1] [Small blackboards, such as are in use in many German churches of this
country.]

4. School-Keeping.

For the instruction of the youth in the doctrines of their Christian faith in Swedish, Nicholas Forsberg, of Götheborg, was taken for the time being. He had studied at the University of Lund, and, after visiting various other parts of the world, came to this country to try his fortune. The congregation were urged to take advantage of the occurrence. At first, for one winter, he was in a private house, and there taught the children, and afterwards, during the summer of 1750, taught school near the church. But as he became unwell towards autumn, and so continued through the winter, and found that the school yielded him a poor support, he gave it up.

5. House Instruction.

The congregation was divided into certain sections, the Provost visiting each in order to hear the Catechism and to make explanations. This was done in the following manner: The beginning was made with some passage of Scripture, which was explained and adapted to the Order of salvation;[1] after this the recitation[2] was attended to, and a suitable exposition was given of both the Law and the Gospel, and the use of the Sacraments, especially of the worthy receiving of the Lord's Supper, inasmuch as a most unjustifiable neglect had prevailed in that respect. Some fruit thereof was perceived, but by no means as much as had been desired and expected. Both the old and the young were encouraged to give an account of their knowledge and faith in answer to the questions proposed, and with most of them a greater acquaintance with the plan of salvation was manifested than had been expected. It could not be avoided that they had sometimes to be allowed to explain themselves in English, as their thoughts thus came most easily. The young were afterwards taken by themselves to read their parts of Christian doctrine either in Swedish or in English; for, from the want of Swedish schools, the young learn mostly in English, until they become more intelligent, and then they use the Swedish Catechism. With all

---

[1] [As given in the Swedish Catechism.]
[2] [Of the Catechism. Suebilius' edition was used.]

22

this, both parents and children were exhorted to a sincere godliness, and to a faithful and holy life. At first many kept away,
fearing too severe admonition and harsh reproof; but after they
became accustomed to the mode of instruction, they not only
attended at their proper place, but also at the meetings in other
more distant sections.

6. DIVINE SERVICE IN ENGLISH.

During the progress of the first year the Provost was frequently
reminded how necessary it was to preach in English. Outside of
the congregation they often lamented the decease of Mr. Tranberg, who made no difference among the people, but was inde-
fatigable, never sparing himself. Within the congregation it
was said that no one could reasonably refuse it; it had been
so formerly, and it ought to be so in the future; so many people
were anxious for it, as they had no other place to go to. There
were also some who had a right to the church who could not
avail themselves of the Swedish service; moreover, it was an aid
to the congregation for strangers also to join in the support of
the Minister. Mr. Tranberg had been loved by all, because he
had ministered to all. Such talk was heard early and late wherever one came, and that, finally, to his deepest disgust. So when
the Provost had allowed the time to run on, some were inclined
to conclude that he was, indeed, well enough disposed, but that
he had not a sufficient command of the English language. They
had instances of this before in others. Finally, he determined to
begin with English preaching in Christina; wherewith the congregation was very well pleased; and thereupon others came
from St. James' Church and desired the same there. The church
was asked about this, and no one was opposed to it, as many
Swedes resided in the neighborhood, and there were good neighbors all around. That was the church in which the Rev. And.
Hesselius had preached every third Sunday, and had received
therefor an annual salary from the London Society. Others
again came from New London[1] and Marlborough, three or four
Swedish miles up in the country, requesting the same aid, as

---

[1] [New London is in Chester county, Pa., northwest of Wilmington, Del.]

otherwise their children would become unchristened heathens, or Quakers; their churches would be changed into stables alongside of Quaker meeting-houses. They praised Mr. Tranberg as a warm-hearted man, who had always assisted them. The Provost therefore took some time to see whether it was possible to please everybody. He preached once a month in all these places. He was at Christina every Sunday; but on week-days and saints' days in the others. That became the rule, and at first was all right; but afterwards each congregation wanted preaching on a Sunday. To these were also added the churches at Concord[1] and Marcus Hook,[2] which presented the same request; and then there were not as many Sundays in the month as there were congregations to serve, and so Christina would always have been vacant. The good old Swedes now began to murmur, partly at the Minister, that they never got to hear him on Sunday in their own church, and partly at the English, who wished to have him with them, and never once paid his expenses of travel. Finally, after the lapse of half a year, it resulted in this, that the expenses were paid by the elders of the church, and the Provost, who neither would nor could meet the unreasonable wishes of everybody, was excused; but he had English preaching only at Christina one Sunday every month — in summer before Vespers,[3] and in the winter before High Mass.[4]

7. HOUSE BUILDING.

April 16th, 1750, a Parish meeting was held. It was there taken into consideration what work should be done during the coming summer, either in repairing the church or in building a parsonage. The Provost declared himself satisfied to live in a rented house in the town if they would first expend the money for the church building. But as they had not for many years had any suitable parsonage, and had for a long time decided to erect one, the most of them were now inclined to undertake

---

[1] [Concordville is in Delaware county, Pa., north of Wilmington.]
[2] [Marcus Hook is also in Delaware county, Pa., 20 miles south of Philadelphia.]
[3] [That is to say, an afternoon service.]
[4] ["Högmässan" (High Mass) is the Swedish name of the principal Sunday service, usually commencing about ten o'clock, A. M.]

it. The foundation was laid in the month of July next following, and the building was completed by the close of the year 1751. The parsonage was built of brick, three stories high, two rooms upon each floor, according to the custom of the town. It stands upon the old church-glebe. The cost amounted to £343 16s. 4d. Of this, £121 13s. 6d. were contributed by the congregation; the remainder, £222 2s. 10d. were taken from the church treasury. The old parsonage is still standing, and serves for a kitchen, store-room, servant's room, and stable — all under one roof.

8. Advantages of the Parsonage.

The meadow at the old church-glebe is sufficient for two horses and three cows, and hay can be gathered twice a year. In the year 1750 that piece of meadow was rented for five years; but the Parish found it advisable to buy back the contract, and give the ground to the support of their Minister. To change the wild land to a better kind of grass cost him a great deal of trouble and expense for plowing, fencing, ditching, embanking, and expensive drain-pipes in a swampy marsh; for the best meadow land was sold before his arrival. Besides this there belongs to the church-glebe a little pasture-lot near the church, upon the ground on which the church stands, together with forty acres of woodland near the town, in good condition. A small vegetable garden is arranged near the house. Some considerable town-lots, that had been rented out, were again taken back by the Corporation, and fenced in at the Provost's own heavy expense, so that they could afterwards be used either for meadow or tillage, in which he always had more regard for his successors' than for his own advantage.

9. Repairs of the Church.

Before the building of the house was completed, the improvement of the church was meditated. The church wall along the south side had yielded to the weight of the roof, as neither an arch nor a wooden beam bound the wall together. They had often taken counsel how and in what manner it might be repaired, whether by an iron band inside or by building pillars outside; but they could not arrive at any conclusion in regard to it.

Nevertheless, that the time might not pass by unimproved, a new roof was laid upon the whole of the south side, which was very necessary.   Then attention was again turned to the wall, as to how it might be secured; but they could not agree as to what was best to be done.   They therefore undertook something else that was very necessary, and made some new windows in the church.   These and similar improvements went on rather slowly, for, although there was no want of a good-will, their resources in land had been greatly contracted by an injurious transaction which could not be remedied.   When the Provost urged his people to undertake these and similar matters, without his putting his hand to them, it was answered by all, that he was the only one who could accomplish such a thing among them, as no one declined to do what he proposed among them; which he also finds it his duty thus to record here to their enduring honor.

10. The Management Conducted Secretly.

The officers were asked in what condition the Corporation and its finances then were?   But this question, of great consequence, could not at once be answered.   The Provost was astonished at their accounts — great sums being expended, and managed in a blind way.   He desired to see their deeds of sale and rent, and the deeds for their lands; also the obligations given by the Trustees for the honest discharge of their duties.   But at one time there was no answer; at another it was one thing here, another there; so that there was no getting at the facts.   He was paid at the pleasure of the officers; but now more, now less.   What was the proper salary?   It was answered, Two parts of all rents of town lots and moneys at interest.   It was further asked, How he was to know what that amounted to, so that he might regulate his expenditures accordingly?   It was answered, That that could not be exactly stated, nor ought they to tell or talk about it!   The Minister would be too cunning for them.   Finally, it also came out that "the Quaker Followel, their book-keeper, had advised them to keep the Priest from looking into their accounts."

11. Representations Thereon.

The Minister represented, both in the Parish meetings and in the Vestry, that this could never have a good ending. If the members of the congregation did not open their eyes in time, they would see into the matter when it was too late. He let every one know that he had not come to look after their money, but after their souls. He appealed to their own testimony that no offensive word had ever passed between him and the officers of the church, or any person in the Parish, in regard to his support, but that he had at all times thankfully received his salary as a free-will offering. But after three years' experience, and some careful consideration of their mistaken management, as also in obedience to the instructions of his Bishop, he could not forbear reminding them of the necessity of acting more prudently with the property of the Parish. The occasion for this was, that the rents and interest were diminishing every year, whilst they ought to have been increasing. The amount of funds in the Parish treasury was known to no one, much less what ought to be there for the lands that had been sold, and for their town lots. The one Trustee honestly acknowledged that he did not know what the other had in his hands. The Quaker Followel had sold land and collected rents equally with the Trustees, but there were no accounts of these transactions.

12. Revision of Accounts.

Finally, they all with one mouth answered, that they would be greatly obliged to the Provost if he would take the matter into his hands and revise the accounts. The old Trustees voluntarily delivered up to him all their papers which could serve to throw any light upon the past. The Quaker Followel was now dead, but had left behind him a correct book of the town lots and annual rents; also of all the lots that had been sold, and the price received for them. A correct account had also been kept of all expenditures and income from the year 1749, when the Provost came into the country, and a young man had been appointed as one of the Trustees, who was well able to write and cast accounts. So the review commenced with the year 1745, when they began to

sell the lots, and thence to the 25th of March, 1749, and for
these four years there was found an undoubted deficiency of
£49 12s. 4d.

13. The Minister United with the Trustees.

When that was shown at the meeting on the 12th of June,
1753, every one was astounded.   The Vestry requested the Provost to become their sole Trustee, and take everything into his
own hands.   But he thanked them for the honor, and represented that a Trustee should be one born in the Parish, and
should possess property to such an amount as would answer for
that with which he was intrusted.   Yet if they had so much
confidence in him as their Minister, he would be a Co-Trustee,
so that nothing should be done in the church corporation without his counsel and concurrence.   The other Trustees should
not be empowered to act before they put their affairs upon a
better footing, and remedied the mischief already done.

14. Injury of Injudicious Management.

The injuries which the Christina congregation has received by
imprudent management are, therefore, very great.   She has been
injured by an unnecessary sale of land, for which no value has
been received.   She has been injured by the giving away of town
lots, when the Corporation was not equal to such liberality;
injured by the unwise setting out of town lots, which now yield
nothing, or are beyond the control of the church; injured by
failure in accounts; injured by want of security for money out
upon interest.   All of which, with something more, amounts to
at least a loss of £1500; to which may be added that the third
part, which was to be kept for the church, has been so squandered
by confused accounts, that it is no longer to be found.   It is impossible to remedy the injury; but necessity demands that an
utter destruction should be prevented.

15. Difference between Former and Present Times.

Posterity are generally wiser than those who have gone before
them, and the errors of others are much easier to see than our
own.   But this is recorded for a testimony to after-times, that

Christina Parish, without the least burthen to its members, was well able to support both the church and its Minister, if the means given it by Providence had been better husbanded. Whereas, it is now doubtful whether the church will come up again, if it is once prostrated. Our Swedish Americans have always been afraid of getting too rich, and have therefore paid little attention to their own best interests. They have rather allowed others to seize upon their advantages, than made use of them themselves. Moreover, the times within fifty years are as changed as night is from day. At the first settlement they could buy land, and within a few years build a church and parsonage, which now they can scarcely support, and with difficulty retain what they have received from their forefathers. But this is nothing wonderful. Formerly, the church people could come some Swedish miles on foot to church; now the young, as well as the old, must be upon horseback. Then many a good and honest man rode upon a piece of bear-skin; now scarcely any saddle is valued unless it has a saddle-cloth with galloon and fringe. Then servants and girls were seen in church barefooted; now young people will be like persons of quality in their dress; servants are seen with *perruques du Crains*,[1] and the like; girls with hooped skirts, fine stuff-shoes, and other finery. Then respectable families lived in low log-houses, where the chimney was made of sticks covered with clay; now they erect painted houses of stone and brick in the country. Then they used ale and brandy, now wine and punch. Then they lived upon grits and mush, now upon tea, coffee, and chocolate.

16. BANK INTEREST.

The church treasury owns at the present time £650 16s. 2d.; of which, however, only £624 16s. 2d, are secure. The yearly interest thereon is £37 10s. The yearly ground-rents amount to ten or twelve pounds that are secure. If the Parish pays its Minister out of this a yearly salary of £50, and also half an acre for the different kinds of grain, he can get along with it. It is well known that the congregation will not allow

---

[1] Wigs made of hair.

its Minister to suffer want; but as the salary is arranged so as to be paid by interest and ground-rents, few make any inquiries as to how he comes out. If he complains of want, all manifest a readiness to help him. Could the Minister live without troubling the congregation, they would rather see it so, and love him all the better.

17. OTHER INCOME.

The income of the church is small. If any stranger is buried in the church-yard, 12 shillings are paid for a corpse over twenty-one years of age, for one under that age 6 shillings. The fee for a bier-pall lent to a stranger is 5 shillings. For seats in church, when sold according to the regulations for pews, from 20 to 50 shillings. This, together with what is gathered in the collection - bags, does not make out more than pays for the Communion wine, the salary of the Sexton, and other small expenditures. Whenever any repairs are made in the church, contributions for the purpose are taken from the congregation.

18. THE PROVOST'S LABORS IN VARIOUS DIRECTIONS.

As Provost, he enjoyed the confidence of his ministerial brethren, and much affection from the Swedish congregations generally. For the upholding of this, it was considered necessary that the Ministers should hold a meeting in every Parish once a year — in the month of May in Christina, in August in Racoon, and in November in Wicacoa. In these they first united in Divine Service on Sunday, when the Lord's Supper was administered. The following days were spent in suitable exercises and consultation on official duties, as also in correspondence with His Grace the Archbishop, and the Consistory. Upon such occasions one or more of the German Lutheran Ministers were usually present at least once a year, as also in like manner the Provost, or one of his brethren, was present in some of the German congregations. This had reference mainly to unity in doctrine; to the fencing out of the erratic sects, which, however, presented themselves in far less numbers at that time than formerly. At the meeting in Germantown in the year 1751, the Provost delivered a short oration, in Latin, "*On the unity of the spirit, in the bond of peace,*"

(Eph. 4 : 3.) At the request of the German Ministers at the meeting in New Providence, in the year 1753, he prepared in Latin a narrative "*On the origin and progress of the German Evangelical congregations in Pennsylvania and the adjacent countries.*" This was presented to the government in Philadelphia, as also to the Trustees of the Free School which had lately been established there. In all official transactions he was not only treated affectionately by his beloved brethren in the faith as a faithful adviser, but also honored as a presiding officer.

The first four years, in succession, he had to undergo severe intermittent fevers, which every year trouble the inhabitants of the country. The numerous official duties, which, even among the English population, increased the more the more he became acquainted with them, and which could not be performed without constant travelling over the country, gave him reason to think that his strength would not continue to be sufficient for this work. He therefore requested his Bishop to relieve him as early as possible, and was assured that this should be accorded as soon as proper advancement could be found for him at home. Nevertheless, this was delayed for several more years, until February, 1756, when the recall home granted by His Most Gracious Majesty,[1] together with a grant of one thousand dollars silver for his travelling expenses from the same Gracious Sovereign, came to hand. Hereupon he was allowed to take his departure whenever he thought proper, and in the meantime Mr. John Abr. Lidenius, Pastor Extraordinary, might be appointed Vice-Pastor, and the Rev. Mr. Parlin Vice-Provost, in his place, until the receipt of further orders. But as he found that in so free a land it was not safe to leave the congregations upon this footing, he delayed his departure until the arrival of the Royal commissions, whereby Mr. Parlin, the Pastor at Wicacoa, was appointed Provost for all the congregations, and Mr. Eric Unander, Pastor in Racoon and Pennsneck, to be Pastor in Christina, and the Pastor Extraordinary, Mr. John Abr. Lidenius, as Pastor in Racoon and Pennsneck. It was also thus settled what was to be done by the Minister Extraordinary, Mr. Peter Nordenlind, upon his arrival

---

[1] [Frederick Adolph.]

in the month of September, which filled up the number of the Ministers.

After he had set all this in order, he could resign and joyfully take his departure, which he did with a sermon at Christina, Dom. XVI., p. Tr. (sixteenth Sunday after Trinity), but not without mutual tears. From the beginning, his hearers had embraced him with so much love, that the separation was with equal regret. Thereupon he delivered a farewell sermon in six different places where he had frequently held Divine Service, to which the people followed him from one place to another, in great numbers, sorrowing most of all that they should never more behold his face. His departure took place on the 9th of November, 1756. After his arrival at home he was, by the Supreme Consistory, through a special grace of the King, appointed to the Pastorate of Fellingsbro, in the diocese of Westerås.[1]

---

[1] [For further notice of Acrelius, see the Introduction to this work. His successors in the church at Christina, or, as it is now called, "The Old Swedes' Church, at Wilmington," were the following:

1. Eric Unanander, who came, as above noticed, from Racoon and Penn's Neck in 1762.

2. Andrew Borell, sent to preside over the Swedish churches in America in 1757, arrived in the country in 1759; deceased in 1768.

3. The Rev. Lawrence Girelius entered upon his duties as Assistant Clergyman in October, 1767; succeeded Mr. Borell as Provost in 1770, and continued in charge until 1791, when he returned to Sweden. With him the Swedish Mission closed, according to the letter of Arpb. Uno von Troil, which may be seen in "Ferris' Original Settlements," pp. 184 and 185; but Ferris has erroneously written "von Troerl" instead of "von Troil."

4. The Rev. Joseph Clarkson, of the Protestant Episcopal Church, officiated from 1792 to 1799.

5. The Rev. William Pryce, from 1800 to 1802.

6. The Rev. Wickes, from 1814 to 1817.

7. The Rev. L. Bull, D. D., from 1818 to 1819.

8. The Rev. Richard D. Hall, from 1819 to 1822.

9. The Rev. Pierce Connally, from 1827 to 1828.

10. The Rev. Isaac Pardee, from 1828 to 1835.

11. The Rev. Adams, from 1835 to 1838.

12. The Rev. J. W. McCullough, D. D., from 1838 to 1847.

13. The Rev. E. M. Van Deusen, D. D., from 1848 to 1852.

14. The Rev. Charles Breck, from 1853 to 1870.

15. The Rev. William J. Frost, D. D., from 1871 to the present time (1873).]

PART SEVENTH.

CONGREGATIONS OF RACOON AND PENNSNECK.

CHAPTER I.

OF THE TIME BEFORE RACOON AND PENNSNECK BECAME PARISHES.

1. RACOON — ITS SITUATION AND NAME.

THE Parish of Racoon lies upon the east side of the river Delaware, in the Province of New Jersey and District of West Jersey, the Government of Burlington, which is divided into the counties of Gloucester and Salem, as also into the townships of Greenwich, Deptford, Pilesgrove, and Upper and Lower Pennsneck. Under the name of Racoon is understood the Swedish Church and Parish, which, extending the width of three Swedish miles, may be called the only one in the Province, with the exception of Pennsneck.[1] Racoon is also the name of the navigable stream which empties into the Delaware, and upon which the church stands. The name comes from the river which the Indians called Memiraco and Naraticon; but the Swedes, in former times, Araratcung, Ratcung, and now, finally, Racoon; in Swedish orthography, Racuun.[2]

---

[1] There was a Minister and church in Salem from 1725 to 1750; but, from misunderstandings, there is now there a church but no Minister, and the congregation is mostly scattered among the Quakers and Anabaptists.

[2] The raccoon is an animal of North America, called by the Swedes "*Äspan;*" * by Linnæus, the American Bear (Ursus Americanus). It is like the badger in color, a hare in its feet, a cat in its claws, a fox in other respects. It feeds upon vegetables, flesh, and fish; it lies in solitary places. The skin is useful for fur and for hat-making, and is counted among the chief products of the country.

* ["Hespan" is the Mohawk for raccoon. See Doc. Hist. N. York, III., 844.]

2. THE FIRST SETTLEMENT OF RACOON.

The first settlement upon that side of the river was, probably, the place which the Indians called *Hermao-missing*, where the Hollanders had their Fort Nassau,[1] which is now called Gloucester. Full forty years had passed before any one felt disposed to settle and establish his home here. It was regarded as a wild land, where nothing could thrive. Mats Matsson, Mr. Rudman's father-in-law, was the first who there built his house. Then, as the people increased, they had their church-services in common with those on the other side of the river, so that from Racoon Kihl, and above on the river, they went to Tenacongh and Wicacoa; below it and down the river, they went to Tranhook Church. When Rudman and Björk came into the country and established new congregations, these Jerseymen also willingly aided according to their means, each in his own congregation.

3. PETER SCHAEFER'S ADVENTURES.

At that time one Peter Shaefer[2] had come into the country from Åbo, in Finland. Nine years before he had fallen into fanatical notions, and, together with three others, Ulstadius,

---

[1] On Lindström's map, after Mackle's Kihl (now Mantua creek) comes Piscozackasings (now Woodbury creek). Then on the map, as well as in Acrelius, p. 63, comes "Tetamekancks (now Timber creek)," immediately followed by "Arwames, Tekoke, Tekaacho, Hermaomissing, Indian, Fort Nassau, Belgian, now Gloucester, English." By this it appears that several names were applied to Timber creek and its branches; and Campanius, p. 38, says "Fort Nassau touched Arwames and Tekoke," which names appear on Lindström's map, and by which it is clear that Campanius means that the fort was situated on the point of land between Big Timber creek and its northern branch, now called Little Timber creek.

In Campanius, however, p. 26, is a map, on a much smaller scale, by Vischer, who places Fort Nassau on the south side of Timmerkil, and makes that stream consist of only two branches; and also incorrectly places the fort and the streams so far too much to the south as to be midway between Philadelphia and Wilmington. — T. W. and J. J. M.

[2] [Ulstadius was a priest (clergyman), Schaefer a Master of Arts in the University of Åbo, and Ulhegius was a student of theology. The principal charge against them was that of believing that the official acts of an unregenerate Minister were invalid and useless. Ulstadius was condemned to death, but had his sentence changed to perpetual imprisonment, and so died in Stockholm after an imprisonment of thirty years. See a sketch of this lamentable history of persecution in C. A. Cornelius' " Handbok i Svenska Kyrkan's Hist., pp. 218, 219.]

Uhlhegius, and Lithovius, had given the Courts and Consistory a great deal to do. Finally, he recanted; but agitated anew by this, wandered through Germany to England, and thence to Pennsylvania. He immediately presented himself to one Edward Shippen, a Quaker and magistrate in the place, and to his wife, Rebecca, giving them to understand that he was to be a guest in their house for six weeks, during which time he was to live upon bread and water. With their approval he remained there at his pleasure, and during that time became more and more involved in his wild notions. Then he went down to Pennsneck to hold school there, by which, however, he effected but little, for soon after he entered upon what he called a " Deathfast," and received a revelation that he should arise and wander about at random. The simple people took him for a saint, and after his wandering, he went up to the Germans in Germantown; and the inhabitants of Pennsneck sent him a call to come down again and be their Minister, with the assurance that twenty-four pounds were ready for his support. He regarded this as a great honor, and always carried this call with him, but never returned an answer to it. Then he came to an agreement with Jonas Aurén that they should go out into the wild forests to convert the heathen; but neither did anything come out of that. So he turned back to England, and in Plymouth, during a fast of fifty days, he received a revelation that he should proceed to Åbo, and there give his judges a new answer, which, in fact, he did. His days were ended in the castle of Gefle in imprisonment and insanity.

4. THE ADVENTURES OF L. TOLLSTADIUS.

The inhabitants of Jersey desired to have a church of their own on their side of the river, but they still helped in the building of the other churches according to their ability. Thereupon there arose a lamentable uproar, which was occasioned by Lars Tollstadius, who had formerly sought to thrust himself into Wicacoa Church.[1] Being excluded from that church, he gave out that he was about to return home to Sweden, obtaining a passport and recommendation. Mr. Rudman agreed to this, with

---

[1] See p. 223, above.

the admonition that Tollstadius was not to go into any of the congregations, and by preaching withdraw them from their proper churches, but confine himself to the catechising of children, in which he might do some good. But notwithstanding this, so soon as he had obtained his wish, he went over to Jersey and preached every Sunday, first in that part belonging to Wicacoa, and afterwards in that which belonged to Christina.

5. MISUNDERSTANDING ABOUT CHURCH-BUILDING.

The Pastors Björk and Sandel missed a part of the hearers in their churches, and could not but rebuke Tollstadius for such an untimely undertaking. They could not conceal that both their congregations and their support were thus diminished. But this they could well have borne, if all else had been regulated by mature counsels. It was true that the inhabitants of Jersey declared that they were too distant from the other churches, and suffered a great deal of loss in their religious services from the dangerous passage over the Delaware, especially in winter-time ; but that was not a sufficient reason. For although they did really require a church and Minister for themselves, yet this was not the right time for it. They were now exhausted by the aid that they had given Wicacoa and Christina, and all debts upon those churches were not yet paid off, so that they could neither erect a respectable church at their own cost, nor expect the assistance of others in so doing. They would have no honor and but little advantage from such a Minister as this Tollstadius had already shown himself to be. Still further, the names of *two* Swedish Ministers had already been sent to the English authorities as about to perform service in these congregations, from which there could not but follow severe animadversion when it was perceived that there were *three*. Moreover, they should draw upon themselves the displeasure of their superiors in Sweden for their ingratitude in falling away from the teachers who had been regularly sent to them, and should never again dare to request any other teachers from thence ; that the Archbishop could not protect congregations which, without his counsel and proper understanding of the matter, made injurious changes among themselves ; and, finally, that no upright Minister would any more dare to come hither, and await the fate of seeing either a part or, what was equally possible, the whole of his people forsake him.   All this, and more besides, was set forth both in letters and by word of mouth, and finally effected so much, that a letter was sent over to the Archbishop for his consent in regard to the undertaking.   Meantime, Tollstadius promised to abstain from official acts, except the christening of children in cases of necessity.

6. The Building of Racoon Church.

But the man did not keep his word.   He abstained for only five or six weeks, and then began to preach here and there, scattered the people, and excited them against their good teachers, so that if either of them came to that quarter to preach, he had but few hearers.   To Pastor Sandel he pleaded that he had, indeed, promised not to preach in that part which belonged to Wicacoa, but he could still preach in that which belonged to Christina.   When reprimanded by Pastor Björk, he fell down and begged forgiveness, but still continued as before.   In the meantime a purchase of land for church ground was made at Racoon creek, and a church built on it, without waiting for any further answer from Sweden.   At first ten acres of land were bought, on which the church stands, then forty acres a little distance from the other, altogether fifty acres of land, for £12. It was bought of John Hugg, Jr., and the deed was dated the 1st of September, 1703.   To this was added two and a half acres of meadow-land, bought of John Jones for five shillings in 1705. The church was finished in 1704, when Tollstadius invited the other Ministers to the consecration on the second Sunday after Trinity.   No one was willing to come after everything had been done in so irregular a manner.   Before that year came to an end, there arose a most disgraceful report in regard to that man, for which also suit was brought against him.   But before this came to trial, the restless life of Tollstadius was ended in the river Delaware, when the canoe, in which he was carried on the 9th of May, 1706, was driven ashore on the Jersey side with his travelling cloak and a plowshare in it, but his lifeless body was found nine days afterwards on the other side of the river, below Upland.[1]

7. Judgment Thereon.

The upright Ministers who, at that time, stood so strongly against the building of Racoon Church, were on this account severely condemned by many.   But they saw further into the matter than people generally, and clearly foresaw the consequences.   Nowhere in the world can it be more plainly seen what injurious consequences result from inconsiderate church-building than in that country.   We have examples of it in many English churches.   Some wealthy and liberal persons erect a church on their burial-place, so as to be nearer to the church, where they can have the services of a Minister for only an uncertain time; or they induce the ordinary Clergyman of the place to visit them occasionally; and afterwards they consider it his duty to do so without any remuneration.   If he cannot gratify them, they blame him; do not come to the proper church any more, and refuse to support either the church or its Minister. Yea, it even happens that they remove to other places, and then people of another creed come into their old home; or they even fall off to other sects.   The congregation is scattered, the church falls into ruins, and the Minister suffers.   Hence it is that many churches are seen without Ministers, Ministers with decaying churches, and without congregations.

8. Thoughts about a Successor.

The people of Racoon were now in a confused condition. Their departed teacher had been but little honor, and still less edification to them, nor did they know how they could get any better.   They did not venture to write to Sweden, as no answer had as yet come to their former letter.   Therefore, that they might have some counsel, they determined to give a call to the Rev. Jonas Aurén.

9. The Rev. Jonas Aurén.

This Jonas Aurén was a Clergyman who had been sent to America by King Charles XI. in the year 1696, at the same time

---

23

[1] [Chester.]

with Rudman and Björk. His errand was to make a map of the country, to describe its character and that of the people, and the like; after which he was at once to return home. Immediately after his arrival the king's death occurred, and then the wars of King Charles XII. He therefore determined to tarry here somewhat longer. During this time he united himself with the so-called Sabbatarians, who regard Saturday as the real Sabbath day. He published in print an Almanac, put his views into it in English, calling it " *Noah's Dove*," [1] whereby a great deal of disorder was produced. This occasioned Mr. Eric Björk to publish, in English also, a refutation of the same in a Tract with this title: " *A little olive-leaf put into the mouth of that so-called ' Noah's* [2] *Dove,' and sent home again, to let her master know that the waters are abated from off the face of the ground, and that for the sake of Jesus Christ—whose servant to the end of my life I shall endeavor to be.*" This work, which was composed with a great deal of good sense, and with strong reasons, accomplished a great deal of good among the people, but little more with Mr. Jonas Aurén, than that he preached for others upon Sundays, but kept Saturday holy for himself.[3]

10. CALLED TO RACOON — BRUNJAN, SCHOOL-MASTER.

Until that time (the year 1706) Mr. Jonas Aurén had been living at Elk river, in Maryland, preaching for the English and Swedes. The people of Racoon called him, in the hope that after he got back among the Swedes they would get him out of his notions about Saturday. He finally arrived there in the autumn, bringing with him his relative Brunjan to be their Lay-Reader in his absence, and also as school-master in the place, as

---

[1] [Acrelius gives the title "*Noae Dufwa*," which I have translated into what I suppose was the original English.]

[2] [Acrelius writes this " Noach's ; " but I presume that the author (Björk) wrote in the usual English form. The remainder of the title is just as Acrelius gives it in English, also translating it into Swedish. I have never seen a copy of either of these curious publications of these Anglo-Swedes.]

[3] [It appears from his letter to his colleague, the Rev. E. Björk, that Aurén actually engaged in Missionary work among the Indians at Conestoga. His letter, dated at Conestoga, January 13, 1$\frac{699}{700}$, may be seen in T. E. Björk's "Dissertatio Gradualis," and in a translation in Proud's History of Pennsylvania.]

he had also had Brunjan there for two years with him in Elk river, they being of the same opinion in regard to Saturday.

11. Aurén Minister at Racoon, but is a Sabbatarian.

Before Mr. Aurén would settle in Racoon, he came to Pastor Björk and desired his advice, against which he would not act. A full consent could not be given, in view of the respect that Mr. Björk had for his Bishop, with whose knowledge and direction he wished everything to be done. Yet out of the kindness that he felt towards Mr. Aurén as a conscientious man, as also towards the people who desired him, he would not in the meantime oppose the arrangement. For the greater certainty, the congregation at Racoon desired the approbation of the Governor of New York, who first called Aurén before him, and then gave his permission. After that he presided over the Parish until the year 1713, when on the 17th of February he left this earthly scene, and also a widow and two sons. His Sabbatarian notions he retained to the close of his life, but never thereby created any offence in the congregation.

CHAPTER II.

OF MR. LIDENIUS' TIME.

1. Lidenius first Adjunct, and then Pastor.

ON the 1st of May, 1712, Mr. Abraham Lidenius, together with the Rev. And. Hesselius, arrived from Sweden; and as there were then several Ministers at Christina, it was found advisable that Mr. Lidenius should, in accordance with the desires of the inhabitants of Jersey, remain with them through the winter in Pennsneck, for which purpose he was sent over on the 5th of December. Then when Mr. Aurén died, two months afterwards, and Mr. Sandel from Wicacoa only occasionally visited Racoon, as he could not come more frequently, Mr. Lidenius supplied them with service, in accordance with the directions of Provost Björk, in such wise that he should preach in each place every other Sunday, which order was observed from October 20, 1713, until April 4, 1714. When the Rev. And. Hesselius succeeded to Christina on the 1st of May, 1714, he exchanged with Mr. Lidenius on both sides of the river, as Racoon and Pennsneck were at that time regarded as annexed[1] to Christina. Meantime the Provost Björk took his journey to Sweden, and as well by writings in regard to the present condition of the congregations, as by verbal reports, stated their case; whereupon the Bishop of Skara, Dr. Jesper Svedberg, who had the supervision of the congregations at that time, by his letter dated Brunsbro, November 24, 1714, gave permission to build a church at Pennsneck, or wherever it was found most suitable, and at the same time appointed Mr. Lidenius Pastor of the churches at Racoon and Pennsneck; and ever since that time these two churches have been united in the same Pastorate.

2. PENNSNECK.

The congregation of Pennsneck is in the Province of West New Jersey, in the Government of Burlington, Salem county, in the Townships of Upper and Lower Pennsneck, Pilesgrove and Mannington, on the east side of the Delaware, and along its strand.[2] The name Pennsneck is derived from Penn and neck, as that strip of land was given to William Penn to occupy and settle with people, and his descendants still receive annual rents from it. But the Penn family have had nothing to do with the government, as in Pennsylvania, the whole of it being under the Royal Government. The land lies low, and consists in great part of moors and marshes. It has good soil in the lower parts, but is quite sandy and poor in the upper parts. It is also as yet but little cleared or inhabited, the air being unhealthy, and producing chills and fever. Good springs are rarely found, and the people generally have a pale and sickly appearance.

---

[1] [In the original, "*en annexe*," which is a technical term for a congregation so connected with another as to enjoy the services of the same Clergyman, like an English "Chapel of Ease."]

[2] [Pennsneck is a sort of peninsula between the Delaware on the west and Salem creek on the south and east.]

3. CHURCH-BUILDING.

Mr. Lidenius was a man of remarkable industry, whereby he accomplished a great deal of good in his congregation : he was also greatly beloved for his zeal and pleasing manners, so that he was able successfully to accomplish his purposes.   His care now was to provide Pennsneck with a church.   After various consultations as to the place, it was determined to locate the church in the middle of the *Neck*, on the highway.   Jean Jaquett gave two acres of land for the purpose.   The deed for the ground was given on the 8th of January, 1715.   The building of the church was immediately commenced, but it was not completed until March 31, 1717, when it was consecrated and called St. George's Church.   It is twenty-four feet square, built of logs, and weatherboarded.

4. THE PARSONAGE.

It was now asked where the Parsonage was to be.   The congregation at Racoon had provided itself with its own church and a piece of land, but the ground was sandy, poor, and unsuitable for grain ; and the Minister's salary from the congregations was also low.   The Pastor, therefore, would not settle himself upon the place, nor advise the people to build, but rather to get a residence which lay in the midst between the churches.   They deliberated about this for eight years, and it was discussed in every Parish meeting, until Mr. Jesper Svedberg [1] and Mans Kyn took it upon themselves to go from house to house, through the congregation, and urge the people to unite and bind themselves for the purchase of a suitable Parsonage.   Göran Kyn's place was found suitable for this purpose, at the distance of about a Swedish mile from Racoon, and a mile and a half from Pennsneck.   It lies in Pilesgrove township, consists of one hundred and seventeen acres of land, and cost £145.   The purchase was made on the 21st of March, 1720.   A fine building was erected upon it with sleeping-rooms in the upper part; and more land for grain was cleared.

---

[1] [The son of the Bishop of the same name; see § 6 below.]

5. THE REPAIR OF THE CHURCH.

In the year 1715 Racoon Church was found to be going to decay; whereupon it was plastered on the outside and white-washed, and thus had the appearance of a stone church. It was also again repaired on the north side in the year 1719; the same year also a vestibule was built before the church door.

6. JESPER SVEDBERG.

Although the Church Corporation remained for a long time in great disorder, yet there was a pretty good succession of schools in Racoon Church, where a school-house was erected, and Mr. Jesper Svedberg, the Bishop's son, spent his time for over a year. During his travels he was to visit that inhospitable land also, probably to see how far he could be found serviceable to the congregations. But here there was neither time nor oppor-tunity for the gathering of a fortune, and so he left the country, and continued his travels to the West India Islands as a seaman.

7. ISAAC BANER.

About the year 1695 Baron Isaac Baner[1] came to Pennsyl-vania. He first lived in Philadelphia, showing his origin both in his dress and in his manners, but was soon reduced to lower cir-cumstances. He had been for some time in the service of King William III. of England, which he used to show by some official papers. After he had determined to spend the rest of his life in this region, he went down to Christina, and in the house of John Stalcop carried on a small traffic at the fort, but without great profit. Thence he went to Pennsneck, married Maria Jaquett,[2] the daughter of a farmer of small means. The marriage

---

[1] [Probably a grandson of the celebrated General John Baner, who succeeded Gus-tavus Adolphus in the command of the Swedish armies — one of the most illustrious of that brilliant school of commanders trained under the eye of the great Swedish King.]

[2] No doubt of the family of John Paul Jaquett, a French Protestant refugee, who, in 1656, was appointed Governor. A descendant of the Governor was the celebrated Major Jaquett of the Delaware line in the Revolution. A more recent member of this family was the Rev. Joseph Jaquett, some time Rector of St. James the Greater at Bristol, and who died in Philadelphia May 24, 1869. This gentleman was dis-tinguished for his philological attainments, and it seems only proper that a learned society should do what it can to preserve the memory of a very learned man. His library, which contains copies of most of the grammars and lexicons that have ever issued from the press, is now in possession of Mr. David W. Sellers, who married his only daughter.   T. W.

was performed by a magistrate in the place, as was the custom there. He manifested his nobility in his quiet, pious, and virtuous life, but he had no means of upholding his distinguished rank. He had bargained for a small piece of land, made part payment upon it, but never got into full possession. His death occurred on the 11th of November, 1713, and his burial was performed in the Presbyterian graveyard, for want of any other place. His widow was left in destitute circumstances to support herself and her four children, Claes, Maria, Gustaf, and Paul. Claes died at the age of two months. The daughter was married to a respectable man, whose mother was of the family of Philip van der Weer,[1] and Gustaf and Paul were apprenticed to trades.

8. HIS CHILDREN.

Mr. Lidenius received his recall home in the year 1723, resigned in 1724, and returned to his native land with his attached wife, Maria van Neaman, together with their children, John, Abraham, and Maria, having received the appointment of Provost and Pastor in the city of Umeå[2] and Diocese of Hernösand. Upon his arrival at home, he represented to the Lieutenant-General, Baron John Baner, and also to the Royal Counsellor, Count Axel Baner, the unfortunate condition of the children of Isaac Baner in America, and excited their active sympathy. Means for travel were therefore sent over to them, and they were brought to Sweden, which was done in the year 1727. Governor Gordon gave orders to the people who had had them in their service to give them their freedom. He himself took the children by the hand and conducted them to the ship. Mr. Lidman took care to fit them out for the voyage, and the Governor's Secretary, Mr. Robert Charles, sailed with them over to London.

9. CHRISTINA IN DEBT TO RACOON AND PENNSNECK.

From the time that Racoon and Pennsneck received Ministers of their own, they began to urge their claim on the Christina con-

---

[1] The Van der Weers were early known, as they still are, in Delaware. Their brick house, yet standing, is mentioned as early as 1655, and was built at Tredie Hook, the third point or promontory on the north side of the Brandywine just below the present railroad bridge.

[2] [In the Province of West Bothnia, and on the river of the same name.]

gregation, for they had contributed in money and labor their heavy share towards the building of that church. According to an agreement in the Parish meeting of October 4th, 1699, they had cut and floated over timber for the erection of the Parsonage; therefore, as they themselves were now at heavy expense, as well in the building of Pennsneck Church as also in the procuring of a church-glebe, so they thought that they had a right to demand a like return from the other side of the river, which had now got into a prosperous condition, and that this was an obligation which should stand for law and right. It is certain that the inhabitants of Jersey, at their first uniting in the Parish meeting of July 30th, 1697, demanded such a connection that when, in the course of time, they should become so strong as to be able to form a separate Parish, to procure and maintain for themselves a teacher of our Lutheran religion, then these on the other side should aid them with as much money as they had aided Christina. But the answer and conclusion was this: "That although we upon this side do not assent to this desire in the manner proposed, yet are we equally bound, for the honor of God, in turn to help those on the other side who have helped us." Nevertheless, when the Pastor, Mr. Lidenius, at the Parish meeting in Christina on the 2d of May, 1720, insisted upon the demand of his Parish, the debt was fairly acknowledged. The vacant pews in Christina Church were to be sold for its payment, and the deficiency supplied by contributions from the Parish. But neither was the amount of the debt determined, nor is any correct account found of that which was afterwards paid. Still it is certain that something was contributed thereto from time to time, and that the payment was finally made *in wheat*, as there was at that time but little money in circulation in the country. Finally, it was liquidated in this manner: Christina Parish was still indebted to Pennsneck Parish, for church-building, forty-six bushels of wheat. On the other hand, Pennsneck Parish was indebted to their Pastor, Mr. Sam. Hesselius, £10 for services rendered for a year after the departure of Mr. Lidenius, and Mr. Hesselius was indebted to Christina Parish to the amount of £9 9s. 7d. On this account, Mr. Hesselius, in accordance with the counsel and resolution of the Parish, gave a general quittance for all debts from the Parishes of Racoon and Pennsneck. The same quittance was also to release him, Mr. Sam. Hesselius, from his debt to Christina Parish, which was done on the 1st of July, 1726. Notwithstanding all this, there is now scarcely any one who remembers that the debt was paid; and so references to it are frequently made [as though Christina were still in debt to those Jersey Parishes].

CHAPTER III.

OF TRANBERG AND WINDRUFVA'S TIME.

1. THEIR JOURNEY.

ON the 1st of September, 1725, the Rev. Peter Tranberg set sail from Sweden to America for the purpose of relieving the Rev. Mr. Lidenius. He was accompanied by the Rev. Mr. Andrew Windrufva as Adjunct Pastor, called, by Bishop Svedberg, in his Ministerial Commission and passport, Drufva, to distinguish him from his unfortunate brother; but he always retained his customary name. These two Ministers had a hard voyage, for the ship, in which they sailed from Götheborg, was driven upon the coast of Norway and wrecked, so that they barely escaped with their lives. But they had the good fortune to be kindly received by Bishop Möller, in Dronthem. Thence they got a vessel to Amsterdam, where they were provided for by the Lutheran clergy. They went thence to England, where the Society[1] provided them respectably with means for travel, besides one thousand dollars silver coinage for each of them, which Bishop Svedberg forwarded to them anew from the King of Sweden, wherewith they prosecuted their journey onward to its appointed end.

2. THE PARISH DIVIDED.

Mr. Tranberg came in the year 1726 to enter upon his place, and was installed by Mr. Lidman on the 30th of June of the

---

[1] [The Society for the Propagation of the Gospel.]

same year. But as his Brother Windrufva, faithful in life and death, had no certain Parish or support, and the congregations were quite numerous, therefore Mr. Tranberg agreed with him that he should preside over Pennsneck, and enjoy its income. This met with the approbation of both the congregations, which were thus all the better served, and also of the Provost in this wise, that Mr. Tranberg was to have forty pounds from Racoon, and Mr. Windrufva twenty pounds from Pennsneck; whilst the latter was also to receive from his congregation a house and provisions, together with a horse for his service — by which arrangement Pennsneck was in better condition than Racoon — though neither Parish fulfilled its engagements. Mr. Windrufva was married into the Jaquett family, but shortly thereafter died, on the 5th of November, 1728. This terminated the contract with the Parishes, and both were again to be united under Mr. Tranberg.

3. PLACES OF RESIDENCE.

Racoon and Pennsneck had now had the advantage not only of obtaining Pastors one after the other, but even had two officiating there at the same time. Mr. Tranberg was very watchful in his office. Besides his own congregation, he often performed service for both the Germans[1] and the English. He was not less careful in his domestic economy. He lived seven years upon the church-glebe; then he purchased a farm of his own in the same neighborhood, and removed to it. Then he exchanged that for one much larger and better, and lived upon that. In the meantime the church-glebe was rented out, and so was greatly run down. In his time a gallery was built in the church, a sign that the congregation was increasing. The pews were also rented out, and the income put out at interest.

4. MR. TRANBERG'S REMOVAL TO CHRISTINA, AND COMPLAINTS THEREOF.

In the year 1740, by the Royal Commission from Sweden, the Rev. Mr. Tranberg was transferred to Christina Parish, and

---

[1] [Probably in the neighborhood of Friesburg, where "Emmanuel" (Lutheran) Church now stands; though the Germans have long since become English.]

entered upon his duties in 1741. The joy at his arrival there was only equalled by the grief at his departure in Racoon and Pennsneck. It is said that those Parishes took the change so hard, that they would not afterwards write for any Minister from Sweden. They thought that he was in·so good a position, that he need not to seek for anything better; everything was interpreted to his disadvantage, even in letters to Sweden. But Mr. Tranberg's age was now advancing and his strength diminishing; the road between the two churches was long, and the congregation widely scattered; his children were growing up, and could not obtain any good education in that neighborhood. It was not, therefore, to be wondered at that, after fifteen years of service, he desired a release, as others had done who had served a shorter time. So when he desired either to come home or to be transferred to Christina, and a Commission was sent him for the latter, he certainly did no wrong in accepting it. They have concluded from this, in Sweden, that the removal of Ministers from one church to another in America was not advisable. But such exchanges of Ministers from one Parish to another are seen here no less than in other places, and in other religious societies also, so that that was nothing new. When removals of Ministers are made upon good and valid grounds, after suitable examination and approbation of presiding officers, then much good is done thereby, and no one has any reason to complain.

CHAPTER IV.

OF AN UNFORTUNATE VACANCY.

1. OL. MALANDER HOLDS DIVINE SERVICE.

HOWEVER that was, yet the people seemed quite careless about their religious services for a long time; but that they might not be entirely deserted, they sometimes had preaching either from Wicacoa or Christina. Finally, they desired to have a settled Minister again. This was Mr. Olof Malander, who came over with Pastor Dylander in the year 1737, with the design of becoming a school-master, but was well exercised in preaching. Pastor Dylander therefore wrote home to Sweden about it. But when answer came back, together with orders from the Archbishop, Dr. John Steuchius, to the Pastors Dylander and Tranberg, to ordain Malander, and also to install him as Pastor in said Parish, Mr. Dylander was now dead, and Mr. Tranberg left as the only Swedish Minister in the country; therefore that ordination could not be performed so soon as had been appointed, viz., the 1st of November, 1741. On this account Mr. Tranberg wrote to the aforesaid congregations on the 9th of November following, and certified them that Malander was selected as their Teacher, although not ordained, and in consequence thereof should have power: 1. To perform Divine Service with prayer, singing, and preaching; 2. To celebrate marriages; 3. To officiate at funerals; 4. To attend to the churching of women; 5. To perform Baptism in cases of necessity. He would himself perform other duties as they might be required. But the people were unwilling to support Malander. He had been unfortunately married to one B. Laurentz, involved in debt; and thus discouraged from entering the ministry, he did not continue to officiate more than a year, from November 1, 1741, to September, 1742, when he is said to have been taken off to Philadelphia by the officers of the Crown on account of his debts.

2. He Publishes a Herrnhuttish Catechism.

The Divine Providence which is manifest in all things, to arrest the evil and to promote the good, undoubtedly had its hand in that change. The time following has shown that this Malander would never have been an edifying preacher. He changed his purpose, under the pretext that the congregations were not able to support him; but the reason was in his own unsettled mind, which he showed in many other ways, but especially in his school-keeping. Afterwards he united himself to the Herrnhutters, who had a strong party in the land at that time; and as he had gone into Mr. Franklin's printing-office, in Philadelphia, to work for his bread and to pay his debts, so he had an opportunity to bring out in print a little work of Herrnhuttish savor, translated into Swedish [1] under the title of "*A short Cate-chism for some of the churches of the Reformed Religion in Penn-sylvania which hold to the Synod of Berne,*[2] *which is the same as the Doctrines of the Moravian Church. First published in the Ger-man language by* JOHN BECHTEL, *Minister of God's Word.*"[3] Its chief articles are twelve:

I. That Christ is our whole doctrine.

II. That God has in Him blessed His people.

III. That He is the ground and foundation.

IV. That God himself should be (immediately) preached under the name of our Mediator.

V. That without Christ there is no word of grace.

VI. That that begins and goes forth from His death.

VII. That just in the same manner He teaches in regard to sin.

VIII. Also, that the law cannot be sufficiently removed from our teachings.

IX. That that is the difference between us and the heathen here.

X. That it is hence that the false shepherds have come, that by their hand the law with its bonds and burdens is introduced again.

XI. That it is the proper course of grace, that we obtain the knowledge of sin from the death of Jesus only.

XII. This precious doctrine is the mystery that should be pro-claimed at all times.

He who has chanced to see any of the Herrnhuttish Cate-chisms, can believe that this is a quintessence of the same, both in its contents and its method. Of this Swedish translation but

---

[1] A copy of this work is in the Royal Library at Stockholm, and was shown to Mr. Mickley in 1870, as a great curiosity. — T. W.

[2] [Guericke, in his "Kirchengeschichte," Vol. III., p. 519, Note 6, says: "The Church of Berne was for a time tending to Lutheranism; a tendency which was especially brought out at the Synod of Berne, in 1537, under Bucer's influence." That is probably the Synod to which Bechtel's book refers.]

[3] [In Swedish, "En kort Catechismus för några Jesu Församlingar utaf den Re-formerta Religionen uti Pennsylvanien, som hålla sig til det Berniska Synodo, hvilket är enligt med Lärone uti den Märiska Kyrkan. Först utgifven idet Tyska Språket af Johanne Bechtel," etc.] The Hist. Soc. Pa. has a copy of the original.

few copies are to be found in the country at the present time, and if one is to be met with, it is in Racoon.

3. The Introduction of the Herrnhutters.

This desolate condition, in which these churches now were, gave an opening for the wily tempter. The people seemed unconcerned about getting another Minister. They were sometimes visited by Mr. Tranberg from Christina, sometimes by Mr. Gabr. Naesman of Wicacoa, who went there alternately, perhaps every third or fourth month, to preach and baptize their children; but this did not guard the churches. At that time Count Zinzendorff came into the country, and sent abroad his apostles as fast as he could. Here were Swedish churches, and he should, therefore, supply them with Swedish Ministers. These were such as Paul Bruzelius, born in Häradshammar in the diocese of Linköping, who had been for some years united with that band in Germany, and was now come to this place to be used for the Swedes. He is also supposed to have been the author of the wretched translation mentioned above. Abraham Reinke, born in Stockholm, and educated in Germany. Sven Rosen,[1] from Götheborg, banished in 1740 for his Pietistic vagaries, and then drawn to Zinzendorff's party, to which also Peter Nyberg joined himself, in regard to whom we shall presently have more to say. It was remarkable that the Swedes ordained by the Herrnhut congregation called themselves Swedish Ministers whenever they came among the Swedish people. They all gave themselves out as Lutherans, and had no other doctrine than that which was established in Sweden. And although they held to the Moravian Brotherhood, which they said was different from the Swedish Church only in church-forms, yet that should make no difficulty

---

[1] [There seems to be some confusion in our author's statement in regard to Rosen. We find no further notice of him in connection with either the Swedes or Moravians in this history. But Skarstedt, in his *"Handbok i Sweriges Kyrko-historia,"* (Stockholm, 1867,) p. 164, Note 3, tells us that Rosen, during his banishment in Germany, "through intercourse with Fresenius, became more reasonable, of which the Swedish Diet being informed in 1747, directed him to travel to the Swedish churches *in the West Indies."* From which it would appear that he came to this country (then called the West Indies) in accordance with the wishes of the public authorities in Sweden. Skarstedt gives a very favorable view of Rosen's character. He wrote it Roseen.]

if they were accepted by a Swedish congregation, for they would there follow the established church-regulations!

4. BRUZELIUS' INTRUSION.

All this, and more, was done in Racoon and Pennsneck. Bruzelius offered his services, and was well received in many houses. The church needed a Minister, and Bruzelius could preach in Swedish, was a very friendly man; and they could have him upon very low terms. He was also looked upon very favorably in Pastor Tranberg's house, and was a great friend of Pastor Nyberg, who had lately come from Sweden to the German congregation in Lancaster. Everything gave the man good credit. But yet not one-half of the church-members were of that way of thinking. One part were strongly opposed to him, and would not receive any Minister who could not show testimonials from Sweden; they would preserve their church from suspected teachers. What happened? A Sunday was appointed for Bruzelius to preach in Racoon Church. The people assembled in great numbers—one party to put him in, another party to keep him out, and a third party to see the fun. But the advantage was on the side of those who were opposed to him, for they had the church-key in their hands. The others, therefore, took the liberty of breaking open a window, creeping in, and so opening the door. When the door was opened, there was fighting to get in, noise and terrible confusion, so that they went away without any service at all, but with great scandal. This happened in the year 1744.

5. INVESTIGATION AND JUDGMENT IN THE MATTER.

The Rev. Gabr. Naesman was greatly excited by this event; went down to Racoon immediately to hold service, and at the same time to investigate the affair. There were mutual complaints. All insisted upon their right to the church. But those who undertook to force in a strange and suspected Minister were found to be very guilty; and therefore the Church-Wardens who were on that side were deposed, and the matter was sent to the proper court for judgment. But although this was a matter of religion between the members of the congregation, a conciliatory course (arbitration) was taken in regard to it. Twenty-five men came together at Gloucester to examine and decide in regard to it, as is often done here when people wish to avoid the expense of a lawsuit. Mr. Naesman did not hesitate to meet the case, and carry it against Bruzelius. He legitimated himself by his Diploma as a Master of Arts, as also by his Minister's letter and Commission, and demanded the like of Bruzelius. He drew up his complaint in nine different specifications, and charged him with an equal number of falsehoods; but Bruzelius did not answer a word. His adherents expected that he would show himself on the occasion as a strong man, but it all came to nothing. He would not, or rather knew not, what he should answer; but still seemed in good spirits. His friends were disgusted with this, and the greater part fell away from him, but were still condemned to £50 damages, of which, however, only £25 were exacted as the costs. Bruzelius and other Moravian Ministers were forbidden to enter into the Swedish and English churches.

6. L. Nyberg mixes Himself up in the Matter.

After Nyberg (in the year 1744) had been shut out of the German Lutheran church in Lancaster with his Moravians, but still remained for some time in the same place among his followers, he took upon himself to go occasionally to Racoon and Pennsneck, all the time urging the people to give up the Church and attach themselves to the Brethren. Immediately after the meeting in Gloucester, he urged the people of Racoon, who still thought well of the sect, to call Bruzelius, and have him preach privately in their houses. This stirred up Mr. Naesman to visit the Parish and preach for it once a month; and he thus held the people pretty well together, whereupon Bruzelius after some time left the place.

7. Abrah. Reinike, the Herrnhutter.

The right-minded were now weary of this disorder, and, upon Mr. Naesman's frequently repeated representations, prepared a petition among themselves to the Archbishop of Sweden for a Minister from thence, which was done August 8, 1744; also, a subscription-list for £30 a year for the support of the Minister, which was subscribed by the names of many members of the Parish. But as soon as the Moravians got some hint of this, they went to Nyberg, and asked him to send them another Swedish Herrnhutter, by the name of Abraham Reinike, who was born in Stockholm. He, at first, on account of the novelty, had a large attendance, so that many left the Church, and the whole body was withdrawn from its undertaking with regard to another Minister. Thus Nyberg prevented them from uniting, and when they were united he scattered them. Neither had all placed their own names or marks to the aforesaid letter, and the smaller number had signed the subscription paper; but seventy-one (71) names had been put down on it, mostly by the Church-Wardens, according to the general agreement. But those who were to put down their marks drew back, and so the paper was of no value. The right-minded, therefore, determined to wait awhile, expecting a better condition. Nor did Reinike's time last long before he withdrew from the place, partly because he appeared to them to be singular and fanatical, at one time keeping them at a funeral in a private house so long with prayers and preaching, that if the people had not stopped him they would not have had daylight to get to the grave-yard. Partly, also, because the Swedes were tired of the frequent journeys of these brethren with their horses, and their numerous visits to their houses, and so the greater part of them fell off from them. Then, again, they thought that the Herrnhut band would be more increased by preaching in English, and Reinike did not understand this language. This gave a new occasion to prepare another letter of call of the same import as the former. This was subscribed by the officers of the congregation and eight other persons, and was accompanied by the above-mentioned subscription list, with seventy-one (71) duly authenticated signatures, which was sent off to Sweden on the 17th of November, 1745.

8. THE STATE OF THINGS IN PENNSNECK.

At the same time Pennsneck was in a still greater desolation. It was agreed between the Rev. Messrs. Tranberg and Naesman that the former should preside over Pennsneck and the latter

24

over Racoon; but however that was, Pennsneck became mostly
a Moravian nest.   Neither was Mr. Naesman ever encouraged to
go thither, as was done from Racoon, and so he could not take
any care of it upon himself.   The English had engaged the
English clergyman in Salem to preach for them once a month;
but the Moravians also had their emissaries, who were going
around there one after the other, and also occasionally came up
to Racoon to hold services there around in the houses.   The
Swedes in the neighborhood of the Neck arranged their plans
secretly with Nyberg how they could get the English Minister
out, and an English Moravian by the name of Rice in his place;
which, however, was never accomplished.   After the Archbishop,
Dr. Jacob Benzelius' letter arrived in the spring of 1746, in which
Nyberg was declared unworthy to be any longer recognized as a
Swedish Minister, he showed plainly what he had long concealed
under certain pretexts, frequently visited and preached in Pennsneck, and busied himself in getting up the Herrnhut Meeting-
House at Olmutz[1] river, in the boundaries between Racoon and
Pennsneck, in 1747.

CHAPTER V.

OF MR. SANDIN'S TIME.

1. JOURNEY AND ARRIVAL.

THE pious Archbishop, Doc. Jac. Benzelius, who had these
Swedish churches in America under his supervision during
these unfortunate times, made suitable arrangements for sending
off the Rev. John Sandin, who was now appointed and provided
with the Royal Commission as Pastor of Racoon and Pennsneck
Parishes.   And for the prevention of like irregularities, which had
been noticed for many years in these Swedish churches generally,
the Archbishop proposed to His Majesty the appointment of a
Provost for all the congregations, with a yearly salary.   The
matter was referred to the examination of the Privy Council of

---

[1] [This is Oldman's creek, or Alderman's Kill.]

the kingdom, who, by their decision given in January, 1747, advised thereto; and it was accordingly so ordered and confirmed by the Royal Commission that there should be a Provost over the Swedish Lutheran churches in [this part of] America, with an annual salary of fifty pounds sterling. His journey was arranged for the worst time of the year, in the most dangerous period of the war, and lasted for eighteen months, during which he was accompanied by his wife, servant, and daughter. The ship landed at New York, whence his journey was continued overland, when he waited upon the Governor in Burlington, who received his passport from the King of Sweden, Frederick I., with much respect, and the greater on this account, viz., that he had been in service in the allied armies under the command of His Majesty. The Governor (Jonathan Belcher) now gave the Rev. Provost his recommendation to his Parishes, through his Secretary, as follows:[1]

"GENTLEMEN: His Excellency, the Governor, hath ordered me to notify to your congregation that the bearer, Mr. John Sandin, Missionary to the Swedish church at Racoon and Pennsneck in this Province, hath waited on him and produced to His Excellency the credentials, passport, and recommendation from His Swedish Majesty, now in alliance with the King our Master, and being therewith fully satisfied, has licensed him to officiate as Minister in the said churches and all others in this Province, by the consent of their particular Pastors, and has kindly promised to give him protection.

"You are, therefore, to conduct him to Mr. Ladd at Gloucester, or to Mr. Gibbons at Salem, before he officiates, and let him be attended by some of the gentlemen capable of interpreting to him the oaths which Mr. Ladd or Mr. Gibbons are authorized to administer.

"Gentlemen: I hope you will in an exemplary manner recommend yourselves to the further care of His Swedish Majesty, by a grateful return for his present favor, in assisting

---

[1] [The original English of this letter is first given, and then a translation into Swedish. We have merely corrected the clerical and typographical errors of the original English.]

Mr. Sandin in everything as far as your circumstances will permit, and beg leave to recommend union and decency in your
church as the proper means for preserving a good reputation
here, and hereafter eternal felicity.

"I am, gentlemen, your very humble servant,

"CHARLES READ.

"To the Vestry and congregation at Racoon and Pennsneck,
in New Jersey.

"BURLINGTON, March 28th, 1748."

2. SHORT TIME, AND DEATH.

A new joy now began. After five years of distressing vacancy,
the congregations seemed to come into perfectly good order.
Their Teacher was beloved by all, even by those who held to the
Moravians. He exerted himself to the utmost to be agreeable
and edifying to all. Pennsneck had not united in his call; still
he attended there, and was received with the same joy as in
Racoon. He preached by turns in each church, and established
good order in both places. New subscriptions were made —
those who had not subscribed before now doing so with a good
will. Some, who had hitherto upheld the Moravians, now left
that party and promised their share. But their joy came to a
speedy end, with new sorrow, when, after the lapse of six months,
in August, 1748, he fell asleep in the Lord, leaving his wife in a
foreign land with a new-born babe.

3. THE HERRNHUTTERS MAKE NEW ATTACKS.

The spirits of the Herrnhutters were undoubtedly raised by
the depression of the Swedish church. Their emissaries immediately began to visit in greater numbers and with greater
frequency than before. Nyberg frequently visited his friends,
and preached in Pennsneck. But now the people had more zeal
for their Swedish services, since they had had such recent proof
of affection on the part of Sweden. Therefore they were all
unanimous, immediately after Provost Sandin's death, in desiring
some one to succeed him, only a few of Nyberg's strongest
friends excepted, who would not be named in it, so that they
might have their freedom until they saw how the Minister who
came next would be.

4. PROFESSOR KALM.

Very fortunately, Mr. Peter Kalm,[1] the Professor of Economics in the University of Abo, was then travelling in this country. His tour was at the expense of the Universities of Upsala and Åbo, and of the Department of Manufactures of the Diet of the kingdom, and his visit to the various regions of North America was for the purpose of discovering and collecting seeds and plants which might with advantage be transferred to Sweden. After the death of Provost Sandin he attended to his surviving family with great care, remained as guest through the winter in their house, and during that time preached nearly every Sunday in Racoon Church. He also delivered funeral sermons, so that the people took him for a regular Minister. His friendship for the widow of Provost Sandin was extended to a marriage contract, which was consummated in Philadelphia in the month of February, 1750, after which the Professor took still another year for his travels, and so spent three years in this country. Then, together with his household, he took leave of this part of the world, experiencing a very dangerous voyage on his journey home.

CHAPTER VI.

OF MR. UNANDER'S TIME.

1. ASSISTANT MINISTER IN THE MISSION.

SO soon as Provost Sandin's death was known, through a letter which arrived in February, 1749, the Jersey congregation was again found to be in its former desolate condition. The Archbishop, Henry Benzelius,[2] had not yet come up to Upsala,

---

[1] [Prof. Kalm wrote an account of his travels in America, which has been translated into English and published in two vols., 8vo. (the second edition in London in 1772). He reached Philadelphia in September, 1748, and remained in the country until the spring of 1751.]

[2] [Brother of the Archbishop James Benzelius, upon whose death, in 1747, he succeeded to the Archbishopric, in which position he died in 1758.]

but was living in his former diocese of Lund; still he took especial thought for that Mission. So soon as he had gained some
insight into the condition of those congregations generally, he
thought it necessary for the Ministers to be provided with an
Assistant, who should be upon hand in case of sickness or death,
and otherwise assist the churches in the instruction of the young,
as found necessary by the Provost; and when his services were
not desired elsewhere, he was to have his place with the Provost.
This was proposed to His Majesty, King Frederick I., and received
his most gracious approbation, with a yearly salary of twelve
hundred dollars copper.

2. THEIR SENDING FORTH.

Accordingly, three Swedish Ministers were to be sent off at
one time to America, the calling of whom was to be given to the
Ecclesiastical Consistory of Upsala; but the Professor of Theology
for the time being, Doct. Engelbert Hallenius, afterwards Bishop
of Skara, was the one who took the greatest interest in the matter.
The Rev. Ol. Parlin had accepted of the call to Wicacoa as Provost Sandin's successor, and so various persons were suggested,
especially three meritorious and honorable clergymen, as suitable
for that Mission; but each of them urged some excuse. Then
the Venerable Consistory turned their attention to the Rev.
Israel Acrelius, who was at that time Preacher Extraordinary to
the Admiralty, who also declined the call; but when his excuses
were not admitted, the call of the Consistory was renewed, and
he was content to yield thereto. In like manner the proposition
was made to several young clergymen to go out as Adjuncts,
but they all, one after the other, declined. Others offered themselves, but were not accepted. Finally, upon the proposition of
Prof. Hallenius, a call was sent to Bergsjö, in Helsingland, to Mr.
Eric Unander, who was then the Adjunct in said church, with
corroborative reasons for his acceptance of the same, urging him
at the same time to get himself ready at once for his departure.
This call was accepted, and the time of departure fixed. The
names proposed were sent in; their commissions from the King
were made out; but before the departure could take place, they
were called to Upsala to receive their instructions and orders, for

now the Archbishop had come up, and he made that Mission the subject of his first public act in the Consistory. Just at that time arrived a letter from Christina giving an account of Mr. Tranberg's death, and requesting the appointment of a successor. Then a fourth Minister was desired. But he could not be so immediately procured; and whilst some time was spent in consultation about the matter, the money for travelling expenses was taken out, and the books necessary for those congregations were purchased. Then the change was made that the Provost Acrelius should, by a later order of the King, be transferred from Racoon and Pennsneck to Christina, and the Preacher Extraordinary, Mr. Er. Unander, was to become a Vicar in the congregations aforesaid until further orders. Mr. Parlin, falling into a severe and tedious fever, remained behind in Stockholm. Acrelius and Unander could delay no longer, as the summer was now passing away. Their departure was therefore taken from Stockholm on the 20th of July, and they arrived at Philadelphia on the 6th of November, 1749.

3. Unander first Vice-Pastor, then Regular Pastor.

As soon as Mr. Unander's arrival was known in Racoon, the officers of the two Parishes came to greet him. The joy was very great, not only to see themselves once again provided with a good Minister, but also one entirely adapted to the wants of the Parish. He was equally beloved by all, even by those who held to the Herrnhutters. All were equally unanimous in obligating themselves to his support. Racoon and Pennsneck remained in their old association as one Pastorate. Nothing was now wanting to the general joy except the assurance of retaining that which they had thus received. For although Mr. Unander now acted as Vice-Pastor, it was uncertain whether another change might not take place next year, which might be less agreeable. On which account, after the Parish had taken counsel with Provost Acrelius on that subject as well as on others, a petition was sent off to the Archbishop, subscribed by the officers of the church, requesting that they might retain Mr. Unander as their regular Pastor. But before that arrived, the Consistory, by a letter to Provost Acrelius dated October 28th,

1750, announced that Mr. Unander had already been appointed Pastor in ordinary. Whereupon also, on the 25th of July of the same year, an order was sent to the Provost to install him as the regular Minister and Pastor, which was accordingly done in Racoon Church on the tenth Sunday after Trinity, 1751, when his Commission as such first arrived.

4. OFFICIAL ACTS.

The wide extent of Parish and the low condition of the public services and of religion gave the Teacher severe labor within his churches. A long road to church, together with double preaching, first in Swedish and then in English, almost every Sunday, also family-hearings[1] once a year throughout the whole congregation, was really more work than one man could perform. But he did not let himself be wearied or prevented from visiting the Swedes at Maurice's river,[2] a place where the people lived almost as heathen, five or six Swedish miles from the parsonage, which, however, could not be done over three times a year. He also distributed his labor to the English congregation in Salem, as also to the people upon Timber creek, though only on weekdays. One who has seen his toil and labor, his zeal and diligence, and this under long-continued sickness, can safely testify that during the time that Mr. Unander lived in Racoon he did not eat the bread of idleness.

5. REPAIRS OF THE PARSONAGE.

During his time the parsonage was considerably improved. The house was repaired with timber and carpenters' work, and had several rooms added to it. The garden was fenced in, and a fine vegetable garden made in front of the house. A log-barn was built, there being none before. The farm was well fenced, manured, and increased by a piece of newly-cleared ground. The meadow was ditched, cleaned up, and increased to many loads of hay. And all this was done in view of the fact that his successors would have the greatest gain from his labors.

---

[1] [Catechization in private families.]

[2] On Delaware Bay, above Cape May. This river was formerly called Prince Maurice, after the Stadtholder. — T. W.

6. Removal to Christina.

It was indeed his desire to return to Sweden with Provost Acrelius, whose seven years of service were ended; and Mr. Unander therefore requested the Archbishop to recall him at the expiration of five years. But as the congregations[1] could not allow the exchange of two Ministers at once, he was therefore content to take a commission to Christina, dated in September, 1755, which arrived in July of the following year, when he entered upon his duties in October, the seventeenth Sunday after Trinity.

CHAPTER VII.

OF THE TIME OF THE YOUNGER LIDENIUS.

1. His Residence in Pennsneck.

IN the year 1750, when Mr. Unander was appointed Pastor in ordinary, Mr. John Abr. Lidenius was appointed to succeed him as the Assistant Minister. He was born in Racoon, taken home with them by his parents in 1723, and had a strong desire to see his native place and his family and kindred. After his arrival in the month of June, 1751, he took up his residence with his mother's brother, Garrit van Neaman, in Pennsneck, so as to aid Mr. Unander in his widely-extended labors. Accordingly, he preached alternately in Racoon and Pennsneck, as well as in the other congregations when needed. Sometimes, also, he visited the Swedish families at Maurice's river, as well as in Manathanim, which are places widely distant[2] from each other. The latter place was more agreeable to him, and he was called thither by frequent prayers, and went to reside there at the end of the year 1752.

2. Services in Various Places.

It is not uncommon to see how the people in this country strive to get a good Minister among them when they are desti-

---

[1] [The original is "staten," "the state," *i. e.*, the associated body of churches.]
[2] [At least one hundred English miles.]

tute of such, and give every sort of inducement to his coming.
Mr. Lidenius preached in Manathanim, and, when he became
more known, was also sometimes invited to Reading, as also to
the place called Little Canestoga.[1] But there he found only a
faint greeting, a weary body, and small pay. Besides, he was
thus debarred from his proper official duties among the Swedish
congregations, and from the faithful society of his ministerial
brethren. He, therefore, allowed himself to be persuaded by his
family to remove back again, and took up his residence at
Amasland, where he preached regularly, the last Sunday in every
month excepted, which Mr. Parlin as Pastor loci retained for
himself. On that day, as also on week-days, he directed his
labors to Marcus Hook, Marlborough, and Folk's[2] Manor, and
was everywhere greatly beloved, as well as highly esteemed for
his services within the Swedish churches to which he was called.
And as he had acquired unusual love in those places, so was the
sorrow no less when, in accordance with the Royal Commission,
he removed to Racoon and Pennsneck to enter upon the charge
of those churches in the place of Mr. Unander.[3]

---

[1] [In the neighborhood of Lancaster.]   [2] Fagg's Manor.

[3] [His successors in this part of the Swedish Mission were:

1. John Wicksell, sent over in 1760, but arriving only in 1762; returned to Sweden
in 1774, and died there in 1800.

2. Nicholas Collin arrived in 1778, and was transferred to Wicacoa in 1786, where
he died in 1832, as above stated. With him the Swedish Mission closed. See
Clay's "Annals," pp. 153 and 154. Since that time the church has had the following succession of Rectors in connection with the Protestant Episcopal Church in the
Diocese of New Jersey:

1. John Wade from 1788 to 1789.

2. John Croes (afterwards first Bishop of New Jersey) from 1790 to 1801.

3. Henry James Feltus from 1802 to 1808.

4. Simon Wilmer from 1808 to 1820.

5. J. M. Douglas from 1820 to 1824.

6. Norman Nash from 1829 to 1834.

7. J. Long Woart from 1834 to 1835.

8. John Woart from 1836 to 1840.

9. Geo. W. Freeman (afterwards Bishop of Arkansas), 1841.

10. J. W. Brown from 1841 to 1843.

11. W. H. Trapnell from 1844 to 1847.

12. E. B. Boggs from 1847 to 1855.

13. W. J. Timmer from 1855 to 1857.

14. Henry Tulledge from 1857 to 1864.

15. C. W. Duane from 1864 to 1868.

16. C. N. Chevrier from 1868 to 1872   To this gentleman I am indebted for the list of Episcopal Rectors, and for the following additional items: "Trinity Parish, Swedesboro, (New Jersey,) is the same as the original Swedish Parish of Racoon. It was not incorporated until 1765, when it received a Charter from the Colonial Council of New Jersey. An attempt was made to have both Racoon and Pennsneck united in this Charter; but the application was denied, as the two places lay in different counties. The present church building was erected in 1784, is of brick, forty-one feet by sixty-one feet, and is on the ground of the old church." The new church was, therefore, built under the Rectorship of Dr. N. Collin. The death of the Rev. C. N. Chevrier occurred soon after the above was written, November 13, 1872. Whereupon C. W. Duane resumed the duties.]

THE CHURCHES OF KINGSESSING AND UPPER MERION.

AN APPENDIX TO ACRELIUS' HISTORY OF THE SWEDISH CHURCHES ON THE DELAWARE.

BY W. M. R.

IT is apparent from the preceding history that the original Swedish population soon spread itself to various points far beyond the limits of their first settlements at Christina, Tinicum, Wicacoa, and West Jersey. We find notices of them on Elk river and various other points on the Eastern Shore of Maryland; at Apoquimeny, in Delaware; and up the Schuylkill, in Pennsylvania. To all these points the faithful Swedish Missionaries followed them with the services of the Church and the Word of God. But receiving no additions from Sweden, their language was soon lost in that of the overwhelming tide of English, and the great mass of them were gathered into the English churches with which they had the nearest affinity. It was only at Kingsessing, a few miles west-south-west of Wicacoa, and at Upper Merion, to the north-west on the Schuylkill, that considerable bodies of them settled together, long retained their native language, and established permanent churches after the type of the National Church of Sweden. Tobias E. Björk,[1] the son of the first Missionary at Christina, tells us that Mr. Rudman, the first Rector of Wicacoa, officiated also at Nitshameneth (Neshaminy) and Kalkonhook, and his successor, Mr. Sandel, at Mahanataunay and Mattzong, the last of which places is, no doubt, the same as Mattson's Ford, near Norristown.

It was not, however, until the year 1765 that the people of Kingsessing, under the name of "St. James' Church," and those of Upper Merion, under the name of "Christ Church," were formed into Parishes distinct from Wicacoa, with which, even long after that time, they maintained the closest connection. It was by the zeal and energy

------

[1] In his "Dissertatio Gradualis," p. 15.

of Dr. Charles Magnus von Wrangel[1] that this was brought about, church buildings erected, and a Charter obtained from the Proprietary Government of Pennsylvania, of which John Penn was at that time the head, whereby they were incorporated under the name of " The United Swedish Lutheran Churches of Wicacoa, Kingsessing, and Upper Merion." Of this distinguished man, a descendant of the illustrious General of the same name, Cornelius,[2] a recent writer of Swedish Church History, gives the following account: " One of the most zealous laborers in that field [the Swedish Mission in America] was Charles Magnus Wrangel. This man, who had studied in Vesterås and Upsala, in 1757 received the degree of Doctor of Divinity at Göttingen, and was then immediately nominated as Court Preacher. But his countryman, *Samuel Troilius*, who, after the death of Henry Benzelius (1758), had become the Archbishop of Sweden, in 1759 called Wrangel to the Provostship of the Swedish churches in America. In that capacity Wrangel accomplished a great deal of good; he directed his attention especially to the instruction of the young. After nine years' zealous service, he left Wicacoa, and returned home to Sweden in 1768, whereupon he was first nominated as First Court Preacher [Öfverhof predikant], and afterwards as Pastor of Sala, where he died in 1786. It should be mentioned that this Wrangel gave the first impulse to the establishment of the Society ' *Pro fide et Christianismo* ' (' For the faith and Christianity '), which was organized in Stockholm in 1771, the object of which was, besides the promotion of the spread of Christianity, to watch over the preservation of the true faith, and especially to resist the progress of Swedenborgianism."

Dr. Henry Melchior Mühlenberg, sometimes called the " Patriarch of American Lutheranism," in his Journal for the year 1760,[3] gives the following account of his intercourse with Von Wrangel, and of some of the labors of the latter:

" On the 24th of August, 1760, I had the honor, for the first time, to meet face to face, in my house in Providence,[4] His Excellency, the Doctor and Provost von Wrangel. I was greatly moved by his mild and humble manners, and edified by his weighty conversation relative to the kingdom of God. On his departure, the Provost invited me to their regular Ministerial Convention, which was to be held at Wicacoa on the 14th of September. On the 13th of September, I arrived at the house of the Rev. Doctor and Provost von Wrangel, where I was entertained by him most kindly and affectionately, and edified by him with solid conversation in regard to the importance of Ministerial labors and other matters relative to the kingdom of God. On Sunday, the 14th of September, at 10 A. M., we went with the Reverend Swedish Ministerium[5] into the church, where the Provost, in a very profound and instructive sermon, directed our attention to the importance of the Holy Supper, after which we made confession and received absolution. The Reverend Provost also delivered the sermon for the occasion, in the Swedish language, from the 5th verse of Psalm 126: ' *They that sow in tears shall reap in joy.*' Hereupon he developed

---

1 He is called " Von Wrangel" by Dr. H. M. Mühlenberg, who was *personally* acquainted with him, and so fully acquainted with his condition. See the " Pennsylvanische Nachrichten, Zehnte Fortsetzung," p. 851.

2 Handbok i Svenska Kyrkans Historia, p. 248.

3 Hall. Nachrichten, pp. 851–862. Halle, 1768.

4 Providence is at the village now called " The Trappe," about 25 miles north-west of Philadelphia, in Montgomery county.

5 The organized body of Ministers.

two propositions: 1. *How God's faithful servants must sow;* and 2. *How and what they shall reap.* These were expounded in demonstration of the spirit and with power, and applied to the hearts of the hearers. After this, the Ministers and people who were present received the Holy Supper with deep solemnity. In the afternoon, at 3 o'clock, there was another Divine Service, after which the remaining time was spent in private edification.

" On Monday, the 15th of September, at 9 o'clock in the morning, the Rev. Provost opened the Conference with prayer. Then he read 1. his Instructions from the Right Reverend the Archbishop of Sweden in the presence of the congregation; wherein, among other things, it was enjoined that he, together with the Swedish Ministers generally, should, so far as possible, live in Christian and brotherly love and harmony with the German Lutheran Ministers, attend our annual meetings, invite us to their regular Conventions, receive us kindly, and consult together for the good of the whole Church. . . . .

" 2. The Rev. Provost gave an account of his labors in his congregations, from which it was evident that he employed unspeakable care and toil not only for the repair of the outward hedge around the Church, and to guard against all sorts of dangerous attacks (Psalm 80), but also especially to bring to life, breath, and growth inwardly the 'dry bones' (Ezek. 37: 1–10) by the power of the Gospel. He has especial gifts and attainments for attracting the young and awakening the old, which are deserving of imitation, and which we should implore from the Giver of all good gifts. A most gracious God has also within a short time already crowned his labors with marked success, and keeps a gracious watch over this his servant. But he also so leads him that when he might be too greatly elevated by one or another marked success and blessing, God permits to descend upon him a proportionally bitter suffering, cross, and temptation in order that he may remain humble and lowly, and give to God alone the glory. And when, on the other hand, the cross becomes too heavy, and would make the heart fearful and shrinking, then the Lord his God allows him to behold a new victory and blessing.

" 3. He earnestly recommended Pastoral visitation and catechization; and, in order that the old might be attracted thereto, he recommended that at the beginning one or another point, taken from the table of Domestic Duties[1] or some passage of God's Word, should be explained, to awaken interest and curiosity. He further showed how we should so extol the Holy Sacraments in such an evangelical manner, according to their use and benefits, that old and young should alike feel a desire for them, whereas otherwise they, unfortunately, usually have only repulsive and legal ideas in regard to them, and gladly put off their use until they come to die. He also added that it was his intention to explain the life of Christ in his private meetings and catechetical exercises with the children.

" 4. The Rev. Provost laid down the rule, that the Ministers should take charge of no vacant English congregations for subscriptions, or for the sake of gain, but should first attend with all diligence to their own with which they were entrusted, wherein there was so much to do that they had no time to spare. But if they could spare the time, and occasionally visit deserted English churches, and supply them with the means of grace according to our Evangelical order and doctrine, this was demanded

---

[1] Haustafel—one of the sections of the Lutheran Catechism.

by Christian charity, and for this they might receive an acknowledgment when such was offered.

"5. The Rev. Provost set forth how necessary it was that Luther's Shorter Cate-chism should be printed anew, and translated into better English for the young, who understood neither Swedish nor German."

A year afterwards, Mühlenberg tells us that, "on Saturday evening, he went to Wicacoa to the Rev. Provost, Dr. Wrangel, strengthened himself by conversing with him on the Word of God, and by prayer with him." For years they lived in this intimate and brotherly manner, assisting each other in every possible way. Thus, on the 29th of July, 1761, we find this entry in M's. diary: "Entered with His Excellency, the Provost, upon a Visitation in his congregations, crossed the river Schuylkill, visited along the road one and another Swedish family, and in the even-ing arrived at the noteworthy island of Tenakum, where the Swedes, over one hun-dred and twenty[1] years ago, established their first colony. We lodged with an Englishman, Mr. John Tailor,[2] who is in possession of a part of the island. Mr. T. had been a Quaker, but was instructed and baptized by the Provost, Dr. W. His pious wife was the daughter of a Brandenburger, but her mother was a Swede, who had lived upon this island. We edified each other with Christian conversation and prayer until we retired to rest. On Thursday we visited the place of the first grave-yard, where we found mouldering remains of bodies, and of the first Christian church in this western wilderness. In the afternoon, accompanied by some friends, we rode back to 'Squire Morton's at Ammesland. A meeting was appointed there to consult about a new Swedish church.[3] The Rev. Provost appointed me one of the Trustees, and I subscribed £5 to the church building." Subsequently he tells of Von Wrangel preaching in the three languages, Swedish, German, and English, and making addresses in holding examinations of candidates for the ministry in Latin. These notices of the Swedish Provost and his Missionary labors continue in Dr. M's. Journals down to the close of the year 1764, after which we have no Journal, or general account of his operations, until after Von Wrangel had left this country and returned to Sweden. But that the Provost continued as active and energetic as ever is evident from the Charter which he procured from the Proprietary Government of Pennsylvania, for the United Swedish Lutheran Churches of Wicacoa, Kingsessing, and Upper Merion, in 1765, and the church edifice which he erected for both of the last named congregations. This Charter may be seen in the Appen-dix to Clay's "Annals of the Swedes," (pp. 161–171,) and it continued in force until 1787, when it was confirmed with some slight changes by the State Government. The most important change made was that of Sec. 6, whereby the people were allowed to elect their own Ministers, who might be "in the ministry of either the Lutheran or the Episcopal Church." This provided alike for the cessation of the Swedish Mission, and for the legal connection of these congregations with the Epis-copal Church of the United States.

The two churches at Kingsessing and Upper Merion continued connected with the Mother Church at Wicacoa until 1842, when they obtained separate charters, and became independent Parishes. Up to that time their Rectors were the same as those

---

[1] This is evidently a mistake arising from the confounding of the arrival of Governor Printz in 1643 with the original establishment of the colony in 1638.

[2] Misspelled for Taylor.   [3] Probably the church at Kingsessing.

of Gloria Dei, already given by our author, and in our Notes. The following sketches will give a connected view of their history down to the present time:

1. St. James' Church, Kingsessing.

"The church-building of St. James' Church, Kingsessing, stands on the Darby Road, between 68th and 69th Streets, Philadelphia. 'Kingsessing,' the name of the old township, is passing out of use, since the whole of the county of Philadelphia has been made the city of Philadelphia. It is about five miles from Gloria Dei. The Parish became independent of Gloria Dei, and was incorporated December 31, 1842. The Rev. S. C. Brinkle was the first Rector. He resigned May 15, 1848. The first Warden (there is but one under the special charter of the Parish) was Justis Culin. The first Vestrymen were. Aubrey Henry Smith, Thomas M. Smith, John C. Knowles, William Harmar, Daniel T. Morton, Samuel Thomas, Charles Palmer, Jr., and Daniel M. Jones.

"The church-building was erected by general subscription. The corner-stone was laid by the Rev. Charles Magnus Wrangel, D.D., in 1760. A Chapel and transepts were added, and the old part of the church was improved in 1854. A Sunday-school building was erected in 1859, and a Parish school-house in 1866. All these buildings are of stone. The original ground (part of which is a cemetery) has been enlarged, so that it now embraces about four acres, nearly completing a square on the city plan. There is a Parsonage also, nearly opposite the church, with about three acres of land.

"The population has changed so much that but few of the old Swedish names are perpetuated here, but the names of Trites, Culin, Yocom, Holstein, and Rambo, are still among us. The number of communicants in the church is about one hundred and fifty, and the Sunday-school numbers about three hundred scholars."

The Rectors since the death of the Rev. Jehu C. Clay, D. D., when the Parish became independent, have been the following:

1. The Rev. S. C. Brinkle from 1842 to 1848.
2. The Rev. J. Brinton Smith from 18— to 1856.
3. The Rev. Chas. A. Maison [1] from May 1st, 1857, to the present time.

2. Christ Church, Upper Merion.

Upper Merion is a township of Montgomery county, Pa., to the north-west of Philadelphia. The building of "Christ Church is on the west bank of the Schuylkill, one mile below Norristown, the county-seat, near the line of the borough of Bridgeport, and sixteen miles from Philadelphia." The first Swedish settlers in this region were Mats Holstein and Peter Rambo, with their families. Mats (Matthias) Holstein is said to have had one thousand acres of land in the neighborhood of what was formerly called Swedes' Ford, where his house still stands. The Ford probably received its name from him, and the place is called by Acrelius, and other early Swedish writers, "Matzong," probably a corruption of Matson's (Mat's Son).

The church-building was erected in 1763, under the direction, as already said, of the Provost Von Wrangel. "Services becoming more frequent here during the time of Dr. Collin, he was assisted by the Rev. Slator Clay, of the Episcopal Church.

---

[1] We are indebted to the kindness of this gentleman for the particulars included in our quotation as given above.

The death of Dr. Collin in 1831 severed our connection with the Swedish Mission. The three churches then, in joint convention, elected the Rev. Jehu C. Clay, D. D., a Swede by descent, also of the Episcopal Church, who had charge of the three churches as heretofore from 1831 to 1843. He was assisted in this church by the Rev. Raymond A. Henderson, Rev. John Reynolds, Rev. Wm. N. Diehl, and Rev. Nathan Stem. After the separation of the three Parishes into distinct churches in 1843, the first Rector chosen for this church was the Rev. Edwin N. Lightner."

The Rectors, then, since the distinct organization of this Parish, are as follows:

1. The Rev. Edwin N. Lightner, from 1844 to 1855.
2. The Rev. Wm. Henry Rees, D. D., from 1855 to 1861.
3. The Rev. Thomas S. Yocom, from 1861 to 1870.
4. The Rev. Octavius Perinchief, from 1870 to 1873.
5. The Rev. Edward A. Warriner, elected in September, 1873, being the present Rector.

"Our church is still independent [of the Episcopal Convention], although we are ministered to by Episcopal clergymen. All the other Swedish churches have formally entered into union with the Episcopal Church." [1]

---

[1] Those portions of this note upon Christ Church marked as quotations, have been kindly communicated to me by Mr. Geo. W. Holstein, now Secretary of the Vestry of Christ Church, Upper Merion, also a lineal descendant of M. Holstein, one of the first Swedish settlers, as above stated, of that part of Pennsylvania.

PART EIGHTH.

OF THE CHURCHES IN GENERAL.

CHAPTER I.

OF VARIOUS ORDERS AND DISORDERS.

1. OF THE INSTRUCTION OF THE YOUNG.

HEN one recollects that the instruction of the young is the foundation of all the rest of the life, he can easily understand what these churches suffer for the want of a proper system of school-keeping. In almost every ridge of woods there is a school-house, but the children never come longer than to learn to read plainly in the book, and to write and cipher. The Quakers, who form the majority of the people, do not permit that their children should learn so much as the Ten Commandments; they must receive through immediate inspiration that which belongs to faith and godliness. Others following much in the same way, it is difficult to remedy this. The people are a mixture of all sorts of religious belief. The school-masters have a different faith from the children, and the children in like manner differ from each other. Hence Pennsylvania is known all over the world for its lamentable destitution and deficiency in the instruction of its children in the knowledge of Christianity.

2. THE SCHOOL-MASTERS.

Forty years back, our people scarcely knew what a school was. The first Swedish and Holland settlers were a poor, weak,

25

and ignorant people, who brought up their children in the same
ignorance, which is the reason why the natives of the country
can neither write nor cipher, and that very few of them are
qualified for any office under the government. None, whether
boys or girls, are now growing up who cannot read English,
write and cipher. In later times there have come over young
men from Ireland, some Presbyterians and some Roman
Catholics, who commenced with school-keeping, but as soon as
they saw better openings they gave that up. Some young
Swedes also have come over from time to time, and undertaken
at first to keep school; such were Lenmayer, Hans Stolt, Arvid
Hernbom, Sven Colsberg, John Göding, Jesper Svedberg, Olof
Malander, Nicolaus Forsberg, and Joach. Reinicke. But either
the support from this was not sufficient, or their mind was unsettled, so that but little was accomplished. As for the rest, the
little knowledge of Christianity which our people have has been
gained chiefly from their parents and Ministers. That the Swedish language has continued for over one hundred and twenty
years, may be ascribed partly to the merciful Providence which
has supplied them with Swedish Ministers, and partly to the
natural love that every race of people has for its own mother
tongue.

3. THE STATE OF CHRISTIANITY IN GENERAL.

The sound remark which some men, not less learned than
zealous, have already made in other parts of the world, exhibits
its truth only too much in Pennsylvania, and the places upon the
Delaware, viz., the further people are from superstition, the nearer
they are to atheism; the further they have gone from the renunciation of Popery, the more does the Christian Church tend
to free-thinking, indifferentism, and naturalism. He who is here
known as a Roman Catholic, is hated as a half devil; but he who
has no religion, is just as much esteemed for it as though he
thereby showed himself quite rational. We here have numerous examples how those who would relieve themselves of all
outward church-service attach themselves to the Quakers.
Those who will not regulate themselves by the strict morality
of the Quakers, and so are excluded from that sect, seldom

attach themselves again to any other religious confession. Our Swedish churches have also cast forth some such apostates from their bosom.

4. ATTENDANCE AT CHURCH.

As many as hold to the congregation are inclined to come to church whenever the weather is fair; but if any severe weather occurs, or bad roads, but few are present. If the next church-day is fine, the churches are full again. To a certain extent the people are justifiable in this. In but few places are there bridges over their streams, so that they have for the most part to be forded. Now when the water is raised by a sudden rain, or the ice forms over it, which will neither bear nor break, then it is impossible to cross. Terrible storms of wind, cold, snow, rain, etc., sometimes occur, so that no one can endure them. Neither can one clothe himself according to the weather: it would expose one to ridicule to wear skins or furs. They talk of their forefathers who used to do so, but laugh at it. The weather often changes very rapidly. Men and women in the summer dress in linen as light as decency will permit. If a warm summer-day suddenly changes to cold rain, then one is in danger of falling into a fever or pleurisy. Again, if a skin is quite useful in some wintry day in the morning, yet by the afternoon it may be quite oppressive. It has also gone out of use to go to church here as they used to do in former times: all must now either ride, or stay at home. But few horses are kept shod in winter-time. Of winter "körslor"[1] nothing is known. To ride in a sled is considered ridiculous. All this implies that public worship is arranged partly according to circumstances, partly according to custom and convenience — all of which strikes a stranger as at once painful and offensive.

5. BAPTISM.

The Sacrament of Baptism is held in due respect within the congregations. In general, it is esteemed an honor to carry one's

---

[1] This is a wagon-body so large as to extend over the wheels. It is about six feet high, is built of open slats, and well adapted for the carriage of hay, cattle, etc. In winter it is covered with cloth, and, the wheels being removed, is placed on runners. — J. J. M.

children to church for the reception of Baptism and Christianity. Yet the carelessness of many persons is such as to keep their children from it until they are four or five weeks old, and often more, under some lame pretext; meantime, if the child gets sick, they send for the Minister. Sometimes they pretend that the child was sick, for no other reason than to avoid the trouble of taking it out, and that the Minister may come to the house, though it be ever so far. No one will hear about "Necessary Baptism." [1] It may be taught and preached about without cessation: no one will believe that any case of necessity can give this power to any one who is not a Minister. No one will venture to become of evil report among others. The strongest reason is that neither the Church of England nor the Church of Scotland allows of " Necessary Baptism."

6. SPONSORSHIP.

Sponsorship is highly esteemed. No one is willing to engage in it unless he is in earnest in keeping his promises. The young are mostly selected for it. The old say that they do not expect to live so long as to fulfil such promises. Some of them have taken the taste of the Presbyterians: the parents will answer for themselves without any one else. They think that none are more suitable for it than they are themselves, and say that many promise what they never perform, and declare that they will never take such obligations upon themselves for other people's children, as Judges and Magistrates never inquire after Sponsors when they are taking measures for the rearing of orphan children, but often put them out to persons of an entirely different religion. And although this is only an unfounded objection, as Sponsors are never prevented from doing their duty if they are willing; yet a Minister has often to talk a long time in explaining Sponsorship before he can proceed to the act of Baptism, or allow parents to stand along with the Sponsors, or, if time and cir-

---

[1] [We have no English term for the *Nöd-Dop* of the Swedes, or the *Noth - Taufe* of the Germans, which can be performed by a layman or a midwife, and so is entirely different from " Private Baptism " in the Church of England and the Prot. Episcopal Church of the U. S., which provides only for baptism in private houses; for which, however, the services of a clergyman are still required.]

cumstances do not allow otherwise, christen the child without any other Sponsorship; inasmuch as Baptism, which is a Sacrament, cannot be delayed for the want of Sponsorship, which is only a ceremony. But, otherwise, Sponsorship is as necessary here as ever it was at its first institution, partly to witness the child's baptism, for doubts have often arisen about it during long vacancies, or in places distant from the churches; and partly to take charge of the child's education. Notwithstanding, according to the law of the country, whenever the parents die or become paupers, the children are, by the authority of Magistrates, put out to service with other people — the boys until they are twenty-one, the girls until they are eighteen years of age. As it may happen that they come in families of entirely different religions, inquiries are only made afterwards about their temporal welfare, and that which is for the benefit of the public. But as no one is hindered in the exercise of his religion, Sponsors may, in such cases, do a great deal of good if they provide the children with suitable books, and keep them in attendance upon church. The Quakers always keep their children among themselves; and so it is not impossible for the Sponsors to find place for the children within their own church, in which matter also a great deal depends upon the prudence of the Minister, who should inquire in his congregations as to the course pursued with children when a death takes place.

7. The Churching of Women.

The churching of women is usually attended to. No one here knows what it is to church a woman at home in her house. Such a thing would be laughed at. The time of four or six weeks, as provided by the Swedish church-laws, is mostly observed. Neither does one see women go into company outside of their houses before they have had their churching. At the same time, according to the old Swedish fashion, some money is put into the Minister's hand. Should it happen to any woman to have illegitimate children, (which, however, is seldom the case,) yet is there no law to compel them to church penance. Cases have also been known in which, under the influence of parents, women have in this matter also obeyed the law of the Swedish Church.

8. Attendance upon the Lord's Supper.

As regards the Sacrament of the Altar, it is to be lamented that there is found some neglect in its use, and in which the present times are more to be blamed than the former. Only a few families come to the Lord's Supper; even their children not doing so. Some think that it is too high a work for the young. A part of the old have formerly attended the Communion with sufficient zeal; but they have afterwards entirely left it off, and do not think of it except in case of severe sickness. One may preach and teach about the use and necessity of the Lord's Supper, late and early, but, God mend it, very little effect is seen to result from it. The most vexatious thing to hear is, when all other objections have been removed, that such and such a Minister never urged any one to attend the Lord's Supper, but left every one his liberty. It has, indeed, been replied that each one should admonish himself and select his own time for it; but when neither will nor inclination for it is shown, then there is no room for excuses. A Teacher can only call and exhort. Those who will not come must bear their own guilt. God give them grace for improvement. The greatest hindrance is found in the evil example of the world. The Quakers do not believe in any Sacraments; and some other English congregations in the country are equally regardless of the Lord's Supper, although their Confession of Faith strictly binds them thereto.

9. Marriage.

Marriage is quick, and not according to rule. To be published three Sundays and then married is only for poor people. The law of the land permits a much shorter way, which is more agreeable and more used, except that it costs money. The Governor has a right to license marriage without the publication of the banns. In every county office marriage licenses are issued in this wise: that the bridegroom gives his bond to pay to the Governor from five to ten thousand dollars copper, according to the ability of the applicants, if it should be found that the marriage of the persons named therein is not lawful. Thereupon a Manifest is issued, which is called a License, in the name of the Governor, to some Protestant Minister to perform the marriage ceremony. And as this gives the Governor a considerable income, so he quite willingly allows the Ministers themselves to keep such a license in blank with his name subscribed, for which payment is made when the bonds are handed in. The abuses of this are indescribable. Yet such a marriage license is usual throughout the whole English government, although now much more restricted than formerly. Our Swedish people, as natural-ized Englishmen, dance to the same tune, and our Swedish men who settle here find an equal pleasure, or are compelled thereto to gratify their brides, who would rather break off their engage-ments than be proclaimed in church. But when such a license comes to the bridal pair, in season or out of season, even if it be in the middle of the night or early in the morning, if they so please, with more or less company, then the marriage immedi-ately takes place. The bride is in her usual dress, so that in that respect she cannot be distinguished from any of the company. Very few celebrate their marriage with a meal and entertainment. Plays and dancing are but little in use, and are usually counted as among loose and disreputable sports. Seldom do the Ministers prevail upon any bridal parties to go to church; but if this is done, the marriage takes place after service. The old speak of the joy with which their bridal parties formerly came to church and sat during the whole service before the altar; but when it comes to the time for their own children to do so, then they either run off to some English Minister with a license, or the parents are afraid of this, or get up some other reason for it, and so it is impossible any more to root out such an inveterate abuse.

10. BURIALS.

Burials also are performed with great haste, the warm climate not allowing of the corpse remaining in the house for over two days. Sometimes the burial takes place on the same day as the death. Some men are sent out on horseback to inform the neigh-bors roundabout of the time of the funeral. If the Minister can be on hand, it is well; but if not, he is not waited for a day. All who desire it are welcome to the house of mourning, and are refreshed with the drinks of the country, according to the ability and means. The nearest relatives sit around the corpse with

downcast looks — the men with large flapped hats on their
heads with long hanging crape bound around them, and with
black gloves at least, if they cannot get anything more. The
women are always dressed in black. When one comes into the
house, it is the custom to go and look at the deceased before
taking a seat. Before the coffin is closed up, the nearest friends,
and others who would show their friendship, go and give the
corpse a farewell kiss. The Swedes take the bearers from the
nearest relatives. Children bear their parents, brothers their own
brothers or sisters. The corpse is borne by the English upon the
shoulders of four men; but the Swedes use the ordinary bier.
On both sides of it go some persons who hold on the pall — old
or young persons, either male or female, according to the age
and sex of the deceased, for whom crape and either black or
white gloves are distributed at the house of mourning. If the
deceased is a person of wealth, scarfs of silk or fine starched linen
are distributed, either white or black, which are hung over one
shoulder and go down to the opposite side. The young women,
who, when the deceased is of their condition, perform this office,
also bear such scarfs, and are all dressed in white. If the corpse
is that of an infant, it is sometimes borne in their arms by young
women; but if there are a number of bearers, they bear it between
them with a towel held in their hands. The Minister also wears
a similar scarf, together with a long crape and white or black
gloves, and goes immediately before the corpse. These customs
are observed according to each one's pleasure, and so also is the
liberality of the entertainment. Funeral sermons are not unusual.
The mourners do not leave the grave before it is filled up. A
corpse is seldom laid out in the church, unless it be that of a
Clergyman. The wealthy have a wall of brick built around the
grave, two or three feet above the ground, and on this lay the
tombstone. Others erect at the head of the grave a large, flat,
and well-wrought piece of marble, upon which the name, age,
etc., of the deceased are inscribed, and a similar but smaller one
at the feet. In general, all have some kind of a flat stone erected
at each end of the grave. The earth is well packed upon the
grave to a considerable height and then covered with turf, so that
the place of the grave can be seen for the life of a man. Some
place boards around to keep up the earth. There is also a custom

to honor the dead with flowers, which grow upon their graves, for which purpose seed is sown — all of·which serves at least to preserve the grave and prevent the dead from being disturbed in their last resting-place.

11. Divine Service.

Divine service is performed, without any objections, according to the Swedish church-regulations, the laws of the country having never forbidden it. All who acknowledge one God, the Maker of all things, have the free exercise of religion in the country. The Swedish Church has the greater freedom, as it is called "a sister of the English Church;" and is, in fact, an older sister. Everything depends upon the union of the people with their Minister, and the prudence of the Clergy in giving their people proper views upon the subject. The genuine Swedes are also greatly attached to their church usages; and many English would be more pleased with the Swedish than with the English Church service, if they understood the language. No objection is made to exorcism at baptism. The singing of the Creed seems strange to the English, as their church retains the custom only with choral music in the cathedrals. Still more singular does the Swedish Mass appear to them. Mass-linen is usual with this; but they cannot be reconciled to the chasuble.[1] Otherwise no attention is excited by the Minister's robe, whether it is the Swedish Kappa or the English gown[2] — a black, blue, or gray gown, as time and circumstances require. But all agree that the Minister's robes are very becoming. That the Minister sings at the grave, and himself casts the earth upon the dead, is regarded as singular; although singing upon this occasion is not unusual with others, and the earth is also cast upon the coffin three different times by the English Sexton. But to read prayers at the grave is customary, as also to preach at the house, or at the grave, or in the church; as also to carry the corpse into the church during preaching is universal both among the Presbyterians and the Quakers, just as one pleases. But the corpse upon the pall, the crucifix in churches, or images or pictures of other saints, should not be even talked of here.

---

[1] [Sw., " Mässhaka " = " Mass-gown."]

[2] [In the original, "*goun*," which may have been the English orthography of the period.]

12. DIVINE SERVICE IN ENGLISH.

It is here necessary to state how far these Swedish churches are inclined to have their service in English. The Swedes formerly dwelt more closely together, used their language more among themselves and daily at home in their houses; whence it happens that the old among our people do not speak English well, can hardly read an English book or clearly understand English preaching; and, in a word, they hate in their hearts everything that is English. They say that they are Swedish people, although they are in an English country. Some of the young people have learnt both languages, and bring up their children in the same manner, as they speak Swedish in their houses, and let the children take their chance of learning English outside of the house. Many others have through marriage mingled with the English, when neither father nor mother spoke anything in the house but what all could understand; or the parents thought it a shame that the child could not speak the common language when they came among strangers, and there-fore so accustomed them to English that they would not after-wards willingly express themselves in Swedish; or when the child was put out to be brought up by strangers, or to learn a trade, the Swedish was easily forgotten, although they had learned that first. From this comes such a confusion in languages as can scarcely be described. All those who understand and speak and read Swedish are entirely in favor of Divine service in their own language. Others, again, whose wives, children, rela-tives, and friends are English, cannot but desire worship for them in that language which they understand, especially as they, upon their side, contribute to support the Minister and church, are descendants of Swedes, and do not wish to fall away from their church, and have also many members of the English church among them, who in like manner need Divine Service, and will help to support the Minister.

13. ITS INCONVENIENCE.

From this it may be concluded with what great difficulties the Minister often has to contend when he is to accommodate people of such unlike minds. Sometimes it is concluded in the Vestry that no more English preaching shall be held, no English any more be buried in the grave-yard. Then the Minister and church officers are decried as persons who regard all English as heathens. They think that it is a failure in duty to water one part of the Lord's vineyard to overflowing whilst many other parts wither and die. So this must be changed again. One will have his child baptized in English, another in Swedish, at one and the same hour in the church. Some refuse to stand as Sponsors if the child is not baptized in Swedish, and yet it may be that the other Sponsors do not understand it. One woman, who is to be churched, will have Swedish, the other English, and this at the same time. When funeral sermons are preached, English people of every form of faith come together, and then it often happens that the one desires preaching in English, the other in Swedish, and that just as the Minister is going into the church. Those who would not find any fault with their Minister, but yet would have something different, commonly say, "The Minister is good enough, if he did not hold so much with the English;" or, The Minister would be more esteemed in the country, if he had not so great a contempt for the English."

14. Occasion Thereto.

The foundation for the reliance of the English people upon the Ministers was laid already in the beginning of this century. The Ministers who then came over built new churches and organized new congregations. At the same time, also, the English Society sent hither its Missionaries, and from this the few English churches here count their age. The Swedes and English united as ministerial brethren : their object was no other than the promotion and extension of Christianity : they preached English in each others' churches; and, as a stronger token of unity, they sometimes sang a Swedish Psalm in the English congregation. They annually held ministerial meetings together; and consecrated each others' churches. No letter was sent home to England, or to the King, Queen, Parliament, or Bishop of London,[1] or to the Society, without the Swedish Clergy also

---

[1] [The Bishop of London was the Diocesan of the English Churches and Clergy in the English Colonies in North America.]

signing it. So, also, were the Swedish Ministers, when they went home, provided with good testimonials from the English Clergy. They were willing to receive the Lord's Supper of one another, as also to administer the Sacraments to each other's hearers. Finally, it may also be mentioned that every Swedish Minister upon his return home received from the Society in London £30 sterling in return for the services which he had performed among the English churches here.[1]

15. FURTHER INDUCEMENTS.

All this and much more was strengthened by the high character of Dr. Svedberg, who was then Bishop of Skara, and by his admonitions to the Clergy to continue all this. The object was in itself good, but the dangerous consequences which were thus produced, even this zealous man himself saw before his death. And although the yearly meetings were soon broken off, especially as the English Clergy did not hold them even among themselves for many years, yet the English and Swedish Ministers still continued, in cases of necessity, to preach for one another in each others' churches. The Swedes also preached English in their own churches at the earnest desire of their hearers, according to the necessity of the times, and the ability of the Minister to express himself in the language. Yet it is certain, that this was done from no other motive than compassion for those who would otherwise be utterly destitute of a preached Gospel. Hence the Swedish churches, no less than those which belonged to the English High Church, were called "Churches," their Teachers were called "Church Ministers," their congregations "church people," "church-men," and "church-women;" but all other sects were called "Dissenters," and their places of worship were only called "Meeting-houses."

16. THE INJURY OF VACANCIES.

The many and long vacancies, which have taken place from time to time, have produced no little injury in these churches. The remaining Ministers could not so well watch over the vacant

---

[1] "America Illuminata," pp. 11, 13, 44, 45, 46.

churches, but the people were compelled to call in the nearest English Ministers to their assistance, so that they might have some public worship.   They were thus also rendered uncertain whether any Minister was to be expected from Sweden, or any who would be suitable for the congregation, and so they doubted whether the church would continue to be Swedish.   This has been poor encouragement for the Swedish language: it was also an open door for prowling sects, and a strong attraction for selfish Trustees to conceal the old Swedish church books, and draw the church property to themselves.   Such lamentable times there were in Wicacoa from the time of Provost Sandel to that of Mr. Lidman, for six months; from Provost Lidman's time to Mr. Falk's, two years; from Mr. Falk's to Mr. Dylander's, four years and some months; from Mr. Dylander's to Mr. Naesman's, three years.   In Racoon and Pennsneck there was scarcely any order from the year 1703, when they separated from the mother churches, until 1715, when Mr. Lidman was installed, which was a period of twelve years.   Then again there was another lamentable period from Mr. Tranberg's removal until Provost Sandin's arrival, eight years; again from Provost Sandin's death, until the arrival of Mr. Unander, one year. Christina has in so far had the least destitution, as she has had only two short vacancies —from Mr. Sam. Hesselius' time to Mr. Eneberg's, one year; and from Mr. Tranberg's death to Provost Acrelius' time, one year.   Into all this the late Archbishop, Dr. Henry Benzelius, had sufficient insight, when he appointed an Adjunct for the whole body of these churches, for the assistance of the ordinary Ministers, and to take charge whenever any vacancy might occur.

17. Deficient Supervision.

Nor can we do otherwise than count among these injurious influences the poor supervision which, during some time, there was over these churches.   The Pastor, Andrew Rudman, received the commission of a Superintendent[1] in 1708, and died

---

[1] [It is evident from this passage that the terms "Superintendent" and "Provost" are synonymous among the Swedes; also, that the Provost was, *de facto*, an "Assistant Bishop."]

immediately afterwards.   In the year 1713, Pastor Björk, of
Christina, was appointed Provost just before his departure from
the country, leaving in his place Pastor Sandel, of Wicacoa, in
1714; in his place, Pastor And. Hesselius, of Christina, in 1719;
in his place, Pastor Lidman, of Wicacoa, from 1723 to 1730.
Here ceased the golden age of the Swedish Church in America.
Bishop Svedberg became old and infirm, and was, undoubtedly,
discouraged by many sad tidings from America.   Correspondence ceased, and no Provost was appointed.   Each one acted
according to the best of his information, or his own notions.
The finances of the churches began to fail, or to get into confusion.   Troubles arose between Ministers and people, but no
one reconciled or removed them.   So it continued until matters
got into the greatest distress, when the pious, zealous, far-famed,
and now forever blessed with the Lord, Archbishop, Dr. Jacob
Benzelius, laid to heart the honor of God and the wretched condition of these churches, and sent out Provost Sandin; but his
time lasted but six months, and so but little was accomplished.

18. Misunderstanding between Ministers and People.

The serious misunderstandings which at various times arose
between Ministers and people have not only hindered a great
deal of good, but have produced a great deal of evil.   It is distressing to think of the time in Christina, whereof they still talk
a great deal, when, if the Minister found any one hostile to him
in the church, he took him by the arm and put him out of the
door.   Also, that for a long time, when one went to church,
nothing was to be expected at the church door but quarrels and
maledictions between the Minister and his people, whereby the
services were discontinued for six months.   What has not
Wicacoa Church suffered through dissensions, partly for honor
and life, on account of gross charges made by a Minister against
an innocent man; partly from dishonest management of the
church property, and the Minister's salary?   For a long time,
also, no Parish meeting could be held without being broken up
by dissension before it had well begun.   Here it is necessary to
have not only a righteous cause to promote, but also to use mildness and prudence in so doing.   The least suspicion should,

so soon as it is perceived, be removed by kindness and discretion. People will have liberty not only to think, but also to say what they please. But he who has justice on his side does not need so many words; the majority will protect him. The opposition that he meets will soon disappear, and his most violent enemies will become his best friends. The Minister who cannot overcome evil with good had better seek a place in another land.

19. OTHER CAUSES.

Among other causes of the decline of these churches may be counted the evil example given by certain Swedes from time to time. Since they have left their country,. which, perhaps. they did not do on account of their virtues, they have visited many parts of the world to seek their fortune. But as they have not succeeded elsewhere, and have understood that there are here some well-to-do Swedes, they betake themselves hither, whither, also, many bad habits, contracted during their travels, accompany them. They appeal to their high or honorable family descent and to their excellent education, but conduct themselves worse than an Indian from the wilderness. Some boast that they were educated as Ministers, are learned, and can preach as well as any one if they had leave, who, however, despise and revile both the Church and the Holy Communion. The poor people who hear and see such things do not understand how those who are educated can live in so unchristian a manner. If one tells them of the good regulations in Sweden relative to attendance at church, and the Lord's Supper, occasion is taken to throw up these abortions. In a word, it has become a proverb, that of the Swedes who are sent hither one is certain that they are good, but that those who come of their own accord cannot be trusted before they become better known. Our good Swedes have always favored strangers who were their countrymen, and have not permitted them to be sold for their passage as others usually do; but when they afterwards see these persons given to pride, drunkenness, profanity, lying, and deceit, and seeking nothing else but to make their children unhappy by marriage, they then become more circumspect in this matter than they were before.

CHAPTER II.

LIST OF SWEDISH BOOKS WHICH WERE SENT FROM SWEDEN
TO AMERICA AT THE KING'S EXPENSE, AND FOR THE USE OF
THE MISSION, FROM THE YEAR 1696 UNTIL THE PRESENT
TIME.

THERE were sent in the year 1696, with **Rudman and Björk**, 30 copies of the Bible — 10 copies printed by **Wankifs** and 20 by Keiser; 6 copies of Postills — 2 Treasuries, 2 of **Möller's**, and 2 of Lütkeman's; 50 copies of the "*Manuale Sveticum*," Stockholm, 1691; 100 copies of "Spiritual Meditations" of various kinds, viz., "*The Garden of Paradise*," 12 of Kelling's "*Meditations*," "*String of Pearls*," and others; 100 Psalm-Books (Hymn-Books) — 50 copies of the Upsala Psalm-Book, in large type, and 50 "*Treasuries of the Soul;*" 2 Liturgies (Kyrko-Hand-lingar); 2 Church Regulations (Kyrko-Ordningar); 100 copies of Suebelius' Catechism, bound in blue paper, etc.; 300 copies of small Catechisms, bound in boards; 500 copies of **Luther's** Catechism, translated into the American language.[1]

---

[1] This was a work of Mr. John Campanius, Missionary in the Swedish Colony. In the year 1696 it was thought necessary, for the conversion of the heathen, to send over this book, which still lay in MS. For this reason it was printed the same year at the Royal expense, with a double C on both sides of the cover. But yet the object was never attained, partly because the Ministers always had so much to do among their widely scattered congregations that they had no time for anything else, partly because the letter R, r, is not found in the language of the Indians, as it is in the book, but in its place L, l. The Swedes, who can still speak the language of the wild Indians, declare that, when one asks for an Indian word, they answer correctly according to the book, but with L, l, in the place of R, r. From this it may be concluded — 1. That Campanius cannot have made the mistake; for as he was able to prepare a vocabulary, dialogues, and translations into the language, so he, no doubt, was able to distinguish between the sounds of R and L in the language. 2. That the Indians upon the Delaware did not use the sound of R; at least the Mynquess or Minnesinks, with whom the Swedes had intercourse, did not. 3. That it is probable that the editor of Campanius' Catechism mistook r for l in the manuscript, being ignorant of the language. 4. That the sound of R, r, was really used in the language of the savages on both sides of the Delaware, as is shown by the following names of places: Akarakungh, Aronamex, Techoherasi. Arfwames, Memiraco or Narraticon,

In the year 1712, with Hesselius and Lidenius: 10 copies of Bibles, King Charles XII.'s Edition, with the double C on both sides; 360 copies of Hymn-Books of three sorts, Doct. Svedberg's Editions — 1, in large type, 8vo, Stock., 1694; 2, in small type, long 8vo, of the same year; 3, in small 12mo, 1695;[1] 12 copies of Guthermuth's "*Fürsten-Lehre*," a gift from Guthermuth's widow.

In the year 1743, with Naesman: 3 copies of Gezelius' "Exposition of the Greek Testament;" 9 copies of Bible in 8vo and

---

afterwards called Araratkung, now Racoon. Also the names of the great lakes Ontario, Erie, Huron. Some admit that the Indians use R, but not in the beginning of a word, for which they give the authority of Conrad Weiser, the old and honorable Provincial Interpreter, who lived among the savages from his childhood. Confirmatory of this, evidence may be given from the streams Ancocus, formerly Rankoques, and Raretan, which means "*the man*." But it is insisted that no word has ever been found in their common conversation which begins with R. But it is a question whether their words may not in later times have lost some of their initial sounds, as in other languages. [Dr. Du Ponceau's suggestion upon this point, on p. v. of the Preface to his Translation of Campanius, is, perhaps, after all, nearest to the truth, namely, that "some of the Delaware tribes made use of the letter [sound] R where others employed the letter L, which is not uncommon among different tribes of the same Indian nation."]

[1] In these editions there has also been found to come from the great and good man, whose ashes our Swedish Church of all times will honor, something that is human. By the order of King Charles XI., he prepared a Church Hymn-Book; but when the Swedish Bishops, in 1695, held a meeting for the purpose of revising this work, they found it necessary to exclude a number of psalms from it; also to introduce others, to correct the text of the Gospel for St. Bartholomew's day according to the Swedish translation, and to strike out a word in the thanksgiving for Christ's assumption of humanity. Hereupon the first edition of the book was called in and stored away in Skepsholm for some years, until His Majesty found it proper to order that a portion of them should be sent over for the service of the churches in America; more were desired, and in the year 1721, by direction of His Royal Majesty, 500 copies were sent off. In the year 1726 His Majesty was again requested by the Ecclesiastical Deputies of the Diet of the Kingdom to accord the sending off of another set, with the proviso that in the thanksgiving for Christ's incarnation the word "*antagit*" (assumed) should be struck out. Upon the application of Pastor Serenius, dated London, July 1, 1729, that he might have a part of them for Swedish seamen who had suffered shipwreck, for captives in Algiers, and for those who travelled to the East Indies, His Majesty, in consequence of the approval of this by the Chancery, resolved to send 200 copies, with the proviso that the same course should be pursued with them as above, and also the order to the officers of the Swedish Church in London not to use any of these in their services. [See an account of the controversy on this subject in Cornelius' "*Handbok*," pp. 200, 201.]

6 in 4to; 1 copy of Scriver's "Treasury of the Soul" with Kock's Register, and 2 without the Register; 3 copies of the "*Concordia Pia*" in Swedish; 24 Psalm-Books. At the total cost of 1012 Swedish dols.[1] 16 ör.

In the year 1747, with Sandin: 200 copies of Suebilius' Catechism, and 200 copies, small; 60 copies of Psalm Books; 1 Bible in quarto; 1 copy of Arndt's "*True Christianity;*" 1 copy of Hallenius' "Concord," three vols.; 1 copy of Gezelius' "*Exposition of the New Testament.*" Amounting to 1000 Swedish dols.

In the year 1749, with Acrelius and Unander: 2 copies of the "*Concordia Pia*" in Swedish; 15 copies of Dr. Ernst Sal. Cyprian's "*Reasonable Warning against the Error that all Religions are equally good,*" translated into Swedish by Provost Eric Beckman, with his introduction touching the Sect of Herrnhutters.

In 1750, with Mr. Parlin: 30 copies of John Walch's "*Thoughts upon the Sect of Herrnhutters,*" with remarks by John Kumbläus.

The same year, with Mr. Lidenius: 50 Psalms-Books of Salvius' edition.[2]

CHAPTER III.

OF THE PRIVILEGES AND MEANS OF THE MISSION.

1. MONEY FOR TRAVELLING EXPENSES.

ALTHOUGH the Swedish Crown has never derived any advantages from America, yet out of zeal for the propagation of the Gospel, and compassion for the children of Sweden remaining there, very considerable expense and encouragement have been bestowed upon the Clergymen who have there done faithful service. To this is to be counted 1000 dollars silver as travelling expenses for every Minister leaving home. No assist-

---

[1] This dollar is equal to about twenty-seven cents. — J. J. M.

[2] [I have translated the Swedish titles of these books into English without giving the original, supposing that those who wish to refer to the original will find the names of the authors a sufficient guide for that purpose. I have left the Latin titles unchanged, as the books will be easily reached from them.]

ance was to be expected for the return home until the time of our pious Archbishop, Dr. H. Benzelius; but by his incomparable tenderness for that Mission, the widow of Provost Sandin, in 1754, received 400 dollars silver mint;[1] Pastor Naesman, in 1754, received 1000 dollars silver mint, as did also Provost Acrelius in the year 1755. Those Ministers who returned home through London, and presented good testimonials to the "*Society for the Propagation of the Gospel in Foreign Parts*," received £30 sterling, in which the present Secretary, Dr. Philip Bearcroft, has shown himself very kind and honorable.

2. YEARLY SALARIES.

For the better ordering of matters, His Royal Majesty, through the representations of the Archbishop, Jacob Benzelius, and in consequence of a resolution of the Privy Council in January, 1747, was empowered to appoint a Provost for the whole body of these churches, at a yearly salary of £50 sterling in addition to what he might expect as Pastor from the usual income of his Parish.   In like manner, by the influence of our present Archbishop,[2] in 1749, an Extraordinary Pastor was appointed, and provided with an annual salary of 400 dollars silver mint.

3. PROMOTION AND PENSIONS.

The Ministers who have satisfactorily fulfilled their duties have, either before their return home, been provided with honorable situations, or have received such immediately after their return. Sometimes also it has been customary to send out the Royal Mandatory[3] to all the Consistories of the Kingdom to bring them forward for appointment;[4] but they have been for the most part promoted without such a proposition.   Meantime 400 dollars silver mint has been a usual pension, which His Royal Majesty, in consequence of the Archbishop Dr. H. Benzelius' affectionate Memorial, by his gracious Resolution of August, 1757, was gra-

---

[1] Twenty-seven cents. — J. J. M.
[2] [Dr. Henry Benzelius, who, as already stated, occupied the position of Archbishop of Sweden from 1747 to 1758.]
[3] [An order of the King and Council of State.]
[4] See "America Illuminata," p. 126.

ciously pleased to increase to 800 dollars silver mint for Provost Acrelius, in respect to his especial services; but for other Provosts, his successors, it was fixed at 600 dollars silver mint annually. This increase was also in a great measure due to the powerful support and recommendation of Mr. Edward Carlesson, the Secretary of State, but now a Royal Chancellor and Member of the Order of the North Star, one of the strongest friends of the Mission.

4. ROYAL BRIEFS, ETC.

The Royal Briefs and Resolutions in accordance with which the American Clergy enjoy their promotions are the following:

"Charles, by the grace of God, King of the Swedes, the Goths, and the Wends, etc.

"Our grace and benignity, through Almighty God, be with our Liegeman[1] and Archbishop.[2] We see by your friendly letter, dated the 21st inst., how you promise, in consequence of our gracious command, to employ your zeal in obtaining two learned and God-fearing Ministers who shall travel to America and instruct the Swedes who are now there in the pure Evangelical doctrine; but as you also kindly solicit for those who shall be sent out thither that they may be assured of their return after the lapse of some years, and then be graciously remembered in some suitable appointment, in which event others may again be sent out in their stead, inasmuch as it seems hard to give up one's native country without any hope of returning to it, and to travel to places so far remote, therefore we graciously assent to the same, and would have you assure them thereof. Wherewith we commend you to the grace of Almighty God.

" CAROLUS.

C. PIPER."

"STOCKHOLM, Feb. 22, 1696."

5. KING FREDERICK'S BRIEF.

Upon the accession of King Frederick to the throne, the Bishop, Dr. Svedberg, requested that the title of "*Magister*"

---

[1] [Original, "Tro-Man," "Faith-Man," is an honorary title applied in Sweden to the highest officers under the Crown.]

[2] [Olof Suebilius.]

might be conferred upon the Clergymen in America, and that they should be excused from maintaining a thesis in the meeting of the Clergy when they returned home to their preferment, and also have the benefit of the Jubilee Fund. The answer of His Royal Majesty was as follows:

"In regard to the title of '*Magister*,' desired for Eric Björk, the Provost of Fahlun, and Andr. Sandel, the Provost of Hedemora, and that they may be excused from maintaining theses at the meeting of the Clergy, His Majesty has graciously agreed to the said proposition; and, in like manner, graciously accords the title of '*Magister*' to the Ministers Abr. Lidenius and Sam. Hesselius, who are at this time serving congregations in America. His Royal Majesty also graciously wills that these Clergymen last named, upon the occurrence of suitable places of promotion, may return home into this our realm.

"The eight (8) pieces of Jubilee-Money desired for the Clergymen who have returned home, as also for the four sojourning in America, and likewise for two Swedish School-masters in the same place, His Royal Majesty will leave, as also their distribution among said parties, to the pleasure of the Bishop to divide it among them. For the rest, we remain, etc.,

"FREDERICK.

"S. BARK."

His Royal Majesty's Order of November 3, 1741, in regard to the Missive[1] and Election appointment for American Clergymen, to make them equal in their promotion with Chaplains of Regiments, Squadrons and Battalions when in the field, or in any command in remote places, is the following:

"ART. 5. In like manner, and as is self-evident, shall those Clergymen be treated who preside over Swedish congregations in America, or elsewhere, as also in the Foreign Missions from this Realm to Constantinople, London, and various foreign parts, after a lawful call, having fulfilled their ministry reputably in

---

[1] [A Missive is an official letter recommending the appointment of the person therein named to some particular situation.]

learning and life, and having received reputable testimony for the same from the congregations which they have served.

"His Royal Majesty's Resolution (Decision) in regard to what his faithful Liege and Archbishop, Dr. H. Benzelius, as also the Evangelical Lutheran congregations in Wicacoa, Christina, Racoon, and Pennsneck in Pennsylvania and America, together with the Ministers ordained for said congregations, as also the Pastor of the Swedish congregation, Ulrica Eleanora in London, have most humbly proposed, viz., the confirmation of the grants hitherto made to said congregations and their Ministers. Given at Stockholm, in the Council Chamber, on the 7th of December, 1752.

"His Royal Majesty has graciously considered as well the humble representation of the Archbishop upon the matter abovementioned, as also the humble petition sent in by the congregations and Clergy. And as His Royal Majesty cherishes no less regard for the upholding and promoting of the Evangelical Lutheran doctrine than his most glorious Predecessors upon the Swedish Throne, so will His Royal Majesty also, at all times, graciously regard the said congregations and their Ministers with His Royal grace, and have them assured that under His Royal Majesty's administration they shall enjoy the same advantages and favors [1] which, in regard to the care of their souls, former Swedish Kings graciously accorded and confirmed to them; permitting also the Ministers after certain years of service to return hither to their father-land, and to be provided with respectable appointments upon their return, and also to send other suitable Ministers to the said churches in their stead. All whom it concerns are to regulate themselves accordingly. For perfect assurance, we have subscribed this with our own hand, and have had it confirmed with our Royal seal. As above.

                                          "ADOLPH FREDERICK.
          " C. RUDENSCHIÖLD."

---

[1] The reformation in Sweden, under Gustavus Vasa, was easily and rapidly accomplished. It left more of the ancient church ritual and ceremonies than was the case in other countries, and the Clergy remained, as they still are, a separate and distinct estate of the Realm. High Mass, with candles burning, the creed sung, and the imposing services, present a spectacle startling to the American Protestant who for the first time witnesses it.—T. W.

VISIT BY THE PROVOST MAGISTER, ISRAEL ACRE-LIUS, TO THE EPHRATA CLOISTER, Aug. 20, 1753.

PHRATA is a place in Lancaster county, Pennsylvania, eleven and a half English miles from the town of Lancaster, in Cocalicoa township, situate on the Cocalicoa creek, between two hills. It is a Protestant cloister, having in possession about one hundred and thirty acres of land, well situated, and built with a number of wooden houses at some distance apart, with apple-trees planted in the intervening spaces. There are also grape-vines there of a good quality, but not in any great number.

The people who live here are called by the English, Dumplers, by the Germans, Dunkers, from "*duncken*" or "*tuncken,*" "to dip," as they are a kind of Anabaptists. From this the town is called by a nickname, but generally *Dunkers' Town.*

The arrangement of the cloister-life was made by Conrad Beisel, formerly a German burgher, who still lives in Ephrata, or Dunkers' Town, as the Director of the whole community, and he is now about 64 years of age. He is a small, lean man, has gray and bushy hair, is quick in his utterance as well as in his movements. Twenty-two years since he first chose for himself the life of a hermit, building for this purpose a small house on the banks of the Cocalicoa. After some time he took a notion to establish a society of his own, upon principles derived in part from other sects, and in part the product of his own brain. His undertaking prospered, and Germans of both sexes came thither, united with him, and made him their priest, chief man, and director of the whole society, not only of the cloister, but of all the brethren in their faith living in this country. From this time he called himself "*Friedsam*" (Peaceful); as it is also an established regulation in their society, that all who are admitted among them shall receive a new name in baptism, as a sign that they have come into a new condition, different from that of the great and wicked world. The brethren and sisters call him Father Friedsam, which is also his common name in the country. He calls himself "*Friedsam, the elder brother.*" He preaches among them, and administers the sacraments as a Minister. As a Director, he makes laws and regulations.

Next to him is a chief over the cloister, or, as they call it, the "*Community.*" His name is Eleazar; suggested, undoubtedly, by the office which he exercises in the economy of the cloister, that is, to receive and distribute the provisions, to purchase clothing according to the wants of the convent, also food and the like. He was now 42 years old, and had lived nineteen years in the fraternity. His father, 60 years of age, was also in the convent, but, as he had come in later, his son was his superior. A similar arrangement also exists among the Nuns.

There was also a brother named Jabez, who, before his re-baptism, was called Peter Müller. He had been a German Calvinistic[1] Minister, came into the country, according to their custom, as a candidate for the Ministry in the Reformed Church of the country, was afterwards ordained by the Presbyterian Minister, Mr. Andrew, in Philadelphia, and for a long time preached in various parts of the country among the Germans before that, eighteen years since, he betook himself to Ephrata. He is a learned man, understands the Oriental languages, speaks Latin, discusses theological controversies as well as other sciences; although, in his present condition, he has forgotten much. He is of a good stature, with a friendly face and friendly manners, on which account strangers always get introduced to him, and seek his society. He is open-hearted towards those to whom he takes a liking, and is modest and genial. The brethren have great respect for him, and not without reason, for he is a prudent man, upon whom their order chiefly depends, although he gives himself no higher name than that of a simple brother. In their Public Worship he reads the Scriptures, and also baptizes when so directed by Father Friedsam.

---

[1] [That is, "Reformed," as distinguished from Lutheran.]

Father Friedsam lives by himself in a little house between the brothers' and the sisters' cloisters, being waited upon by the brethren, and has his food from their kitchen. He lives in entire solitude, except when messengers go out or in, or he performs his duties in the congregation.

The brethren have their convent below, for the houses stand near to each other, with their rear running back to the stream. It is three stories high, and contains about one hundred rooms. The cells are about four paces long and two broad, and there are usually three cells to each antechamber.   There is one man to each cell.   One iron stove usually serves to warm two or three rooms. The house has a wing. In the lowest story is the brethren's church, in the next their refectory, in the uppermost their store-rooms for their economical purposes. All their doors are unusually narrow, the stairs steep and narrow, so that other people find difficulty in getting along them.   The windows are in like manner small.   No chair is seen in their rooms, but only narrow benches; but these as well as the floor are just as clean and bright as though they had been newly scoured.   The inside of the house is plastered and whitewashed.

The sisters' convent, standing by itself, is built on the hill above, and arranged in a similar manner, having its own refectory and its own church in a wing of the house. They have also some other small houses for work close by.

The business of the brethren outside of the house is to work in the fields, meadows, and woods, as also at their mill.   The greater part of them seemed to be brought up to agricultural labors.   Others labor inside of the convent at all sorts of handicrafts, such as shoemaking, tailoring, weaving cloth and stockings, and the like, partly for the use of the cloisters and partly for sale, and so as to enable them to purchase other necessaries.   Others attend to other domestic duties, such as cooking, baking, housecleaning, washing clothes, etc., for all the work is done by the brethren without any female assistance in the men's cloister.

The sisters also live by themselves in their convent, engaged in spinning, sewing, writing, drawing, singing, and other things. The younger sisters are mostly employed in drawing. A part of them are just now constantly engaged in copying musical note-books for themselves and the brethren. I saw some of these upon which a wonderful amount of labor had been expended.[1]

The dress of the brethren is a long, close coat, the skirts of which overlap each other, and are fastened with hooks quite down to the feet, with narrow sleeves, and the collar fitted close around the neck; also a girdle around the middle of the coat. When they wish to be well dressed, a habit is also worn over the close coat, like a chasuble in front, which is thrown over the head; but back of the head is a cape or hood to draw over the head in bad weather, and below this a round cape which hangs down over the back. In summer-time the clothes are of linen or cotton, and entirely white; in the winter-time they are of white woollen cloth. On work-days they have coarse coats usually fastened around them by a leathern girdle. But upon their Sunday-clothes the girdles are either of embroidered woollen stuff or linen. Members of the congregation living in the country dress like those in the cloisters when they come to their church. However, they have clothes of various colors and of the usual fashion. Some have inserted in front on their hoods a piece of pasteboard, which serves as a guard to the capoch when it is drawn over the head. The brethren of the convent wear no shirts, but have their woollen coats next to their body. In summer-time they go barefooted; if they wear shoes, they are either of the usual sort with strings, or they are of wool above and a leather sole below. Some wear straw hats when they are travelling over the country; but most of them use their cape or hood as a hat or cap.

The sisters' dress was also a long, close coat; but we noticed that they all had linen girdles. The hood which they always had over their heads was sewed on to the coat. Their coats are also of linen or cotton stuff in summer; in winter of wool, without any linen next to their body. They also go barefooted in summer.

This dress makes them look quite thin, which their scanty

---

[1] [In a visit made to Ephrata in 1860, the translator also had the pleasure of seeing these remarkable and beautiful musical collections. One of these beautiful books is in the collection of the Historical Society.]

food aids, as shall be described hereafter. Hence they are very quick and rapid in their movements, are not troubled by their narrow doors or their steep and narrow stairs. It seemed strange that they could go so thinly clad in the autumn.

Sometimes the brethren and sisters come together, when they invite each other to their *love-feasts*, which, however, are celebrated in a very sparing style. If either party wish to hold a love-feast, it must be first notified to Father Friedsam, who grants permission thereto. If any of the brethren out in the country wish to hold this, he lets Father Friedsam know that his house can hold all the brethren and all the sisters, who are invited at the same time through Father Friedsam. If he informs them that his house can hold only a portion of them, then he has permission both to invite and to select his guests. If any love-feast is made within the convent, the brothers invite any sisters, or the sisters invite any brothers, at their pleasure. Sometimes the invitations are so secret that the others know nothing about it until the meal is prepared. No one goes to a love-feast without an invitation.

They are very hospitable to strangers, friendly, and cheerful. When, on the 7th of September, 1753, I went to visit them in company with Mr. George Ross, we were received and treated as old friends. He had visited them several times before, and was also a man of importance in the country, which had something to do with the matter. We first announced ourselves to Müller, and were heartily welcomed. I informed him that I was a Swedish Minister, and had long been desirous of seeing them. "So," said Müller, "will you also see this poor place? But however poorly we live here, and although we live almost entirely by ourselves, yet we have the advantage of seeing the most distinguished people in the country; for no one comes to the land, who wishes to be honored for his knowledge and understanding, without visiting us in our isolated retreat, even though our visitors be the proudest people in the country. We thus get acquaintance enough, though but little advantage therefrom. If any new Lawyer or Advocate comes to Lancaster, it is certain that we shall soon make his acquaintance." He had known almost all the Swedish Ministers who had been in the country. I begged leave to remain over night among them, so that I might see their worship, which would take place on the next day, being a Saturday. He answered, "Why not? We shall entertain you as well as we can; if you will be satisfied with that."

We requested Mr. Müller to show us the various rooms in the convent, and thereupon went into the brethren's church. In the middle of the church was a broad seat, or place for a chair for Father Friedsam; this was turned towards the congregation; back of this were two others turned towards each other and making a square; this was said to be intended for Eleazar, the Superior of the convent, and the oldest of the brethren. Back of this again was an altar, or a small and high table, and a pulpit to lay a book on. The altar stood somewhat away from the aisle, so that he who ministered there might always turn himself towards the congregation; on the right side of the altar there was also a little room screened by a curtain, within which no one was to enter except their Minister, which was called the *Sanctuary*. There were also places for benches on both sides of the church, which are used for the brothers and sisters of the congregation. Above, there was a gallery on both sides, so arranged with extending lattice-work that one could look through the openings and see down through the church. Müller said that that was built for the sisters, so that if they should come to look at the brothers' service, they should, for the sake of modesty, be concealed, as also that the women's place in the temple at Jerusalem was arranged in the same way. "True enough," said I; "for we still see the same thing in the Jewish Synagogues; but why should modesty prevent the men from seeing the women any more than the women from seeing the men? Neither do I understand why they should not see the sisters of the convent just as well as they see the other sisters of the congregation down in the church." "O, well!" he answered, "it is still an old and becoming custom."

We sat ourselves down to rest on a seat in the church, and I asked him whether the Lord's Supper was celebrated at the altar? He answered, "Yes, that is done by Father Friedsam, when one after another goes forward and receives the Sacrament in Bread and Wine; but this must be done on some evening, and with feet-washing afterwards." "That," answered I, "may be as proper as for the Lutherans in some places to use burning lights, although in the middle of the day. But," I asked, "cannot the Lord's Supper be celebrated at any time in the day, although it is not the evening?" Müller answered, "A supper cannot be held at mid-day; its time is in the evening." I replied, "That which regards time cannot be anything more than an external ceremony. We know that the disciples of Christ, almost immediately after His resurrection, most carefully considered almost every circumstance in the institution of the first Supper, such as to receive the Supper in a sitting posture, to sit reclining against each other, to celebrate the Supper in a house of entertainment, up one flight of stairs, and various other things. But after they understood that the service of the New Testament is not inseparably connected with any church usages, but that these are only to be regarded according to circumstances of convenience and propriety, then one external matter after another was omitted; and it is enough for us Christians to regard the Sacrament as it is in itself." Müller answered, "It is our duty as Christians to regard *the primitive state of the Church*,[1] and not to make changes therein at our own caprice." I said, "*The spirit of the primitive Church*[2] is sufficient for us; everything else that is external is less necessary, as also difficult to ascertain, and we now live in other times. How many Societies give themselves out as still retaining the usages of the primitive Church, which churches are, however, very different from each other?" He answered, "We can prove ourselves to have both the *spirit* and the *state of the primitive Church*. We keep our vows of chastity, we have all things in common among us, we observe the washing of feet, and other things." I said, "Each of these things were enough to talk about for half a day; but let us abide by the ceremonies of the Lord's Supper. If you will make any of those necessary which were in the first institution, why not all?" He answered, "It is enough to retain those which contain in them something that is symbolical, and which exhibits the value of the Lord's Supper." I said, "Take them all together, and the act thus

---

[1] [Orig., "*Statum Primitivæ Ecclesiæ.*"] [2] ["*Spiritus Primitivæ Ecclesiæ.*"]

becomes more symbolical. There is none of those just mentioned in which I cannot show something especially notable; yet I regard them all as indifferent.[1] If, now, you will regard them as absolutely necessary,[2] then show wherefore this and not the others?" Thereupon I perceived that the man was somewhat changed, and he answered, " The brethren live in the simplicity of their faith, and do not place a high value upon disputations. You must consider that we have lived here more than twenty years, and we must have learned something from our immediate intercourse with God during that time." " Well," said I, " if that is so, it is more than I know." From that hour I determined not to go any further into controversy than he himself occasioned and took pleasure in, so that I might not make myself a disagreeable guest.

We went into the sisters' convent, and saw their rooms in some parts. The church was arranged in the same manner as that of the brethren above described, with the exception of the gallery. Upon the one side were benches for the brethren of the cloister, when they wished to come thither. The Lord's Supper is administered at the altar in both churches by Father Friedsam, so that they come one by one each time. He is also the Minister in both churches.

Mr. George Ross had a desire to see the sisters and hear them sing. Müller, however, would not go to them to urge this upon them, but said, " You may yourself ask them for this, and perhaps you can effect more with them than I can." We went and knocked at the convent door. Their Prioress came out, and when she heard our request, she bade us remain in the church until the sisters came in the proper order to sing. We received an invitation, and went up a still narrower set of stairs than any that we had before seen, and came into a large room; in that there were long tables, with seats upon both sides of them. Here there were some of the sisters sitting, and writing their note-books for the hymns — a work wonderful for its ornaments. Six of them sat together and sang a very lovely tune. Both before and after the singing, the sisters talked both with us and with Müller quite freely about one thing and another, and seemed

---

[1] [Orig., " *Indifferantia.*"]   [2] [Orig., " *Absoluta.*"]

to be quite pleased.   Both at our entrance and our departure we shook hands with each of them, and they testified their friendship, according to their custom, by a peculiar position and pressure of the hand.

Mr. Ross returned home and left me alone.   A knot of brethren, to the number of ten, met in Müller's white and clean anteroom — I cannot say whether to visit me or to show their respect for Müller.   At six o'clock they broke up and went to the sisters' convent one by one, after each other, up the hill.   I asked what that meant?   Müller answered that they were going to a love-feast among the sisters.   I said, "Come, I will go along." Müller declined, as he had not been invited, and also said, "I knew nothing of that meeting until they assembled here.   You can have your supper with the brethren, which will be just as pleasant to you."

The time came for the cloister brethren to go to their evening meal, and thereupon each one came out of his room immediately, and all went one after another up a pair of stairs into the refectory. This was large enough for one hundred persons, with two long tables; but now they were mostly seated at one table, as the number of the brethren at that time was scarcely twenty.   Around the hall in the passages were small cases, each large enough to hold a Bible, for which indeed they were intended, and each had a small white linen curtain before it.   The cloth was spread on the table, the food placed in deep stone dishes.   The courses were pealed barley boiled in milk, with bread broken into it; another course was pumpkin mush, with slices of soft-crusted bread on a plate.   Between these was butter, but only for me, as the brethren for themselves had a kind of cheese-curds on platters[1] all around the table.   Each one took his place, and I was shown to mine, where the greater part of the brethren were behind my back. After they had sat for some time with downcast eyes, one of the brethren at the table read a passage out of the Bible, after which they sat still for some moments; then each one took out of his pocket a bag in which there was a wooden spoon and a knife. The spoon and knife given to me were taken out of a drawer

---

[1] These platters are of wood.   Two of them are in the collection of the Historical Society.—T. W.

under the table. We all ate with a good appetite, first of the
barley, then of the pumpkin mush, and finally of the butter, in
which this economy was observed — that when, at the finishing
of the dish, one could no longer use the spoon, the remainder
was taken up with pieces of bread. There was no other use for
a knife than to take the butter and cut the bread; neither was
any plate needed, as, in fact, none was there. I did not see that
any piece of bread was broken. At the close, each one licked
his knife and spoon, dried them with a cloth which they had in
the same bag, and then the knife and spoon were restored to
their former place. During the meal not a word was spoken;
at its close another chapter was read out of the Bible.

After the meal, Müller and Eleazar remained with me in the
refectory, and then Eleazar asked me what I thought of their
arrangements? If I knew what I had eaten? And how long I
thought I could live upon such a diet? We agreed that nature
is satisfied with a small quantity of food; that both moderation
in eating and drinking, and food suitable to the human body,
preserves from sickness, makes the body active and the mind
cheerful; that if all which may properly be called superfluous in
meat and drink and clothing should be used for the suffering,
there would be no need of so many hospitals in the old countries, and Christianity would have a very different aspect from
that which it now presents. Eleazar said that the English, who
could not live without flesh at every meal, wonder at our style
of meals; but the German taste is different. many peasants in
Germany do not taste flesh five times a year. I asked if they
regarded the eating of flesh as sinful? Müller answered, "Nay;
but the brethren do not incline to the eating of flesh. Our food
is usually of vegetables, such as cabbages, roots, greens, also
milk, butter, cheese, and good bread always. At the love-feasts,
the provision may be somewhat better than usual. We forbid
none among us who desire it to eat meat. Wine is used when
some one is sick."

I saw at the table a man who was not in their usual dress, also
without a beard, and was told that he had lately come into their
society; that he was a Doctor of Medicine, born in Saxony, educated at Halle. After he had visited a great part of Europe and

Africa, without finding any genuine Christian society, he had finally remained with them, as, in his opinion, the best that was to be found. Müller said that he had had a Christian sickness; which means consumption, and is an abiding cross until death. It is to be observed that, according to their received opinion, the cross and affliction are the surest token of a genuine Christianity, whether they come through God's providence, or they take them upon themselves of their own accord. I said that, according to this, all incurable sicknesses are Christian, or, more correctly, with some they are preparatory, and with others means of strengthening in Christianity. But no suffering, whether external or internal, can, of itself, make us Christians, or be regarded as the surest token of Christianity, for "Pharaoh's magicians had boils as well as Job." "True enough," said he; "we may make a difference between God's punishments and God's corrections, but a Christian without the cross is no Christian."

I asked further about their arrangements with regard to eating, and they said that in the morning, on working-days, the brethren usually took their meals by themselves in their rooms; at noon they went into the kitchen, and received whatever was at hand. Their supper they all took together.

We went down again into Müller's room, and there he showed me the "*History of the Persecutions of the Anabaptists*," a large and thick folio volume, which he himself had translated from the Holland into the German language, and had afterwards had it printed there in Ephrata, saying that it was the largest book that had been printed in Pennsylvania[1] as also that he had labored for three years upon the translation, and was at the same time so burthened with work that he did not sleep more than four hours during the night. He believed that the Anabaptists had not suffered any persecutions in Sweden. I, however, gave him to understand that King Gustavus had in his time had great difficulty in curing their infectious reformatory sickness, which would otherwise have gone very far, although he did this without persecution. The edition of Müller's book was one thousand two hundred copies, of which seven hundred have been

---

[1] A copy of this work, together with the press on which it was printed, is in the collections of the Historical Society.—T. W.

circulated, and five hundred are still on hand.[1] He said that they could be sold within ten years. I think he meant twenty. The price is twenty-two shillings. I asked him how they could be sold at so low a price! "Why not," said he; "for we do not propose to get rich?"

They conducted me to a cell, up a set of stairs, where there was a chaff bed laid upon the floor, a coarse sheet spread over it, with two blankets, and then a figured bedquilt. They told me to use this just as I pleased. They, themselves, lie upon their hard benches, having either a stone or a piece of wood under their head. After I had lain down, I heard a splashing and shuffling late into the night, which was caused by their washing the feet of some strange brethren who had come from the country to make them a visit, whose feet the Brethren of the Cloister then washed.

On Saturday morning, at 6 o'clock, the cook came to waken me, and said that Divine Service would begin in half an hour. This was a black-bearded old man, very serviceable; but I did not know why he should have such a long coat of black cloth, when all the others wore white, unless it was that the pot-black might be better concealed in this way. I was soon dressed, and came to Müller. There the brethren were as white as snow, and the room smelled of rose-water, which they put on their clothes.

Whilst we were waiting for the service, we fell into conversation on the hallowing of the seventh day. I wondered that they who professed to be *Christians* should so regulate themselves by the Jewish law, and separate themselves from all others who confess the Christian name. Müller answered, "That is no Jewish law, but a perpetual natural law [2] which is written upon the hearts of all men, and is of the same force as all the other nine of the ten Divine Commandments, none of which can be changed, but stands to all eternity." "Pardon me," I answered, "that I, upon this your Sabbath, and at the same hour that you are proceeding to hallow it, take upon me to show that you have

---

[1] Part of these five hundred copies were used during the Revolutionary War for making cartridges.—T. W.

[2] ["*Lex naturalis perpetua*," in the original.]

not got the correct meaning of the *third*[1] commandment, or, as you prefer to call it, the *fourth.* The hallowing of the seventh day is a moral, not a natural law, and thus perpetual, but is so without being fixed to any certain time. The subject is extensive, and our time short, and I shall therefore confine myself chiefly to your words. Is it a natural law which is inscribed upon the hearts of all men, why then did not the wise heathen regard the seventh day, whilst they externally observed the other commandments? Still more, if it is a perpetual moral law, the seventh day should be observed in heaven also. But where do we see that there are there six working-days, and the seventh a day of rest? Are not all the days there one eternal Sabbath?" "My friend," answered Müller, "has not God commanded, *Six days shalt thou labor and do all thy work, but on the seventh is the Sabbath of the Lord thy God*, etc. Where do you anywhere see a command to hallow the first?" "Beloved, do you not understand," said I, "that I have already answered thereon how far that command extends. But if it is so necessary that this should come upon the seventh day, do you believe that this Saturday is the seventh day in your week, according to the original arrangement? Consider that a whole day, or twelve hours, were abstracted from the natural course of time in the time of Joshua. (Josh. 10 : 2.) Again, ten degrees, or five hours, in the time of Hezekiah. (Is. 38 : 8.) Palestine has one meridian and Pennsylvania another, and how now will your seventh day coincide with the first arrangement?" Müller answered, "We hold no other day as the seventh than that which you yourselves hold? Is it not sufficient that we observe the general computation of the country?" "Well, my friend," answered I; "but if the general computation of the country does not coincide with God's reckoning, as He instituted it, how do you observe God's commandment? Is not that an erroneous conscience?"[2] "Ah!" answered he, "is not that a command of the Lord? *The seventh day is the Sabbath of the Lord*, etc. Who has changed that com-

---

[1] [It is well known that the Lutherans, following Luther's Catechisms and the usage of the Western Church before the Reformation, make but one Commandment of what are considered by Protestants generally as the first and second.]

[2] [Orig., " *Consciencia erronea*."]

mandment? Not God, but men. To them Christ says, 'Who has demanded this at your hands?' Everything that stands in the Scriptures is ancient and true; all that does not stand there is new and false. The Scripture is our rule." I said, " It is just by the Scriptures that I will show that the Saviour himself changed the first command in regard to the seventh day, if not in express words, yet by express acts, which in an equally strong manner explained this holy will. He hallowed the first day as our day of rest when upon that day He arose from the dead, as a token that as the seventh day was in the Old Testament hallowed in commemoration of the creation, so should the first day be hallowed in commemoration of the resurrection. On the Jewish Sabbath Christ was laid in the grave, and so took away the eating of their Paschal lamb, and the celebration of their Sabbath. On the Christian Sabbath the Redeemer arose, and at the same time instituted a new church order. Throughout the whole of the Holy Scriptures you can nowhere find that the Redeemer after His resurrection at any time met His Apostles on the Jewish Sabbath, or that the Redeemer during the whole of the forty days had any intercourse with the Jews, a clear sign that the Old Testament had now passed away." My opponent now seemed to be somewhat warm, and it just then came to pass that the bell rang, which broke off our conversation, which otherwise might not have been terminated with equal satisfaction upon both sides.

He referred to Jonas Aurén, who had come into the country along with the Pastors Rudman and Björk, but afterwards turned to the Sabbatarians, and asked if I had been informed of that. I let him understand that I was aware alike of his fall and of his uprising. How, during the time that he held with the observers of the seventh day, he had written an Almanac called "*Noah's Dove*," which flew through that country to favor said sect. In opposition to which, the Provost Björk, with manly sense and spirit, had written a reply entitled "*A little Olive-Leaf put in the mouth of that so-called Noah's Dove, and sent home again to let her owner know that the waters are abated from off the face of the ground*."[1] The Rev. Provost saw from this the blessed result

---

[1] See above, p. 320.

that the man came back to his flock, and often afterwards performed service in his church.

This last conversation was held between us whilst we were going out and a part of our way, for in a moment the brethren were out of their cells and in full march. We now went to the third church, which stands on the hill by itself, in which service is held once a month, and the whole congregation comes together from both convents, as well as from the country. The people of the cloisters walk in their usual way, one after the other, the sisters as well as the brothers; and their walks are, therefore, all narrow, like footpaths. I took my place in the ranks of the white brethren, whilst Müller went upon my left side.

During our walk up the long hill, Müller asked me if I believed that the pains of hell were eternal? To which I answered, "Just as certainly as the joy of heaven is eternal. How else?" I asked, in reply. "Nay," said he; "I do not believe that the soul, which is a part of God's being, can perish eternally." "But," said I, "I understand that you believe that this part of God's being lies for thousands of millions of years in the punishment of hell as in a sort of purifying fire. Dear Mr. Müller," said I, "you are a benevolent man, but let not your charity extend so far as to wish to extinguish the fires of hell. Remember that there was a great gulf between Abraham's bosom and the rich man's place of punishment, so that no one could go from the one place to the other." "Yea," said he, "as long as you are evil and I good, we shall never agree; but if we are both good, then we shall well agree. When thirty-nine thousand years have passed, the great Jubilee comes, when the Devil shall be chained." I understood well whence that came and whither it tended. When we had made the distinction between *æternitas* (eternity) and *æviternitas* (a great period), we arrived at the church door, and that was the end of the matter.

The church was not large, and could be filled by some hundred persons. The forepart of the church was the third part of its size, the floor of which was some steps higher than the other part, and there sat the cloister brothers in their order. Müller and Eleazar, together with some others, sat on cross-seats opposite to one another, the others on long benches on both sides,

and also in the rear. Above, the sisters of the cloister had their
gallery, so arranged that neither they could see the congregation
nor the congregation see them. Father Friedsam had his seat
separate between that high choir and the rest of the church. The
cloister brothers went in through a little door to the high choir,
whereupon the sisters immediately followed. But Müller conducted me in through the large door, and gave me in charge to
the sexton, who immediately showed me my place in the foremost seats. In the church there were people both of their own
and of other forms of faith.

When they were all assembled, they sat for some moments
perfectly still. In the meantime Father Friedsam was seen to
be preparing himself; he held his hands upon both his sides,
threw his head up and down, his eyes hither and thither; pulled
at his mouth, his nose, his neck, and finally sang in a low and
fine tone. Thereupon the sisters in the gallery began to sing,
the cloister brothers joined in with them, and all those who were
together in the high choir united in a delightful hymn, which
lasted for about a quarter of an hour. Thereupon Müller arose
and read the third chapter of Isaiah.

Father Friedsam recommenced his former movements, and
appeared rather ridiculous than devotional. Finally, he arose
with his hands clasped together and his eyes turned upwards,
and began to speak of the natural darkness of man's understanding, and prayed for enlightenment and a blessing. Then he sat
down and preached about holiness of life, the danger of temptations, and the need of watchfulness. Examples of this were taken
from the soldiers in Germany, who call out, " Who goes there?
Who goes there?" Finally, he began to speak of faith, hope,
and charity. Faith and unbelief are the points between which
man fluctuates. Faith saves, but unbelief condemns. That hope
and charity follow faith. But when he should have developed
this point, he made faith the foundation of hope and love; but
then again immediately said that just as love is so are hope and
faith. All turned upon this, that faith was nothing else than an
inward fear of God, and devotion. It seemed to me that Father
Friedsam himself did not know where he was at home (what he
believed). All this was spoken with an incomparable rapidity,

in hasty language, with rapid gestures. Now he struck out his hands, now he pressed them to his breast, now he placed them upon one side, now upon another, and now upon both. Again, he scratched his head, then patted himself on the nose, and then wiped his nose on the back of his hand. Meanwhile, in the congregation, which he frequently called Jerusalem, some were moved and shook their heads, others wept, others slept, and so on. The sermon was concluded with an Amen.

Müller went forward to Father Friedsam and proposed that a psalm should be sung. It is to be remarked that every one has the liberty of speaking and suggesting anything profitable to the congregation. Then Father Friedsam hinted to a brother, who sat on a bench nearest to him in the church, that he should begin, and himself raised the tune; the said brother began the psalm and led it. Father Friedsam also united in it, as also the brethren and sisters, who sat in cross-seats in front, having psalm-books and also note-books; but the cloister people, as well as the rest of the congregation, were silent.

It is to be observed that to every psalm there are three different melodies, according to which the note-books are written by the sisters of the convent. Different brothers, as well as the sisters, understand vocal music, as also does Father Friedsam. When they sing, each one holds a note-book as well as a psalm-book, both of which are of quarto size, looking into both alternately, which custom would be more difficult if the singing were not performed so regularly every day.

After that psalm, Father Friedsam asked the brethren generally if any one had anything to suggest for the general edification? Thereupon a little man, quite old, with a heavy beard which concealed the greater part of his face, and with a soft voice, answered, "That he pictured the Gospel to himself as a beautiful flower, which had a delightful odor of still increasing strength, and that should bear glorious fruit. Also, that he had both a right to that flower and pleasure in it, when he could appropriate it to himself with a broken and contrite heart." Whereupon he burst forth into tears, so that the rest of his well-meant discourse was broken off and suppressed.

This part of their service consists, as it were, in common conversation, wherein each one relates what he has upon his conscience, in what state he finds himself, and what may be suggested as to the edification of the congregation. When any one announces anything of the kind, Father Friedsam gives his judgment thereupon.

When the service closed, it was eight o'clock. The women went out of church first, in such manner that those from the benches nearest to the door first marched off one after another, then those that were next, and so the whole of the women's side of the church. The same order was observed upon the men's side, whence they went through the large door of the church; so also did the brethren and sisters go through the smaller door from their high choir. They are not accustomed to many hours of attendance at church, as Müller stated to me; whereupon I asked him how the rest of the day was spent among them? Whether they go to visit one another, etc.? He answered: "The brethren remain most of their time within their cells; they work hard during the week, and so they must rest." Whence it followed that as the work was bodily, so must their rest be chiefly of that character.

I further asked why there were no prayers in their service. That question seemed to excite him, and his answer was "That the heart is not always open for prayer; that to pray with a closed heart is only hypocrisy." "What," said I, "are there not many hearts in church? How can you tell which are open or which are not? You scarcely know your own heart, how much less that of others. But he who does not find his heart open, ought to pray that it may be opened." He answered, "Prayer is a gift of the Spirit. They whose heart is not open have not yet received that gift, and cannot pray." "Pardon me, my friend," I answered; "God, through His prepared grace, gives us sometimes the will, but not at all times the immediate power; but if we persevere in prayer, we obtain both. We are now talking about general church prayers, which ought to be applicable to the condition of all in general. Ought not such to be made, that they who receive the spirit of prayer may unite their thoughts and offer their devotion therein? I hope that you, who are spiritual, do not come before the Lord with closed and hardened hearts." "All right," said he; "he who has a desire to pray has also liberty so to do among us, only he must report it to Father Friedsam." "So," said I, "one must ask leave of Father Friedsam to pray to God." "Nay, nay," said he; "but he keeps order in our congregation, and we cannot do less than pay him this respect, as he is the founder of the brotherhood."

It is to be remarked that, as they hold their Sabbath on Saturday, they are in the midst of their work on Sunday, which is not only in conflict with all Christian order, but also against the fundamental law of the land, which expressly declares that Sunday shall be a Sabbath for all. In consequence of this, the Magistrates of the country, when they first took up their abode there, took their horses and oxen from the plow, and imposed fines upon them; but this did not produce the slightest change in them. They were therefore arrested and driven in great flocks to the jail in Lancaster. But they were not cast down by this, but sang hymns in their place of imprisonment; but neither ate nor drank for many days; neither did they lie down to rest any further than that they leaned against one another as they sat. All which, with other things, moved the Governor and other Magistrates to leave them in peace from that time.

After Divine Service, whilst I went hither and thither among the brethren in their cloister, talking now with one and now with another, most of them being very stupid, Father Friedsam came to make me a visit, — an honor of which not every one can boast, — as is the custom of that place. He came in a white woollen coat, with a bare head and rapid gait. He bade me welcome to their brotherhood with friendly words and gestures. I perceived that the brethren had induced him to show me this politeness, as they also seemed to take pleasure in my society. We went into Müller's room, and the old man seemed more full of life than the others.

He asked what I thought of their Society. I answered, "It is not to be wondered at that, in a country where there is such toleration for all forms of faith, some well-meaning Christians should choose such a peculiar mode of life for themselves, according to the best of their understanding, and as tending to the promotion of that rest of conscience for which they long. I understood that they had seen in Germany every form of cloister-life, and established something of the kind for themselves here, retaining what appeared to them to be good."

"I doubt not, my friend," said he, "that you are aware that the cloister-life is older than the Papacy; as also that the Christian Church, whilst still in its state of innocence, had within it certain flocks that chose a life of celibacy, and had all things in common." "That is not denied," said I; "neither do I myself undertake to judge that manner of life, only through this, that no merit is aimed at before God. Or, how is that, my friends? Do you believe that you are nearer to the door of heaven than I am, because of your hard life — because you sleep upon these hard benches, and are so lean and haggard?"

"We by no means think of meriting anything hereby," said Father Friedsam. "God guard us from that. But we are commanded to depart from Babylon, or the sinful world; and as we are left at liberty to separate ourselves in this manner, so we have had a desire to do so." I answered, "Do you mean that the world, the flesh, and the devil do not trouble you here in this house?" Müller fell into the conversation by saying, "We believe that these enemies are everywhere, and even here also; but here we are not so much oppressed by them as you are in the great world, where there are more temptations. And you should also remember that the Apostle enjoins that each one shall walk in the vocation wherein he is called. We have found our calling to coincide with this mode of life. In this we are secure."

"But think you," said I, "that no one has the spirit of the Primitive Church except those who live in a community of goods?" "As regards that," continued Müller, "we admit that such a community can be observed only by those who arrive at the highest degree of perfection. It was not all Christians in the first Church who had received that gift. Among us, also, we have paid dearly enough for it, as several false brethren took the money which we had gathered for the common good of the congregation and, under the pretence of purchasing a piece of land for a new residence on the other side of the river Susquehanna, ran away with it, which placed us in such straits that it was nearly the end of our mode of life here. To him who can live among us the door stands open. Those of our brethren who have their farms around us are of the same mind, although they do not live in the same way; so that if we should need the whole of any one's place, he would willingly give it to us out of love to the brethren."

I again turned myself to Father Friedsam, and said, "It gives me great joy to learn that you love the Lord Jesus Christ, honor His Sacraments, and speak of His gracious dealings in your Divine Services." He answered, "God preserve us from anything else; it is upon Him that we must hope, obeying His commands and walking in His footsteps." I said, further, that I had not expected to see the brethren and sisters with such smiling faces and friendly demeanor beneath their outward cross. I doubted not that each one had his inward sufferings, which sometimes weighed heavily enough upon their hearts, which they kept silently within themselves without disturbing others therewith. I told them of a sort of Pietists, who over twenty years ago arose in Sweden, who were self-conceited, morose, and bitter, just as if they would eat other people up. One could not take it as a proof of Christian love and spiritual meekness, although they wore long coats like these of yours. Müller replied, "Indeed you touch my heart by your conversation. Such are also our thoughts. The children of God need not always show a sour countenance. That would be nothing else than to show one's self impatient of their Father's will. One never sees a discontented mind with a glad countenance, nor a contented mind with a sour face. If we are contented with our Heavenly Father's will, we shall always show ourselves satisfied, and with a glad countenance, even in the bitterness of death."

When I inquired whether the place where they live was healthful, Father Friedsam replied that, during the twenty-two years of his residence here, he had suffered from fever but once, and then he immediately got up and ran around through the hills until his sickness disappeared, and did not return again. There are seldom any sick among them, although the country all around is subject to various fevers and pleurisy. They are indebted to their diet for such good health. Eleazar related, in the presence of Father

Friedsam, that Peter Kalm, the Swede, who was with them some
years ago, had spoken to me about the brotherhood with great
kindness, after which I had had a desire to come hither. They
are very fond of hearing what others say in their honor. They
now asked a great deal about Peter Kalm. Others again reported
my age, and that I had hitherto lived unmarried, which greatly
pleased the old man. Thereupon he took a friendly leave, and
wished me happiness.

The time was further passed away by conversation between Müller and myself. I requested him to inform me as to their mode of
baptizing, which he also did. " We seldom receive any others,"
said he, " than such as have been already baptized, and who thus
have some knowledge of Christianity; but if they have been
brought up in our Society, we first instruct them. When they
come to the water, the Minister there puts to them the necessary
questions, which are to be answered. Then the person falls down
upon his knees in the water, places both his opened hands before
his mouth, with the ends of his fingers turned towards his nose,
so as to keep his nostrils closed, and the same with his mouth.
The Minister then lays his right hand crosswise over the other's
hands and presses them closely together, holding his left hand
behind his neck, and thus plunges the person under the water.
When the person who is to be baptized makes resistance during
the performance of the rite, force and strength are employed for
its completion. Without dipping them under the water, there
can be no baptism. Is it not so ? "

I answered, " I have nothing against your amount of water,
but cannot understand why you will not allow of less water.
When our Saviour, in St. John iii., speaks about what belongs
to a true baptism, He says, '*water and the Holy Ghost;*' but not
that it should be a whole river, more or less." " Nay," said he,
"that cannot be sufficient, for the person must be submerged.
When Christ sent out His Apostles, He commanded them to
baptize, which word cannot receive its significance in a small
cup of water."

I referred to the English Baptists; how the Minister takes the
person who is to be baptized, with one hand back in his collar,
and the other in his waistband from behind, and so hurls him

backwards, that his head is dipped into the water, and his feet
turned up into the air, which must thus require the strength of
two men in the Minister. On the other hand, the German Anabaptists, who are called Mennonists, conduct the person to the
water, and there with their hands pour the water three times
over his head. You of Ephrata, again, have your peculiar manner, which was never heard of nor seen before your time. You
all profess to be Baptists, appeal to the first institution, and despise others. Which class of you all has now found the right
way?" He answered, "I believe we have." I said, "I will
believe the same, but not before it is proved."

I asked if he had been in Bethlehem and seen the Herrnhut
Brethren? Whether Herrnhut and Ephrata could not become
one brotherhood? "Nay," answered he; "there is a great gulf
between us. Some years since we had a brother who had been
in Bethlehem. He praised the Moravians, and exhorted us to
union with them. Then four of us went to Bethlehem and stayed
upon the other side of the river, sending over to the Moravians
and desiring to hold a meeting with their Society. Thereupon
they took counsel for two hours, after which they answered.
'That the Saviour did not will that their congregation should be
called together on this account; but that on the following day
they should be allowed to come over and see whom they would
individually in their houses. In the meantime they should stay
in the tavern that was there over night, either at their own
expense, or that of the Moravian Brethren.' The plain meaning,
however, was that the brethren of Ephrata should pay for themselves, which they also did. The messenger from Bethlehem
had also to report that the Saviour had informed them of it the
same hour that they set forth from Ephrata, so that their arrival
had been known already for some days; although it had required
two hours to decide whether they should be received or not, as
Müller said. The next day two of them turned back homewards.
The other two crossed over the river to continue their journey to
East Jersey. But when they went through Bethlehem, all the
windows were full of people, who stared at them. The Swede
Nyberg was here several times after he had joined himself to the
Moravians," said Müller. "He asked me if I could explain

mystic words for him; but I said that I could not, and that I did
not busy myself with such things." He also informed Müller of
one Israel Simor who had lived a half year with them, but last
autumn had given himself up to drinking, lying, and deceit, and
finally went over the country to Carolina. He said that they
could perceive when any one was about withdrawing himself from
the cloister — they showed themselves discontented at home, and
desired to wander out into the country, until they finally returned
no more.

We had much other conversation about marriage, defensive
war, oaths, etc., which it would be too tedious to relate.

Among themselves these brethren live in great love, always
calling each other brother or sister along with their proper name.
They kiss each other when they meet, and wash each other's
feet.

Their rules, whether of the church, the household, or other
usages, are as yet only oral, and are frequently changed, as seems
to be demanded by edification. It is said that the brotherhood
lives in the freedom of its conscience, and therefore without
laws; and it is thought that some of the brethren do not yet
know what the others believe. At first they regarded it as a sin
to kill any animal, and still more so to eat flesh. Now they say
that this is left to each one's freedom to eat it or not; but what
liberty is there in eating what is not found in their storehouse?
At first, also, it was regarded as a sin to use horses for working,
and they themselves dragged home their own wood, and for this
purpose put on themselves a suitable harness. Now they labor
with horses and oxen, which, however, they treat very kindly.
This, with other things, causes me to think that their work is
still in its beginning, and stands, as it were, in a state of ferment
as to whether anything shall come of it hereafter or not; also,
that the freedom so much talked of is nothing but an encouragement to others to unite with them. I am sure that no one is regarded as a genuine brother in that house, unless he sleeps upon
a hard bench in his usual clothes, however they may prate about
their freedom.

They talk there of Christ, of justification, of faith and unbelief;
there Christ's Sacraments are used in the form and manner that

have been mentioned, but I doubt much about the true meaning of all this; neither could I within so short a time investigate everything. Some persons in Lancaster told me that they were Arians, who denied Christ's godhead, or equality with the Father. Of the congregation in general, I believe that I have been right in thinking that their justification is "*infused, not imputed;*"[1] that their salvation is not a fruit of faith, but worked out by a severe life. Regner, who lived among them for some time, testifies the same in Fresenius about the affairs of Herrn-hut. He calls them Beiselian Eckerlings; testifies that he united with them that he might gain sanctity by a severe life, and the forsaking of this world. That they offered him the Lord's Supper before he had had an opportunity to be baptized by them; that he constantly insisted that such a holy life should be begun, as had often been spoken about; that they directed him to regulate himself by the brethren; that they built him a hut for himself, wherein he became deranged. Then they took him into the cloister, and removed him from one room to another. When he finally came to his senses, they would no longer tolerate him among them. Müller told me about all this, and also that he was a severe burthen to them, and that the brethren were glad when they got rid of him.

They have a great many Jewish customs. They all have their beard growing up to their ears. This, together with their white dress and their spare diet, is well adapted to gain their object, namely, to look pale, thin, and wretched. They go barefooted in summer, use feet-washing, keep the seventh day as holy, count their hours after the Jewish fashion, from the beginning of the day, so that our six o'clock is their one, and our twelve their seven. To which may also be added that when I heard them read the Scriptures five different times, it was always out of the Old Testament, the Prophets, and the Psalms, but never out of the New Testament. So, also, they had a taste for the Old Testament in their "Sanctuary," and their "Women's gallery."

They hold with the Quakers, inasmuch as they are a sort of Enthusiasts. They do, indeed, read the Scriptures, but believe

---

[1] "*Infusa, non imputata.*"

themselves to be possessed of an "inward light," which transcends the outward. They, therefore, despise all outward instruction; give out that their sermons come from the immediate light and impulse of the Spirit in the same time in which they speak; that each and every one has liberty to teach publicly in their congregations, when the order therefor comes; that we are to use "thou" in conversation; to shake hands; exhibit absolute perfection in our life, and to use no prayers, unless they come extempore into the head.

They agree with the Anabaptists in that they take no one into their Society unless he has been baptized by them; baptize those who come from other churches; baptize only those who have come to years of discretion. Their baptism is performed with an abundance of water by immersion; other things, as already mentioned. They also hold services in their churches late at night. Father Friedsam, who lives in a little house between the brethren's and sisters' cloisters, has a rope, which goes upon both sides over the garden, with a bell at each end in both cloisters. When it so comes into his head, and he pulls thereon, and the bell rings, and even if it were in the middle of the night, all must get up and assemble in their church to hold service; a small paper lantern in each one's cell is used upon such occasions.

With the Papists, also, they have much in common, although they call themselves Protestants; they follow the same cloistered life, and have a cloister dress, and also rules for their meals; they seek their justification by a severe life, and perfection in a life of celibacy; they believe in a purgatory, or purifying fire after death; on which account, also, Father Friedsam at certain times offers prayers for the dead. Many Roman Catholics from Germany have been received into their Society, and live among them. The number of people in the cloisters was much greater in former years. Now the brethren are not more in number than twenty-five (25), and the sisters thirty-five (35) or thirty-six (36). However earnestly they strive for a chaste life, the untimely intercourse of some of the brethren and sisters with each other has subjected the whole society to the unfavorable judgment of many. Father Friedsam himself is not free from such charges, which are made with great particularity. They cannot deny that some members have been licentious, but say that they have been immediately discarded; during the time that Conrad Weiser lived among them, he once took the liberty of visiting his own house and family in another place.[1] But upon his return, after a strict examination, he had to submit to a severe punishment for having slept with his own wife, which he willingly underwent. Around the Convent and its land, families belonging to their Society have settled themselves and bought farms and homesteads. In this there is a policy, namely, that people of other faith may not come too near and disturb them. They are also so peaceful with their neighbors, that if any dispute ever arises, they would rather surrender their rights, or give the matter into the hands of others in whom they have confidence, than trouble any Judge with it. Their congregations are widely scattered in several places in Chester county, and also in East Jersey. But at some distance from the Convent several Hermits live in houses by themselves, built mostly at the expense of the Society.

They have one Society in New Virginia, upon New river.[2] There, however, they dwell in separate houses, but in one neighborhood, and so by themselves that they neither help nor desire help from other people. The land that they cultivate has an excellent soil. The brethren often receive messages in these nests from travelling brethren, who always journey on foot, two and two together, never more and never less. Sometimes, also, the sisters are thus seen upon the roads.

In the cloister there is a printing-office, with a press, together with new type, fair and clear, brought from Frankfort.[3] But it has not yet repaid either its expense or its trouble. Some books have been printed there written by the brethren themselves. The "*History of the Persecutions of the Anabaptists*" has given them the most trouble and least return. They have had a proposal to print the Classic Authors for the Philadelphia Academy;[4] but Müller said that he was now tired of that work,

---

[1] [At Heidelberg, in Berks county.]

[2] In the western part of Virginia.

[3] [On the Mayn, from which place Beissel came. This printing-press is now in the collection of the Historical Society.]

[4] The old Academy, in Fourth Street below Arch.—T. W.

28

was alone in it, and his sight was growing weak. In the printing-office there were large pieces, some two, others three ells long, engraved on wood, for printing tablets, which were placed either in their churches or in their cells, consisting of verses or passages of Scripture. There were also some school-books lying there. I inquired for their owner, and Müller answered that some time ago a German student had come to them, but became tired of their way of life, and took his departure. He, as well as many others, I understood, had made the trial, but had found neither pleasure nor profit in the regulations of that spiritual corporation.

The mills which belong to the convent are both a useful and an ingenious work. There are flour-, saw-, and paper-mills, a fulling-mill, and a flaxseed-oil press at the same place, and operated with the same water-power. The greater part of their support is derived from the oil-press. The flour-mill makes good flour, so that in view of this, and also because the toll is moderate, the people pass by other mills to come to this one. The saw-mill is also in a good condition. The paper-mill makes the best kind of card-paper. The fulling-mill was burnt down. About this, Müller related that one evening, when the brethren were together consulting about the next day's work, word came that the mill was in flames. That was occasioned by the carelessness of some of the brethren, who did not look after the fire before they went away from it.

As I had now been among these brethren from Friday noon until Saturday afternoon, it was time to return to Lancaster. The brethren asked me several times when I would come again to see them. This seemed to me as though they thought that I had some desire to unite with their Society. I took leave of the brethren, and invited them to visit me if their way was so directed. Müller, who, during all this time, had kept me company, followed me down to the mill a short distance from the cloister, where they had my horse. He bore my travelling-sack the whole way for me, and when I objected to it, he said, " You may permit me to carry it now, perhaps I can never do it again." The day was warm ; and when I said that the weight was troublesome, and I would help him a little, he answered again, " You can see very well that what I do is done from love. If I did not love you, I would not do it."

Finally, I took a friendly leave of my companion. I thanked him that he did not dislike me for being of a different way of thinking. I hoped that if we did not see each other any more in this life, we might meet with joy in that place where there should be one fold and one Shepherd; where all controversies in theology would cease; where love should abide forever after all other gifts disappear. He took me in his arms and kissed me, thanked me, and said, "That is a good wish. I hope we shall meet in that place, although we travel different roads. I shall also pray to God for you. Farewell."

A VISIT BY THE REV. PROVOST ISRAEL ACRELIUS TO THE AMERICAN CLOISTER AT BETHLEHEM,

IN COMPANY WITH THE REV. PASTOR PETER BRUNNHOLTZ, PASTOR ERIC UNANDER, AND MR. SLEYDORN, WHICH WAS MADE ON THE 18TH AND 19TH OF JUNE, 1754.

ETHLEHEM is a Protestant cloister belonging to the Herrnhut Brotherhood, established in the year 1743[1] by Count Zinzendorff, the founder of the Brotherhood, and instituted by David Nitschman, Spangenberg, Anna Nitschman, and others, as the Elders and Officers of the Society. There belongs thereto a good tract of land, bought of William Allen, Esq., who was the first to take up said tract.

It is situated in Pennsylvania, North Hampton county, Bethlehem township, where the Menakesi[2] creek falls into the west branch of the Delaware river, and so has a very convenient location, with running water upon two sides. Bethlehem is situated upon a hill, and has the Lecheigh[3] Hills around it, with the Delaware[4] on one side and the Menakesi on the other. On the north and east sides is an orchard of seven or eight acres' extent. On the south, where the hill slopes to the river, there are vegetable gardens — two or three for vegetables, another for medicinal plants. On the west side, where the Menakesi descends,

---

[1] Bethlehem was founded in the spring of 1741, at the instance of Count Zinzendorff, by whom furthermore its inhabitants were organized into an ecclesiastical body in June, 1742. The Count was in America but once, *i. e.*, in the interval between December, 1741, and January, 1743. — W. C. R.

[2] [Now generally written Monocacy.]

[3] [Now written "Lehigh."]

[4] The west branch of the Delaware is meant; it is now called the Lehigh. The Lehigh Hills are to the south of Bethlehem.—T. W.

are their workshops.[1]   Below, there is a handsome field, smooth and even.

As one comes on the road from Philadelphia, travelling fifty-three English miles through a wooded and flat country, the road eighteen miles from Bethlehem being very rough from stumps and stones, and when he finally draws nigh to Bethlehem, reaching a hill two miles away from it, there it shows itself in a glory which is not much inferior to that of Konungahof.[2]

The houses do not form regular streets, as the beginning of Bethlehem was very small, and far from the expectation that the cloister should increase as has subsequently happened.   The Brethren, at first, took no pleasure in that place.   After they had dwelt there for a short time, they withdrew from it.[3]   Perhaps they were at first left to support themselves by their labor as well as they could.   But after considerable sums of money were collected from other places, wherewith splendid houses were built, they changed their minds, and returned.   The Brotherhood is now thinking of bringing their houses into better order as the old ones fall down and they build new ones.

1. Here is to be noticed the house of the unmarried Brethren, not unlike a castle,[4] built of sandstone, five stories high, containing about seventy rooms, large and small.   The Brethren, who are mechanics of every trade, either sit there together, those who are of the same trade, or each one by himself.   There are shoemakers' and saddlers' shops, where the unmarried Brethren work. In the other stories there are two dining-halls, in each of which are five tables, each table large enough to seat twenty persons. The third story forms a dormitory, which stretches from one end of the house to the other, in which beds stand side by side to the number of two hundred, each for a single person.   There were good bed-clothes on each bed, but without sheets, and the

---

[1] The mechanics' shops, in part, and several mills were built along the creek. — W. C. R.

[2] A summer residence of the King in the south of Sweden. — J. J. M.

[3] This statement is altogether erroneous, and is doubtless based upon a misapprehension on the part of Acrelius. — W. C. R.

[4] In 1814, this house was evacuated by its occupants and fitted up for a boarding-school for young ladies. It is the central building of the present well-known Moravian Seminary.

beds were mostly of feathers, as the Germans commonly have them.   In the fourth story was a place for the rearing of silk-worms.   In the fifth hung the Brethren's clothes.   The roof was Italian, flat, with a parapet around, so that one could conveniently walk upon it, where also the Brethren aired their clothes.   Over the north door were the words : [1]

Vater und Mutter und lieber Mann,
Habt Ehre vorm Jünglings Plan. [2]

Over the south door stood a sun-dial with this inscription : " *Gloria Pleuræ.*" [3]

2. Two houses of the unmarried Sisters, about a musket-shot from the other, of stone, three stories high.   This is built with a main building [4] and two wings.   The rooms are arranged in the same manner as in the unmarried Brethren's house.   In the left wing, the lowest story was the Sisters' dining-hall, roomy enough for four hundred persons.   In the other story was the church, or, as they called it, hall ; in this there were long, loose benches for seats — first lengthwise, and then others crosswise, in both ends of the room.   The seats of the Sisters were above, those of the Brethren below, each sex taking up half of the length of the church.   On the other side was only a set of loose benches along the aisle, where the Elders and Officers of the Society had their seats — the men below and the women above.   Upon that side, and apart from the Brethren's seats, stood a small square table, at which the Minister sat when he performed Divine Service.   Back in the church was a gallery, with a small unsightly

---

[1] These mystical inscriptions were framed by young Bishop Cammerhoff, of Beth-lehem, who, as the reader of Moravian history will remember, was for a time deeply imbued with the spirit of fanaticism to which his church, as is well known, was in bondage in the interval between 1745 and 1750.   The first of the two purports to be an invocation of the three persons of the Trinity, and may be rendered : Father, mother, and beloved husband, despise not what we propose to do with these disciples ; the second, " Glory to the Side," is descriptive of glory to Christ for His meritorious sufferings and death as typified by His pierced side.—W. C. R.

[2] [" Father and Mother and Husband dear,
Duly the youthful plans revere."]

[3] [" Glory to the Side," the pierced side of the crucified Saviour.]

[4] Orig., " *Corps de Logis.*"

organ. Under the organ-gallery was the door for the Brethren ; in the middle, on the east aisle, which separated the seats of the Brethren and Sisters, was the door for the Sisters, who there went into their house. That house had been built so carelessly, and upon such loose ground, that it had afterwards to be supported by pillars set all around it, which gave it a very singular appearance.

3. With that a frame house is connected, which forms a wing of the Sisters' house, two stories high, boarded, and painted red. Through that the Brethren go out from the church, under the organ. Therein live the most distinguished married Brethren, and also their Ministers.

4. A log-house, with the interstices filled in with mortar, two stories high, without any ornamentation, is the oldest house in Bethlehem, from which it is seen that the first settlement was very small. In this is the workshop of the weavers, in which there are six looms with their equipments, and which are all in constant operation. Here, too, is the shop for making women's shoes, in which five or six married Brethren are at work. The other rooms were residences for a number of married Brethren and their wives.

5. Directly opposite is a stone house, two stories high, where the women are kept during child-birth, and remain there until their child is weaned. They were building a large stone house for the married Brethren, who were now more numerous than the lodgings for them, on which account they had to be housed among the unmarried Brethren, and their wives among the un- married Sisters. A stone house a short distance off was used for a nursery. A stone house higher up the hill, upon the great highway, and seeming to be separated from Bethlehem, was the abode of married persons who mostly live at their own expense, or are upon trial as to whether they will or will not unite with the Brethren. Here also a store is kept on the Brethren's account.

6. Along the Menakesi creek, and within the town of Bethle- hem, were workshops and places of labor for tailors, carpenters, smiths, etc., likewise a milk-house ; also a tan-yard, but not of any value. The mill by which the bark was prepared was turned by a water-wheel. In the same house they were now arranging

water-works,[1] which were to drive the water up the steep hill, and then through pipes distribute it to every house, which work a Jutlander had undertaken to accomplish. The Brethren were now working at this very actively and industriously. This will be a very useful work for the cloister, for hitherto it has kept a man busy from morning till night to carry the water up the hill to the houses.

7. The mill stands upon the Menakesi, within Bethlehem, and has two pair of stones. One pair is used for the cloister, the other works for strangers for toll.

8. A cattle-yard of considerable size; it holds eighty milch cows, besides young cattle, oxen, and horses. The stable and barn are quite large. This is the largest cattle-yard in the country. There is a summer-house on a hill on the other side of the Menakesi, in a thick grove, to which also a broad walk has been made and levelled. The walk corresponds to that which lies between the houses of the unmarried Brothers and Sisters, stretching straight through the orchard to another summer-house built in similar style. These summer-houses are used by the Brethren or Sisters, or children, when they go out to enjoy themselves, to protect them against rain, or the great heat of the sun, or for any one who wishes to enjoy an hour of solitude; at times also for music, which is heard most pleasantly from such a distance, when made by horns and trombones.

9. The wash-house in the orchard, a little way from the cloister, on the east, down by the Delaware river, only for the use of the Sisters. A short distance from this is the soap factory, in the orchard, for the whole society. Westward, at the same distance in a field down by the Delaware, is another wooden house, for the use of the Brothers only. The Brothers wash their own clothes; and it is said to come quite handy to them both to wash and starch them.

10. The tavern, with its appurtenant houses, all of logs, on the south side of the Lehigh, and on the road from Philadelphia, belongs to the Brethren. It has fair accommodations for travellers. The ferry over the river is also kept by the Brethren. There is also an inn of stone in Bethlehem, on the other side of

---

[1] The first water-works in the United States.—J. J. M.

the Menakesi, which is only for the use of the Indians, and its arrangements are accordingly. Whether they belong to the Brethren or not, all are welcome there. The host and his wife are both Indians, and live and dress themselves in their way, but have been baptized, and belong to the Brotherhood.

11. Nazareth is a Herrnhut settlement, twelve miles further up the country. There are connected with it one thousand five hundred acres of farming land, first taken up by the head man of the Methodists, Mr. George Whitfield, when, twelve years since, he had a mind to erect here an Orphan house, but afterwards changed his mind, and sold the land to some persons in England, from whom Count Zinzendorff purchased it before he became the owner of the land at Bethlehem. Here is an Orphan house, which is represented as more considerable and important than it really is. There are also some houses for the families of married people who cultivate the land, and an inn[1] belonging to the Brethren.

12. Gnadenhütten[2] is a place thirty (30) miles from Bethlehem, where the Moravians are said to have their converted Indians. Together with the children they are said to amount to one hundred and fifty persons, live in huts after their manner, but are baptized, and belong to the Brotherhood, and have all things in common. Those that hunt, hunt for all; those that fish, fish for all. The Moravians converse with them in English. It is remarkable that they do not count their numbers higher, for the work of conversion must be very easy, without reading, and without instruction in the fundamental points of Christianity. It seems as though these Indians believed more in the Brethren than they do in the Holy Trinity. When they first connected themselves with the Indians, complaints came to the Government that they were seeking to get possession of the land by

---

[1] This was the well-known house with the sign of the Rose, one mile north of the village. As Acrelius did not visit Nazareth, his statements were sometimes founded on incorrect information.

[2] [The first settlement in Carbon county, Pennsylvania, was made in 1746, near the site of Lehighton, on the Mahoning creek. In 1754 the Mission was transferred to the other bank of the Lehigh, on the site of Weissport, and received the name of New Gnadenhütten. The old settlement was destroyed by hostile Indians, November 24, 1755, and New Gnadenhütten, on the 9th of January, 1756.]

private contracts with the savages, which was contrary to the laws of the land, as it is the exclusive right of the Proprietor to buy land of the Indians, after which others are to buy of him.

13. Gnadenthal [1] is also a place where the Moravian Brethren have a society. Some German families have settled there. Gnadenthal and Gnadenhut both lie on the other side of the Blue Mountains.[2]

Our Intercourse in Bethlehem.

When we had come to the inn, where all travellers first stop when coming to the cloister, I let the host [3] know that I had a letter to Mr. Spangenberg,[4] and a recommendation from Mr. Paul Bruzelius,[5] that I should be received and informed as to the condition of the Brotherhood in Bethlehem, and the character of the place. I inquired whether Mr. Spangenberg was at home, and directed him to send him the letter. The host seemed quite inquisitive in regard to that commission, as though he expected some new Brethren; went over on the errand, but immediately came back with the answer that Brother Spangenberg had just gone off to Nazareth, and was not to be expected back for some weeks, but that another person would at once come over and wait upon us. We waited about half an hour, and, as it seemed to be drawing towards the evening, we determined to go over without waiting for a convoy. Whilst we were going down to the ferry, two gentlemen met us, whom I saluted in this manner; that as I was a stranger in the country, and ever since my

---

[1] [About one mile nearly west from Nazareth, Pennsylvania.]

[2] Gnadenhütten only lay beyond the mountains.—W. C. R.

[3] The Bethlehem Inn (the Crown) was, at this time, kept by John Godfrey Grabs, a Silesian by birth.—W. C. R.

[4] [Bishop Spangenberg, who, perhaps next to Zinzendorff, has exerted the greatest influence in the development of the Moravian system of both faith and practice He superintended their churches in America for upwards of twenty years.]

[5] The Rev. Paul D. Bryzelius, of Bethlehem, was at this time laboring in the Gospel, under the auspices of the Moravian Church, among the descendants of the early Swedish settlers on the Delaware, whither he had been sent by Count Zinzendorff in January, 1743. His appointments, and those of his assistants, were along Maurice river, at Cohansey, Pennsneck, Racoon, Ammasland, and Calkoens' Hook. Mr. Bryzelius severed his connection with the Moravian Church in the autumn of 1760, and united himself with the Lutherans.—W. C. R.

arrival had a great desire to see their community at Bethlehem,
for which I had never before had an opportunity, I hoped that
they would now give me that privilege. They answered with
much politeness that I should be welcome, and that I should receive all the information that I desired relative to everything
within their place of abode. They also turned to the gentlemen
who were in my company, and gave them the same assurance.

One of these gentlemen was Mr. Benzien, a native of Livonia.
He said that he had been a good friend, and well acquainted
with Mr. Th. O., and had associated with him in Livonia. He
was thus one of the first who had entered the Brotherhood, and
well acquainted with the difficulties of the Herrnhut Society
from its first commencement. And as he has shown himself a
steadfast brother, Count Zinzendorff has employed him as his
Secretary during a year that he spent in London, to carry on
his correspondence with all parts of the world, to receive such
of the Brethren as came to London, and promote their further
journey, etc. He had been in Bethlehem only six weeks, having lately come from London to New York in the Brethren's
galliot, and thence directly to Bethlehem, so that he was still a
stranger in Pennsylvania. At present he was the Brethren's
Secretary, and kept their Journal; he carried on their correspondence, kept their archives, etc., and he also· received strangers.
The other was Mr. Rodgers,[1] formerly a Minister in the English
church, afterwards a teacher among the so-called New Lights,
Whitefieldians, or Methodists, but now an influential brother and
preacher in the Moravian Society. From his blue coat and black
vest one was made aware that he belonged to the ministry, for
the Moravian Ministers sometimes find it advantageous to dress
themselves as the Ministers of other churches. But few Ministers of the Church of England, so far as known, have gone over
to the Moravians. Does any one ask who he is? It is, for the
most part, answered that he is a Minister of the Church of England, but that he no more holds to the articles of faith or liturgy
of the Church of England than to the Koran. In England he
went over to the Brethren. It is said that he has greater gifts in

---

[1] The Rev. Jacob Rogers, of Bedford, England.—W. C. R.

the delivery of his sermons than is common among them, but this is not strange, as he has been educated as a Minister, and the others as mechanics. In New York, some years ago, he had drawn many over to the Brethren by his sermons, and was greatly beloved, but when his fame had reached its height, he was called away, in accordance with one of the strongest maxims of the Zinzendorffians. During the past year, one of my Parishioners, who had heard him preach in Philadelphia, came and inquired of me whether I would allow him to preach in Christina Church? He had been an English Minister, and still held to the church, although he lived among the Brethren. I replied that he was no better for having left his Church and gone to that Sect, and that it was not strange that he gave himself out as holding with both, as he was a Herrnhutter; but that as to preaching in my church, I could not grant it, if I desired, etc. How far Mr. Rodgers now remembered me in that matter, I could not perceive. These two gentlemen regretted that Mr. Spangenberg was not at home. He had gone to Nazareth, and thought of going to Gnadenhutten the next day to visit their Indians. They would take us over to Bethlehem, and do their best to gratify us. I understood at once that they had broken open and examined the letter that I had brought to Mr. Spangenberg, as is their custom. During our passage over the ferry we had not been able particularly to examine each other's faces, but it seemed to us that we had seen each other before, especially Mr. Benzien and myself. If I had ever seen him elsewhere, it must have been upon the streets in London. Pastor Unander and he were certain that they had seen each other in the Brother's community in Fetterlane, in London. We first went up to the church, where Mr. Ritz[1] played for us on the organ. He was one of their Ministers, who was acquainted with Pastor Unander when he had charge of their meeting-house at Oldman's creek, in Racoon. He afterwards came down and joined us. There was nothing remarkable there to see. The room was large and empty, excepting

---

[1] The Rev. Matthew Reuz, who was occasionally sent out from Bethlehem to preach to the Swedish settlers on the Delaware. Other Moravian Evangelists to these people were the Rev. Abraham Reineke and the Rev. Sven Roseen, both natives of Sweden.—W. C. R.

the many loose benches which stood there, and the small square table.   Thence we were taken to the house, where the store was upon the hill.   A lady was there from New York to see her brother, who was married in Bethlehem, but still held his own property, and was therefore obliged to dwell in this house apart from the others.

We next went down to the cattle-yard, mill, milk-house, the tannery, a place where the bark-mill was for preparing the bark, and where the new works were being arranged for driving the water up the hill.   Finally, our walk terminated at the door of the unmarried Brethren's house.

During all this time our guides, the two Brethren, seemed to be somewhat troubled about us.   What they said seemed to be spoken with great caution.   At every word they turned their eyes sometimes at both of us, sometimes at each other.   It seemed that they already began to distrust our object.   This came either from their having learned the names of Pastor Brunnholtz and Mr. Sleidorn, who some years since had been the severest enemies of the Brethren here in America, or that they did not perceive that any of us greatly admired their set-tlement.   In fact there was nothing very much to admire beyond what I have noticed in passing.   It was evident that there was some strong interest connected with all this, and that it could not be carried on without some considerable expenditure, as they also stated, and added that it was entirely the Brethren's own work.   All worked for one another, and each worked for all.

We had asked whether it was not possible to hear their music. Mr. Benzien answered that he did not know how that could be done, as the Brethren were weary from their work.   But just as we were standing before the unmarried Brothers' house, there came a blast from two trumpets up in the summer-house, which stands on the forest-hill.   They gave a charming sound, and admonished us to go and behold more of the glories of Bethlehem.

We were standing before the door of the house aforesaid, and were weary of our long standing.   We inquired about Nazareth, and said that we thought of going thither the next morning. They regretted that we would not remain longer with them in Bethlehem.   But it seemed as though we were already overlong there. We sometimes looked at the singular inscription, "*Vater und Mutter*," etc., and the Brethren also looked at us; but no one said a word. We took it patiently, although we saw that they were already wearied of us. We inquired about the arrangements in that house, but got only half answers, upon which no reliance could be placed. Mr. Ritz was a friendly man. He sought to make the time somewhat more pleasant for us. Therefore, when I asked about the arrangements in the house for the unmarried Brethren and the others, and Benzien and Rodgers would not come out with anything, Ritz said, "Come in, good gentlemen, and you shall see how things are here." He first conducted us into one of their dining-halls, where there were five tables, and each table large enough for twenty persons. Thence he took us up into their dormitory, of which we have already related. The others, Benzien and Rodgers, remained still upon the street. When we came down again, a new standing took place. They had no heart to invite us to go anywhere, neither could we take leave, as they invited us to remain with them until their hour of prayer, which was to be held at nine o'clock. Neither did they invite us to eat or drink anything, although it was late in the afternoon, and the whole Brotherhood there had had their evening meal. We could get a glass of water if we desired it. To pass the time, we went out into their vegetable garden, which was full of vegetables for the table. They showed us many of these, and Mr. Rodgers said that their household was large, and they must have a great many such things. I asked him how the German diet agreed with his English stomach. The Germans live mostly upon cabbage, salad, roots, and other green things, and also upon soups, whilst the English must have meat at every meal, and do not wish anything else. He answered that there must be a dispensation for that, and every one may exercise his freedom in regard to his table arrangements. Benzien said that since he had been so long in England, it was now very much the same with himself in regard to diet. He then asked me if I did not look with contempt upon Sweden since I had seen England. I asked him what he had seen in that country that could throw contempt upon any other in comparison. That it might be a prejudice which he had not yet been able to overcome, etc.

Meanwhile it became dark so that we could no longer stand upon the street, neither could we walk about anywhere, and then we were invited into the red house next to the church, and into a chamber which seemed to be for Mr. Rodgers. We sat there for a short time, and no one had anything to say. Some of the Brethren came in to see us, but said nothing. They are generally Germans, of whom, however, the greater part understand English. Every Sunday preaching is held in both German and English. Mr. Rodgers was now their English Minister; he understood German, but did not speak it with the ease of a native. His business was to translate books from the German into the English. They said that all within that community had their daily work, and that no idlers are tolerated among them. Pastor Brunnholtz inquired whether their people, who work so hard, are not sleepy when they come to the evening service, which is held so late. Mr. Ritz answered, "What then? Although they may sleep, the Saviour is awake."

The Brethren had their passage through that house, and went up stairs into the church. Finally, our turn came. The Brethren were divided in their opinions as to whether we should sit in the organ-gallery or down in the church. It was finally arranged that we should sit below, as the music sounded better there. The organ had the accompaniment of violins and flutes. The musicians were back in the gallery, so that none of them were seen. The men and women were in about equal numbers — between three and four hundred — all clean and neat. It was especially observable that the women all had white caps, which were tied under the chin with a rosette of ribbon. The cap fits tightly to the head, and is made in plaits, and finished out with long ears. Over them passes a band, two fingers broad, of thin linen, which is fastened behind. They had short jackets of the usual kind. The men had either the usual clothing or linen roundabouts with long linen trowsers. After all had been collected during the playing of the music, one of their Ministers seated himself at the little table and read some verses of a German hymn-book, after which they were sung with excellent music. Inasmuch as we, their guests, were, as they well knew, Lutherans, they were so polite as to read and sing some verses of our

German hymns, e. g., "*Come, Holy Ghost, descend, we pray*,"[1]
etc.; "*Zion with deep grief bewaileth*,"[2] etc. This was their
service which they called "hour of singing." And so it was,
for the verses were alternately read and sung, five or six verses,
as directed. We went out, and expressed our gratification with
the music, with which they were well pleased. We remained
awhile before the door, where Mr. Sleidorn and Pastor Brunnholtz talked with one after another as they came out. Mr.
Rodgers thought that the time was too long for him, and bade
us good-night. Mr. Benzien was better mannered than to leave
us in that way amid the thick darkness. Whilst we stood there,
a new hymn was started in the church, and the music struck up
again. Mr. Benzien said that that was the unmarried Brethren's
hour of relaxation, when none but themselves were present; also
that the unmarried Sisters had a similar hour in their house.

It was now time to return over the river, and to get our entertainment for the night in the inn. Mr. Benzien was so polite as
to express his regret that he could not entertain us as he ought.
He accompanied us upon the way, and was very attentive that
we might not fare badly in the thick darkness and on the uneven
ground. After he had delivered us over to the care of the ferryman, he bade us good-night, and then turned back.

The ferryman[3] was an Englishman with a loose tongue. We
now commenced an examination with him by asking how he
came hither. He said that he had for some years followed the
sea in the Brethren's galliot or sloop, but had now determined
to spend the rest of his life upon their ferry-boat. I asked him
if the Brethren had not other vessels besides the sloop. "Not
at the present time," he answered. "During the late war they
had had a large ship, which the Spaniards had seized.[4] They

---

[1] [The well-known German hymn, "*Komm H. Geist kehr bei uns ein.*"]

[2] [The German hymn, "*Zion klagt mit Angst u. Schmerzen.*" In the original, the
first lines are given in Swedish.]

[3] The ferry at this date was in charge of William Edmonds, a native of Coleford,
England, and some time cook in the Moravian *Snow Irene*, on board of which
colonists were transported across the Atlantic in the interval between 1748 and 1758.
He afterwards represented Northampton county in the Assembly.— W. C. R.

[4] The *Little Strength*, bought by the Church for the transporting of colonists to
America, on her voyage out to Amsterdam was taken by a Spanish cruiser in the
Chops of the Channel on the 1st of May, 1744.— W. C. R.

sought, through their agent, to get it back again, as it was great injustice to make a prize of a vessel which had been sent out for the sake of promulgating the Gospel to the world; but it was still retained." I inquired whether it had any lading. "Yes," said he; "it went from New York to London, and carried some brandy, sugar, etc." "So," I answered, "do brandy and sugar belong to the promulgation and extension of the Gospel? Those were English goods, and as the ship sailed under the English flag, so it is not strange that the Spaniards took it for their own when they could lay their hands on it."

What remained of our little time we employed for the gratification of our curiosity. During our supper, the host informed us that the Brotherhood in Bethlehem retire to bed at ten o'clock. Notwithstanding this, lights are burning in all the windows the whole night, and every night.

For supper, in the summer-time, they had cold milk and bread, or rye-meal mush, or whatever the season presented. That they had no fixed rules for eating or diet, but were regulated by the season of the year and convenience.

They eat meat only once a week. The reason for this is good enough, for the whole of North Hampton county would not be sufficient to supply them with butchers' meat if they were to eat it every day, as the English do. Mr. Sleydorn asked, "How often do you eat meat in your house?" The host answered, "As often as I wish to. And so, so," said he, "I am better off than any of them." It was asked again, "What was the object in building the new house?" The host answered that it was for the married Brethren, who were now so numerous that they had not room enough for themselves, but had to sleep along with the unmarried Brethren, and their wives with the unmarried Sisters. "I understand," said Mr. Sleydorn, "that you are by all means better off here than they are there."

But we had not yet seen enough of Bethlehem. We had thought of going on to Nazareth; but as the way was long, the time short, and the heat great, and we, as well as our horses, quite tired, we determined to stay in Bethlehem on the following day, and towards evening to turn our faces homeward.

The 10th of June was Wednesday, when Mr. Sleydorn con-

29

tinued his journey further up into the country, on the other side of Nazareth, to hunt up and sue people who had purchased land of him, but failed to pay. And thus he separated from our company.

Whilst we were dressing ourselves on the following morning, and were going back and forwards in the inn, we fell into conversation with the ferryman. We did not know him, although we had talked a great deal with him the night before, for then it was quite dark. He spoke quite freely, as though he wished to get up a controversy with us, which we also understood when the host said to us, " Good gentlemen, you had a great deal to ask me yesterday evening; now here is a man who can answer you much better than I." I asked him about the Brethren's order for eating in Bethlehem. He answered that there was no fixed rule in regard to this, but that they regulated themselves by the season of the year, and what it was possible to get for the table. The Brethren who had come in, but retained some of their own property, could get one thing or another as they liked between meals. Those who would rather board themselves at their own expense were at liberty to do so. One must understand that the Brethren were not brought up all in the same manner, and so were accustomed to different modes of diet; their Society made no change in their modes of living. They could all be faithful Brethren, although one might live better than another, just as they had been brought up.

I further asked him how he had come into this association, and who had drawn him to it. He answered that no one else than a plowman or peasant had converted him. I said, " That is quite possible, especially if one understands this in the same way as when it is said that a cock converted St. Peter. Conversion is a work of God, but not of a plowman. The occasion for it is given in all nature and the works of creation. The means are no other than God's Word and Sacraments. The persons who are ordinarily employed are the Gospel Ministry; yet, without the usual order, one Christian may edify and advance another of whatever condition he may be, and so one plowman another." Then he began with much zeal to set forth the order of salvation, and showed himself more apt therein than could have been expected. He further said that he belonged to a congregation of sinners, but that he was assured that no one was so great a sinner that he could not expect forgiveness, and that he also believed that even the traitor Judas was saved. Pastor Unander reminded him that the Saviour had called Judas "*the son of perdition,*" (St. John 17:12,) which was not a sign of his conversion, to say nothing of other passages of Scripture. "Yes," said he; "but we find again, in another place, that the Saviour says to His disciples, '*Ye shall sit upon twelve thrones, and judge the twelve tribes of Israel.*' Certainly Judas must there be one of them." I answered that I saw in Luke 22 : 30 only *thrones* mentioned, without any special number. "That," he said, "was more than he knew." Then I informed him that it is no article of faith whether Judas was or was not saved. We can, indeed, see in Acts i. what was the end of Judas, and that the number of the Apostles had to be filled up after the departure of Judas, so that twelve thrones could be filled without him. I asked him whether that was his own individual opinion or an accepted article of faith among the Brethren. He answered that it was his own opinion, and he could not say whether any others of the Brethren believed the same. "Then," said I, "you must pardon me, my friend, for not believing with you." When the other Ministers also opposed his views, and he began to talk very loudly and obstinately, I told him not to flatter himself that he could, on so small a subject as that was, out-talk three Ministers at once, and that we would rather let him have the room to himself, which we also did.

Meanwhile the host went over to Bethlehem to inform them there that we had concluded to remain with them until the afternoon. For between the inn and the officers in Bethlehem reports are continually made, so that nothing can take place there of which they have not immediate information. In accordance wherewith, Mr. Benzien now immediately came over to keep us company for the day. He expressed his pleasure that we would still spend another day in Bethlehem, and we equally assured him that we could not return satisfied without having spent a few hours more in that place. We hoped that he would now show us the other arrangements of the Society. He answered that we should be at liberty to see everything that was there.

I especially expressed my desire to see their Children's House, and their arrangements for the training of children. "Yes," said he, "that is certainly worth seeing. Many come hither from great distances for no other purpose than to see how we bring up our children." I said that I had also heard a great deal talked about it, but had never had any clear idea in regard to it. Pastor Unander was reminded that a young woman of a Swedish family had, in the past year, come down to Philadelphia and Amas Land, to see after her inheritance, when her friends and relatives found her in such a state of ignorance that she could not read in the least, nor answer any questions in the knowledge of Christianity, etc. That so provoked them that they took her to the Mayor's in Philadelphia to be examined, of which Pastor Parlin, in Wicacoa, was a witness. Mr. Benzien could not possibly believe that. He regarded it as an envious story about the Brethren. He was assured that his children, who were now in that place of nurture, could not be as well taught by himself as by the masters and mistresses under whose oversight they now were. At two o'clock in the afternoon the children would have a meeting in the church, and we should see them there. We determined to spend the morning in a walk on this side of the river. Whilst Pastor Brunnholtz was dressing himself, Pastor Unander and I sat before the inn on the side towards Bethlehem. We had determined not to trouble him with controversy, as that might destroy our pleasure for the whole day. Notwithstanding this, Pastor Unander came forward with the serious question, "What is the meaning of the inscription which is read over the door of the unmarried Brethren's house, '*Vater und Mutter und lieber Mann*,' etc." "Ah," answered Mr. Benzien, "that is something that he devised who built the house. I, for my part, have never approved of it." I fell into the conversation, and said, "Be assured, gentlemen, that although the words are altogether mystical, yet we well understand their meaning." "I doubt not, gentlemen," he answered, "that you do indeed understand it, and that you are not ignorant of the Brethren's arrangements in other places." "But," said Pastor Unander, "would it not be better if those words did not stand there?" "Yes," said he; "so I also think that it would be better. Yet no one can doubt

that the man who first put that up had a good meaning with it."
It was undoubtedly Mr. Benzien's idea that that should be kept
among the secrets of the Brethren, and not stand before the eyes
of every one, whereby their Society might be misjudged. For
that he is one of their chief men, who approves of all their
inventions, cannot be doubted. Upon the same occasion I asked,
in regard to their marriage, how they do therewith. Whether
they unite as husband and wife who have never before known
each other. "Yes," said he; "we do so. In view of the great
number of unmarried men and women whom we have, how
would it do for them to come together and seek spouses for
themselves?" "But," said I, "is not that a compulsion?"
"Nay," he answered; "they may object if they please, which
also sometimes happens." N. B. — They may refuse, but the
Brethren will not love them the more for that.

We directed our walk up one of the Lehigh hills. The Brethren
had there made a broad road, which was also quite smooth.
During our ascent, I related about Mr. Arv. Gradin; how he had
sought to introduce the Brethren's Society into Sweden, first in
the year 1740 in company with Dobern, when he got in with
Doctor Alstrin, and procured license to preach in the great
church in Stockholm as one who had returned from the Dip-
pelians, though it was not yet known that he was a secret
Herrnhutter. Also how he afterwards misused Dr. Alstrin's
name. Again, how he came back in the year 1748, and created
great disturbance in the Royal College of Chancery in Stockholm, in the City Consistory among the Clergy, as also in the
churches, and how he was finally banished and carried out of
Sweden by a guard. Mr. Benzien thought that this was a severe
forcing of conscience. I answered that in Sweden there is no
coercion of conscience; every one can believe as he chooses;
but if any one undertakes to spread abroad and publicly defend
doctrines different from those which accord with the Augsburg
Confession and the other Symbolical Books, he is regarded as a
disturber of the general good order. The fundamental laws of
the Realm declare that no other doctrine shall be received in the
kingdom. The Estates of the Realm have made the law, and
so the Estates of the Realm are bound to uphold it. We also
spoke of the expulsion of the Moravian Brethren from Herrn-

hag.   Mr. Benzien said that none of them, whether old or young,
were left there: all were immediately ready to leave when the
command came.   That the Count of Budingen had exercised
violence in seizing their property, selling their houses, and
keeping the proceeds.   They might call him to an account
for this before a Romish tribunal, but they would rather suffer
than contend for their rights.   I inquired why the Brethren
did not themselves sell their houses before they departed.   He
answered that time for this was not given them.   I stated that three
years had been given them to dispose of their property as they
pleased.   He at first denied this, but afterwards admitted it.

When we arrived at the top of the hill, we saw Nazareth in a
valley at the distance of twelve miles.   We saw there two stone
houses,[1] which must be quite large, as they appeared above a
thick forest and a low country.   That valley is formed by the
Blue Mountains, which run in a long chain through North
Hampton county, and appear to meet the skies high up in the
air.   They are, however, as we saw, cut through in various
places by valleys, through which the roads pass to the people
who live upon their other side.   From the other side of the river
the road leads to the mountains, and is used by those who trade
with the Indians, who, however, live far on the other side of
these mountains.   Bethlehem has great advantages from these
traders, who here purchase various goods, as also what is necessary for their journeys, such as saddles, powder, balls, lead, etc.
Between Nazareth and Bethlehem is a great road, broad and
smooth as a King's highway, all made by the labor of the Brethren,
although the road goes over the lands of many of their neighbors.

It is remarkable that although this region is so covered with
forests, so well watered by rivers and creeks, and though so few
places of abode are occupied, yet one seldom sees a deer there,
and the savages have all disappeared.   On the contrary, the
places upon the Delaware inhabited by the Swedes have had
deer in great numbers until within the last thirty years, and the
Indians prospered well among the Christians.   It is also related

---

[1] These are, first, Nazareth Hall, intended for Count Zinzendorff's residence, and
now used for the seminary; and the other, the celebrated Whitefield House, the
upper part of which is used for the Moravian Historical Society, and the lower part
as a retreat for retired Missionaries.—T. W.

of those who go back into Virginia[1] to hunt, that they find wide districts, upon beautiful rivers, filled with deer, where no Christian has yet taken up his abode, and no savage is to be seen, although so convenient for the chase. From which it may be concluded that this people is, at the present time, a rapidly declining race. I asked what use they could make of so much land as was now lying waste around Bethlehem? He answered that they were thinking of dividing it into separate residences for the Brethren.

Upon this hill we found a mussel-shell, which led us to speak of the height of the Flood. In the Philadelphia Library are shown a great many mussel-shells gathered upon the Blue Mountains, twenty miles from where we stood, and it was held that the Flood had carried them thus far, and then left them. No certain conclusion could be formed from our mussel-shell, as it lay upon a place to which people frequently came.

In descending, we visited a Brother who lived on that road in a small cottage. He was an old Swiss,[2] about seventy years of age, and his wife was not much younger. This pair had cleared a little land around their house for meadow, enough for a cow, broken up the stones and built a fence with them. As I came to the old man, who was sitting before his house, he greeted me with a kiss, which had a strong flavor of his tobacco-pipe, and called me his brother, when I called him father. He greeted my companions in the same manner. Thereupon he immediately asked Mr. Benzien if we were not their brethren? But when he answered that we were strangers who had come to see them, the old man said, "So, so; are they the inquisitive people?" and then sat down with his tobacco-pipe, and had not another word to say. Here Mr. Benzien fell into conversation with Pastor Brunnholtz about the Lutheran candidate in theology, Pastor Walter in Gotha, who, in the beginning, when the Zinzendorffians first came in, at first fell in with them, but afterwards fell away

---

[1] [The allusion seems to be to Kentucky, which at this time, and long after, was a part of Virginia. But Daniel Boone is usually represented as the first explorer of Kentucky in 1769 and 1770.]

[2] John Jacob Lescher, the remains of whose little improvements on the mountain's side were long designated by the Moravians of Bethlehem as "The Old Man's Place." The site of old Lescher's homestead is included within the park of the Lehigh University. — W. C. R.

from them entirely. Mr. Benzien said that he was deranged;
insisted on taking his wife and child from the Brethren, to which
he had no right. The mother believed herself to have as good
a right to the child as the father. I made the suggestion that it
would be well to have the decision of a judge upon that point,
and that the laws of nature and of nations gave the father the
highest right to his minor children. Pastor Brunnholtz denied
that he was deranged, and proved it in very strong terms.

We returned to the inn. The day was very warm. Mr. Benzien
took his dinner with us. One of our dishes was trout, which are
taken in the streams of the country, but were a rarity for us.

During the dinner, Mr. Benzien stated that Count Louis Zinzendorff has now been for seven years in England, and transacts
his business there. With him lives Anna Nitschman. The
Countess is in Germany, at Great Hennersdorff, which is the
Count's own property.

. I asked if the Count is always much engaged. "Yes," he
answered ; "he always has his hands overfull, and wishes that
he were entirely released." "What is the reason," said I, "that
he cannot get away from his troubles?" "He wishes to see his
affairs in good order before he leaves them," answered Mr. Benzien. I said again, "Perhaps the Count will extend his views
further, to obtain the object that he first had in view?" "That
is quite probable," was the answer, and therewith he laughed.
He further asked whether none of us saw the Count when he
was here in this country? We answered that none of us were
then here. Pastor Brunnholtz said that there was then no
German Lutheran Minister here except Pastor Mühlenberg.
"Well," said he, "how did he agree with the Count?" Pastor
Brunnholtz answered, "That he could not exactly know, as it
was before his time, but believed that they were not very great
friends." "My good friends," said I, "it was not wonderful that
they could not draw together, as they both came to the country
at the same time to establish churches, and were so unlike in
their principles. However, notwithstanding this, Pastor Mühlenberg has made great progress ever since."

After our meal, we made our way up to Bethlehem. It was
two o'clock, and the children were assembled in the church. They

came two and two together, holding each other's hands, the boys and girls through different doors. The boys were divided between seven or eight masters, each of whom had hold of a boy's hand as they were going. Without doubt, these boys were especially recommended before all the others. The girls came in like manner with their mistresses. Among the boys were two mulatto children and an Indian. The dress of the children had nothing special about it, except that the girls had the same kind of caps as those of the women already mentioned, with green ribbons under their chin. Their mistresses had red ribbons. The number of boys and girls was about equal, altogether one hundred and forty-four. In that meeting none of the congregation were present except the children and their teachers.

The meeting consisted in this, that when they were seated in their places, a man came and seated himself at the little square table. There he first read some verses, then sang some verses, then read some more verses, and sang again, and so read and sang alternately. During the singing the organ was played. Finally, he made a little address to the children, and recommended to them six other children, who were then introduced. There were but few of the children that sang. The great heat made most of the little things sleepy. The whole meeting was over in half an hour.

We went down into the room where we were the evening before, namely, Mr. Rodgers'. We saw him pass by the window, but he did not come in, nor did he say a word to us during the day. They asked us whether we would like to see the Swedish Minister Nyberg's children, about whom I had inquired several times before, and desired that they might be brought to us. They came, two little girls, quite lively, and kissed our hands. In truth, we were greatly moved when we saw them. The elder one, who was six years old, had the apple of her eyes like those of a cat or an owl, and was greatly to be pitied, although she was otherwise a fine child. Her mother had looked at a cat, which came running towards her when she was *enceinte*, and, instead of shutting her eyes so as not to see it, she put up one hand before both her eyes, and thus injured her child. The other, a year younger, was a fine child. I asked her whether she would go with me to Sweden and see her father's family. She answered, "Yes," and seemed to be at once ready.

When they had gone out, I asked what kind of nurture they had for their children. Benzien said that they had a house for women who were lying-in, where they staid with the children as long as they were at the breast. After that the children are taken to Nazareth, and remain in the Children's House until they are four years old. Then they are brought back to Bethlehem again, as we had seen done that day. The man who read and sang for them in the church is called the "Father of the children in Nazareth." He has an oversight of their treatment. In Bethlehem they are under the care of their masters and mistresses, as we saw.

I asked, "How are the children taught?" Mr. Benzien answered, "They receive instruction in everything that a Christian ought to know. In regard to their manners, they are always under supervision, so that they may not form any bad habits. All those who know what excellent order is kept among them cannot but wonder at it. Many also send their children hither to receive such an education, and afterwards take them home, paying for the time they were here."

I asked again, "My friend, how are they taught? What do they learn? Have they any Catechism? Do I understand that they are required to learn the Ten Commandments and the Articles of the Creed? No, no! I am speaking too fast. I recollect that it is in fact contrary to your doctrine to learn the Ten Commandments. You go at once to the Articles of the Creed? Is not that so?" Mr. Benzien could not refrain from laughing when so many questions came out at once, and especially when I recalled, as a hasty speech, their being required to learn the Ten Commandments as conflicting with their doctrine. "It is true," he said, "they do not learn the Ten Commandments in our schools; we find the way of salvation without them." "But," I further asked, "do they learn our three Articles of Faith? I should think that they ought at least to learn the second, if not the first and third." "Nay, nay," answered he; "they learn neither the one nor the other." Again I asked, "Do

they learn the Lord's Prayer?" "Yes, yes," he answered;
"they learn that." "But," I asked, "do all of them learn the
prayer?" Then he hesitated, with the answer, "I believe so."
Finally, I inquired, "Do they read any in the Bible?" He
answered, "No." Then it was clear what the good man had
before denied, viz., that they brought up the children in a terrible
ignorance, as Pastor Unander had already shown by a well-
known case, and also that they afterwards lead them into
mysticism.[1]

Yet once more I took it upon me to ask: "Would it not be
well for the children to be accustomed to prayer?" "Yes, yes,"
said Mr. Benzien; "they have, indeed, prayers also." "Do you
use prayers yourselves, my friends?" I inquired. Then another
person who was present noticed that Mr. Benzien held back, and
would not come right out with the truth, and therefore answered,
"You must understand that our prayers consist in verses, and
therefore we alternately read and sing our hymns. Our Litany
is a general church-prayer, wherein all other forms of prayer are
included."

They took down from a shelf their Litany, which formed a
volume by itself, and one of their new hymn-books, about which
they were quite reserved. They thought that no hymn-book
so fine ·had hitherto appeared. Both were' new editions, in German, lately brought over from London. The hymn-book, Mr.
Benzien said, was printed in London. The Brethren have their
own printing-office there, but at that time the office was so busy
with other work that they had to employ strangers. It was a
collection of hymns gathered from the Greek, Latin, Samoyede,
ancient Moravian, Lutheran, Calvinistic, and other churches.
Now it was being translated into English. I said that I hoped
that the Brethren would be more fortunate with that hymn-book
than they had been with the one before. Mr. Benzien asked,
"What was the matter with that one?" I answered that I did
not know what it contained, but I well know that it was something too much. "What," said he, "was too much?" "That,"
said I, "which over four years ago was published in the 'London Magazine,' as something very strange to be used in a Church

---

[1] [Orig., "*Enthusiasteri.*"]

hymn-book." Of that he knew nothing; he could not believe it; it might be something of the Saviour's doctrine which the world does not understand, and therefore ridicules. Here Pastor Unander fell into the conversation, and said, " My dear sir, there can be no folly in the Saviour's teachings." " What do you call folly?" said Mr. Benzien. " If the Saviour does not choose to reveal His mysteries to you, what can I do about it?" And therewith he seemed to be excited. I begged him not to misunderstand our conversation, and assured him that it was not by any means our purpose to be offensive to him, inasmuch as we, who were ignorant of their arrangements, might not interpret them correctly. But he would not deny that their former hymn-book had exposed them to censure in all parts of Europe. This he acknowledged, and said that this was just the reason why this new one had been published. Pastor Unander again observed, " Dear sir, your hymn-book which was published in 1749 does really contain some passages which give people reason to wonder at you." He answered, " There are, indeed, some passages that might have been omitted." Pastor Unander said, " I wish that hymn-book had never been published." He answered, " And such is also my wish; and it is just for this reason that we do not give out this our Litany, for it should not be published to the world."

During this conversation Pastor Brunnholtz was turning over the leaves of the new hymn-book, and at length said: " I see here some of our hymns spoiled; it is only a few verses at the beginning of each hymn that I recognize, after which come additions or changes of another character." Mr. Benzien believed that these were improvements, not corruptions. At our request, he promised to send each of us a hymn-book when more should come over, for now they had very few. They were to be in German, for Pastor Brunnholtz and myself; in English, for Pastor Unander, at the price of five (5) shillings apiece. I desired to buy their Litany, cost what it might; but he said that they had so few copies of it that they could not spare any of them. A little before he had said that that Litany ought not to be published to the world. The day after, upon our road home, when we met Mr. Paul Bruzelius, he, both with hand and mouth, promised me

a copy of it, and said that they had them in great quantities!
In that room were two copies of copper-plate engravings of
Count Louis Zinzendorff himself, apparently designed to place
after the title-page of a book.   Upon the one also stood some
passages of Scripture which refer to the Saviour himself.   I expressed my surprise that they had not good evangelical pictures;
but it was said that they had not yet any such artist among
them, and that it would be expensive to pay for such things.
They have, however, a room filled with portraits of their saint,
etc.

We went from there to see the silk-culture, which was carried
on in the house of the unmarried Brethren.   Here were worms
of various ages — some lately come out of the egg, others full
grown, and near to their spinning.   Two Brethren were attending to them.   They said that they had nothing to do but to
supply them with mulberry leaves, for when they had finished
spreading out the leaves at one end, new ones were already required at the place where they began.   There was also a cocoon
of a wild silk-worm obtained in a forest.   This was much larger
than they ever become when raised in the house, and the colors
were most beautiful.   One of the Brethren who was attending
to the worms, and had gotten this from the forest, believed that
its silk would be as good as that of the domesticated worms.
But no one there yet knew how the cocoon of the wild species
was to be managed, for that must be done in a different way
from that of the other kind.   The same person thought that they
might expect £20 as the product of this year.   They had a
larger cocoonery in Nazareth, but everything was still in its in-
cipiency, so that they could not say what gain they might expect from it.   I asked whether they thought that it would pay
for the trouble.   Mr. Benzien answered that, at all events, they
could not lose much from it, as they always had people enough
who could not be employed for anything else.   From this we
understood that these Brethren who attended to the silk-worms
might be some of the musicians, who are always regarded as indispensable in the Brotherhood, and so cannot be put to any
hard work.

They further took us up on to the roof of the house, where

there was a balcony. The prospect was not very extensive, on
account of the great hills all around. But from this we saw a
little summer-house on an island down in the Menakesi creek,
with earthen walls around it; a very neat work, small as it was.
A Brother from Germany had made it for his own pleasure
during a visit here.

We directed our walk up to their burial-place, situated on the
north side of Bethlehem. That was a portion of their orchard
ground, though there were no trees within the graveyard.
During our walk I inquired what ceremonies were used in their
burials. Mr. Benzien answered that there was nothing especially
remarkable, except that the unmarried Brethren bore the corpse;
all appear satisfied and joyful; none are buried without music.

The graveyard, which is by them called "God's Acre," is in
the form of a square, containing about one acre. It is divided
into two halves by a broad walk; as you enter, the right side is
for the women, the left for the men. On both sides the graves
are arranged in three rows. The first is for the married, the
second for the unmarried, the third for children. Each grave is
separate and in a square covered with turf, and flat as a garden-
bed, only a hand's-breadth above the surface of the earth, separated
from each other by straight sanded walks. On the broad walk
was a grave by itself, with a handsome tombstone of white marble
on it. An inscription was cut upon the stone in German, and
the letters filled with lead, so that they could scarcely be read in
the sunshine. The name was *Juliana Nitschman*, with her birth-
place and her death, which was called a going to the "little
lamb" (Lämmlein). I asked why she should be so distinguished
from all the others, and Mr. Benzien answered that her husband
was still there, and that this had been done by his labor and at
his expense. Upon many of the other graves there were only
small flat stones lying loose, with the name and date upon them.
He said, further, that the Brethren were indeed willing to have
such tokens of love over their dead, but they had not yet had
any stone-cutter among them, nor were they in a situation to
pay strangers for such work. In the first grave on the men's
side lay their Bishop, Cammerhoff. There were more graves on
the men's than on the women's side. The line of children's

graves was longer than that of those who were older. Altogether there were about one hundred and eighty. The place is reported to be very healthy, and it is said that there are seldom any sick among them. But when we consider the short time that Bethlehem has stood, and that its inhabitants are Germans, strangers to this climate, the graves also show that death has as great a privilege among them as among others.

During the time that we were there, girls were at play in the graveyard. Their mistresses sat by themselves with some work in their hands. Mr. Benzien's and Mr. Bruzelius' daughters were there, and kissed our hands, and we also kissed them. They talked and laughed as freely as other children.

It was said that the mistresses get up at certain times in the night and engage in singing, and thereby wake up the children. Perhaps some of these are also able to sing along with them. But we saw how the children slept in their meeting during the day, and how much more at night? What is said here of the girls applies also to the boys.

Directly opposite the graveyard, on the other side of the great highway, is the house where the store is kept. We went over there to buy something that was required for our journey. The goods are sold at a reasonable price; some were presented to us, though they were of no great value. The Brethren are not allowed to take out of the store whatever they need or desire without the knowledge of the officers. They are said to live as sparingly as they possibly can; that their Society is still quite poor, and that no one shall be a burden to the others. They have their bread-stuff without pay, mostly from Nazareth. They can also sell to their neighbors the grain that they have need of. Most of that which is required by their necessities they have within themselves; yet several hundred pounds currency more are expended every year than they receive.

We visited the weavers' workshop, the shop of the shoemakers for the unmarried women, as also that of the unmarried Brethren; also the saddlers' shop, in which the work is done partly for the Brethren's use, and partly for that of other people in the country. Mr. Benzien was now minded to show us whatever he could. But we wished to get ourselves ready for our return; however, he said we must still come into the smithy, although it was some-what out of the way. We went thither, but there was no work under way. He wondered where the people had gone. There I talked with a man, but he did not understand English, and very little German. He said he was a Swede, and very glad to see his countrymen there. He related that he was born in the Parish of Wåling, in Sörmanland, whence his ancestors had removed to the city of Scheninge, and that he had left Sweden in 1749. His name was Hasselberg, and his business that of a tinner, but now he was working in copper, brass, and iron, and seemed to be clever at his work. Whilst we were talking Swedish, Benzien seemed to be somewhat disturbed; his eyes flew rapidly from the one to the other to learn what we were talking about. For he had become used to the Swedish whilst he was brought up in Livonia, but could not now recollect a great deal of it. We wondered that we had not before heard that we had a countryman in Bethlehem. Mr. Benzien apologized for himself by saying that he had forgotten to tell us about it. But, undoubtedly, the reason was that he was afraid that we might entice him away if we had time for it. Now he took us there just as we were about to take our departure. The man seemed to be more beloved by the Brethren on account of his work than he loved them for his support. Pastor Unander asked him how he got along there. Just so so; it would not take much to make him bid farewell to Bethlehem. But the crafty Brethren have many arts to retain such simple strangers in their clutches if they see that they are useful to them. Mr. Benzien stated that although the Brethren labor very hard during their work-days, yet nearly half the time is taken for rest. They not only keep the Sabbath-day, which is Saturday, as well as Sunday, but also many festivals and Saints' days during the week.

Finally, we went back over the river to the inn, Mr. Benzien keeping us company to the last. We paid our reckoning to the uttermost farthing, not excepting the ferriage over the river, which is said to be free to those who come to visit the Brethren. But the ferryman had no scruples in taking this as a gift for his trouble. We understood that the hospitality which strangers saw in Bethlehem some years since was now at an end; that there was no house left for strangers, however severe the weather, or poor the inn, or however great the need; that the Brethren at the present time really need all that they have, and that they also have due regard to their interests. Bethlehem is now more populous than ever before, and they are therefore building new dwelling-houses. Many families have come hither who were banished from Herrnhag; many from other places, and now lately from London. But it cannot be concluded from this that they have taken any capital with them, and that the Brotherhood at Bethlehem is more wealthy. We may much rather conclude that when they do not succeed in other places they throng hither, and live as well as they can. At the present time there are three Bishops — Spangenberg, acting as Pater Prior, and having now all things under his direction; Nitschman, a cripple, cannot do anything more for the good of the Church; Hehl, for what purposes I know not. There are five or six of their Ministers, of whom Ritz works as a carpenter, and Bruzelius as a watch-maker.

For the rest, there are nearly as many consuming as supporting members. Their Bishops, Ministers, Elders, and Officers live more expensively than the others. There is a house full of women with children. One does not go many steps upon the hill without meeting a woman with a child in her arms. The number of children in the Children's House is one hundred and forty-four, who have their masters and their mistresses; none of these labor, and yet must have food. We leave out of the question how their housekeeping tallies with their income; that may well be charged among the inscrutable accounts.[1] Yet there is no doubt that they now stand considerably behind-hand, according to their own statement. The land around Bethlehem was mortgaged[2] to Wm. Allen, Esq., as soon as Count Zinzendorff felt his hard blow from a fraudulent bankruptcy. The land around Nazareth, from the beginning to the present time, has laid under mortgage to the Benezet family in Philadelphia.

Meantime, whilst we were preparing ourselves for our journey,

---

[1] Acrelius, during his short visit, could not have attained a full knowledge of the Moravian œconomy, which continued until 1762, and resulted in the prosperity of the Society and of the individuals composing it.—T. W.

[2] This is incorrect. The mortgage referred to was given at the time of the purchase of the land.—T. W.

30

Mr. Benzien desired to know our names, which he wrote down in his note-book. Pastor Brunnholtz inquired whether he thought of putting us into his Journal! He asked in return, Is no Journal kept in your church ? I asked whether he thought of remaining much longer in the country ? He answered that, as he had travelled to so many countries, he was now tired of that, but that if he should again go over to London, he would come back and close his days here. " Then," said I, " you think, sir, that you will remain among the Moravian Brethren until your dying day ? Should you not be still satisfied with your former faith in the Augsburg Confession ? What is the necessity for so many ' inventions,' ' maxims,' ' secrets,' and ' mysteries,' as you have in your Society ? A Christian faith and a Christian life are open-hearted, and not so artificial." He answered, " Be assured, gentlemen, that I was a strict Lutheran, but that doctrine could never satisfy my soul, and never can to all eternity. I find a secret excellence in my Brotherhood which I cannot fully describe, and which will keep me there as long as I live." " Pardon me, sir," said I, " for taking such liberty in conversing with you. But what think you yourself of the condition in which you found yourself when you first had a desire for true godliness ? Perhaps you were then under the guidance of blind leaders, who so led you under the terrors of the law, that you did not once dare to think of any consolation by the Gospel of Christ. But now, since you have got a real taste of precious grace, other teachers have led your thoughts to such a freedom that you have a hatred to all that is called law, sorrow for sin, and improvement; in regard to which you have hitherto kept yourself altogether in extremes, both of which are by-paths, but not the middle way, which is the right way. I confess, honestly, that as soon as I saw your face, I took you for one of those who, some twenty years since, were their own martyrs under the law, and most cruelly mortified themselves for the sake of their own righteousness, and nothing else. Of these, you know, sir, Livonia had enough in that day, as well as other countries, as also that the greater part of them went over to the Moravian Brotherhood. I am greatly mistaken, if you are not one of them."

He answered, "It is true enough that I was once under the guidance of such blind leaders. I had no rest nor peace in my heart. All was dark and terrible before my eyes. Those who kept me company went out with me into the fields. We lay upon our knees until I had worn off the skin from the caps of mine, and I could scarcely drag myself home again. Notwithstanding this, my soul was as lean and empty as before. Many of those who then held companionship with me now live as carelessly as ever in the world. Our leaders were the blind Hallensians, who themselves knew no better, and would soon have made an end of us, both in soul and body, if the Saviour had not come to our aid."

Pastor Brunnholtz here took up the conversation, and said, " I am a Holsteiner by my birth, and I have also studied in the University of Halle; but, so far as I know, no such errors ever came out of that place. The pure evangelical doctrine was taught there and preached in my time, and ever since. It is true, that the Theological Faculty at Halle has fought hard against Count Zinzendorff and his adherents, but that is no proof that they are erroneous in the doctrines of salvation," etc.

Mr. Benzien proceeded. " Certain as I am that the infection was in Halle, as well as in other places, and that many went out thence who infected others; yet am I equally certain that if your fathers, Francke, Horbius, etc., were living, you would see them hold with us, but not with you." " That is idle talk," said Pastor Brunnholtz, " and is easier said than proved. These men were not reeds driven hither and thither by every wind of doctrine," etc.

As the words seemed to come out pretty strong, the voice to rise higher, and the blood to boil in the veins, on both sides, I thought it best to terminate the conversation in this wise. " My friends, we have associated together for two days in peace, let us now, therefore, separate in peace. It is possible that, if we had opportunity for more intercourse, we might understand each other better. It would be a pleasure to me to see Mr. Benzien in my house, and I am assured of the same in regard to my brethren and fellow-travellers, when we recall to mind the great trouble that we have given him here in Bethlehem, and we assure him that we have great regard for his person and character, although we do not agree in our doctrinal views." And thereupon we took leave.

These are the remarks upon the Brotherhood in Bethlehem suggested by the circumstances of our visit. However slight they are, they yet give some idea of the character of that place. Some may think more, others less, of them, especially as that sect and its friends proclaim it to be Paradise itself, and have made their Bethlehem known all over the world. Others again represent it as declining, and so of less account than it really is. That we have not gone further in our remarks is not for want of attention, but of occasion. Those who rightly know that class of people, and what mysteries they have among themselves, will not suppose that some travellers could, within a few hours spent in their society, make any great discoveries. Many hundreds may go thither and not arrive at the half of what we saw. It is enough that they say that they have much which ought not to be revealed to the world, and also that, if it happens to slip out, it is just that of which they are most ashamed. To be convicted of untruths will never make them blush or turn pale. Those who have for some time lived in their Society, and afterwards turned their back upon them, are the best witnesses of their condition.

APPENDIX.

REGISTER of members of the Moravian Church, and of persons attached to said church, in this country and abroad, between 1727 and 1754, has just been prepared for the Transactions of the Moravian Historical Society, by the Rev. William C. Reichel, of Bethlehem. The introduction thereto, and that portion relating to New Jersey, are here given as an appropriate appendix to the work of Acrelius.

This contribution to the early history of the Moravian Church in the northern British Colonies of America, is based upon a record of members of its congregations, which the Rev. Abraham Reincke made, in the course of his ministry in this country, between the years 1744 and 1760. The record, though meagre, is an unusually interesting one, in as far as in its entirety it acquaints us with the men and women, who, in various ways, wrought together in the beginnings of a religious movement, which, with remarkable singleness of purpose, aimed at the extension of Christ's kingdom upon earth. It carries us back, in fact, to the very origin of the Renewed Church of the United Brethren (better known in this country as the Moravian Church), — to that time when, among the Moravian and Bohemian refugees settled in the village of Herrnhut, in Saxony, there was a blending of spirits by which they were knit together into a brotherhood, and thereby strengthened to enter upon a mission for which they believed themselves to have been specially called.

It was from Herrnhut that the infant Church sent out her first evangelists. Thence, too, her religious teachers went forth, seeking, wheresoever they came, those who were in spiritual darkness, or doubt, or in bondage to sin, that they might instruct them in the way of salvation. From Saxony they passed into the other states of Germany and the Continent; next into Great Britain, and then into the North American Colonies of the British Crown.

The Province of Pennsylvania, which, since 1718, had been annually receiving large accessions to its population from the states of Germany, chiefly from the Rhineland, was, we are told, one of the first foreign fields which arrested the attention of the Moravians of Herrnhut as having a claim upon their Christian philanthropy. And it was, in fact, the necessitous condition in spiritual things of the Pennsylvania Palatine, as much as the heathenism of the North American Indian, which induced the Moravians to send evangelists, and then colonies, into the New World. Such was the beginning of the Moravian Church in America. With the agents in this transatlantic movement inaugurated by the Brethren, and with those who were brought under its influence, the major part of the register which constitutes the subject-matter of this paper is concerned. The spirit which pervaded this movement, the policy and mode according to which it was prosecuted, and its success, are matters of history. No farther comment on either is necessary, save such as may serve to elucidate terms employed occasionally by the recorder, in the rubrics of his several enumerations, and allusions made by the editor, in the course of his necessarily brief historical introductions.

As was intimated above, the early Moravians were deeply impressed with the belief that it was their Church's mission to extend the Redeemer's kingdom. Hence they not only obeyed the last injunction of their Divine Master to his disciples literally, as often as they sent out missionaries into the dark corners of the earth, but they also sought, wherever occasion offered, to preach and teach Christ in Christian countries, to those who were ignorant of him, or who, as they believed, failed to apprehend him aright. No wonder, then, that on their arrival in this country, the condition of the religiously destitute Germans of this and the adjacent Provinces enlisted their sympathies. They found them without church organizations, without places of worship in the rural districts, and without a stated ministry; — themselves become neglectful of or indifferent to the things of God, and their children growing up in ignorance. These they now visited in the character of evangelists, preaching the Gospel, and administering the sacraments to them in houses, or in barns, and gathering their children together in schools. At some points they organized congregations, and then incorporated them with their Church, at others they formed the attendants upon their ministry into "Societies," — content to have the members of these adhere to the tenets of Luther or Calvin, and to the churches of their birth and education, provided such a course would only secure them willing hearers of the Word of God. For ten years this Catholic work, on the part of the Moravian Church, was carried on with surprising energy, and whether we consider the men who engaged in it, the field in which they wrought, the difficulties under which they labored, the activity which they displayed, and the faith by which they were actuated — it will always remain an interesting chapter in the early annals of that Church in America.

Abraham Reincke, a son of Peter Reincke, merchant, and Magdalene, m. n. Petersen, his wife, was born on the 17th of April, 1712, in Stockholm, Sweden. In his eighteenth year, at the instance of his mother, who designed her son for the Church, he was sent to Wollmirstadt, near Magdeburg, in Prussia, to pursue a course of liberal studies under the direction of his uncle, Pastor Jacob Petersen, who was a Lutheran clergyman in that place. In his house he remained two years, and then entered the gymnasium, or high-school, in Brandenburg, old town. Here, he tells us, he became deeply concerned about the welfare of his soul, having been moved to a serious consideration of spiritual things by the godly walk and conversation of the co-rector of the academy. In this frame of mind young Reincke, in 1735, repaired to Jena. It was at the time of a religious revival among the students of that then world-famed University. Peter Boehler, from Frankfort-on-the-Main, was one of these, and by him the subject of this notice was counselled in his distress, and led eventually to unite with a brotherhood of young disciples of Christ, which included in its ranks men who subsequently became shining lights in the Moravian Church. To this brotherhood belonged Christian Renatus, the son of Count Zinzendorf, after whom it was named "Christian's Economy." Accompanying this association in its movements, in 1738, we find him in Berlin engaged with several of his comrades in reporting a series of discourses[1] which the Count held in that capital,— and subsequently a second time in Jena. In the autumn of the last-mentioned year he was admitted to church fellowship with the Brethren, at the castle of Marienborn, in consequence of which step he incurred the sore and lasting displeasure of his father.

Having spent upwards of a year in St. Petersburg, where he preached the Gospel, and acted as tutor in the family of Baron von Nolken, counsellor for the Swedish Legation in that city, he returned to Marienborn in June of 1741. In December following he was sent to England, and labored in the Gospel in London and Yorkshire. In 1744 he returned to the Continent, and in July óf that year, at Herrndyk, Utrecht, married Susan Stockberg, from Sunmoer, Norway. This was preparatory to his departure to the New World, whither he had been called by the authorities of the Church of his adoption.

In company with Bishop Spangenberg, accordingly, he sailed from Amsterdam in the autumn of 1744, for New York, and arrived at Bethlehem on the 9th of November. Of Mr. Reincke's career in the ministry in this country, we will state the following facts : Having itinerated in West Jersey among the descendants of the early Swedish settlers, to whom he preached in their native tongue, he was in November of 1745 settled at Nazareth, where he filled the office of "Ordinary" until in May of 1747. Thence he removed to Philadelphia, preached in the Moravian church in that city, and for a second time itinerated in West Jersey, and along the shores of Delaware Bay. We find him next in Lancaster, then at Bethlehem, and in the summer of 1751 a second time in Philadelphia. The following years were spent by him in visiting the rural congregations of his church, during which

---

[1] "*Des Herrn Grafen von Zinzendorfs einiger œffentlichen Reden, welche im Jahr 1738 vom Januario bis zu Ende des Aprils in Berlin an die Frauens Personen daselbst gehalten worden.*" Leipsic und Altona, 1749.

period he dedicated a house of worship in the Pennsylvania Minisinks, and also opened a door for the Moravian Gospel ministry in "The Oblong," on the eastern confines of the Province of New York. His last charge was the Moravian congregation in New York city. In consequence of failing health, he retired to Bethlehem in 1754, where, in addition to assisting in the ecclesiastical affairs of that church, he was employed as a copyist, a writer of diaries, and appointed custodian of the Archives. His wife died on the 31st of August, 1758. He followed her to the eternal world on the 7th of April, 1760.

Abraham Reincke was the father of two children, one of whom, Abraham, born in June of 1752, in Philadelphia, survived him, and entered the Church. He was settled at Heidelberg, Hebron, York, Litiz, Lancaster, Hope, and Nazareth, during his long ministry, and died at Litiz in February of 1833. Abraham Reincke, Jr., was the father of six children, to wit: Abraham, who died while a tutor in Nazareth Hall, in 1806; Mary Susan, who died in Lancaster in 1793; Mary Theresa, who married the late Christian Busse of Nazareth, and who is still living; Johanna Augusta, who married the late John Beck of Litiz, and who is still living; Benjamin Rudolph, who died while a pupil at Nazareth Hall, in 1810; and Samuel, born at Litiz, 12th August, 1791 — ordained a Bishop of the Moravian Church in October of 1858, and residing at Bethlehem, Pa., whose three sons, Amadeus A., Edwin E., and Clement L., are all in the ministry — the first, pastor of the Moravian congregation in New York city (he was ordained a Bishop in August of 1870); the second, Superintendent of the Jamaica Moravian Mission; and the third, a Professor in the Moravian Theological Seminary at Bethlehem, Pa.

In annotating this register, the editor has availed himself of material he drew from various authorities in the course of researches conducted by him in the field of early Moravian history. He trusts that this essay at illustrating some of its pages may gratify the antiquarian student; and should its perusal induce such a one, or others, to prosecute farther research in the almost inexhaustible mine in which he has occasionally wrought, the time and labor expended upon this effort will cause him no regret.   W. C. R.

BETHLEHEM, PA., Oct. 1, 1873.

NEW JERSEY

1748.

Paul Daniel Pryzelius, who had been ordained a Minister of the Gospel by Bishop David Nitschmann in January of 1743, was thereupon sent by Zinzendorf to preach the Gospel to the descendants of the early Swedish settlers on the shores of the Delaware, and Delaware Bay. His appointments were on Maurice River, Cohansey, Penn's Neck, Raccoon, Ammasland, Potomock, and Calkoen's Hook. He labored in this mission for upwards of two years. Meanwhile, however, the Swedish churches had been supplied with pastors from abroad, the Moravian movement met with opposition at their hands, and in 1745 Pryzelius was recalled. But the Brethren, nevertheless, continued to minister to the spiritual wants of such families as had become attached to them, visiting them in their houses, and preaching, also, wherever they found a church or school-house unoccupied. It was seldom, accordingly, that one or more of their evangelists from Bethlehem or Philadelphia were not on the circuit of the old Swedish settlements in Delaware, in the interval between 1745 and 1755. Among these were the Brethren, Owen Rice, Matthew Reuz, Abraham Reincke, Sven Roseen, Hector Gambold, and Thomas Yarrel.

At the date of this register (1748) there were four principal points in this domestic mission, viz.: Raccoon, Piles' Grove, Penn's Neck, and Maurice River.

1. RACCOON.

The old Swedish church, which, according to Evans' map of 1755, stood on Beaver Creek (about five miles above its mouth), within the limits of Gloucester County, and which was standing within the recollection of men living, was closed on Pryzelius in December of 1744, and thereupon to all Moravian evangelists.

NAMES OF PERSONS ATTACHED TO THE BRETHREN IN RACCOON.

Dennis, Thomas.
Guest, William, and wife.
Gill, Matthew,   do.

Halton, James, and wife.
Hopman, Andrew.
Hopman, Lawrence.

Jones, Stephen.
Jones, John, (widower.)
Kyn, John.
Lock, John, and wife.
Lawrence, Nathaniel.
Matson, Peter.
Matson, Matthew.

Matson, Jacob.
Mullicas, Eric.
Petersen, Zacharias.
Rambo, Peter, and wife.
Sehnes, Robert, (Quaker.)
Stanton, William.
Wallace, William.

2. PILES' GROVE.

In December of 1747, the Brethren were preaching in a church on Oldman's Creek, in Piles' Grove, then building for them by friends of theirs (principally English, some Germans, however, and others, descendants of the early Dutch and Swedish settlers) residing in Raccoon and Piles' Grove. It was five miles distant from the old Raccoon church, within the limits of Gloucester County, and was dedicated to the worship of God in 1749, by Bishop Spangenberg and Pastor Lawrence T. Nyberg.

NAMES OF PERSONS ATTACHED TO THE BRETHREN IN PILES' GROVE.

Avis, George.
Dahlberg, ——, and wife.
Dorsaw, Charles.
Holstein, Andrew.
Holstein, Lawrence, Sr.
Holstein, Lawrence, Jr.
Hopman, Lars.
Kett, Michael.
Kyn, Mouns.
Lauterbach, Peter.
Lehberger, Adam.
Lynch, Samuel.

Linmeyer, Christoper.
Lloyd, Bateman.
Lloyd, Obadiah.
Mueller, Alexander.
Roalin, John.
Samson, (Lynch's slave.)
Van Immen, Garret, and wife.
Van Immen, John,   do.
Van Immen, William,   do.
Van Immen, Andrew,   do.
Wood, Jechoniah.
Wood, Jeremiah.

3. PENN'S NECK.

At the date of this register, the Brethren again occupied the pulpit of a church that stood in this district, perhaps either in Salem, or near the site of Fort Elfinsboro'. It is stated by Moravian writers of that day to have been seven miles distant from the church on Oldman's Creek, in Piles' Grove. In 1746 its doors had been closed on Moravian preachers.

NAMES OF PERSONS ATTACHED TO THE BRETHREN IN PENN'S NECK.

Bartelsen, Sarah, (widow.)
Cornelius, Carl, and wife.
Graceberry, William, and wife.
Kalkloeser, ——.
Masslander, Abraham.

Philpott, William, and wife.
Philpott, Nicholas,   do.
Senecksen, Senec,   do.
Van Immen, Jacob,   do.
Van Immen, Peter,   do.

4. MAURICE RIVER.

Thirty-six miles south-east from the Penn's Neck church, and on the bank of Maurice River, stood a meeting-house, which had been built for the use of the Brethren, and then dedicated to the worship of God by Abraham Reincke, Pastor Lawrence T. Nyberg, Owen Rice, and Matthew Reutz, Dec. 18th, 1746. From this point the resident missionary would occasionally itinerate by way of Cape May, along the Jersey shore, as far as Great and Little Egg Harbors.

NAMES OF PERSONS RESIDING ON MAURICE RIVER ATTACHED TO THE
BRETHREN.

Cabb, Samuel, and Catherine, his
    wife.
Camp, Paul.
Hopman, Nicholas, and wife.
Hopman, John,   do.
Hopman, Peter,   do.
Hopman, Frederic,   do.
Jones, Joseph.
Jones, Abraham, and wife.
Kyn, Eric,   do.
Lommus, ——.
Masslander, Peter.
Margaret, ——, (widow.)

Mullicas, Stephen, and wife.
Mullicas, Eric,   do.
Petersen, Lucas.
Petersen, Lars, and wife.
Petersen, Aaron.
Petersen, Thomas.
Powell, Gabriel.
Purple, ——.
Shiloh, an Indian.
Van Immen, Samuel, and wife.
Van Immen, David.
Van Immen, Peter.
Van Immen, Gabriel.

SUPPLEMENT.

Abraham Reincke's private record of official acts performed among his countrymen and others, in New Jersey, on Delaware, during his occasional ministry in the Brethren's mission of that Province.

1. *Baptisms.*

April 18, 1745. — *Eric,* infant son of Eric and Catherine Kyn, of Maurice River, born Dec. 25, 1744. The act was performed in Goevan Kyn's house.

May 4, 1745. — *Deborah,* infant daughter of Lorenz and Molly Hopman. On the same day, *Seth Samuel,* infant son of Samuel and Sarah Ward. Both acts were performed in Lorenz Hopman's house in Raccoon.

May 7, 1745. — *Priscilla,* infant daughter of John and Rebecca Locke. The act was performed in the parents' house in Raccoon. She died in Aug., 1748.

June 20, 1745. — *Elizabeth,* infant daughter of Nicholas and —— Philpott. The act was performed in the church in Penn's Neck.

June 21, 1745. — *Mary,* infant daughter of John and Rachel Kyn. The act was performed in the parsonage in Raccoon.

June 22, 1745. — *Margaret,* infant daughter of John and Margaret Roal (the father a Swede, the mother Irish). The act was performed in William Graceberry's house, in Piles' Grove.

June 27, 1745. — *Jeremiah,* infant son of Lars and Susan Petersen, in the new church on Maurice River, at the close of the first sermon preached within its walls.

Dec. 18, 1746. — *Rebecca,* infant daughter of Abraham and Gunla Jones, born Dec. 5. On the same day, *Elizabeth,* infant daughter of Abraham and Elizabeth Masslander. Also, *William,* infant son of Samuel and Caroline Cabb. These families are all residing on Maurice River. The act was performed in the church on Maurice River, immediately after its dedication to the worship of God.

Oct. 20, 1748. — *Christina,* infant daughter of Christoph and Anna Linmeyer, born in Piles' Grove, in West Jersey, March 27, 1748. The act was performed in the new church on Oldman's Creek, on the twentieth Sunday after Trinity. Garret van Immen and William Guest, and their wives, were sponsors.

Nov. 24, 1748. — *Rebecca,* infant daughter of John and Rebecca Locke, born in Raccoon, Oct. 31, 1748. The act was performed in the father's house, in the presence of Garret van Immen, John Jones, old Stephen Jones, Eric Mullicas, and ten other witnesses.

Nov. 27, 1748. — *Mary,* infant daughter of Lorenz and Molly Holstein, born in Piles' Grove, Nov. 11, 1748. The act was performed in Yerred van Emmen's house. (N. B. Her mother deceased on the 19th of Nov., eight days after the birth of the child, and was buried near the new church on Oldman's Creek.   Hers was the first interment there, after the erection of the church.)

Nov. 30, 1748. — *Frederic*, infant son of Frederic and Catherine Hopman, born on Maurice River, Aug. 1, 1748.   The act was performed in the church on Maurice River, at the close of the Swedish sermon.

Jan. 19, 1751. — *Abraham*, infant son of Frederic and Catherine Hopman, born in *Marantico*, Dec. 10, 1750.   The act was performed in the father's house in *Marantico*.

Jan. 20, 1751. — *Sarah*, infant daughter of Joseph and Margaret Jones, born Oct. 30, 1750, at *Menomuskin*.   The act was performed in the church on Maurice River.

Jan. 22, 1751. — *Catherine*, infant daughter of William and Christina Guest, born Nov. 18, 1750, in Raccoon.   The act was performed in our church on Oldman's Creek.

April 21, 1751. — *Mary*, infant daughter of Matthew and Mary Gill, born in Raccoon, March 16, 1751.   The act was performed in the father's house.

April 12, 1752. — *Charity*, infant daughter of Obadiah and Rebecca Lloyd, born in Piles' Grove, March 12, 1752.   The act was performed "at the close of the public service in our church on Oldman's Creek."

August 16, 1752. — *James*, infant son of George and Jane Avis, born in Piles' Grove, Dec. 2, 1751.   The act was performed in the church on Oldman's Creek.

2. *Marriages.*

June 8, 1745. — George Kyn, a widower, aged 64, to Margaret Justis, a widow, aged 53, after the bans had been thrice published — first in Raccoon, next in Penn's Neck, and for the last time in Maurice River. The ceremony was performed in the groom's house on Maurice River, in the presence of the entire Swedish congregation of said neighborhood.

INDEX.

[Where the article cited is not in the text, it may be found in the notes.]

445

31

THE

HISTORICAL SOCIETY OF PENNSYLVANIA.

FUND

FOR THE PUBLICATION OF ORIGINAL, AND THE REPRINT OF RARE AND
VALUABLE WORKS ON STATE AND NATIONAL HISTORY.

A payment of twenty-five dollars obtains the right to receive, during life, a copy of each publication; for Libraries, twenty years. Subscriptions may be made to the Librarian, at the Hall of the Society, No. 820 Spruce Street, to the Secretary, or to the Collector.

WORKS ALREADY PUBLISHED:

History of Braddock's Expedition.
Contributions to American History, 1858.
Record of Upland, and Denny's Military Journal.
Republication of Memoirs of the Society, Vol. I.
Minutes of the Committee of Defence of Philadelphia.
Penn and Logan Correspondence, Vol. I.
Penn and Logan Correspondence, Vol. II.
Acrelius's New Sweden.   Translated by REYNOLDS.

LIST OF SUBSCRIBERS

TO THE

PUBLICATION FUND.

Abbett, Henry M., Baltimore
Aertsen, James M., Germantown
Agnew, Daniel, Beaver Court-House,
  Beaver County
Allen, Samuel, Hainesport, Burling-
  ton County, N. J.
Allen, William H.
Allibone, Thomas
Alofsen, Solomon, Holland

Alter, Solomon
Altemus, S. T.
Anspach, Jr., John
†Archer, Ellis S., New York
†Armstrong, Edward, Germantown
Arnold, Frederick K., Portland, Ore-
  gon
Arnold, Simon W.
Arrott, William

† Deceased.

(459)

†Ashbridge, William
Ashhurst, Henry
Ashhurst, John
Ashhurst, Jr., John
†Ashhurst, Richard
Ashhurst, Jr., Richard
Ashhurst, Richard L.
†Ashmead, Samuel B.
Ashton, Samuel K., Germantown
Askin, J. Henry, Radnor, Del. Co.
Atlee, Washington L.
†Audenried, Lewis
Austin, John B.

†Bache, Franklin
†Backus, F. R.
Bailey, E. Westcott
Baird, Alexander
Baird, Henry C.
Baird, John
Baird, Matthew
Baird, William M.
Baker, Joseph B.
†Baker, R. L., Economy, Beaver Co.
Balch, Thomas
Bald, J. Dorsey
†Balderston, Jonathan
†Baldwin, Matthias W.
Ball, George W.
Bancroft, George, New York
†Barton, Isaac
†Barton, Thomas Pennant, N. Y.
Bates, Joseph William
Bayard, Thos. F., Wilmington, Del.
†Beck, Charles F.
Bell, Miss Helen
Benners, William J., Germantown
†Benson, Jr., Alexander
Besson, Charles A.
Bettle, Samuel
Bettle, William
Betton, Thomas F., Germantown
Biddle, Alexander
†Biddle, Charles J.
Biddle, Clement
Biddle, Edward C.
Biddle, Henry D.
Biddle, James S.
Biddle, Thomas A.
Bigler, William, Clearfield
Blanchard, William A.
Bleck, Ernest F., Bethlehem
Blight, Atherton
Boardman, Henry A.
Boker, Charles S.
Boller, Frederick J.

†Bond, James
Bond, L. Montgomery
Borie, Adolphe E.
Borie, Charles L.
Bourquin, Frederick
Bowen, Ezra
Boyd, W. Stokes, Nice, France
†Bradish, Luther, New York
Brady, Patrick
†Breck, Samuel
Brereton, Thomas J., Pittsburg
Brewster, Benjamin Harris
Brick, Samuel R.
Bringhurst, John H.
Brock, John P.
Brockie, William, Germantown
Broomall, John M., Chester
Brotherhead, William
Brown, D. P., Pottsville
Brown, David S.
†Brown, Frederick
†Brown, John A.
†Brown, Joseph D.
†Brown, Washington
Browne, Charles, Boston, Mass.
Browne, N. B.
Browning, Edward
Brunot, Felix R., Pittsburg
Buchanan, R., Cincinnati, Ohio
†Buck, Francis N., Chestnut Hill
Buck, William J., Jenkintown
Bullitt, John C.
†Bunting, Jacob T.
†Burgin, George H.
Burnham, George
Burroughs, Horatio N.
Burt, Nathaniel, Lancaster Co.
Busch, Edward
Bushnell, Charles J., New York
†Bushnell, N., Quincy, Illinois
†Butler, John M.

Cabeen, Francis von A.
Cadwalader, John
Cadwalader, Richard M.
Cadwalader, William
†Caldcleugh, William George
Caldwell, James E.
Camac, J. Burgess, Paris, France
Campbell, Archibald, Germantown
†Cannell, S. Wilmer, Beechwood,
     Philadelphia County
Carey, Henry C.
Carpenter, Edward, Hanover Mills,
     Burlington County, N. J.
Carpenter, J. Edward

†Dundas, James
Dungan, Charles B.
†Dunlap, Thomas

Earl, Harrison
Earle, James S.
Early, William
†Eckert, George N.
Eddy, Richard, Gloucester, Mass.
Eisenbrey, Edwin T.
Eisenbrey, William Harrison
Eldridge, G. Morgan
Elkin, S.
†Elliott, Isaac
†Ellis, Charles
Ellis, Thomas H., Richmond, Va.
Ellmaker, Peter C.
Elwyn, Alfred Langdon
†Ely, John
Ely, Miss Louisa
Ely, Richard Elias, New Hope, Bucks
    County
Ely, William, New Brighton, Beaver
    County
Emery, Titus S.
Emley, Gilbert
Emory, Charles
Emory, John, Montgomery County
†Errickson, Michael
Evans, Horace
Evans, Joseph R.
†Evans, J. Wistar, Germantown
†Everett, Edward, Boston, Mass.

Fagan, George R.
†Fagan, John
†Fahnestock, B. A.
†Fahnestock, George W.
†Fallon, Christopher, Delaware Co.
Fallon, John
Farmer, James S.
†Farnum, John
Fay, William A.
Fell, Franklin
Fell, J. Gillingham
Felton, S. M., Chester
†Fennimore, Jason L.
Fernon, Thomas S.
Field, Francis K.
Firmstone, William, Easton
Fish, A. J.
†Fisher, Charles Henry, Brookwood,
    Philadelphia
Fisher, Miss Elizabeth R., Wake-
    field, Germantown
Fisher, J. B.

†Fisher, J. Francis, Alverthorpe
Flanagan, James M.
Flanagan, Stephen
Fitler, Edwin H.
Foltz, Jonathan M.
Foote, William Henry, Romney, Va.
†Forster, Jr., William B.
†Foulke, William Parker
Foust, Robert M.
†Fox, Charles P., Champ-lost, Phila.
Fox, Miss Mary D., Champ-lost,
    Philadelphia
Fox, Philip L.
Fox, William Logan
Fraley, Frederick
Franciscus, A. H.
Freas, P. R., Germantown
Freeman, Chapman
Freytag, Godfrey, Germany
†Fuller, Henry M.
†Fullerton, Alexander
Furness, Horace Howard

Gardette, Emile B.
Garrard, Kenner, U. S. Army
Garrard, Lewis H., Westervelt, Minn.
Garrett, Thomas C., Germantown
Garrett, Walter
Garrett, Jr., William E.
†Gaul, Frederick
Gaw, Alexander G.
†Gerhard, Benjamin
Gibbons, Charles
Gibson, Jr., George, U. S. Army
Gibson, Henry C.
†Gilbert, David
Gilbert, John
†Gillis, John P., U. S. Navy, Wil-
    mington, Del.
†Gilpin, Henry D.
Goforth, John
†Gordon, N. P.
†Gorgas, John, Wilmington, Del.
Graff, Frederick
†Graham, James D., U. S. Army
Grant, Jr., Samuel
Grant, William S.
†Gratz, Robert H.
Gray, Andrew C., New Castle, Del.
Greble, Edwin
†Greeves, James R.
†Gries, John M.
Griffiths, Jr., William F.
†Grigg, John
Grimshaw, Arthur H., Wilmington,
    Del.

Jordan, Francis
Jordan, Jr., John
Justice, Philip S.

Kane, Robert P.
Kane, Thomas L., Kane, McKean County
Kay, J. Alfred
Keating, William V.
Keim, De B. Randolph, Reading
Keim, George De B., Pottsville
†Keim, George M., Reading
Kelley, William D.
†Kelly, Charles, Kellyville
Kemble, William H.
†Kempton, James C., Manayunk
Kent, Rodolphus, Gwynedd, Montgomery County
Kent, William C.
Kern, William H.
Kessler, Jr., John
Keyser, Charles S.
†Keyser, Peter A.
†Kimball, Stephen
Kimber, Jr., Thomas
King, C. Murray
King, D. Rodney
†King, Robert P.
Kirkbride, Thomas S.
†Kirkham, William
Kirkpatrick, Edwin
Kirtley, Thomas H.
Kneass, Strickland
Kneedler, J. S.
Knight, Edward C.
Knowles, George L.
Koecker, Leonard R.
†Kramer, Allen
†Kuhn, Hartman
†Kuhn, J. Hamilton

Lambdin, James R., Germantown
Lambert, John
Landreth, Oliver
Lardner, James L., U. S. Navy
Lardner, Richard Penn, Graydon, Montgomery County
Larimer, Jr., William, Omaha, Neb.
†Latimer, John R., Wilmington, Del.
Laux, James B.
Lea, Henry C.
Lea, Isaac
Lee, George F.
Leedom, Benjamin, J., Germantown
†Leibert, James, Bethlehem
Lejée, William R.

Lenox, James, New York
†Lennig, Frederick
†Levering, Lemuel S.
†Levy, Lyon Joseph
†Lewis, Ellis
Lewis, George T.
Lewis, Henry
Lewis, John T.
†Lewis, Mordecai D.
Lick, John H., San José, California
Linn, John B., Harrisburg
Linn, J. Merrill, Lewisburg, Union County
†Lindsay, John
Lippincott, J. B.
Littell, C. Willing, Germantown
Littell, John S., Wilmington, Del.
†Livermore, George, Boston, Mass.
†Lloyd, Franklin, Bay City, Michigan
Locke, Zebulon
Logan, J. Dickinson, Baltimore
†Longnecker, Henry C., Allentown
Longstreth, William C.
Loper, Richard F., Stonington, Conn.
Lovering, Joseph S., Oak Hill, Phila.
Lowry, Robert O.
†Ludewig, Herman E., New York
†Lukens, Casper P.
Lukens, Henry Clay
Library, Athenæum, Philadelphia
Library, Athenæum, West Chester
Library, Carpenters' Comp'y, Phila.
Library, Cliosophic Society, Princeton, N. J.
Library Company, Philadelphia, two copies
Library, Delaware County Institute of Science, Media
Library, Lafayette College, Easton
Library Association, Portland, Oregon
Library, Presbyterian Historical Society, Philadelphia
Library of Cincinnati, The, Cincinnati, Ohio
Library of Seminary, Bethlehem
Library of Seminary, Nazareth
Library of Seminary, Salem, N. C.
Library of State, Boston, Mass.
Library of State, Harrisburg
Library of Swarthmore College, Delaware County
Library, Wilmington Institute, Wilmington, Del.

McAllister, John A.

McAllister, Wardale G., N. Y.
McArthur, Jr., John
†McCall, George A., West Chester
McCall, Harry
McCall, John C.
McCammon, David C.
†McCanles, John
McCauley, Edwin H., Lebanon
McDowell, Robert, Slatington, Lehigh County
McElhone, John J., Washington, D.C.
McHenry, George, London, England
†McHenry, Isaac, Pittsburg
McIntyre, Archibald
McKean, H. Pratt, Germantown
McKibben, William C.
McMahon, George W.
McMichael, Morton

†Macalester, Charles
Maceuen, Malcolm
Mackellar, Thomas
Maddock, Edward
Magarge, Charles, Germantown
Magee, James
Malone, Benjamin
Man, William, London, Eng.
Mann, William B.
Markley, Edward C.
Marsh, Benjamin V.
†Marshall, Benjamin
†Martin, George H.
Martin, John Hill
Mason, Samuel
†Massey, Robert V.
Mathias, John T., Baltimore, Md.
Maule, Edward
Maus, Philip F., Danville
Maxwell, Henry D., Easton
Maxwell, Volney L., Wilkes-Barré
Meconkey, David, West Chester
Megargee, Sylvester J.
Mellor, Thomas, Chelton Hills
Menzies, William, New York
†Meredith, William M.
†Mercer, Singleton A.
†Merrick, Samuel V.
Messchert, M. H.
Michener, Israel
Michener, John H.
†Michler, Peter S., Easton
Mickley, Joseph J.
†Middleton, E. P.
Middleton, Nathan
Mifflin, Samuel W., Columbia
Miles, Edward Harris

†Miller, Andrew
Miller, E. Spencer
Miller, John, Oxford, Chester Co.
Milliken, James
†Miner, Charles, Wilkes-Barré
Miskey, William F.
Mitchell, James T.
Mitchell, John C.
†Mitchell, John K.
†Mitchell, Thomas S.
Mitchell, William A.
Moore, Bloomfield H.
Moreau, John B., New York
Morris, Anthony S.. Pemberton, N. J.
Morris, Casper
Morris, Charles M.
Morris, Israel
†Morris, Jacob G.
Morris, Wistar
Muhlenberg, Heister H., Reading
Muirheid, Charles H.
Munsell, Joel, Albany, N. Y.
Murray, James B., Pittsburg
Murray, Joseph A., Carlisle
Myers, Joseph B.

Neill, John
Newbold, James S.
Newbold, John S.
†Newbold, Thomas H.
†Newbold, William H.
Newell, Samuel
Newhall, Thomas A., Germantown
†Newkirk, Matthew
Newland, Edward
Nicholson, James B.
Nicholson, Richard L.
Norris, George W.
Norris, Isaac
†Norris, Samuel
†Notman, John

Ogden, Charles S.
Ogden, John M.
Okie, J. Brognard
†Orne, James H.

Packer, E. A., New York
Palmer, Jonathan
Pardee, A., Hazleton
Parker, John B.
Parrish, Charles, Wilkes-Barré
†Parrish, George D., Burlington Co.,
  New Jersey
Parrish, Samuel
Parry, Richard Randolph

Parry, Charles T.
Paschall, Robert S.
Patten, William
Patterson, Robert
Patterson, Robert
Paul, Bettle
Paul, James
Paul, James W.
Pawson, James
†Paxton, Joseph R.
†Peabody, George, London, Eng.
Peace, Edward
Peirce, William S.
Pemberton, Israel
†Penn, Granville John, Pennsylvania
  Castle, Isle of Portland, Eng.
Pennock, Mrs. Caroline, Howellville,
  Delaware County
Pepper, George S.
†Pepper, Henry
Pepper, Lawrence S.
†Peters, Francis
Phillips, Henry M.
Phillips, Horace
Phillips, Moro
Pickett, John T., Washington, D. C.
Plate, J. Theophilus, New York
†Platt, Jr., William
†Pleasants, Samuel
†Plitt, George
Porter, William A.
Potts, Joseph D.
Potts, William John, Camden, N. J.
Powell, Washington B.
Powers, Thomas H.
Preston, Miss Ann, Stockport, Wayne
  County
†Preston, Paul S., Stockport
Price, Eli K.
Price, J. Sergeant
†Price, Richard
†Priestly, Jos. R., Northumberland
†Primrose, William
†Pringle, James S.
Purves, William
Putnam, George P., New York

Quay, Matthew S., Beaver Court-
  House, Beaver County

†Randall, Josiah
Randall, Robert E.
Randolph, Edward T.
Randolph, Evan
†Randolph, Nathaniel
Rau, Edward H.

Rawle, William Brooke
Read, Jr., John M., Albany
Reed, William B., New York
Reeves, Samuel J.
Remington, Thomas P.
Repplier, George S.
Repplier, John G.
†Repplier, Joseph M.
Resor, Jacob, Cincinnati, Ohio
Rice, John
Richardson, Richard
Richardson, Thomas
Riggs, George W., Washington, D.C.
†Ritter, Jacob B.
Robbins, John
†Roberts, Algernon S.
Roberts, Charles
Roberts, George H.
Roberts, Solomon W.
Roberts, William R.
Robins, Thomas
†Robinson, Hanson, New Castle
  County, Delaware
Roepper, William Theodore, Bethle-
  hem
†Rogers, Alfred W.
Rogers, Charles H.
Rogers, Fairman
Rorer, David, Burlington, Iowa
Ross, Andrew
Ross, M. A., Addison, Somerset Co.
†Ross, William S., Wilkes-Barré
Rowland, Jos. Galloway, Quincy, Ill.
Rowland, William
Rupp, I. Daniel
†Rutter, R. L.
†Ryerss, Joseph W.

Sabin, Joseph, New York
Sanford, E. S., Brooklyn, L. I.
†Sargent, Winthrop
Scattergood, George J.
Schenley, Mary, Prince's Gate, Hyde
  Park, London, Eng.
Schuyler, Jr., P. C., Portland, Ore-
  gon
Schwartz, Jacob E., Pittsburg
Scott, E. Greenough, Wilkes-Barré
Scott, Lewis A.
Scott, Thomas A.
Scull, Edward L.
Scull, D. G., The Laurels, Hounslow
  Heath, Eng.
Scranton, Selden T., Oxford, War-
  ren County, New Jersey
Seal, Joseph H.

Seitzinger, J. J.
Sellers, David W.
Sellers, Jr., John
Sellers, William
Seltzer, J. H.
Sergeant, J. Dickinson
†Sergeant, Thomas
†Sergeant, William
Sexton, John W.
Shaffer, Charles, Concordville, Delaware County
Sharp, Joseph W.
†Sharpless, Henry H. G.
Sharpless, Samuel J.
Sharswood, George
Shea, C. B., Pittsburg
Sheafer, Peter W., Pottsville
Sheppard, Furman
Sherman, Roger
Shipley, Augustus B.
†Shipley, Joseph, Rockwood, New Castle County, Delaware
†Shippen, Franklin
†Shippen, William
Shober, Samuel L.
Simons, Henry
Sinclair, Thomas
Singerly, Joseph
Slack, J. Hamilton, Bloomsbury, N. J.
†Slocum, J. J., Wilkes-Barré
Smedley, Samuel L.
Smith, Aubrey H.
Smith, A. Lewis
†Smith, Beaton
Smith, Charles E.
Smith, Davis R.
Smith, Ellwood M.
Smith, James C.
Smith, Jesse E., Windlawn, Phila.
Smith, John F.
Smith, Joseph P.
Smith, Newberry A.
Smith, Richard
Smith, Richard S.
Smith, Robert
Smith, Robert P., Germantown
Smith, Samuel Grant
†Smith, William Prescott, Baltimore
Snowden, James Ross, Hulmeville
Snyder, George W., Pottsville
Solms, Sidney J.
Sower, Charles G.
Spackman, John B.
Spangler, C. E.
Sparks, Thomas
Spencer, Charles, Germantown

Spencer, Howard
Spooner, Edwin
†Sproat, Harris L.
Steele, Hugh E., Coatesville
Steele, James L.
†Steever, Henry D., Germantown
†Stevens, James E. P., Germantown
Stewart, William H., Paris, France
Stillé, Alfred
Stillé, Charles J.
Stocker, Anthony E.
Stokes, William A.
Stone, Frederick D.
Stone, James N.
Stone, William E., Germantown
Stuart, George H.
Stoddart, Curwen
Strong, William, Washington, D. C.
Struthers, William
†Sully, Thomas
Swift, Joseph

Taggart, William H.
Tasker, Stephen P. M.
Tasker, Thomas T.
Tasker, Jr., Thomas T.
Taylor, Samuel L.
Taylor, Stephen
Thomas, David, Catasauqua
Thomas, George C.
†Thomas, John Dover
†Thomas, Joseph M.
†Thomas, Martin
Thomas, William B.
†Thomson, George H., Germantown
Thomson, J. Edgar
Thompson, E. O.
Thompson, John J.
†Thompson, Oswald
Tobias, Joseph F.
†Toland, Henry
Townsend, Henry C.
Traquair, James
Trautwine, John C.
Trotter, Charles W.
Trotter, Joseph H.
Trotter, Newbold H.
Trotter, William Henry
Trump, Daniel
Tucker, John
†Turnbull, William P.
Turnpenny, Joseph C.
Tyler, George F.
Tyndale, Hector
Tyson, James, Titusville
Tyson, James L.

†Tyson, J. R.
Valentine, Robert
Van der Kemp, John J., Paris, France
†Van Rensselaer, Cortlandt, Burlington, N. J.
†Van Syckel, James J.
Vaux, George
Vaux, Roberts
Vaux, William S.
Verree, John P.
Von Utassy, A. W., Germantown

Wagner, Charles M.
†Wagner, Samuel, York
Wagner, Mrs. Tobias
Walker, Jerry
Wallace, John William
†Waln, S. Morris
†Ward, Richard Ray, New York
Ward, Townsend
†Warder, Benjamin H.
†Warner, Joseph
Warner, Redwood F.
Washburn, Daniel, Ashland
Watkins, Jr., Samuel P.
Watson, George N.
Weber, Paul, Germany
Webster, David
Webster, Thomas
Weightman, William
Welsh, John
Welsh, Jr., John
Westcott, Thompson
†Wetmore, Henry C., Fishkill, New York
†Wharton, George M.
Wharton, Joseph
†Wharton, Thomas I.
Whitall, John M.
White, C. Brooke
White, J. Claude, Swatara
White, J. DeHaven
White, William R.
†Whiteman, William A.

†Whiting, William, Boston, Mass.
Whitney, Asa
Whitney, John R., Glen Brook Farm, Bryn Mawr, Delaware County
Whitney, Thomas H., Glassboro', New Jersey
Wicht, William V., Nassau, Germany
Wight, Jr., Andrew, New York
Wilcocks, Alexander
Willcox, Mark
Williams, Edward H.
Williams, Henry J.
†Williams, James W.
Wilson, John H., St. Louis, Mo.
Wilson, Oliver Howard
†Wilson, Thomas B.
†Wilson, William S.
Winsor, Henry
Winthrop, Robert C.
†Wistar, Mifflin
†Wistar, Richard
Wister, Casper
Witte, William H., White Marsh
Womrath, F. K.
Wood, George A.
Wood, George B.
Wood, James F.
Wood, Richard
Wood, Robert
Wood, R. Francis
Woodward, Harry Conrad
Woodward, Warren J., Reading
Workman, Henry Weir
†Worrell, James C.
†Wynkoop, Francis M.

Yarnall, Charles
†Yarnall, Edward
Yarnall, Ellis
Yarnall, Francis C.
Yarrow, Mrs. Matilda
†Yost, J. S., Pottstown

Ziegler, George K.

DATE DUE
